Emma Spaulding Bryant

Emma Frances Spauling (Bryant), c. 1863. Photo courtesy of Josephine Zeller Megehee.

Emma Spaulding Bryant

CIVIL WAR BRIDE, CARPETBAGGER'S WIFE,
ARDENT FEMINIST

Letters and Diaries
1860–1900

Edited with Narrative by

RUTH DOUGLAS CURRIE

Fordham University Press
New York
2004

Reconstructing America No. 7
ISSN 1523–4606

Library of Congress Cataloging-in-Publication Data

Bryant, Emma Frances Spaulding, 1844–1901.
  Emma Spaulding Bryant : Civil War bride, carpetbagger's wife, ardent feminist : letters and diaries, 1860–1900 / edited with narrative by Ruth Douglas Currie. — 1st ed.
       p. cm. — (Reconstructing America, ISSN 1523–4606 ; no. 7)
  Includes bibliographical references (p. 485) and index.
  ISBN 0-8232-2273-X
  1. Reconstruction—Georgia. 2. Georgia—History—1865– 3. United States—History—Civil War, 1861–1865—Personal narratives. 4. Bryant, Emma Frances Spaulding, 1844–1901—Correspondence. 5. Bryant, Emma Frances Spaulding, 1844–1901—Diaries. 6. Feminists—Georgia—Correspondence. 7. Feminists—Georgia—Diaries. I. Currie, Ruth Douglas. II. Title. III. Reconstructing America (Series) ; no. 7.

F291.B88   2004
973.8'092—dc22   2003022907

Printed in the United States of America
08 07 06 05 04   5 4 3 2 1
First edition

For Ken

CONTENTS

FOREWORD AND GRATITUDES

In 1905, Emma Alice Bryant Zeller wrote to the widow of William A. Pledger, an African-American political colleague of her father's, to inquire about the Bryant library, furniture, working papers, and private letters, supposedly under the care of the Pledgers in Atlanta. The response was somewhat disappointing: the furniture and most of the library had been sold. But the papers and letters remained, still kept in long wooden boxes; they would be shipped to Illinois for the sum of two dollars. Thus began the effort by the family—through three generations and multiple moves west, east, and finally south—to preserve the political papers of John Emory Bryant and the personal correspondence between Bryant and his wife, Emma Frances Spaulding Bryant.

As a new graduate student in the early 1970s, as I explored ways to deal with an interest in the era of Reconstruction, my advisor at Duke, Dr. Robert F. Durden, suggested that I check out the large manuscript collection recently acquired by the University. From the first perusal, I was hooked on the John Emory Bryant Collection. With 1,818 items in forty boxes of documents and letters, it was a magnificent opportunity. What better way to deal with the complicated politics of Reconstruction than through the eyes of an assertive carpetbagger from Maine, one who struggled for almost thirty years on the "foreign" soil of Georgia. With the support of Dr. Mattie Russell in the Manuscript Department of Duke's Perkins Library and the guidance of Dr. Durden, the dissertation took shape. In 1987, after a decade of Reconstruction scholarship by other historians helped to define Bryant's work further, the University of Georgia Press published *Carpetbagger of Conscience, A Biography of John Emory Bryant*.

From the outset, it was obvious that while John's was a significant political career, the story still to be told was that of the carpetbagger's wife, Emma Spaulding Bryant. Her diaries and the correspondence between Emma and John were engaging and revealed much about the public as well as private lives of them both. Anonymous readers at the press as well as later book reviewers asked for more information about Emma. At the time, several associates remarked: "I didn't know that carpetbaggers had wives!"

Scholarship in the academic field of women's history has come light-years since those days, but still little is known about the wives of the carpetbaggers as a group. From existing sources, however, it appears that Emma's struggles were not very different from those of other northern women who came South after the Civil War. Their courage and resolve in the face of hardship and southern hostility provides another dimension to the political reform efforts of their husbands.

At first the work went slowly. The correspondence seemed voluminous and my own career brought new interests and other projects. But to my delight, the descendants of the Bryants read *Carpetbagger of Conscience* and agreed to support the publication of a second volume. The idea of telling Emma's narrative through her own letters and diaries began to seem possible. Emma's great-granddaughter, Josephine Zeller Megehee, and I talked about the sources. Then, serendipity: yes, the family had an additional cache of letters and papers, photographs, and artifacts. While they had provided Duke with the bulk of JEB's political papers and many letters, the family had retained much of the personal correspondence, particularly that from the later years, the period that had remained something of a mystery to me up until then. Moreover, there were paintings that Emma had done and charming line drawings in her own sketchbook. Through her writings and artwork, Emma herself could come into focus. The letters from the last years of her life would reveal the woman she became and the causes she supported, as well as the deepening bonds of devotion between husband and wife despite their differences.

In 1999, Fordham University Press published a reprint of *Carpetbagger of Conscience*, adding several photographs of John and Emma. In working on the new introduction for that edition, a re-evaluation of the Bryants brought a deeper appreciation for their dedicated lives and increased my determination to continue.

I am deeply indebted to the Zeller family for their assistance, including all the daughters of Bryant's grandson, Raymond Bryant Zeller: Louise Zeller Wicker, Dorothy Zeller Knight, Beverly Zeller Herring, and Stephanie Zeller. But especially I want to thank Josephine Zeller Megehee and her husband, Dan, who opened their home to me, made copies and copies and copies, and graciously shared all the Bryant photographs and artifacts.

My years at Appalachian State University allowed more progress on the Emma project. Dr. Clinton Parker made possible grant funds, released time, and support for research trips. I am grateful for this tangible assistance and also for Dr. Parker's consistent encouragement. Pamela Price Mitchem helped to check the excellent transcription work of Renee Taylor and also transcribed additional letters. Both Pam and Mark Brittain assisted with clerical support.

The headmaster at Kents Hill School, Mr. Rist Bonnefond, graciously welcomed me to the campus, while archivist Mrs. Marjorie Gordon enthusiastically guided me through records related to Emma's education at the school's antecedent institution, Maine Wesleyan Seminary and Female College. The archives at Kents Hill house the small coffin the Ku Klux Klan sent JEB as a death threat. Bryant had presented this reminder of his harrowing years in Georgia to his alma mater through the Calliopean Society, the school's literary society, of which he had been a member as a student.

I am grateful to Dr. David Ferriero at Duke for his interest in Emma's life and for the cooperation I have continued to receive from the University. Ms. Janie Morris in the Rare Book, Manuscript, and Special Collections Library has been outstanding in her assistance throughout my latest work with the Bryant Collection. At the Bell Library of Montreat College, Ms. Elizabeth Pearson and Ms. Sue Diehl have been helpful in providing microfilm reading time, interlibrary loan service, and reference assistance. David O. Bradshaw and Ms. B. K. Segall in the Ellison Library of Warren Wilson College also have provided reference service.

My profound thanks and gratitude to all who have assisted and encouraged me in this effort, especially my sister Lynn, who listens so well and has sustained me through every crisis, and her husband, Jim Wallace, who patiently answered endless computer questions. Most of all to Ken, my husband and "dearest friend," whose love and support have given me the renewed spirit to complete the project.

EDITORIAL NOTE

The diaries and correspondence between John Emory Bryant and Emma Spaulding Bryant in this volume were selected from two major collections. The first may be found in the Rare Book, Manuscript, and Special Collections Library, Duke University, Durham, North Carolina. Until recently, the second had been held privately by the Zeller family, descendants of the Bryants. I have worked from the originals at Duke, some microfilm for the second reading, and from copies provided by the family. I am delighted to note here that the Zellers have generously allowed the Bryant papers and correspondence to be reunited; the entire collection is now housed at Duke.

This book represents selected letters, approximately two-thirds of the extant total. Also included are portions of the diaries and journals Emma kept in 1866 and 1876, and then John's diary through his last days in 1900, continued by Emma after his death. John's political papers and letters are not included here, but are abundantly referenced in *Carpetbagger of Conscience*.

For the most part, these are Emma's letters, with a number of John's during the Civil War and several of his through the years. John and Emma were themselves selective in what they kept; references to additional correspondence not preserved are sometimes tantalizing. Inevitably, some papers and letters have been lost or damaged over the years.

I have selected the letters that tell best the happenings of their lives, their reflections on the political climate and events of the time, and of the relationship between Emma and John. A few of the many existing letters from their daughter Emma Alice Bryant (Zeller) are included, as are excerpts from Alice's autobiography (typescript at Duke) which add details of her parents' lives. A few letters from friends are included to help to describe or explain certain events.

Emma and John's letters have been transcribed as they wrote them, without updating their spelling or punctuation. The only exception is an occasional period and/or capitalization at the distinct ending of a sentence and the next beginning. When their meaning or usage is clear, I have not changed it—as in their consistent omission of an apostrophe (as in *dont*) or possessive (as *Johns letter*), or their omission of any punctuation with ending quotation marks (as *of the event*"). As much as possible, the reader may see the sentiment of the letter as the writer expressed it through dashes, paragraphs, underlining, etc.

The final step was my own reread and check of every original (or copy) selected. I regret any remaining error on my part in accurately deciphering John and Emma's handwriting.

RUTH DOUGLAS CURRIE
Warren Wilson College
August 2002

INTRODUCTION

One's initial impression of Emma Frances Spaulding assesses her as a typical woman of her century. In 1863, the dark-haired, demure college student smiled shyly for the camera, her hands folded ladylike in her lap. Surely, here was a "true woman," ready for her task of obedience and support for the future husband who would determine the contours of her life. Doubtless she would accept passively her prescribed role, blind to the earthshaking "other civil war" emerging in the nineteenth century from the fiery pen of Elizabeth Cady Stanton and the actions of other women also challenging the norms of society.

More interesting, seemingly, would be her husband, the daring John Emory Bryant, handsome and aggressive young teacher who would command African American troops during the Civil War and become one of the notorious Radical carpetbaggers who transformed Southern politics of the Reconstruction era. JEB served in the Freedmen's Bureau and the Georgia Legislature, and was a key player in Republican politics in the state for almost thirty years. His self-defined mission to "Northernize" the South was a consuming passion as he plotted strategy, worked for equal civil rights for African American males, and wrote countless newspaper editorials and tracts on the evils of the slave society. His self-righteous, arrogant character would embroil him in endless controversy, and while his ambition for national elective office was never realized, he would hold various brief patronage positions in the South. Bryant is a fascinating study in the ambiguity of Republican politics. Was he the scoundrel his critics claimed, or an upright "political missionary" as he maintained? It would take immersion into the couple's private lives to uncover the best, most intriguing evidence. Further knowledge would reveal Emma's personality as vastly different from the original supposition; but indeed, the contours of her life would be determined by her husband. In a sense, she would become the conscience of the carpetbagger.

The correspondence and diaries of Emma and John provide an open window on the nineteenth century. John's political career spanned the bedrock public issues of Reconstruction and civil rights. For Emma, the drama unfolds in the small events, the "teaspoons" of their daily existence. The reader not only becomes part of their personal relationship, beginning with courtship and marriage during the Civil War, but cheers the emerging character of this woman, follows the child-rearing practices of the day, and through Emma's surprisingly candid descriptions of her own treatment, learns something of medical practice concerning women's health in that century.

The list of Emma Spaulding Bryant's activities is impressive. In addition to what she considered her primary task, that of rearing her daughter to her own standards of "real womanhood," she assisted her husband in his work, did massive amounts of sewing both for the family and for hire, taught Sunday school, and volunteered in various mission projects such as visiting in jails. After taking classes as a student, painting was a talent and skill she nurtured throughout her lifetime. (Samples from her sketchbook may be seen in this volume.) Determined that her daughter would have a first-rate education, at the age of forty-three Emma began teaching mathematics, the subject in which she had excelled in her own schooling. The Woman's Christian Temperance Union, in which she enjoyed a prominent leadership role, took much of her volunteer time in her later years.

By the end of her life, clearly Emma had read deeply in reform literature and had become a profound thinker, suffragist, and (though she did not use the word) an ardent feminist. She analyzed closely held traditions of the church, the "cheap grace" of Gilded Age theology, and challenged biblical interpretations that dictated a submissive role for women. In her letters she commented on the treatment of Native Americans and advocated citizenship for them as well as for women. In eloquent language she coached her husband's understanding of women's rights: "it is always unfortunate when a woman needs to assert that which she should simply use as her natural inheritance." With remarkable dignity, she endured her indigent life, remaining faithful in her duties and never wavering in dedication to her family.

The adult Emma Spaulding Bryant was far different from the demure student photographed in the 1860s, nor did life match her schoolgirl expectations. By her own admission, she had "looked forward to a house full of happy children and a home to rear them in," but with stoic realism she later believed "that infinite wisdom and infinite love" had given the couple "just what we ought to have. . . ." The grueling years in the shadow of her husband's political career gave her a backbone of steel and unrelenting faith in the worth of each individual. Clearly, the revolution for women's rights taking shape in America "had begun from within," deeply affected her values, and was then reflected in her actions.

One tiptoes into the private correspondence between husband and wife with trepidation and a certain awe, as it becomes a kind of long-distance eavesdropping. The letters between Emma and John reveal a love affair spanning more than forty years of devotion and turmoil. Their long separations, which engendered these letters, also determined the parameters of the relationship. Forced to rely on her own resources, Emma forged a persona of strength and independence, even while sustaining total support for her husband and his causes. "Our married life has never grown stale and common place," she wrote him. Their love, she felt, had retained "its first warmth and freshness"; the "charm of courtship."

Having been a party to this long courtship, one reads the closing chapter with a measure of sadness—also with deep affection for both Emma and John, and profound respect for the character and commitment they gave to their mission.

Emma Frances Spaulding Bryant proved far different from any facile stereotype. She shows once again that the wives of public, even prominent men have lives of their own. Emma's story is significant in itself, not only as an advocate and reflection of her husband's work. Her life became increasingly complex, even heroic as she courageously met the adversity that she faced. In that, she typifies the legion of women who fostered the woman's cause through a determination to live feminist values, balancing family duties with public reforms, and thereby laying the foundation for wider acceptance in following centuries of a belief in the equality of all persons. "God grant," Emma wrote, "that our own little daughter shall never need to <u>assert</u> her rights in her own household, that she shall never rear a son who shall consider woman inferior to man. . . ."

LETTERS: 1860–1864

Emma Frances Spaulding was born into a prominent family in historic New England, in an era of activism and religious piety in the state of Maine. Her entire life would reflect the influence of these early priorities and deep roots. Born February 16, 1844, Emma was the third daughter, fourth child of James Spaulding and his wife, Cynthia Bray.[1] Her sister Zilpha died when Emma was eighteen, while Margaretta ("Gretta") lived until 1894. Gretta would provide not only a home for her father but safe lodging for Emma herself during long separations from her husband. Throughout her life, Emma also remained close to her brother James Greenleaf.

Buckfield, Maine, a small farming village nestled in a "grand and beautiful" landscape with "rugged formation," was a community with Protestant and Universalist congregations and citizens of strong moral character. A few miles to the west, the larger town of Augusta boasted a plainspoken newspaper, the *Kennebec Journal*. The *Journal*, Whig as well as thoroughly antislavery, also lauded the outreach of missionaries from New England to the Pacific. During the years of Emma's youth, the paper faithfully reported the religious conversion of natives to "Christian civilization" and advocated American annexation of the Hawaiian Islands.[2] Many carpetbaggers and teachers carried that same sense of mission to the South after the Civil War. Having been imbued with abolitionist zeal for eliminating the evils of slavery and its injurious effects on both whites and blacks, they went with conviction for the "glorious cause" of "Northernizing" the South. In addition, the state held strong sentiments regarding drunkenness, as evidenced by the action of the Legislature of

---

[1] "Birth & Death Records," Municipal Center, Town of Buckfield, Maine; Alfred Cole and Charles F. Whitman, *A History of Buckfield Oxford County, Maine from the Earliest Exploration to the Close of the Year 1900* (Lewiston, Maine: The Journal Printshop, 1915), 18–19, 687.

[2] Edward P. Crapol, *James G. Blaine: Architect of Empire* (Wilmington, Del.: Scholarly Resources, 2000), 4–6; Tom Coffman, *Nation Within: The Story of America's Annexation of the Nation of Hawaii* (Kane'ohe, Hawaii: Epicenter, 1998), 97–98; Noel J. Kent, *Hawaii: Islands under the Influence* (New York: Monthly Review Press, 1983), 26.

Maine in 1846 to prohibit the manufacture or sale of intoxicating beverages in the state.

In 1787, Emma's great-grandfather, Benjamin Spaulding, had been the first settler in the Buckfield area. He, along with the other original proprietors of Buckfield, set aside twenty-eight acres for educational purposes, and by 1801 the settlement had a schoolhouse. Later the town was divided into eight school districts. The Spauldings continued to be leading citizens of the town. Benjamin's grandson, Dastine Spaulding, as selectman and treasurer in 1860, was instrumental in bringing education to the youth in the community.[3] With no state-mandated public education yet available, local district adults took major responsibility for the "subscription schools," which brought traveling scholars to the area for agreed-upon terms of six to ten weeks of lessons with the children.

Such a youthful instructor was John Emory Bryant, who asked about the possibility of lodging in the Spaulding home during a teaching assignment in Buckfield. Boarding with the families of students was the custom for these schools, and Dastine agreed to accommodate Bryant, if he could "'grin and bear it.'" Childless, Dastine and his wife Clarinda apparently lived with extended family, perhaps the brood of his nephew, James. James had the reputation of being a stoic and upright man and was described as a "popular captain in the militia."[4] His youngest daughter, Emma Frances, would be one of Bryant's students.

There was good reason to examine Bryant's credentials before taking him on as teacher. He came with a checkered background of strong support and just as strenuous condemnation from the town of Wayne, a few miles northeast of Buckfield. A graduate of Maine Wesleyan Seminary at Kents Hill[5] (a few miles from Augusta), Bryant's academics seemed sound. Clearly, he was an intelligent young man. He was also upstanding, if somewhat self-righteous. Pledged to total abstinence in infancy by his father, a Methodist minister, John was proud of his ability to uphold that promise. Finding the temperance unit in Wayne too lenient, he had established

---

[3] Cole and Whitman, *History of Buckfield*, 25, 31, 100–104, 687; Charles Warren Spalding, *The Spalding Memorial: A Genealogical History of Edward Spalding of Virginia and the Massachusetts Bay and His Descendents*, 2 vols. (Chicago: American Publishers' Association, 1897), 547, in Maine State Library, Augusta, Maine. The memorial shows alternate spellings of Spalding and Spaulding for the family name. Emma's family consistently used Spaulding.

[4] Spalding, *The Spalding Memorial*, 547.

[5] At the time, the name was Kent's Hill, though the school has since dropped the apostrophe. In their letters, John and Emma also usually omitted it.

there a rival lodge—presumably with stricter rules for membership—and, of course, with himself as president.[6]

Most unsettling perhaps was the reputation John carried for being a strict disciplinarian to the point of cruelty. Spaulding, however, thought this a plus and commiserated with Bryant that it "must be very unpleasant" for a teacher "to have trouble in school" with his scholars. But, he agreed, were he a teacher, "I should be master."

Emma Frances Spaulding was sixteen when she sat in John Emory Bryant's classroom and looked into the face of her future husband. From the time he was teacher and perhaps even a resident in her home, he was her "brother," while she became his little "sister."[7] As John was eight years her elder and in a position of authority as instructor, it is understandable that in the first stages of their relationship, he seemed a surrogate parent and guide. When John enlisted in the military in 1861 in response to Lincoln's call for troops, Emma became one of the several young women who corresponded with him—as well as with other local heroes serving in the Union army.

The Civil War correspondence between Emma and John documents the developing bond between them even as Emma matured while attending college at Kents Hill, where John's alma mater had become Maine Wesleyan Seminary and Female College. Along with its lovely campus and placid surroundings, the college offered a rigorous curriculum for women, which compared favorably with that required for men. Emma's course of study included literature; languages: Latin, French, and German; and mathematics, including algebra, plain and analytical geometry, and trigonometry.[8] While the extant letters from this period are mostly John's, they contain glimpses of Emma's personality as she cultivated dear "chummies," laughed "at anyone," engaged in "flirting" (to the consternation of her mentor), took painting lessons, and learned to enjoy composition.

In the exigencies of war, John's character emerged as well. The determination and even arrogance that southerners would soon despise served him well at times and poorly at others. From the outset, John resented the restraints of officers higher in rank than his own captain's commission,

---

[6] See *Carpetbagger of Conscience*, 1–41, for details of JEB's early life and career in the years 1860–64.

[7] Platonic "brother-sister" relationships were not unusual in American society in the nineteenth century, perhaps to compensate for the prevalent ideology of "separate spheres" for females and males.

[8] E. R. French, *History of the Maine Wesleyan Seminary* (Portland, Maine: Smith & Sale, 1919), 35; *Catalogue of the Officers and Students of the Maine Wesleyan Seminary and Female College, Kent's Hill, Readfield, 1863–64* (Portland: B. Thurston, 1864), Kents Hill School Archives, Kents Hill, Maine.

men whom he considered inferior to himself in leadership ability and/or moral character. Throughout the rigors of a court-martial for insubordination, he continued to believe in his own rightness and expected—and received—the allegiance of Emma, his "little angel," during the ordeal. His advice for her included warnings that she should beware of other men, drop her "little beaux," abandon her correspondence with any "of southern sympathies," and evaluate carefully various friends, all as he groomed her to become a "proper lady."

Emma's feelings of ambivalence toward the handsome captain's pursuit were evident, but throughout the courtship, mostly by mail, her genuine affection for him deepened. Also apparent with maturity were Emma's moral convictions, intelligence, diligence in her studies, and conscious spirituality.

By 1864, when John's enlistment came to an end, he had served in some of the most sensitive theaters of the war, including the coast of South Carolina and Georgia with the Department of the South, where he recruited African American troops and engaged in scouting expeditions to free slaves from plantations on the mainland. Having redeemed his name and restored his reputation by his exploits as "the Scout," he returned to the Eighth Maine Infantry and briefly commanded his regiment at the Battle of the Crater in Petersburg, Virginia.

By this time John had successfully wooed Emma, and they were married on June 26, 1864. Like so many Union soldiers, while stationed in the Sea Islands John had been seduced by the southern climate and dreamed of living in the South after the war. Emma's vision of the future was somewhat different, as she expected his law career to flourish closer to home. After he left the army in September 1864, he did read law for a brief time, preparing for admittance to the Maine bar, which he accomplished in December 1866. But the promises John made in the last months of their courtship would be hard for him to honor.

D Spaulding
Buckfield, Jan. 31ˢᵗ, 1860

Friend Bryant,

I suppose you have been looking for a letter from me for some time, in answer to yours of the 12ᵗʰ inst. We were very glad to hear that you got out of your trouble in school as well as you did, and hope that you will not have any more. It must be very unpleasant for a teacher to have trouble in school with his schollars [*sic*],[9] because there will not be the same kind feelings there would have been if there [had] not been any trouble.

I hope you will not have occasion to chastise any schollar, for it must be an unpleasant duty or a duty I should consider it for as long as I was teacher I should be master. You asked in your letter if you could board with us if you came to B.[uckfield] in the spring. I think there is no doubt but what you can if we are all well, if you can bring your mind down, and conform, to that passage of scripture of the old womans, "<u>grin and bear it</u>."

The people here seem to be pleased with the prospect of your comming [*sic*] here to keep school this spring. I think you will have a good school but not so large a school as you would have in the fall. . . .

We are having a "singing school" this winter kept by Mr. Thorp of Portland, he kept here some 20 years ago. he is a verry [*sic*] good teacher, & we are having a verry good school, have some 25 or 40 schollars: it keeps two evenings in a week. . . .

Clarinda & I went to Lisbon[10] last week visiting was gone from home two nights had a pleasant visit. We have had pleasant weather this months [*sic*] & first rate sleighing. I hope it will continue so through the winter.

We had a town meeting yesterday in regard to the Defalcation of our liquor agent who is minus some six or seven hundred dollars. Chose a committee of three to investigate the matter. Messrs. Chase Russell & Gardner are the comm, "Defalcation" is the order of the day. All well.

Write soon. Yours, with respect
D[astine] Spaulding

––––––––

Farmington Hill
July 16th, 1861

Dear Sister

I have moved around so much since I saw you that I have had poor chance to write any one. I am in the store of my friend Chandler and can write a few words.

––––––––––––

[9] As described in the editorial note, original spellings have been preserved throughout the book. A few words are correct in some instances, wrong in others. In the interest of readability, not all incorrect spellings have been marked. Certain consistent misspellings are indicated only once per page or letter.

[10] Village near Buckfield.

Your friend Miss Beede[11] (is that spelled right?) was in here a moment ago but I did not conclude to get an introduction. I shall be in Buckfield next Saturday and you and the Lord being willing I will call up to <u>read</u> with you Sunday in the afternoon. I saw Henry[12] last we[ek] He told me that he was in B- last week. Good by and give my love to Sewell[13] when you write.

All from your affectionate Brother
John

————

Camp Hill
Augusta
Sep 1 1861

My Dear Little Sister

I sit down to write a good many letters and the first one I will write to my little sister. You see that I am "in camp" but not as a soldier. I have aided Col Strickland[14] to get up his company I aided McDonald[15] to be 1st Lieut and now I am aiding Strickland to become Col of this Reg. I am full of business and all is for aiding me in the future. I am very successful. But I should rather see my little sister today than almost any one. I shall see you the first of the week. I think I shall be successful this time as usual.

After leaving you Tues eve I went home all safe arrived about 3 ½ A.M. Went to bed and did not wake until 9 ½ A.M. got a horse and started for the Falls as soon as I could arrived about 15 minutes before the cars started and came through all right. I am in the officers tent I camp with them I guess that your particular little self would turn up her nose at our accommodations but yet I like it. We have beans hard bread soft bread and coffee for breakfast; coffee hard bread soft bread and beans for dinner and soft bread hard bread coffee and beans for supper and soft beef three times per day and yet I am not "homesick." I would not go a private I would not go unless I were Cap but If I were elected Cap and my little sister would give me up I think I should go. It is a curious sight

————

[11] Clara and Emily Beedy, from Farmington, were Emma's classmates at Kents Hill.

[12] Probably Henry Irish, fellow student at Kents Hill.

[13] Rival of John's for Emma's attention.

[14] Colonel Augustus H. (Lee) Strickland commanded the Eighth Maine Infantry.

[15] Bryant, first elected Second Lieutenant, refused to serve under John P. Swasey, who had defeated him for First Lieutenant; JEB accepted a captain's commission; Isaac H. McDonald, first elected captain, probably replaced Swasey. See Cole and Whitman, *History of Buckfield*, 405.

to see about 100 tents spread over the beautiful state grounds and inhabited by 600 or 700 men all or nearly all of whom are to leave their homes and many never to return. Some have wives and children to leave behind some parents brothers & sisters some sweethearts and perhaps some <u>sisters</u>. We have all kinds of men some good and some very bad. . . . I shall come to see you Tuesday Wedns or Thursday and bring you to Augusta if you want to come I do not know when I shall go to Buckfield not until his Reg goes I think unless I go with them.

. . . I hope you are not homesick. I want you to stand A 1 in your class.

I suppose you will receive this tomorrow if you do please write Tuesday and tell me all.

All from your brother John

––––––––

Sep 18 1861
Headquarters 8th M.M.V.

Dear Sister

At last I am able to write a few lines to you. I wrote you from Phil just to let you know that I was alive.

With that exception and a letter which I wrote for my trunk I have not had time to write any since I left Augusta and now for a good long letter. After leaving Augusta we passed rapidly through the intermediate places and arrived in Boston. It was wonderful to see the enthusiasm of the people throughout the entire town.

Although thousands of people had passed along this route yet the people were carried away with enthusiasm. Old & young rich and poor clean & dirty cheered us on. We arrived in Boston about 4 P.M. and marched from the cars to the [illegible] There the good people of Boston had prepared for us a most bountiful dinner (Supper?) We were hungry as bears (Oxford) and did justice to what was placed before us.

We did not finish until dark and then marched to the depot and took the cars for Providence R.I. which place we reached the night. There we took a boat for N.Y. . . .

The next morning at an early hour we started in the cars for the famous Jamaca Islands. . . .[16] Friday I went to New York city—that famous place

––––––––

[16] Jamaica Bay in New York harbor.

filled with almost every thing known to America. One of my men who was acquainted in the city went with me. We were on the famous Broadway went into [illegible] & I cant tell you all about it for I have so much to write. I returned Saturday through Brooklyn and reached the camp ground about four PM all was bustle. The report was that a great battle was raging in Washington and we were to go immediately some thought we would go and some did not know. At last the order came for us to start in an hour. Before the hour was up we were ready. Our tents and baggage were to be left behind. Wm Cole (my boy) stayed with my things. The order came again for us to start at 10 P.M. We did not get ready until 1 A.M. . . .

We are now encamped in Washington in plain sight of the Capitol where laws are made for this great nation or rather for the loyal part of the nation. We have a good church but have had a hard time of it since we left Augusta. It is a great amount of work to feed so many men as there are in this Reg and in moving around as we have since leaving Maine it is difficult to get every thing ready and for a few days our men did not get all they wanted to eat but now we have things enough.

Fri Sep. 20. I commenced this letter Wedn but can write only at certain hours.

For a few days we have had things in better shape this morn. I had beaf steak toasted bread with sugar and water. Our men had coffee. We must expect to have hard times i.e. not as easy as at home but we do not suffer and I do not think we shall immediately. I like full better than I expected But we are near the seat of war I can hear heavy cannon every day sometimes the Rebels some times our folks firing we are surrounded by about 300,000 men ready to defend their country. . . .

I must close but will write again in a few days. I want you to write often and I will do the same.

> Direct
> Cap. J E Bryant
> 8th Maine Reg
> Washington D.C.

I am well and hope my dear little sister is enjoying herself and progressing finely with her studies. I want to see you and shall if nothing unforseen prevents me about three or four months. Write soon and often.

> From your brother
> John

Head Quarters
8th Maine Reg
"Dec 4th" 1861

Dear Little Sister

I received a letter from you yesterday dated Nov 21st. It had been a long time since I had received a letter from you about 18 days and I was somewhat disappointed at receiving but one. But I suppose the sore eye must be the excuse. You dont give me a bit of gossip from 13. Not a word about your friend Pray's leaving. Not a word of the school, Lyceum, Division or the flirtations of the young folks. In your next after receiving this please gossip one or two sheets full.

I received a letter from Joseph Stevens yesterday. He thinks you rank the best scholar in your class and perhaps the best in the school. I was very much pleased with this good report 1st because it was my little sister and again because you had been a scholar [in my school] for several terms. I have known from the first what you could do and that was one reason why I was and am so anxious for you to finish a collegiate course. Please sister do not allow any thing to prevent you from completing your course. Whenever your father thinks he cant send you let me know it. I know that you will continue to hold the position you now do and when I return I shall find my sister a very dignified miss. I suppose you will be at Kents Hill when this reaches you but I will direct to Buckfield. If you are at the Hill let me know of the news from there also.

We remain here on Hilton Head Island in a cotton field where the dust (sand) flies almost constantly. My company has become well drilled and I have learned something of military affairs. I am now in my tent—a round one twelve feet on the ground and coming to a peak about twelve feet from the ground. Mc Willie and I occupy it. Willie lies on a bed reading Mc is writing by the table and I am writing this on my knee by his side. The ground is covered with long grass and straw for a floor. My bed is on the ground I have a frame without legs and upon it a matress [sic] and three thick army blankets to keep me warm. We eat from tin dishes and live very well for soldiers. I suppose you are all froze up down in Maine here we have had but one frost. Today is about as warm as a pleasant September day with you. The nights are cool. i.e. for the days day before yesterday the mercury was about 80° above 0 and at daylight the next morning it stood about 10° above. Such sudden changes are bad. We expect to leave here every day. Where we shall go to I cant tell. I am satisfied the danger is not a[s] great as I thought it was when I enlisted and I hope and expect to see you next season. It does me good to hear from Buckfield. I like to hear from no other place so well. If I could only spend one week there I could be satisfied. But I cant. In my last I stated that I had sent to you a toilet basket and a boll of cotton. You will find bunches of cotton bursting from the bur and buds not ripe. The cotton will be handy for good use. When we first came onto the island nearly every officer went out and got what he could. We all thought it perfectly right to get what we could from these South Carolina traitors but Gen Shurman[17] for political effect stoped [*sic*] it and ordered us to give up what we had got so I have lost everything except the basket which I hope my little sister has got ere this. Nearly all of the officers have sent something home to their friends I expect some of my enemies will write home about it if they do I shall answer them and if they are not careful they will get themselves into a hard fix. If you see anything about me in the papers either of praise or censure please let me know and if you can send me the piece stating in what paper it may be found.

You may expect to see in several of the papers favorable mention of me about the first of January. It is not certain but quite sure.

Write soon Direct as I said in my last Capt J E Bryant

> Co C 8<u>th</u> Main Regiment
> Gen Shermans Division
> Core of D D Tompkins No 6
> State Street New York City
>
> All from your absent brother
> John

P.S. I have been able to get some postage stamp and in future I will try and pay the postage

> John

---

[17] Brigadier General Thomas West Sherman.

Head Quarters 8<u>th</u> Me
Hilton Head S.C.
Jan 19th 1862

Dear Sister

I received your letter of Jan 10th two or three days since and was as ever very very glad to hear from you again. I am very much disappointed if I do not get one or two letters from you each week. A week here appears 2; and yet I enjoy myself hugely. If I could come to Buckfield and see my friend even once a month I should be satisfied, but it is for the best that I should remain here at present. I shall try to come in May or June. You ask me what I ment [*sic*] by saying that you would see me favorably mentioned about the first of Jan. It was this I knew that Col Strickland would resign about that time and I expected that influence enough could be brought upon the Gov[18] to secure my appointment for Maj. I wrote to my friends but by some unaccountable reason they were not received until some two or three weeks after they were sent and in the mean time another man had written and his letters went direct the result was the Gov had appointed before my friends saw him but the Gov said he recollected me and that I would be favorably remembered by him. My time will come by and by. I am content where I am. Indeed am now glad that I was not appointed Maj for I am doing better. Every time I go out to the field review Gen Viele[19] compliments me. Today (Sunday) yes Sunday, we had a grand review . . . as my company passed thru the Gen said to our Col who was on his horse close bye, "That is the best company in your Regt" That you see does not sound like the stories some are pleased to tell in B- [Buckfield] In your next please tell me what they say now about my S.C. affairs. Also tell me what the people say and do—Do they have parties sleigh rides etc etc? Do you remember our last New Years ride What a glorious time! Some difference between then and now.

Today had been as warm as June in Me tonight is also warm. We had been here about nine weeks with only two days rain but the rainy season commenced the 16th and we have had rain all the time since then until today. It will rain most of the time—"They say" for six weeks Then no more until July How should you like such weather?

---

[18] Governor Israel Washburn of Maine.
[19] Brigadier General E. L. Viele.

Please tell me of the changes that take place with you Buckfield folks. I am as much interested as though I were with you.

I had a letter from Augusta by last steamer she was well and teaching school near her home. Maria had lost her hair—Those beautiful curls, How "pretty" you would look with your hair gone (?) or with it "for that matter."

I hope your sister is better. It makes me feel bad to have you so sad and then I want her to get well soon so that you may go and see your friends at the Hill I fear they will loose [*sic*] their hearts if you do not return. Oh! how I should like to see my little sister to night. While I write she is just before me and as I write I look up at her but then it is only her Ambrotype. I often <u>very</u> <u>very</u> often think of her and long for those pleasant times to return. How I should like to be in the arm chair as of yore.

But I must close by saying that as usual we expect to move this week. "My health is good and I hope these few lines may find you enjoying the same blessing."

Write soon and often Direct as usual

> Good night sister pleasant dreams
> John

P.S. This letter does not look <u>quite</u> as bad as the last

————

> S.C. 8th Me Vols Port Royal
> Feb 8th 1862

Dear Sister

Your letter of Jan 29th was received yesterday. I . . . was very very glad to get this letter. I wrote day before yesterday to you saying that I had not heard for nearly a month. . . . I learned by a letter to Billy that your sister[20] was dead and I knew how bad you must feel and so excuse the long delay in writing. I learned first by your letter and again by papers from Maine that the 8th and 9th Reg's had seen battle. . . . So you see you were ahead of us in news. . . .

We have not only not seen battle but so far as this Reg't is conserned [*sic*] are not likely to soon. For weeks we have expected to leave "<u>very soon</u>" but now do not expect to leave at all.

————

[20] Zilpha Prince Spaulding Packard.

We think we shall be left to defend the island. If so we shall be safe but cant gain much honor. Which should you wish us to do remain here safe or be exposed and gain some honor?

I continue to enjoy myself. My health is good I live tip top but want very very much to see my sister. You ask if I have been homesick No—and yet I want very much to see my friends. I never allow myself to be homesick. It will do for <u>young ladies</u> and <u>little</u> girls to be homesick and cry but men should not be. I would rather much rather be with my friends if it were as well for me but in this world we must consult our interest and not allow our feelings to rule us. For instance it is much more pleasant to be in Buckfield at home with <u>Mother</u> where you are surrounded with friends and can have a good time than at Kents Hill where nearly all are strangers and all are busy, and above all, with <u>some</u>, where the boys and girls can't be together as much as <u>some</u> like. But there the mind is cultivated. . . . you meet with some of the best minds in the State and learn to measure your own abilities. But Emma to be <u>serious</u> although Kents Hill is not as pleasant as Buckfield yet until you complete your Collegiate course it is very much for your interest to remain there you must allow your <u>studies</u> to engross your attention and not think of being homesick. Desire to keep at the head of your class and graduate with honor. But dont let those young men fill too large a space in your thoughts. Of course you could not live without devoting a portion of the time to them. I shall expect a <u>very</u> long letter from you about Kents Hill affairs & remember me to Alice.[21]

> Good by sister be a good girl and study
> not too hard but about hard enough. . . .
> John

> Daufuskie Island S.C.
> March 14th 1862

Dear Sister

Then you did not feel like writing me. Why Emma how strange. I did not write more about your trouble because you felt so bad that I thought I would not add to it. I am sorry that you in the least doubted me. Remember I am

---

[21] Emma's closest friend, Alice M. White, also from Buckfield.

your brother and hope to be true to my sister. Pour out all your troubles into my ears and I will sympathize with you and if I do not write about it remember it is not because I do not feel for you but because I do not wish to add fuel to the fire. But Emma do not doubt me again. In my last before this I was obliged to say that I have been pained by words showing distrust. Please banish such thoughts in future.

I have not written any one in two weeks, and I have time to write only to you and my father today. Since I wrote before honors have piled themselves upon me thicker and thicker. The General has given me command of a company of boatmen and placed me in command of transportation from this point to our batteries. This is a mark of esteem unexpected. I prize it highly mostly as another answer to my enemies in Maine. It has been a hard place for me since I was appointed. I have about 10 boatmen under my charge [in] my company to look after twenty boats at [and] attend to and a steamboat to keep at work. I have been obliged to work day and night but now things are being arranged and in a few days I hope to write you a longer letter although this is longer than your last. I am well and enjoy myself finely. You may read to Mrs. Dastine[22] so much of this letter as related to my promotion if you are in Buckfield and wish to. I send you a copy of the order giving me my present position.

> Goodby sister Please write often.
> A kiss from your
> John
> Direct as before

———

> Co C 8th Me Vol's
> Daufuskie Island S.C.
> April 18th 1862

Dear Sister

'Tis a beautiful day I sit in my tent with my linen coat on. How odd it sounds to have you tell of snow drifts. Upon my table is beautiful bouquet of roses sweetwilliams etc etc—wish I could send it to my sister much rather give it to her. The birds are singing . . . blackberry sauce cherries will be ripe

---

[22] JEB's supporter and perhaps mentor.

soon Figs and peaches are quite large. . . . Strawberries have been ripe . . . [but] not many of them but blackberries are very plenty [*sic*] and taste just like those we get in Maine. If I could live in this climate during the winter and in Maine during the summer it would be delightful.

A few days ago I wrote to you sending a bouquet which you will no doubt receive before this as soon as I received your last I wrote again taking back all I had written in the other. . . . Hope in future I shall not feel like writing such letters guess I shant. It has turned out as I expected. I thought that as you became better acquainted at the Hill your homesickness would subside especially after you could flirt am glad <u>very very</u> glad you enjoy yourself so will hope you will continue to be pleased with your new home. . . . You will excel Emma in composition if you still try and in time you will learn to love composition as much as you hate it now. . . . I shall do my best to be at exhibition[23] so you will of course do <u>your</u> best. If I come I shall of course wish for my sister's company at [illegible] How will you arrange it with your little beau? Be sure sister and play your cards wisely and you may "entrap a pretty smart man" dont waste your time on <u>little beaux</u> if you do smart men may "pass by on the other side" Smart men you know are more particular than drones. . . . I wish Julie was your roommate she is such a good girl. You ask why the men do not pay attentions to Julie . . . those young men with whom I am acquainted feel that Julie will not flirt and they fear that she will not care to become too familiar as for myself I regard Julie as one of the most desirable young ladies [in] my acquaintance for a companion and I am not sure but I shall "play my cards" How do you think I should succeed sister?

I want to see you Emma very much there are many things which I wish to say of which I do not care to write—be a good girl do your best with your studies and write often to me. A letter from you is worth more than any other I get. Please remember that.

John

---

[23] Special event closing the school term, at which students displayed writing and oratorical skill by reading their own compositions.

[Notes on birch bark—Emma's handwriting]

May 14th 1862
Kents Hill May walk

Poem by [illegible]
lovely day beautiful & sunny
pleasant company
happy afternoon
Emma

———

No 1

Hilton Head SC
May 19th 1862

Why Emma F. Spaulding!
My Dear Sister

Before me lay your letters of May 5th & 9th and how different that of the 5th "My Dear Brother" etc from that of the 9th "Mr Bryant" etc. It seems that it was my letter of April 23d which produced all of the change. You say that showed a "lack of confidence" and was insulting. Now my Dear Sister—for I shall consider you as such for the present at least—so far as lack of confidence is concerned. No person lives in whom I place such implicit confidence as in my sister Emma and I would as soon insult any other person living as her. We have always joked. Indeed I do not know which began it you or I. But certain it is both have done it. In regard to "the boy" of which you refer no doubt my sister first mentioned him and although I have often writen [*sic*] of him I had no more idea of distrusting you than I used to Mrs. Spaulding when I joked her about Dr. Childs or some one else. You have sent the dollar back and so I suppose you felt insulted because I sent it. Although I gave many reasons for sending it the real one was this. The one dollar gold piece is the handsomest piece of money in use—so I think—and I have sent one to my sister not because it was good looking but because I thought being pretty it would be an acceptable "keepsake" to show the friendship I felt for my sister. I do not remember what I did say but I must have said some foolish thing I suppose as it would not have been sent back [otherwise]. I will send it again in this as a token of continued friendship and confidence not to be judged by the smallness of the money but being quite pretty I judge it a proper present for my sister. Do not be offended at that for if you knew my feelings better I know you would not have been even offended at all. I guess in future I will stop joking until I see you for if I can explain myself I know you will not be offended.

Did I show lack of confidence? I thought you did and after hearing from you I was satisfied. Did I insult you? Why Emma! I insult my sister? I would as soon take off an arm as to intentionally insult you. Nothing could be further from my thoughts.

No 2

In the last letter, I think before these you say "Nothing done on my part shall ever break the relation of brother and sister "between us" or words to that effect. . . .

Now Emma if I have shown lack of confidence I say as you did certainly nothing could be further from my thoughts. I have most perfect confidence in you. If I have insulted you with all my heart I ask to be forgiven and trust it will be granted. Why Emma should I lose the letters from you and the friendship which they indicate my stay here would be almost unendurable. Nothing around me—hardly—is pleasant. Almost every thing is calculated to make me homesick but when I receive your letters so full of fun when the world moves smartly with you I laugh and for the time enjoy myself.

But now my sister gets mad with her brother, and, are those letters to stop?

I hope not. My sister will forgive her brother this time and hold him on his good behavior in future. Is it not so Emma?

Now for reply to the letter of the 5th.

So my sister has been sick with the measles was quite sick I suppose. Not long for which I am glad but your eyes will be weak and I hope you have not used them enough to injure them since. Be careful Emma of your health. It is a great blessing to be as healthy as you are and I hope you will continue healthy for a <u>long</u> time. Then Mr Scott has gone to his long home. How sad. Of late I have stood by the death bed of two of my men and it was sad to see them as life ebbed away and they so far from home, brothers and sisters how would my sister feel if her brother should fall a prey to this climate but hold, let me see, she is no longer his sister. But I was answering the letter of the 5th <u>now</u> and she <u>is</u> in that. As yet I am quite well. While others are sick I stand the climate well. If I could come North it would be better for me I shall if I

---

[24] Colonel John D. Rust, commander of Eighth Maine Infantry.

can. I have writen you concerning it. Col Rust[24] says he is sure I will be Lieut Col and he wishes me to stay as he wishes to go home in July and leave the Reg't No 3

with me and he thinks I have better stay and get the "hang of business" that it may be easier. But now you may expect me during vacation perhaps not at exhibition then we will talk of every thing for I know you will forgive your brother so long as there was nothing intentional on his part. The Reg't is yet in Tybee[25] I am here (Port Royal) on business. Direct as before

> Now Emma be sure and write me.
> With much love and a kiss for my sister
> I remain as ever your brother John

Co C. On Picket At Rosa's Plantation
Port Royal Island ten miles from Beaufort S.C.
Sept 1st 1862

Dear Sister

I have writen [*sic*] three letters to you and have received none. . . . But knowing that my sister has written and supposing that you would like to know something more of soldiers life I will write again. Day before yesterday we had orders to be ready to march . . . yes yesterday (Sunday). . . .

If you please me of course that <u>villain's</u> face will not disgrace the album for I know that my sister does not regard him as a friend who would disgrace himself before a dieing [*sic*] wife. Tell me what did he say when you refused to correspond with him. Who your friends are to be is for you to judge of course As my <u>dearest</u> <u>friend</u> I know you will be careful. Oh Emma how often I think of you! I know the temptations which surround young ladies and I almost tremble: but I know that my sister is <u>good</u> and I have perfect confidence. How happy I shall be when the war is over to return and feel that I alone enjoy the love of a good and pure young lady And how sad I should feel if my hopes were disappointed I feel sure that it will not be so and I will try that I am worthy of such love. I have sent to [Mrs] Dustine Cecil Dreme of which book I have spoken before. I wish for you to get the book and keep it

----

[25] Tybee Island near Savannah, Georgia.
[26] Theodore Winthrop (1828–61), author of *Cecil Dreme* (Boston: Ticknor & Field, 1861).

for me. Densdeth was a terrible character but I know of just such men not possessed of as much power as Winthrop[26] represents him to have, perhaps, but yet just like him; and, Emma those men are more pleasing than you suppose ready to overcome and disgrace the fairest and purest of the other sex One of these men caused me to know and love my sister You remember! Shun such men as you would death. . . .

I will not forget your poney [*sic*]. As soon as I can find one that I like I will send him to my sister.

Jim was left in New York. He left the steamer while I was away and did not return before she sailed I have just received a letter from a man in New York saying that Jim is with him. I shall send for him. Beneath his dark skin is a soul which perhaps has been entrusted to me. He had a mind which I will try to develop and send him out to do good to his race.

I was pleased Emma with your journal as you called it. . . .

> It is a beautiful night as ever in July in Maine the moon is bright I wish I could see my sister but as I can not I will send a kiss and bid her good night John. . . .

————

Beaufort S.C
Sept 13th 1862

My Darling Sister

I feel sad I hardly know why. It is not often that I feel so and if I do I do not give way to my feelings. I have been up reading the war news of the 4th— the latest we have received—That may be a part While I feel sad I will do as you do have a chat; and I will chat with my sister. If I could sit by the window in the chamber with my sister by my side looking down onto those beautiful trees I think I should feel better. . . .

But every day I want to chat with you . . . as long as our relations are as they are now. Do you know that I sometimes fear that something will arise to change matters. . . . I think a kiss would do me good Not from every one no not even from Julie or my equally good friend Mattie. Do you think Willie[27] and Alice are particularly partial to each other? As for your opposite as you

---

[27] Willie Bryant, JEB's cousin.

call him if he is secesh of course you with two brothers in the Union army will have nothing to do with him No not even regard him as a friend.

I have written to Greenleaf [28] tell me in your next when did you hear from him. . . .

I feared when I left home that I was not quite well but am now very well and quite fleshy. You may depend I will look after my health and we will yet be happy together then we will talk of the dangers past and look forward to happiness.

Sunday eve Tis raining At home I do not feel as well during a storm as in fair weather here I feel better. I do not feel sad as when I commenced this letter. I feel cheerful but would give my poney for a good chat with my darling sister. I too have a rocking chair and unlike yours it has arms As I write I sit in it wish my sister was in it with me and we were in B- [Buckfield] I wrote you a few days since at your request about Sewell and did not express a wish I will now Emma I have been reading Gold Foil.[29] 'Tis a charming book I will send it to you soon As I read an idea was discovered which has changed my mind. The idea is this. "Avoid temptation" and I reason thus Sewell loved you and you had a regard for him. He loves you still and every time you write to him the old feeling is awakened in his breast. The more he thinks of it the stronger his desires are. You cannot correspond with him as you could with Henry Irish. Now it is your duty to withdraw the temptation from him and in time he will forget if he receives no letters if he does every one fans the flame and we are told that love begets love and you are tempted also. Perhaps you have not been already; you know. You have told me that you loved me well enough to marry me—I have told you the same. Now is it not better for both to avoid temptation. I have most perfect confidence in my sister I know she is good and pure but we all are subject to temptation and the only safe way is to avoid it. I was delighted at the way you treated the young Florida gentleman because you kept away from temptation I know that but few young ladies of my acquaintance have a stronger will than you but drops wear the stone in time. I do not suppose that you were made for me above all other girls neither do I suppose that I was made for you. I know that I shall be tempted when I return and I know you will be I shall shun it and I trust you will. When you see that a young man wishes to be more than a friend

---

[28] James Greenleaf Spaulding, Emma's brother.

[29] Josiah Gilbert Holland (1819–81), *Gold Foil; Hammered from Popular Proverbs* (New York: n.p., 1859).

avoid him and give him no chance to be tempted. So Emma although I have most perfect confidence in you and am happy that I have yet I must now ask that you do not correspond with Sewell unless you chose to select him. In that case I will talk as a brother and will tell you things of which I have never spoken. Good night my love with a kiss good night

John

Monday morn Tis raining again I have been reading Goldsmith[30] like his writing much. Have you read "The Traveller["] and "The Deserted Village["]. . . . If so what do you . . .

. . . Wonder how my sister is this morning [illegible] and would she like to see her brother with a kiss I [illegible] go to reading again. Will the time ever come when she will run into my office find me reading alone have a chat and with a kiss be away again—That is in the future

John

Monday eve 12 ½ midnight

The mail has just arrived and brings a letter from my sister Glad very glad to hear from you. Sorry to hear the sad war news: As for Greenleaf if he is the grade Post Master, I think he is safe. I fear the most will fight for many months wish I could help defend Washington but here I am as safe from Rebels as though I were at Kents Hill but not half as happy. Will write more tomorrow or next day so with a good night kiss I will retire.

Thursday 18th

'Tis a beautiful morning and as I learn that the mail leaves today at noon I will finish this long drawn out letter. You speak in your favor of the 4th of not hearing from Greenleaf. I see by the papers that no letters are allowed to be sent from the army of the Potomac and if you do not hear from him 'twill not be strange. . . .

But I must not write any more this time Good bye my sister write soon with a kiss goodby

J

---

30 Oliver Goldsmith (1728–74), author of poems "The Traveller" (1764) and "The Deserted Village" (1770).

Co C 8th Maine Vols
Beaufort S.C
Sept 30th 1862

My Dear Sister

I finished my letter of the 21st etc this morn and as I have leisure and feel in the writing mood I will write again.

What you say in your last of Mr Packard proves what I said when I first knew of his disgraceful proposition to you. "Straws tell which way the wind blows" and I trust under no circumstances will you be tempted to treat him otherwise than as a villain. No not even if you are obliged to let your mother know the reason for when a good person has any thing to do with one of the other sex <u>known</u> to be a villain they are injured. You also speak of Mr Brown[31] wife & child coming North. You are glad I do not wonder, but I am sorry for the reason I spoke of when at home. Not that I suppose he will overcome you for I am certain he will not but I am sorry that one so nearly related as you should desire such a thing and sorry that he will be in Maine. I shall of course feel that you are as safe as though he were not there knowing the goodness of my sister and the strength of her will. But you know that it is much better to be with the good and those who desire our welfare. No good person can have constant intercourse with a bad person and not be injured such is the opinion of Dr. Holland[32] and also of your humble servant. So my dear be more guarded than you would if the remark had not been made which was made. It is hard I know not to feel like allowing such brotherly attentions as refined society permits but you know what is best and of course I leave all with you only putting you on your guard and giving you the opinions of two such sages as Dr Holland and myself. If he comes please tell me what you think give my warm regards to your sister and the little nephew. I have been thinking of having my moustache shaved off and now that I learn that Julie does not like one I am determined so give yourself no uneasiness on that account. I am sorry that Julie and Alice do not like [it] but that my sister has so good a chum and is pleased with the school pleases <u>me</u>. I never wanted to see you so much as since I returned from the North and am determined to

---

[31] Emma's sister Margaretta (Gretta) J. Spaulding Bisbee Browne's second husband, Jacob W. Browne.

[32] Josiah Gilbert Holland, author of *Gold Foil; Hammered from Popular Proverbs.*

leave in the spring unless we have fighting then. I shall go to Augusta and expect a pleasant time. . . .

The news from the North by the last steamer was very cheering if it continues as good the war must end before many months.

Sunday Oct 1st

'Tis a beautiful day and I am feeling tip top my health was never better, but I want very much to see my darling this afternoon. It would drive away those fears which trouble her and of which you speak in your note of the 21st etc and which was received yesterday. No I shall not laugh at your fears. It is quite natural for after such a dreadful outrage I do not wonder that young ladies see their danger but I must say that I think some of the girls carry their fears too far for what can be the danger in the College. I think that young ladies should not go far from home without a protector unless two or more are together and the crime of which you speak will no doubt be a warning to all careful young ladies. Not only that they have a protector but that it is one in whom they have confidence for a bad protector is much worse than none, but my sister is a very proper lady and I know does just what is proper.

I received a letter from Joseph[33] by the same steamer which brought your letter and he speaks of seeing "Miss Emma" from whom he says he hears of me frequently "I am pleased to meet her frequently and always find her the same <u>fine</u> <u>Laidy</u>" [sic] he says. So you see that Joseph is pleased with my sister and perhaps if she likes my [sic] get ahead of Miss Chadborn but if you desire that you must be quick for I guess Joseph intends to be married the first of November. Instead of being "mouse in the corner" perhaps you might give him lessons. Joseph courting! much better could I do preaching. He is an odd genius but a prime good fellow. I have reason to like him for he has been a good friend to me and never tires of telling of my exploits—should not care to have him know some that my sister knows. Should you? As for love between he and his Chadborn I never supposed there was any and since your description of her am confirmed in my opinion.

I have been thinking that I ought to look after one child and now that you advise it guess I will. Perhaps I will adopt it and the mother to [sic] if you think best.

---

[33] Probably Joseph Stevens; JEB also has a cousin Joseph Bryant.

I am more determined than ever to resign in the spring and am more and more disgusted with this Reg't.

> I shall not send the money in this but in another letter which I send with this

————

> Co C 8th Me Vols
> Beaufort SC
> Oct 23d 1862

'Tis a beautiful day

My Darling and I will commence one of my long letters to my sister. Wish I could see you this afternoon and have a good long chat feel just like it. Our forces landed on the mainland yesterday morning and we learn were badly cut up. Our Reg't was about the only one in this part of the Department which did not go and so you see luck is with us again. Everything works so far in favor of my returning to my friends again and no doubt we shall be happy together again. In your letter written while we were at home I notice you look on the darkest side. You would be much happier if you would have more hope and it would be as well I may be killed, and I may not. If I thought I should be I should be unhappy all the time. I expect to return to my friends and am happy in that thought. If I am killed it will be no worse than it would have been had I expected to die. If I died I shall have been much happier by being hopeful. I always look on the bright side and things come out right in the end. Yes if I were at home I would keep my sister as hopeful as I am. . . .

I am pleased that you have concluded not to correspond with Sewell. You say that "he may have been wild in the past" That he behaved himself well on Kents Hill. I have reason to know first from my sister and second from many others That he has been wild in the past you intimate and others inform me is true. You say he is noble and generous. I never saw a sailor that was not generous and they have qualities which pass for noble. I admire a sailor and have from my childhood. Indeed I desired to be a sailor and should if my parents would have consented but although I admire certain traits in sailors yet I have seen but few young men who went to sea that I would be willing to be the associates of a sister of mine. The very qualities we admire in them make them dangerous; for they gain the affections where a different person would not. But all I have said is of no use for your mind was already made up.

Sunday 26th

I have had no chance to write since Thurs for Friday I went after your poney and yesterday I was on duty. Yes I have got your poney and he is a splendid little fellow. Everybody admires him. Willie says he would like to buy him to send to Sarah. Others want him but if he lives and I live my sister shall have him. He is light red very kind and just large enough for you. I have not seen so pretty a poney since I have been in the State. I could now sell him for three times what I gave. I shall send him as soon as I can. I call him "Secesh Jim" and if he is admired as much in Buckfield as here he will be a great pet.

The expedition has returned they had nearly four hundred killed and wounded and accomplished nothing. I am glad that I was not there. It is a cold day for these parts the wind blows hard and my tent shakes but 'tis not cold enough for a fire. I suppose you have a good warm fire today wish I was sitting beside the fire with you But here I am away from home and home friends. . . .

You speak in one of your letters of of [*sic*] the trees looking beautiful and ask if the foliage South changes its colors to those bright tints. No we have nothing here so beautiful as the gorgeous tints of the woods of New England in autumn. I have somewhere read that they are the most beautiful of any in the world. The foliage here is always green. The leaves which fall off the trees in spring are green. 'Tis singular to see leaves just bursting from the buds on the tree with green leaves a year old.

Your experience in learning is the same as mine and I suppose of every one. While at school you can see that you make but little [progress] but when term closes and you look back and see how much you know that you did not know at the commencement you then perceive how much you have learned.

I continue to be more and more determined to leave this Reg't as soon as Spring. Every day I am more and more disgusted. I am obliged to obey men that I know are my inferiors and yet superior in command—men corrupt as they can be and I do not think it my duty to stay under such men and I will not unless we are in active service. If I should leave under such circumstances my motives would be misunderstood And I would rather be shot than do any act which should seem to be from cowardice.

Monday eve

The poney looks better and better each day. He is a great pet with my men.

I have been teaching school today and it seemed like old times.[34] When I came South in Aug a lady from New York came in the steamer and while in New York she was put under my charge, but there were several officers on board and as they were very attentive and she was not very handsome I gave up all attentions to them to tell the truth I did not think she knew much and I hardly spoke to her during the passage. Not very polite was I. If she had been better looking it might have been otherwise. Some weeks after I came here I met her and another teacher more plain if it were possible. She was very glad to see me and introduced me to teacher No 2. I talked with them a few moments and both invited me to call upon them at their house and also at the school room. A few weeks more passed and I called at the school room and found teacher No 1 alone with 140 black brats who had come to learn. She was neglected by the gents because, of course, she was not handsome. I was mad with myself because I had entirely slighted a young lady away from home and friends and I offered to assist her. She said she should be very happy to have me and today I fulfilled my promise and what do you think. I found an assistant in the person of a pretty young lady and she had picked up a young man who I noticed was very attentive and assisted also in teaching. I was mad again that this teacher No 1 should have been alone so long and No 3 should have got an assistant so soon. I therefore asked to have a class and so helped to learn some of these little black children to read and not satisfied with this I told No 1 of my poney and offered her the loan of him to ride. She was much pleased and I will show these pretty young misses that not they alone shall receive attention. Although to tell the truth to my sister I should like it better if it was a certain little black eyed girl I know of with me then when we were out of sight I would steal a kiss. But if I could I would as soon kiss my hand as this teacher No 1. I have not heard from you since I wrote my last letter before this. I am a bit lonely this eve wish I could see my sister this eve but as I can not will kiss you good night

John

---

[34] For details of the schools operated by Northern humanitarian organizations under the protection of the Department of the South, see Willie Lee Rose, *Rehearsal for Reconstruction: The Port Royal Experiment* (New York: Vintage, 1964).

Co C. 8th Me Vols
Beaufort S.C
Oct 28th 1862

I have just read a letter from you

My Darling and of all the letters I have ever received from you I think 'tis the best. When I opened it I felt a little sad but when I finished I felt different than I ever have after receiving a letter from you and now that I feel very well I am going to tell you something which I did not intend to speak of. When I have opened your letters it has been almost with a dread of something unpleasant a fear that "Mr Bryant" would first catch my eye but no 'twas "My Dear Brother" And when I had read the letter I found it every thing I could expect and yet there was a longing for something beside if I had been asked what I could not have told. And I lay down the letter with a sigh. I have longed my darling for one heart which as you so beautifully express it I might clasp to my heart and feel that it beat in unison with my own. I never felt fully that such a heart was in existence until this night away down here in S.C. far away from all friends who are <u>dear</u> to me. I could not blame you if you did not feel towards me just as I wished I was glad that you loved me as a brother. But Emma as much as we have been togather [*sic*] and as many evidences of affection as I have had nothing has ever reached my heart like those few simple words of yours writen [*sic*] on the 18th. I tonight long to press to my bosom my little sister and have her nestle in my arms as of yore. Now have I not been very silly to speak thus? A large man as you say, and a soldier— Captain of a company I talk so because my heart is moved by the heart far away which I feel is true to me. God grant that I may be true to her! I will write more tomorrow. Good night my darling receive a warm kiss and have pleasant dreams.

Thurs eve

Your favor of the 16th was received two days before that of the 18th. . . . I notice by what you say in yours of the 15th that you intend to attend school next winter. I sent $20.00 with this letter and if you attend will send more as soon as school commences. What you say of Alice I have no doubt is true of all young ladies viz that she is pleased to receive attention from the gentlemen. Those who profess indifference but take up the cry of "sour grapes" Indeed I do not think it wrong to desire attentions from the other sex before a selection is made and not afterwards to a proper extent. I am sorry of your objection to my plan for a library but until I return let it rest as it is you having charge of my books and pictures. I did not see that your letter was any better for having been kissed by Miss Beady [*sic*] should much rather she had kissed me.

Poor unfortunate girl! What untold suffering you have endured since you commenced to board at Mr Pattersons 1st—if I remember well—the bread was absolutely unendurable. Then the fish troubled your sensitive little nose and now the water is not to be endured. I fear you will not live through your schoolgirl days(?) Was sorry that your favorites the frogs caused the trouble(?) Give yourself no trouble about money. . . .

Your little Jim is improving finely Willie has been riding him today and he pronounces him a splendid saddle poney he "lopes" so easy. He is a little beauty. What fun you will have next summer and fall. You must be a good girl to pay for him (?) And beside he is as gentle as a lamb but as smart as you will wish I would not take a hundred dollars for him. Within a few days our Reg't has been placed under the command of Gen Saxton[35] military Governor of S.C this insures us an easy task during the winter and exemption from battle. So my darling rest easy about me. Let me know immediately if the $20 which I send in this is received. Good night and receive a kiss from your brother John

———

Co C 8th Me Vols
Beaufort SC
Dec. 25th 1862

I wish you a "Merry Christmas" "My Love" I have wished all day that I was at home and that we were having a pleasant sleigh ride this beautiful day. It has been a beautiful day here the mercury about 80° above 0 as warm as July in Maine and now 7:00 P.M. it is 60° above—moderate—It has been a merry Christmas here I assure you. The officers were drunk and raced horses Lieut's. Capt's, Maj's, and Lt Cols together. Men would not dare do so in Maine. I have seen more of the soldiers drunk although no doubt there are many instances. I am more and more disgusted with the army. Down here gamblers and drunkards rule. I am thankful that I did not form such habits when I was a boy for now instead of desiring to join with those who "indulge"

———

[35] Brigadier General Rufus Saxton served in the Department of the South as Chief Quartermaster. On April 29, 1862, he became military governor of the Sea Islands, under the direct command of the War Department.

I loath it. I passed a very pleasant eve last night with Maj Strong he was formerly a Methodist minister. He lives with the Rev Mr French[36] who has become quite noted in this Department or rather stops with him nights. The house is the headquarters of the anti-slavery people of Beaufort. The parlor is well furnished there were several ladies and gentlemen present and they had prayers. All knelt but myself but my love I prayed. I used to pray often but do not now as often as I should. I do not know that I have ever told anyone but you that I pray because I do not profess religion and if I told others that I prayed they might think I was a hypocrite and I would much rather be thought to be irreligious. I love to be in a room of prayer as I was last eve where all around were religious but a noisy meeting I do not. Wont my "little angel" pray often for me; that I may be no worse and much better than now. A steamer has arrived from the North today and no letter from you. Write often love for I want so much to hear from you. I am yet in arrest and no trial granted me.[37] The common remark in camp is, "They are afraid either to try Bryant or release him he will whip the whole gang yet" so your brother has thought for some time, but an end will come to this matter—I hope soon. I intended to have sent you a "Christmas present" but shall send one "New Years" am waiting for an answer to "that letter" before sending it For perhaps it might make a difference in the kind next steamer will most certainly bring a letter from you tell me when do you think of attending school.

Good Night Love

With Christmas kisses
Good Night
John

Fri 26th Another steamer arrived yesterday Emma and no letter from you. I am disappointed, sorry, cross, surprised etc. because I do not hear from you. Is it so cold that you have frozen up and closed business for the winter. It has been a delightful day as pleasant as June at home and I have been sitting all the eve in my tent without a fire.

---

[36] Reverend Mansfield French, Methodist minister and later army chaplain, representative of the Port Royal Relief Committee in conjunction with the American Missionary Association, was one of the missionaries to the Sea Islands.

[37] JEB awaited court-martial trial after his arrest for insubordination, stemming from his lack of respect for Colonel Rust's authority. Rust discounted Bryant's letter of apology after the primary incident and pressed charges. The trial began a few days after this letter and lasted about one month.

I am not yet allowed a trial and know not when one will be granted me.

Good Night

John

Fri eve 11 P.M. After I had written what you have read on the first page of this sheet one of my men handed me a letter and as soon as I saw the well known direction I felt better. I had hardly finished writing when the letter was handed me it appears that it was too heavy for 3 cents when you write more than two sheets full it is safest to put on two stamps. My aunt Harriet would say make your letter light enough for 3 cents but your brother does not say so. I take back all I said the first of the eve and will answer your letter in a few days. I have only one think [*sic*] to say tonight I don't like those "<u>Kind</u> Good Nights" of yours—if you cant send a kiss or say something else say "Good Night" I prefer that with the "<u>kind</u>" omitted. It sounds too much like a girls writing to a disconsolate lover wose [*sic*] love was not returned but she was willing to be "<u>kind</u>." The "Good Night" is better for being blunt and cold which I much prefer to a patronising air. But "My Love" I received your letter now with a much different feeling from what I did a few weeks ago. Indeed I receive them as I should your own self with open arms or like a little boy would a bit of coke(!) This was a charming letter guess you had a December "Thaw"(!) but Emma without joking I was highly pleased with it twas really so frank just like talking with you it appeared to be from the heart of my own "little angel" Harrietlike[38] to have you talk to me thus.

I mistrust that instead of that being Mary Whitney 'twas Hat herself for I know no Mary Whitney and she lies so easy and I wish you would see if you can find out. 'Twas just like her she never forgets me and although she abuses me yet really loves me such is the characteristic of woman. Excuse me my dear I almost dodged my head when I said that for fear you would give me rap know you would if I were in reach

But My Love

Good Night

I will write no more in this letter but send it and answer yours soon.

With much love and kisses

Good Night

John

---

[38] JEB's friend Harriet Whitney, from Wayne, former classmate at Kents Hill.

P.S. Womans style—The poney is safe and [illegible] of how near he came of being deprived of the pleasure of carrying your little self I dreaded to tell him. I shall keep him and bring him North if I can

"Most Kindly"
John

There is the Miss Whitney now in Wayne and I never knew any other but Hat and a younger sister now married.

————

Co C 8th Me vols
Beaufort S.C
Dec 27th 1862

I have sent a letter to you today "My Love" but will this eve commence another.

Yours of the 13th did atone for that of the 11th but as I have writen of that no matter tonight. You say "Believe a mans heart is supposed to be situated in the vicinity of his pocket" It is well it is so for the ladies hearts are fixed upon what they put upon their backs and if it were not for these pockets they I fear would be heart broken. I should think you had been reading Fanny Fern[39] and had attended a womans rights convention besides having been desperately in love with a man who had proved false to you, by the way you talk. Poor unfortunate creature(!) What horrible creatures the men are (!) how can that much abused sex of yours condescend to associate with them. Do tell me dear I am sorry to pity you my little darling. Will you allow me to kiss you when I return—As for the letter I guess I will keep it to read to you some time.

Now be sure to find out if it was Hat Whitney who was with Miss Armstrong. I am quite sure it was. I think Gold Foil is a charming book did you notice many places which I had marked The same chapter you speak of—Vices of Imagination—particularly attracted my attention and I think is marked more that any other chapter in the book. I am thankful too, my darling, that you have been spared and I too pray that you may be preserved for you are my angel and I am glad to feel that I am worthy of one so good. Pray for me will you not that I may continue worthy. You see nothing of

————

[39] Sarah Payson Willis Parton, under the pen name of Fanny Fern, wrote in Boston magazines and later the *New York Ledger* on the role of women and various controversial issues.

drunkenness in B[ryant.] I thought before I entered the army that I knew
something of it but find that I knew but little. Here it is popular to be a
drunkard and gambler and unpopular to be a temperance man. Nearly all the
officers drink but I am thankful that I remain true to my pledge. I have a
charter and shall organize a Division of S[ons] of T[emperance] very soon
and called Army Division No 2. Will Alice ever really truly and warmly love
anyone? Has she not a cold temperament so much so that she cannot warmly
love any one but self? Willie is much like the girls indeed has been scooled
[*sic*] by them or rather has seen and followed their example. He is every bodies friend and does not mark out a course for himself to follow and dislike
those who do not come up to his ideas. The girls are so too They appear to
love every body and as I said I can't help being a friend to such but I don't
want my lady love too common. That which we get easily we prize lightly. We
may be pleased and flattered at the attention of a lady but when we see that
every one comes in for a share we conclude that tis cheap. We like to have our
ladies a little exclusive For if they love too many 'twill be like a small plaster
spread over a large space too thin. Now I think Willie is that way and perhaps
on that account may make a good companion for Alice.

In regard to your attending school Emma you must do as you think best
always remembering that I wish for you to attend every term unless your
own health or that of your parents make it more prudent to stay at home. . . .
I have sent you $20 for the winter term. . . . Do not stay at home on account
of money my dear for it will pain me if I know 'tis so. I do not offer to do
what I do not wish to do and am not perfectly able to do, and if you have
such pride that your conscience is uneasy about it I will loan it and we will
after you graduate fix the payment. So my love do not let that stand in the
way. The books you send to Ticknor & Field[40] for come by mail as well as
any way. I am glad you are going to send for books. Government now owes
me $525 and I propose to save a part of that sum to buy books with and as
I owe no man—to my knowledge I do not know as it is any bodies business
how good a library I get. I propose to buy some few romances and shall
want you for critic. . . . Now another word in relation to Mattie. The very
idea of her speaking well of every body I dislike. Mattie is a fine girl but
that—in my opinion—is one of her faults. To strangers 'tis best to speak
well of all we say any thing of but we should not always speak well of all.
The vices of some should at times be spoken of to warn others to shun the

---

[40] Boston publisher.

evil. I shall come in the spring <u>sure</u> if I can get away and I think I can. I shall try to be at exhibition. Poney Jim will accompany me. You ask me what you should do about attending school. If you wish to attend and if your father and mother think best I should go. Never be afraid of annoying me always say all you wish to I am glad to have you. If you get all of my letters you must hear from me often for I send one or more every week.

Good Night Love With a kiss
John

Thurs Jan 1st

I wish you a "Happy New Year" Love Wish I was in Maine tonight would have a sleigh ride to Turner or some other good place. Now would you like that?

I have tonight received your letter of Dec 22<u>d</u>. Cant say I am satisfied and as <u>you</u> say wish to see and have a talk with you I will not say what I would like to. Do not under any circumstances allow any one not even your parents to know of the contents of the letter of Dec 1<u>st</u>. It would have been proper if you had thought best to answer as I wished to have informed your parents as it is I desire that you will not allow any one to know what it contains. If you have already informed your parents be sure it is known to no more of your folks at present. You will please me in this will you not? If the letter is not all I desired yet it is very good at least the first part. I have assurances which are partly what I desired. Yes, of course you may be my little sister longer. I do not think as you do of an engagement. If I were engaged to any one and they wished to have it broken off I should give my consent and should expect the same treatment from a lady but to love one as I wish and feel that there is no <u>certain</u> tie that binds us is what I do not like and our letters have been until quite lately unsatisfactory to me and my letter has accomplished one object—It has caused us to express to each other our feelings more than before. It had become a fixed policy with me to have no expressions of mine in the hands of another which if an enemy by accident should see, could be used to my disadvantage but I am away from you so long that I can persue [*sic*] this policy no longer. How abserd [*sic*] for us to caress each other as we do when togather [*sic*] and when we are absent be cold and formal in our letters. It is too childish. It would show us to be too much the creatures of impulse and so I shall run the risk of having my letters by any accident fall into <u>other</u> hands than yours and trusting all to the honor and love of my little sister. I will say what I please. It appears to me that in your last you hold back some things you would say. Do not fear of having your letters seen by others. Your letters before I went North are in the trunk which I left at Mrs Spauldings locked up and if I die please take them and these I now have shall be sent to you or destroyed. I know we cannot write as we talk. But we may be openhearted to each other. I love you my darling ever so much tonight and live for you I shape my life in future in a measure to please you. Now that I have said as much let me be very frank a moment. Until I went North last summer I did not suppose we should ever be other than brother and sister. But I saw then plainer than ever before that our relations to each other were wrong. We gave people to understand by our conduct that we bore to each other a different relation. You knowing the true state of the relations felt justefying [*sic*] in receiving some attentions from Sewell my friends having other ideas thought it wrong. I then saw that we must no longer bear to each other simply the relation of brother and sister. If that was the case I must write to you not so frequent and must show you less attention. You have chidden [*sic*] me for a lack of gallantry. It was not that I was constantly quarreling with myself whether or no I was doing right. I commenced you know how. When we were togother [*sic*] oftener and oftener I changed and yet I feared it was not proper for us to marry. I could not break off on account of my own feelings and so did as I did perhaps it was not right one thing is certain my motives were pure and if I did wrong I was <u>lead</u> [*sic*] <u>into it</u> by my own feelings and did intend no wrong. When I was at home I thought very much on the subject and of course my friends talked to me of that I have told you. . . .

I know that women are led away by men but they are bad men. As I said the most lovely are ensnared and cast off. How can we men know who are These young ladies appear to us as good as good ones. Sometimes we learn that those we have admired are not good and as I said when we learn that several are not good we learn to distrust all for we can know no difference by seeing them. I have talked with many <u>good</u> men about this very thing and I know that they feel as I do. One of our Captains is keeping company with a beautiful girl in Manchester N.Y. Those who know her tell me she is a fine lady and yet I would distrust her. Why askes [*sic*] my sister. Because I <u>know</u> him to be a <u>villain</u>. I am satisfied he would as soon rob a young lady of her virtue as he would kiss her. I know by letters which he has shown me from her that she loves him (Do not suppose that I show your letters after they reach me—my eyes alone see them) I do not know but he has "taken advantage of that trusting love." She was a lovely girl and is now I judge yet I should distrust her and would never marry her. Henry Irish has been intimate with Kate Hinder.

They have been alone—past the hours which your mother thinks proper. If they parted and I wished and could I would as soon marry Kate as though she and Henry had never been intimate Why? Because Henry is honorable and would as soon die as ruin a virtuous girl so I think I do not distrust Kate. . . . Since I have known her I have learned to see more clearly the temptations of the sex and get to see the nobleness of their virtue. . . . Now I say I do not distrust your sex as I did before I knew you and is it true that after knowing me as long as you have you speak of men in general as you do. Men are as true as women—both are oftentimes bad. It is not the man who ruins a woman that alone distrusts but he who has often been deceived or rather, found those he considered good different from what he supposed. You were right in supposing that I should not have allowed you to continue such a lecture. I should have placd [*sic*] my moustache over that saucy mouth of yours until you would change the subject. You find fault with me because I say some things of your sex but you say harder things of the gentlemen. But remember this If you keep the company of honorable gentlemen alone you will have no occasion to doubt but there are honorable men and your virtue is sacred to them. . . . Do not talk so again plase [*sic*]. It destroys the pleasure I take in receiving your letters.

Now Emma in regard to Mr Brown[e] he is the husband of your sister as such you must of course show him certain attentions. If he comes for you or offers to carry you to school or to any other proper place I should think it best to go with him as though you had never heard a word but I would think it best to be sure that you gave him no chance to attempt any thing wrong and if he did you know very well what to do. I do not know Mr Brown[e] and all I know about that was what Isaac said and under the circumstances and time when it was said I did not doubt it. If I had most certainly I should not have mentioned it. If you should be satisfied that he meant wrong you would not under no circumstances allow yourself in his way. I hope and trust it was not true. I pity you my darling and wish I could take you in my arms this eve and kiss away all unhappines [*sic*] as I used to do. One rule my darling please adopt. If you know it do not allow yourself to receive any attention from any man you know to be bad but be quite certain before you judge. Bad men I have found are usually favorites with ladies if they can hide their badness for they try so hard to make themselves agreeable and by experience know how to reach a womans heart Some good men do also.

In your note of the 5th you speak of being sad and of writing "doleful epistles" I did not think that of the 22d which I have just answered was very doleful. You speak of the death of Genl Mitchell.[41] We met with a great loss when he died. But your fears of yellow fever were unfounded. Genl Mitchell and Staff came from Hilton Head sick with the fever—with those exceptions I have known of no case of Yellow fever in Beaufort. Beaufort is one of the most healthy places on this coast. I have been very well since I returned from the North and as we have had heavy frosts shall have no more danger from Yellow Fever. So my darling give yourself no uneasiness on that account. I am glad that my little sister has such an interest in her brother. Camp life would sometimes be unendurable were it not for the remembrance of loved ones at home.

So you presume to laugh at me for my fancy of a novel. My sister laughing at her brother and attempting to give him information of novels just as a parent would talk of a child "Such as I used to read in my child hood" ha ha Did you suppose I was about six or eight. I beg to inform you my dear that that was an extract from one of the best Italian romances writen by one of her best writer[s] and I will pardon your poor judgment from the fact that you gave it "slight attention" If you can please get the book for me. Dont be alarmed I shall not be offended at any of your nonsense. You ask "had this Hattie Whitney a sister Mary" No Why did you ask? please answer This beats all the letters I have ever writen but as I am in the writing mood will fill one more sheet. Here before me is your letter of the 12th Nov. How different from some parts of the 22$\underline{d}$ Oct For instance "would have welcomed you very <u>very</u> gladly"

"If I had known that was your opinion then I most certainly should not have received your attentions" How do those sound side by side. You do not write doleful letters but all kinds. I have been expecting one beginning "Mr Bryant" before this. But my little darling write as you wish and please do not say hard things again I am sorry my love that you are so uneasy about me I shall live and we will yet be <u>so</u> <u>happy</u> togaher [*sic*]. Shall we not. Your arguments about commencing the practice of law are very good and it was only after the most careful thought and the advice of some of my best friends that I concluded to join the army. If I live I expect to return in the spring and will then give you all arguments which have governed me if you desire to know. As for the poney I have got him he is a little beauty. If my sister had not wanted him I should not have bought him Now I have got him I will send him home and we will see then whether or no you want him.

Now I think I have answered all you have writen and suppose we have a bit of a chat. I am more than ever disgusted with this Regiment You know I have

---

[41] Major General Ormsby MacKnight Mitchel, newly appointed commander of the Department of the South and the X Corps, died on October 30, 1862, of yellow fever.

always liked the Colonel[42] but of late he has shown himself to be a rascal. I have befriended him and got enemies by doing so and of late he has done things that I disapprove. In a word he has shown himself to be a different man from what I supposed him to be. At another time I will speak more fully I am well but want more than ever to caress my darling once more. But I have writen too much already I will close receive a hundred kisses and much love

"Most kindly"
John

———

Company C 8th Reg Maine
Beaufort S.C
Jan 4th 1863

'Tis Sabbath eve "My Love" and will you excuse me if I write to you tonight. On the 1st I wrote to you two very long letters and ever since have felt that I should write another to explain some things I fear you may be offended by some of the remarks made there. I said I used to be happy when with you but unhappy when away. Now if I repeat in this some things I said in those letters excuse me please. You were my scholar. I was pleased with you because you were a good scholar. A young man I feared was plotting your ruin—I told you of it. This of necessity made us intimate and we were frequently togather [sic] I learned to love you and called you my sister. I thought I could love you as my <u>sister</u>. When with you I was very happy we had pleasant times togather. You know that at every interview we were more and more intimate. As time passed I felt that it was not proper for me to be so intimate and I would promise myself to be more "<u>proper</u>" when with you but it was not so when we were alone. It was by accident that we became intimate and I had no intention of becoming so intimate and did not suppose that we would ever be to each other more than brother and sister. As time passed I felt that I gave you reasons to think it more than brotherly friendship. I thought I was doing wrong and yet I could not refuse myself the pleasure of being with you this made me unhappy. I raised objections, to myself, to our being other than brother and sister and yet I could not prevail upon myself to act properly or rather prudently so time passed and every month it grew no better very fast. At length

---

[42] Colonel John D. Rust.

I came into the army. Before I came I had so far changed my mind that I was willing to promise to be engaged to no one but my sister until I returned and when I returned felt that we should have an understanding. The affair with Sewell and your being absent in Portland almost separated us. But the last time I was in Buckfield I felt differently. And so I came out here. One after one the reasons against your being other to me than a sister vanished and I was ready to say what I did. If I interpret your answer aright I am satisfied but I wrote as I did for this reason. We have been togather a long time, love. It is wrong to be as intimate longer unless we look upon each other in a different light than brother and sister. I see and feel it—I can love you as my darling little sister but have expressed my wishes. If we are to be brother and sister then we must look for a dearer friend in some other one. I have opened my feelings to you very plainly, for our letters have been of that non committal style which I am heartily sick of. Let us understand each other and act accordingly?

My trial progresses finely my counsel says I am all right. The trial will probably last a week longer.

I shall look for a letter in answer to this and the two last—which I suppose will go by same steamer—very anxiously. Be as plain with me Emma as I have been. It is due to yourself and to myself to understand each other.

Although I have writen perhaps in a businesslike manner I am very anxious for your reply. I know you love me Emma but are you willing to be my "Love," shall I learn to give you all, every bit of my love? Can we when togather be perfectly happy and when away feel not a bit of unhappiness on each others account? Do not hold one thing from me open your heart to me as I have mine. Now please do so

> Good Night Darling
> And have a kiss from
> Me

―――――

> Camp 8th Regt Me vols
> Beaufort S.C
> Jan 27th 1863

My Darling little Sister

I have just received another one of your letters marked "Due" and so it appears that my letters are marked the same. I feared it might be so because yours came marked that way. But if yours are too heavy they are delayed at Port Royal and it is some days before I get them. For instance the mail reached here last Friday and I get this letter (which came on same steamer) today. The reason is there is no Post Office at Beaufort or has not been until within a few days.

As for money darling let us say no more about it. You can not receive it with the same pleasure with which I give it I dont like you any the less for your feelings and let us drop the subject. Only let me know how much money you wish to use and leave the rest with me. When I commenced to give you money, you were my little sister. 'Tis true a little more but yet my little sister. Now you are my little darling and if we should be again brother and sister I should be glad I had done as I have. Only one thing would make me sorry and that can never happen I <u>know</u> viz for you to throw yourself away as many young ladies have done as good as my little pet too. But they had not such a wise brother (?) to advise them as you have and did not "play their cards wisely" I have not answered your other letter yet for I have been returned to duty and find <u>very</u> <u>much</u> to do in my company. I will answer it as soon as I get things in my company straight. As for the <u>present</u> you will receive it in due time and I know you will be delighted Be sure to tell me when it is received. Poney Jim is well and I know you will be in love with him when you see him. My boy Jim has not come yet.

I think I have answered your letter, except one thing of which in a moment, all that I propose to. We are so far away and it takes a letter so long to reach me that we can not touch upon disputed points safely and let them pass. Your letter before this is a charming letter I have read it more than once and shall not at present put it away. This one I shall at once file away. It does not displease me But is just the kind that once would almost. Of course I would not allow myself to be displeased with you.

One thing I did forget and asked you pardon in my last letter I asked you not to show my letters I told you why. I did not distrust you but as I said; one who has been burned is cautious even where there is no danger. In future let us have no arguments until I return. They do no good and if you are as sad when you get my letters of that kind as I when I get yours I pity you and so enough. Let the past go. When I see you I can satisfy you that I have acted as I should. But never asked the advise [*sic*] of my friends on that one point Although they have talked to me But I will stop. Dont allude to it darling.

But my little pet does not wish to write love letters do not for the world(?) No doubt she has become sick of them from reading those flashy love stories and can not allow her self to be guilty of such an impropriety. One thing I am glad of though you will stop your "kindly." But Emma pardon all I have said or done to make you unhappy. I am a wayward youth I know and you must make me as good as your little self talk to me as you feel; write when and what you like only do not mention any of our old arguments. You have told me that you love me that we might be to each other as dear friends and yet we will if you like call each other brother and sister for we will <u>always</u> be as near to each other as that certain.

I cant write more now but will in a few days. I want to see my little darling sister ever so much and will come in the spring if my life is spared. Shall we be happy then without a drawback? I trust so.

Good bye, with kisses
Good morning
John

Camp 8th Regt Me Vols
Beaufort S.C.
March 8th 1863

Tis beautiful weather my "Darling Little Dovie" like a warm June day at home. The peach trees are in blossom some of which blossoms I send to you. They look pretty on the trees. I was just reading one of your letters telling me of your skating. Our weather has not been very favorable for skating the past winter. The water in tubs froze but twice I think and then not more than ¼ of an inch. But give me New England after all. I suppose I shall allow interest to govern me somwhat [sic] but shall try very hard to find a home in Maine. I think I shall know how to prize my home and friends when I return Oh! how I want to see you dovie I would give—a kiss if I could. Will the time come when we will be happy togather again. If so we will be happier than ever before Oh! that this war might close that I might return. But I shall leave this Regiment in a few months let the result be as it may. I have learned how to prize Christmas holy days since I have been in the army and think that next Christmas I will have some fun. Wont <u>we</u>? Perhaps skating togather

I am so glad Darling that you are happy at Kents Hill. I thought you would be and that was <u>a</u> reason why I laughed at you when you were homesick. I had been just so myself and learned to think that no place was like Kents Hill. My folks are all Methodists and I am glad you like them. They have often tried to make me one perhaps my little angel will succeed. I need some one to make me good although I am not remarkably bad now.

You speak in one of your letters of my arrest and say, "My faith is of course strong that all will be well" I have told you in a previous letter that it is well with me. I can not tell you all the particulars now will when I see you But had it not been for villainy I should have been acquitted the first time. As it is I have lost more than a hundred dollars and at length been acquitted of all. But that does not annul the previous sentence. As it is I loose [sic] my money but gain very much in position. In the end I will be the gainer all round. I think I can see into the future and see that I have been benefitted.

8 ½ P.M. Since writing the above two officers came to my tent and wished for me to defend a Lieut of the 6th Conn who is to be tried tomorrow before a Court Martial. I consider that a great compliment Because one of the officers who came has been for several months Provost Marshall and is considered a smart officer and because they being from Conn select me a Maine man to defend a Lieut a particular friend of theirs and because I am and have been for four months to their knowledge in arrest. I will own to you dovie that I am pleased. One of these days when I am at the bar I will try to be pleased by success there. Success is what gives us friends. Not such friends as my little dovie I do not mean but fair weather friends who can be of service to us even though they leave in a storm. I am fortunate always in having friends then who stand by me—then Wont you congratulate me on my success. You who are a friend in rain and storm as well as sunshine. I know you will be pleased dovie. I am glad you have so much confidence in me. I pray My Father that I may never loose [sic] your confidence I want just such a friend and I love my darling better and better.

You say men have a particular tallent [sic] for lounging you made a mistake it is women who do but little but lounge and gossip. I hardly know which they enjoy best perhaps you can tell me.

Now see here do not tell me any more that you cannot write composition. Do you tell me so to get me to compliment you? No matter I think not if I did I would not do so But thinking that you do really get discouraged I will say that but few I might say not any lady of my acquaintance has the tallent for composition which I think my sister has. I do not flatter you Emma. When you get so you love to write composition and are satisfied to write as you feel for the pleasure of writing then you will succeed depend upon it. Write your thoughts upon such subjects as you feel an interest in and I will [illegible] you. Tell me about your Exhibition piece please. When you want to talk to me take the pen and talk as you would if I were in the great rocking chair. No matter if you send a letter every day. If you can not do that write a little each day and send one a week only be free and <u>talk</u> with me. If you are very happy tell me; if not happy talk with me about that. I feel an interest in all that <u>you</u> do.

Some of your last letters do not commence "Dear Brother" I like to be called so. You told me once you liked to keep up the farce I did not then know how well I liked to be called so. I know it is only a farce but you were my darling little <u>sister</u> once I thought that was it and I learned to love to be called brother somehow it sounds better. But of course I do not ask you to please me love. Please yourself and that will please me but I thought perhaps you concluded by some of my letters that I did not wished to be called so I do sister.

I expect to send Poney Jim to Fayette by next steamer. He needs to be bitted and broken before you take him. I will tell Joseph all about it and when I come in the summer will get a saddle and bridle and make a formal present of him to you. But remember he is yours <u>now</u> I claim no ownership in him and when he arrives you can do with him as you like only I think he had better remain with Joseph a few months and unlearn some of the bad tricks the boys have learned him he is as smart as Black Jim but a good saddle poney. If I never come Jim is yours for life. You may marry him if you like. But like him for his masters sake. . . .

It <u>did</u> give me pleasure darling to be told that your confidence was the same in me in adversity as in prosperity. If my little darling stands by me I should be happy though all others leave me but I have many friends here and some even among the ladies. I think (pardon the egotism you know I <u>am</u> egotistic) that I might perhaps have a <u>particular</u> friend down here if I wished a mans lady—from Bangor. But I will try to practice as well as preach although sometimes I wish I was with a darling friend.

Let me tell you a bit of gossip. It is not to whip you but to prove what I have before said. A Miss Thompson from Philadelphia came to this Department. She is handsome and accomplished and of course had many admirers. When she came there were on the steamer several ladies and several officers among the latter Lt Alford from whom I learn some of the facts. Most of the officers were bad But of course appeared good. They tried hard to pay attention to her but could not she hardly spoke to them after the first day. The other ladies received the attentions of the officers and the Lieut thinks that if they had virtue before they came they lost it there. Miss Thompson slighted their attentions and I learn from a lady friend of hers knew very well that the officers were not honorable. I think that Lt Alford was the only exception. After she arrived she received much attention but was prudent. At length Genl Saxton, a noble man, who has passed some thirty five years in single blessedness was enamored with this young <u>wo</u>man and proposed was accepted and she has now gone North to prepare for a married life and will in few days return to become Mrs Saxton. Such ladies dovie learn us to love the sex. She has slighted all until she gets a noble man who has worked his way from a poor boy to distinction. If she had yielded to the seductive influence of some gay young man she would not have been Mrs Genl Saxton.

[copy ends here; no signature]

———

> Camp 8th Regt Me Vols
> Beaufort S.C.
> March 9 1863

I have just received a letter from you Dovie and as Something very important has happened to me today I will write you although I put a long, long letter into the office today for you I will write again tonight. I was a bit disappointed to receive only one letter from you in three or four weeks but not vexed nor any where near it. You do not know how happy I feel Dovie in thinking that I have such a darling little angel to advise me. You have asked me several times of late not to seek revenge and I will try and please you although I have the best possible chance. When I was placed in arrest nearly four months ago, Rust had several friends upon whom he could rely now he has but one and I was told today that <u>that</u> friend was not to be depended upon by Rust. I have ten friends today where I had one then. Nothing could have done me more good.

I was informed today by General Saxton that I was to be released from arrest and would report to him—Genl Saxton—for duty. This Emma is a great victory and is so regarded by officers and men in this Regiment I feel tip-top wish I could see you and talk with you all about it. But if fortune smiles as I think it will the future has honors in store for me which I will speak of in due time. I now have a great stimulus to urge me on for I feel that my little sister will be happy at my success. With her counsel and love to help me I will have <u>honors</u> if I live. My aim is away up I may never reach it but I will work. Now Darling the clouds have broken I expect in a day or two that the sky will be clear then for a bold push for success. Pray for me Darling. I pray for myself but do not know as God will hear the prayer of one no better than I. He will hear <u>you</u> only ask that I may succeed when I do right.

I have <u>completely</u> <u>triumphed</u>. How do your parents feel about my troubles? Are they perfectly willing for you to be my <u>friend</u>? I am anxious to hear if the watch and money was received by you 'Twas a charming little watch and chain. I long to hear that you have received it.

> Good night Dovie
> With lots of love and kisses
> John

I have received a letter from Willie Bryant tonight he says in speaking of his friends "As to Alice of whom you spoke in connection with myself, now Alice, Emma & Julie" (see he puts Alice first) "I think [they] are three of the finest young ladies I ever met and I prize their friendship very much" Then he goes on to make excuses and protestations which put me in mind of a bashful boy in love who in trying to make people think it is not so shows that it is just so. Willie is a good honest honorable young man a good friend to my sister of which I am very glad glad because I know him to be honorable and my sister can be his friend safely. If she wants an advisor among the gentlemen he is one in whom she may place perfect confidence so far as his honesty goes. For instance suppose you wanted an escort and some young man should ask for "the pleasure of your company" and suppose you were not quite certain whether or no he was a proper person to accompany you. If Wille [*sic*] was at Kents Hill and you there he would be a good friend to speak to and would never mention it not even to his sisters. You ask me was it proper to receive attentions from a certain "engaged young man" on a certain occasion Perfectly if he was a suitable person. His being engaged or not engaged does not matter in my opinion. So far as I am concerned Emma I do not wish to interfere with your escorts. You are free as the air you breathe I shall never if I know it marry a woman who does not love me. I shall never buy or coax any person to love me. This Darling does not refer to <u>you</u> for I have never attempted either and never shall. What I say to you of others in regard to love matters is said as a <u>brother</u>. It may seem strange to you but if I know my heart that is the fact. What money I loan you is from a brother to a darling little <u>sister</u>. If I had no idea of ever being nearer I would do the same. As a lover it would be quite improper for me to give my advice same of how you should conduct with others and as a <u>lover</u> simply I should not I think consider it just right to offer you money. It is the first instance in my knowledge where a brother proposed to his sister But you know I am a strange mortal. No Emma as a lover

I shall leave you to do as you like and when you have decided as a <u>lover</u> I shall say nothing if you choose some one else. As a brother I may advise you against the one you choose. I shall not be easily offended nor very jealous but perhaps not easily reconciled when once <u>offended</u> which will never happen with you and I for we are <u>never</u> to be <u>offended</u> with each other. If we cant be lovers we can and will be brother and sister. I do not doubt you Dovie. Perhaps I shall never feel <u>certain</u> until we are engaged but I know you are so good and true that I am happy I know you will be honorable. If you cannot at any time love me better than any other young man that is enough my wife must love me <u>best</u> if I know her feelings. I would not for the world marry you if I could if you in the <u>least</u> regretted it. So as a lover I can never say a word about others unless it should be as a reason for breaking off. You must love me as free as I do you and as you do me. I shall never offer any inducement for you to love me except what my <u>life</u> shows. You must take me for "betterer or for worser." But Dovie as a brother I will advise you if you wish. One thing I would advise. Have a dear lady friend in whom you have confidence. One whom you <u>know</u> to be <u>good</u> and whose experience has given her a chance to form a correct judgment and if you have any doubt of the propriety of any course ask her advice. Mrs. Dustine is one of the best lady advisers I know of and a good friend to you. But do not let her know that we are other than brother and sister for I always told her so and I was honest when I told her and would rather she should see by my actions that I have changed my mind. Julie is another. But perhaps she may be a little envious. (Am I right?) Julie is a dear good girl and one of my warm friends I think but somehow I could not love her I do not know why myself. I will always as a brother advise you. Were I a girl and loved a man who was away I think I should on all proper occasions want an escort I suppose I should be <u>very</u> <u>careful</u> that his character was without suspicion. I should not be particular whether he was engaged or not but should want him agreeable. If he was not I should not go very often where he was. But the moment I saw a friend was too much interested in me I should always for the future avoid his attentions and if I found that I was too much interested in him I should do the same. Above all I should be sure of his character and if I had doubts should ask some gentleman friend of mine in whom I had reason to believe good. But Dovie how I run on. I did not intend to write but one sheet and here are three full.

Good Night again
"Most Kindly"(?)

Camp Saxton
Beaufort S.C.
March 28 1863

It is nearly if not quite two weeks since I had time to write a letter to my darling little Dovie. I have written two or three notes in one of which I put twenty
dollars for you. I directed that note to Kents Hill supposing you were at school.
Our Regt has gone to Florida and for that reason I have not heard from you for
a long time. I do not know whether you are at school or no and as I directed the
letter in which I sent the money to Kents Hill I will direct this to Buckfield.

You will be anxious to know why I am not with my Regiment. I have told
you of my troubles. I had been in arrest nearly four months and without doubt
should have remained in arrest some time longer. The only way to stop Rust
from arresting me if I remained with the Regiment was to report him and if possible have him arrested and tried. It was not certain that I could bring that about
and if I did a love of revenge would work in and my little Darling urged me not
to seek revenge and I wished to please her because she tries to please me and
because she is my little angel. I will acknowledge Emma that the love of revenge
is as strongly implanted in my nature as the love of flirting is in yours. You have
broken yourself of that and I will break myself of this. No one ever had a better chance than I to revenge themselves upon an enemy and it was not altogether
revenge either for I should be ill treated until I learned Rust to look out if I
remained with the Regt. Therefore I determined to leave the Regiment. But I
did not wish to leave the service yet. The rebellion must be crushed Emma and
I wish to help crush it. A young man at home will be looked upon by those who
have been to war, when the war is over, as a coward. I do not see how a young
man of pluck can stay at home. If I leave the army just now when Charleston is
to be attacked I should be looked upon as McDonald was when he left just
before the battle of Fredericksburg and I know you would not wish for me to
do that. The only thing left for me to do was to get another position in the army.
Fortune favored me as she usually does. Although I had been in arrest four
months and was then in arrest yet Genl Saxton who commanded the Brigade
asked Genl Hunter[43] who commands the Department to relieve me from duty
in the 8th Maine and have me report to him on special service. Gen'l Hunter
did so and I was released from arrest and ordered to report to Gen'l Saxton on

---

[43] Major General David M. Hunter, controversial commander of the Department of the
South, raised the first regiment of African American troops, the First South Carolina.

special service. That of itself was a great compliment and was so regarded. Genl Saxton made me the superintendent of the draft of colored men in this Department and gave me the command of the camp in which they were placed. That was a greater compliment than the first but of a different nature. The first relieved me from arrest and placed me on special service in a Generals command which as much as said that I was not to blame although I had been in arrest four months and was a severe rebuke to the Col who had placed me in arrest. The second placed upon me duties which would be intrusted to a man only in whom Genl Saxton had perfect confidence and shows that he gives me credit for considerable ability. I hope I may be able to fulfill his expectations.

I may accept [the offer] of a position as field officer in one of the colored Regiments. If I do it will be after considerable thought has been given to the subject and I will give you my reasons for so doing. I am quite certain that you will approve of what I have already done. Billy Cole[44] is with me.

So Dovie I am all through with my difficulty and it has pushed me up a considerable distance. Congratulate me again wont you?

I shall be more certain of coming home at Exhibition time. I may resign then or I may come home on a furlough as circumstances dictate. I shall certainly do one or the other if possible and I have a way of bringing about what I attempt.

I want to see my Darling this morning. Every night at sunset I ask my Father to not only guide me but her also. What a happy time we will have Dovie when I come home next time.

With love and kisses
Good Bye
John

———

Direct Capt J. E. Bryant
Beaufort S.C.

Beaufort S.C.
April 9th 1863

I was delighted to receive a letter from you last eve Dovie and glad to have it commence "My Dear Brother" If you have a formal commencement to

---

[44] JEB's servant, identified earlier as "my boy," probably justified as "contraband of war."

your letters I would rather that would be it or rather I am not very particular only that sounds a little better. I know not quite consistent but you know I am not a very consistent mortal and so long as you and I <u>now</u> understand each other <u>fully</u> I like to be called brother and you will be "<u>sis</u>." We will "<u>play</u>" that "<u>you know</u>." I am very busy and like it very much. I have not time to tell you how I am situated and perhaps you would rather I would tell you of other things When I get time I will write you all about my situation and prospects. Since the war commenced I have not had <u>near</u> <u>as</u> <u>good</u> prospects as <u>now</u> and I know my little (?) "sis" will be happy to know it. I shall certainly come home this spring or next summer and shall be at exhibition if <u>possible</u> I cannot now tell whether I can come the last of May or last of June. If I live you may expect me either in May or June. I want to come and see My Darling at exhibition and <u>shall</u> if <u>possible</u> So prepare yourself and commence early. But do not neglect other studies and do not study hard enough to injure your health Take pleanty [*sic*] of exercise. I would rather you would be at College a year longer than injure your health by too hard study. I wish you had <u>Jim</u> so that you could ride poney back every day. I will bring him when I come. I know you are very busy but write as often as possible. . . . If a steamer comes without a letter from you I am disappointed. I do not love you less or distrust you because I do not hear as often but tis a pleasure to hear often. I think You misunderstood my <u>last</u> letter if you thought I distrusted you now or I wrote what I did not intend to write and what I did not think. I do not distrust you <u>a bit</u> I have <u>perfect</u> confidence in you I only sometimes have feared that you might sometime find out that you could not love me with that depth of affection which my nature requires. I should think as well of you if that were the case as now although I should not love you as now and would not if I knew it marry you for the world because I would not make you unhappy. But Dovie I do not distrust you for an <u>instant</u> I know you are good and true and have no doubt that a sense of honor would cause you to do what you might not wish to do and if I knew it I would not consent to make you unhappy for life that is what I meant. I have no reason to fear this. I do not really fear it but sometimes I think <u>perhaps</u> it may be so some time. But I will not think so any longer. My little Pet is so good and true that I will fear no more You do not know how much I have thought of this whole subject from that eventful time when you first saw that letter of C. C. S's until now. I have already told you much I will say no more until I see you. My conscience is clear and has always been upon this whole matter but at first I hardly knew what to do but I am on forbidden ground. Excuse me Darling for speaking of this again. I am more than satisfied now delighted to know that you can love me wayward as I am see that now for an instant troubles me is the fear that sometime you may find that you can not love me as you now do but Dovie I will not think that any more "Sufficient unto the day is the evil thereof"

When the sun sets I try to pray to our Father and I ask Him to watch over my "Darling Little Dovie" 'Twill be pleasant to feel that at Sunset in Maine nearly the same time as sunset in South Carolina my little Pet is also thinking of her brother far from home and friends for I trust I have friends <u>here</u> also. Not such as I have in Maine though. This is an importent [*sic*] era in my life and I think if I live I will press away up in a few months. I have something now to urge me more than my own ambition I feel that another persons happiness is to some extent in my keeping. I will try to be true to my trust. So far as attentions shown to you are concerned I leave all with you. Do as you think right Only be careful that the person from whom you receive attentions is one I would associate with as a friend were I at home. I will try that my lady friends shall be those my little Dovie would be willing to have as friends. Have you received $20.00 which I have sent to you?

I was pleased that you answered my letter (lecture) as you did—Not that you were remarkably meek. Because if you were a very meek person I should not love you; but as indicating that you wished to please me which was the best possible proof of your love for those who love each other always try to please each other and are willing to overlook very many things. A meek person I dislike a person who yields to others to please them. I like my little Pet I love. My sister thought I had grown stern from the way I wrote and yet I did not think so. 'Twas only her fancy of course. I hope I am not stern to my friends.

Was I ever stern to my little sister? I hope not. Our forces are now attacking Charleston the contest is not decided I think we shall take the place. I am very busy sometimes when the sun sets I am on my horse and try to pray on horseback.

> Good Bye Dovie
> love and kisses
> John

———

> Beaufort S.C.
> July 19th 1863

A steamer has just arrived from the North but brings no letter from my darling. I was hoping that she might have written although you would have written but a very few days after I left. I want so much to see my pet tonight. I can not tell you how happy I feel since we were engaged. It is a new feeling to me. Life is commenced anew. Indeed I cannot tell you just how I do feel but certain it is that there has been a great change in my feelings. I did not suppose it would be so for we had been very dear friends and I was aware that my feelings had undergone a great change but now I am so happy. The one thing lacking has been supplied and my dovie is willing to make me happy for life. I love you darling more and more and may God preserve us both to be a blessing to each other. The more I see of your photographs the more I am pleased with the vignette. 'Tis a charming picture. Did I tell you in my last that I got an Album in New York? Such was the fact and your vignette is on the first page (The proper place) But I want a good Ambrotype of you. Say was [sic] you offended with me because I destroyed the Ambrotype you had taken in Hallowell? It did not look like you a bit and I could not bare [sic] to look at it.

I am enjoying my life quite well if my darling was here I should be happy. The weather is hot but I do not suffer I suppose we are to have much hotter weather. I wish you could have some figs, peaches, apples (yes apples and ripe ones too raised here this year), watermelons; green corn, new potatoes cucumber, tomatoes etc etc. It would give me the greatest pleasure to furnish you with these luxuries but I fear that away in that cold region where you live you must get along without these and put up with such few luxuries as that region affords. " 'Tis the land of the" South "'Tis the clime of the sun" where Nature is most productive.

Then again we have other luxuries unknown and camparitively [sic] unknown to you. Such as fleas musquitoes [sic] sand flies etc etc etc.

But after all give me my New England home where I can see her hills and be refreshed by the invigorating air and cool water.

I think I told you in my last that Charleston was being attacked again. Our troops have attacked one fort twice and lost heavily both times. The 8th are not there. The 54 Mass was in the fight and all agree that they fought with the greatest bravery and desperation. Charles Bridgham[45] was not injured but nearly all of the officers of that Regt were killed & wounded. More than a thousand were killed and wounded in both engagements. All think that the fort will in time be taken and with it Charleston.

---

[45] Probably the son of Thomas J. Bridgham, in 1858 elected supervisor of schools in Buckfield, Maine.

Monday

A letter did come in the steamer after all from my darling. You thought right when you thought that I would like to hear from you. I was delighted to receive the letter. To be sure I had been gone but a few days when you wrote but I was so glad you did write. I received the letter this morning.

I was pleased to have you say that if your mothers health continued to be as good as now that you might go to school this fall. I think it would be better to go in the fall and, if you <u>must</u>, stay at home in the winter. It appears to me that it would be better but I leave all with you. I shall be delighted to have you go and if you conclude to do so tell me in your next. You know it will give me the greatest pleasure to send you the money so I will say nothing about that. If you go do not study <u>hard</u> now remember. Please me in that will you not?

I told you in my other letters the reason why I could not go home. I was really disappointed but <u>could not</u> go. If [sic] expect mother will say that it shows that I think more of you than of her. I am in a great hurry this morn and must write no more. Will try to write another letter before the steamer sails for the North.

> With much love and many very many kisses
> Good Bye
> John

————

Beaufort S.C.
Aug 12th 1863

I received a letter from you darling written Aug 3^d, seven days after it was mailed I think I have never received one as soon before. Same time received a letter from my sister Lucy. The dear good girl was very much disappointed because I did not come to see them. Says, "I think it is cruel in Miss Emma to steal <u>all</u> of your heart she should have left one little corner for other friends who loved you as dearly as herself" What have you to say to the charge of theft?

I would like to be in Buckfield this morning although I do not suppose you would be up at so early an hour 9 A.M. I would send up my cord[46] and wait. This is the season when Buckfield people enjoy life to their hearts content.

---

[46] In the book of Joshua in the Old Testament, Rahab used a scarlet cord from her window as signal.

When city folks spend days and weeks in pleasure seeking. Wish I could spend six weeks there But no here I am where the mercury is 100° above 0 and fleas mosquitoes etc annoy us so that life is just bearable. Our luxuries are fast leaving us and harvest is come Corn is nearly ripe . . . Rice will be harvested soon and potatoes gathered; then the cotton will be picked. I am sorry your father and mother are going West with the prospect of living, but if your mothers health will be benefited I will not say one word. . . . As for yourself dovie Do not think of going until we are married. If you should desire it I will go West after I am admitted to the bar if you will please me by staying East until we are married. I shall leave the army as soon as spring at the furthest. Now darling we have been apart for nearly two years and now just when we love each other most I am coming home I do not want you away. Promise me darling that you will not go West until we are married and as I said I will settle West after I am admitted to the bar if <u>you desire it</u>. Do not forget to write me upon this matter will you and <u>say will you not please me</u>? How can I think of living away from you for two or four years more or for life. If you go West and I East who can tell what may arise to estrange us. No dovie please do not think of going West for the present will you? Now tell me in your next without fail For really I am troubled about it. You will not think of going at any rate until after you graduate.

I shall certainly come as soon as spring if you do not go West. Shall be governed somewhat by what you conclude to do. If you go West with your parents I may conclude not to hurry out of the army. I shall await an answer to this letter with impatitents [*sic*] so do not keep me waiting please. . . .

With much love and a thousand kisses John

Ladies Island near
Beaufort S.C.
Oct 21st 1863

My darling Pet

I was delighted to read your letter of Oct 3^d and it was singular that I read it between 8 and 9 Saturday eve last when you were writing to me no doubt. 'Twas a charming letter darling and as I read it I felt almost that you were talking with me I love you my dear girl today and would give any thing almost to see you. . . .

I miss you more and more and as the time draws near when I shall return I feel more anxious to come than when I thought of staying many months But as for my joining the "Home Guards" "I can't see it" I shall be too happy to guard my pet and escort her the dark nights when she is frightened I do not wonder that you do not wish to go out unprotected. If other ladies are with you it is safe But I should not like to have you go out alone I shall be fully prepared to do "escort duty" when I return and at your service Will that do?

Do please <u>if possible</u> attend school next winter and spring. I am anxious for you to graduate.

I am sorry that you had such luck in joining the church you will not of course give it up.

You ask me if I attend church on Sunday. When I am in Beaufort; while here I have none to attend. I shall be glad when I return to civilised society again.

I shall be much pleased to have Nellie room with you she is so good and amiable. You ask if I hear from my sister Lucy. Quite often I fear she will never enjoy good health. The last time I heard she was quite sick.

Evening—I suppose this eve is quite cool with you. Perhaps you need a fire I am sitting in my tent on the bank of Coosaw river with the door open. The mercury is 78° above 0 (almost summer heat) The moon is shining pleasantly and all I need to be happy is my pet She is far away Wonder if her thoughts are of the "soldier boy" tonight.

I am well darling and prospering finely
With love and warm kisses
Good Bye
John

Ladies Island, S.C.
Jan 1st 1864

I wish you a "Happy New Year"
My Darling Girl

Yes a year of happiness without sorrow. Who can tell what this year will bring forth? At its close where will you and I be? Shall we during a part of the year be happy in each other's society? Shall war cease during this year and shall we again enjoy the blessings of peace? God only can answer and wisely He keeps the book of fate closed and we read only as time passes.

Do you know my pet that I miss you every day I live; yes almost every hour. May our Father watch over and preserve your life and health. The world would be dark to me without my little angel.

Greenleaf is to be my Quartermaster. I have been trying for many weeks to have him consent to accept a position and at last he has done so. He can be commissioned at any time. I think he will be in a few weeks unless something new turns up with me. I am intending to commence in a few days a history of my struggle to raise a Regiment.[47] I guess you will laugh But I have succeeded so far to my satisfaction although have not progressed as fast as I wished and expected. But I have done it without the aid of influential friends. I have done it myself. Obstacle after obstacle has been removed and now I have smooth sailing. I think I will make more visible progress in four weeks to come than I have in the last ten months. I have progressed slowly but I am the only officer in the Department who has made any progress and very many would be glad to take my present position but they would not perhaps begin where I did and work as I have.

As you say, I think I have "played my cards shrewdly enough" considering that they were all poor cards to begin with. I have large hopes and plans for the future but dare not tell you for fear you will laugh at me and say I am building "Air Castles." When the time comes I will tell you all. I tell you all these things because I wish to tell someone and I know you feel and [sic] interest in my affairs.

Beaufort 7 P.M. I came down today to attend the celebration of this day by the colored people. This is the anniversary of their freedom. . . .[48]

This is a grand day for the freedmen. Upon this anniversary they have more reason to express their joy than we have to express ours upon the 4th day of July. We were not slaves; families could not be separated, wives and children sold and separated never to meet again on earth. These freedmen and women have been raised from a condition as low as the bruit [sic] creation and now have the rights which God desires for all his people

---

[47] Recruiting for a regiment of African American troops.
[48] The Emancipation Proclamation was effective in January 1863.

Today hundreds of these people came together from the different plantations on these islands and had a day of Jubilee. Last year they came together and were told that the President would issue a proclamation of freedom upon that day. Now they come together to celebrate the day. Then but few understood the importance of the change; now very many more do.

A sword was presented—Genl Saxton and one to Col Higginson[49] by the colored people and speeches made by several of the friends of freedmen.

I wish I could have been with my pet during the Christmas holldays [*sic*] now past.

I hope the time is not far distant when I shall be with you

Good By Darling
With much love and a thousand kisses
Good Bye
John

Beaufort S C
Jan 18th 10 ½ P.M. 1864

I am thinking of you tonight my Pet—far away—Do you love me tonight. Shall I tell you that I love you 'tis not necessary—you know I do. . . .

The wind howls without and it rains hard but 'tis a warm rain just think of that my girl; you who have the pleasure of a Northern winter. 'Tis a pleasant eve in my room I am alone, my table is covered with books and papers (as usual) But here also is my photographic album and another, A New Years present for my pet, partly filled with photographs of Generals.[50] I have been waiting for others but can not purchase more here now that suit me. When I can I will send them.

Wish my darling was with me tonight—I would then be happy.

I send in this ($20.00) twenty dollars more accept it please as a renewed pledge of my love.

---

[49] Colonel Thomas Wentworth Higginson commanded the First South Carolina Volunteers, one African American company that remained in continuous service after Hunter's regiment was disbanded.

[50] This album is now a part of the Bryant Papers in the Rare Book, Manuscript, and Special Collections Library at Duke University.

One more term and you will graduate. Only think of that. Who would have thought four years ago when you recited to me in the old Buckfield schoolhouse that you would so soon be a graduate from a college. What happy days we will spend together. Do you know I think of it constantly.

> With a heart full of love
> And warm kisses
> Good Bye
> John

————

> Beaufort S.C.
> Feb 15th 1864

My Darling Girl

I wrote you yesterday but will write some more today.

The President has issued a call to draft 500,000 more soldiers. This has caused me to again think of what has often come into my mind of late. The war may not close next year and it is impossible to tell how many more soldiers will be raised by draft. If I return in the spring I may be drafted and then should have lost a position as Captain with prospects of a better position. I think I have told you that Genl Gilmore[51] will offer me the position of Colonel of a Colored Regiment but that I shall not accept—and yet be obliged to again enter the army as a private or pay $300. These things I have often thought of before but never so much as since the late call of the president for more troops. These facts and arguments I present to you. I have promised to resign in the spring and I shall do so unless you release me from my promise. I intend to show you that I can keep my promises with you. Of course you have as much interest in my affairs as I have myself and in this matter after presenting the facts and arguments to you I shall if I have any doubt about what is best to do, be governed by your decision.

If you think I had better remain longer in the army will you fix upon a day when I am at home in the spring for us to be married. I have thought of this subject <u>much</u> very <u>much</u>. If I am married I know my duties as a husband and can I feel assured perform <u>all</u>. It would make no difference about my reading

---

[51] Major General Quincy Adams Gillmore became commander of the Department of the South and the X Corps on July 10, 1863.

law. There are <u>very many</u> reasons why I wish to be married then if I remain in the army. What my reasons are you do not care to know. What you do want to know is, can I do my duty to you as your husband. I think with the blessing of Providence that <u>I can</u>.

You need not reply immediately if you wish to think more of the matter.

If you do not wish for me to remain then I will not ask your reply to this question but we will speak of it after I return.

I kiss you warmly and with much love
John

———

Beaufort S.C.
March 8<u>th</u> 1864

My Darling Girl

The anxiously looked for letter has been received I was impatient to hear from you and although not quite satisfied yet cannot complain. I have after considerable thought upon the subject decided to settle West after I am admitted to the bar, unless—of course—you wish to remain in New England. But it is not for my interest to go until I am admitted to the bar. I feel certain that I shall return to Maine in a few months But can not tell <u>positively</u> now that you do not insist upon it. In war time a few days or weeks may make a great difference in our plans. I thought formerly that I could lay very good plans for many months to come. Now I can not <u>certainly</u>. One of two promises I am <u>very</u> anxious for you to make me. One—to be married if I remain in the war. I do not urge for you must judge what you think best. I wish for it to be so you must decide. If you do not think best that we shall be married then I do urge that you will not go West until we are married. I have often spoken of this I know and you can judge by that the importance I place upon your decission [*sic*]

I would grant any request you made of me that you were as anxious about as I am on this subject. Now Emma if you love me grant this request for I shall regard your answer almost as a test of the warmth of your love for me. Do not be offended with me will you for my earnestness on this subject? I wish I could see you and show by my manner and words <u>how much</u> I feel upon this subject. If your parents go and you do not think best to be married please allow me to furnish you with a home in Maine unless your father is perfectly willing to do so. He may think I am foolish to insist that you stay and conclude he does not wish to provide you a home away from himself. Really My Darling, I am very anxious upon this subject. I know I repeat this often but cannot help it.

Yes my pet I will most gladly frame and defray all expenses upon all pieces you will paint and I think myself a fortunate man to have so good an opportunity to have a collection.

No My girl I do never think that your expenses are too much. I have concluded to <u>allow you</u> (?) $100.00 for the spring term. It is your last; you graduate and of course need many things not desired other terms. If that is not enough let me know You shall have <u>all</u> you want. You know I shall be at exhibition and I do not wish to see my pet outdone by others. You will be sure to see me then. Remember me to my friends; the Hines girls; White girls; Parsons girls &c &c. I was delighted with the rose you sent. It was fragrant when I received it.

If we are married and you desire it I will take you South with me. You shall have a chance to know how a plantation looks with "darkeys" upon it and to know something of camp life.

May our Father help you to decide wisely. But Emma for my sake please me In the <u>urgent request</u> I make.

I am well and as happy as I can expect to be away from you. I am <u>longing</u> for the time to come when we shall meet to part no more this side the grave. My warmest love is for you may nothing arise to estrange us. My duties are arduous but pleasant I have never before had so good a position Step by Step I ascend the ladder. May nothing hurl me down. I feel that I do not toil for myself alone. I love my pet better than myself. For her I will toil.

I love you warmly tonight darling and wish so much to caress you again.

Good Bye My Pet
With kisses
John.

Beaufort S.C.
March 13th 1864

My Darling Girl

Your letter from Buckfield which came by last steamer was not received for several days after the other letter which came per same steamer which you sent from Kents Hill. One more term and your school days are over. How time flies. 'Tis but a few short years, they seem like months so quickly has the time passed, when I first went to Buckfield and you were a wild little flirt. Pardon me, please. I trust time has improved both of us. A few years longer and we shall—but I will not prophesy. What has passed we know the future is uncertain. God grant that I may bring happiness to you and I.

My pet wished that I could be home so, I wished I long so much to see you. I think of you <u>so much</u> and pray that you may be spared to me and I to you, and that no evil may befall either of us. You are my own darling girl. If I live you may feel assured that I shall be at exhibition. Do you know my pet I was glad to know that you had joined the church. You will always be my little angel, wont you?

In regard to my remaining in the army I have decided to remain until summer or fall, if I am promoted. If I am not, I shall return in the spring. If I am promoted I shall have a chance to be Colonel after a time if I am not I have nothing to hope in the 8th and will turn my attention to law. I think now I should look to interest as well as duty. The future is before me and I must provide for it. My pet of course expects me to do so.

I have sent by express "Birth Day" presents for you. A gold necklace and cross and a beautiful opera glass. I send at the same time the ring made from a rebel shell which I told you of before but which I failed to send. I send in this ($100) one hundred dollars for your spring term. Please receive all as a token of my love. May they indicate the strength of the love. I thought you would prize the glasses because there are so many views to be seen from Kents Hill.

Jim is in good health and spirits and no doubt is anxious to see his mistress.

I was <u>greatly pleased</u> I assure you to know that you went to Division meeting and to hear that it was prosperous. Never before did I feel the importance of temperance societies more than now. I believe it has been a good thing for me. I have not broken my pledge since I was first pledged at six months of age. I feel a great interest in the Buckfield division because I first proposed to organize it. I trust my pet will give her influence to the Division.

We are having most delightful weather. The mercury is in the shade 64° above 0. The grass is green the peach trees are in bloom The birds sing sweetly and the frogs add their beautiful (?) songs at night and as there are no <u>semi-savages</u> here, no one wishes to <u>eat</u> them and they are allowed to live.

Thursday March 17th

Since I commenced this letter a Mail has arrived from the North and I learn that I am not promoted. I shall resign about the middle of May and arrive in Maine the first of June.

Much love and many kisses to you
My Pet
John

Please give my warm regards to your father and mother.

————

Beaufort S.C.
April 24th 1864

My Darling Girl

My letters of late have been short and hastily writen [*sic*] but now I can spare time to think and write and I will be more particular. I should judge by the way you write that you run through the letter as a schoolgirl would a lesson when she wished to go to play But then I know you must have two thousand things to do. I can stand it a few weeks longer. On your account I am so glad that I remain in Beaufort For had I gone to the Army of the Potomac I could not have seen you in all probability until September. On the 7th of September my time is up and then I shall leave the army at any rate. You may be sure to see me at exhibition if it is <u>possible</u>.

Please give me your opinion upon this matter Had I better resign. I did not intend to do so until June which will be only three months before my time is up. I shall come to exhibition at any rate and shall be with you nearly one month of the three. If I do not resign I can have it to say that I served my time in the army. I have not thought of this much until lately. What say you my pet Tell me please in your next. I thank you darling for saying that we shall not disagree. You never said a word more pleasant to me. Not even when you said yes on a certain <u>momentous occasion</u>. Not that I really thought that we should disagree. But the talk of your going West had made me feel so badly that this word was dear to me. No my darling we will not disagree. It shall be my study to please you and so we will always be happy will we not. I think very much of late of being married and as the time approaches when I hope to call you my little wife—How funny that sounds. It is a most pleasant thought my darling. God grant that nothing may arise to delay my happiness.

So you have got your name in the paper. I notice that you were one of a committee to draw up resolutions upon the death of one of your schoolfellows. I was very much pleased with them who drew them up! Don't forget to answer me please. I judge that you have learned to like composition better than formerly for you do not complain as much as you did. Just like a woman to think that the men engross their time just as though they did not know that they waste more of the time of men than all other causes combined. Did I ever ask for you to tell me what you noticed laughable in me? I must have been thinking of something else and did not know what I said if my pen was induced to put that on paper. Just as though I did not know that <u>you</u> could find a thousand things laughable in anyone <u>you</u> saw. I always knew that you was [*sic*] noted for such things.

I remember that you did not like to see me wear shoes and I had determined to please you. I will always do so in dress if I can. I know that my taste is poor indeed I never cared much and I will employ you now as my teacher in that branch. So please commence and in your next tell me just how I shall present myself at exhibition.

So the old bugbear haunts you still and the main reason why you do not wish to be disappointed in my coming is that you would run a risk of being left beauless Poor girl!

I will not however disappoint you if I can <u>possibly</u> help it.

We are having delightful weather Mercury 70° above 0 in the shade. I have on my table a beautiful bouquet mostly roses one of which I send in this letter.

I have learned to love this climate and would like to live here if 'twas for the best.

I love my pet tonight more than all beside and wish <u>so much</u> to see her.

> Good Bye Darling
> With warm loving kisses
> John

———

> May or June [1864?]

Miss Spaulding

  Allow me to present to you
    Jim
      Seecesh
  Poney and a splendid fellow

> J. E. Bryant
> Capt 8th Me Vols

Astor House New York
June 28th 1864

My Darling Wife

How funny—I arrived in this city this morning at six and am stopping at the Astor House and this eve before I retire will write to my pet. I love you darling and wish you could sleep in my arms tonight and if I could have known that a steamer would not sail until Friday I should not have been in so great a hurry to reach this city. How does my darling do tonight—does she feel so very much different as she expected she would—is she happy. My wife must write often very often to her absent husband to cheer him. I think more and more of your mother leaving. I fear she will be overcome if she goes West. If she is not better very much better do discourage her. If she should be overcome by her journey and die on account of it how sad it would be.

Good night Darling
Pleasant dreams

With much love and warm kisses
John

Wednesday

I fear I cannot get away until Sunday. The [illegible] which was to leave Friday has been for some cause taken off the route. It is very unfortunate for board here is $3.'s a day for myself and about as much for my servant I expect. I have looked at the city today and took a ride to the City Park. It must be six miles from here and all for 5 cents. I went in the horse car. It rained when I got there and I was not able to look at the Park. I may go again before I leave the city. If I do I will tell you of the sights.

Good night darling

With a thousand kisses
John

Thursday

I cannot go until Sunday how sorry that I could not have known it last Sunday.

I went to Barnums Museum today and do assure you that I have seldom passed a pleasanter half day. I can give but a poor description of what I saw.

Birds and beasts—stuffed—of every kind almost in the world some of the most rare fish alive. One most remarkable fish I must describe. It was obtained from the river Gambia in Western Africa. . . . Mr Barnum held in his hand a lump of lard clay and informed the audience that in it was a fish who had been imbedded at least nine months. The clay was sawed in two parts and the fish exposed to view he was then exposed to the air for a few moments and put into a tank of water. After a few moments he swam like other fish. . . .

Miss Maj Cushman was there who has served as a union spy and scout. I send you a photograph of her as she appeared in her uniform. I saw two giants a man and woman—the woman 8 feet and an inch high and the man two or three inches taller—also two boys one 14 years old and 22 inches high and the other 12 years old and 23 inches high. Beside these there were many other sights too numerous to mention.

Someday I hope to take you there and show you the curiosities.

Good night darling

> With a thousand kisses and much love
> John

Friday

I do not go until Sunday. I wish I could be off. I am tired of remaining here and beside it costs so much. When I left you I had $75 and It will all be used up in board and travel. I did not dare to have any cards printed here for fear I should not have the money. I have written to Mr. Pidgire of Paris to print some and send to you. I have told him to send the bill to you. You need not pay until I send you money from Beaufort.

> Good Night Darling
> Pleasant dreams
> John

Saturday

I am off tomorrow at 9 A.M. I have today had my life insured for $6000 so that if I should be killed or die my darling wife have some money to make herself comfortable.

I will send the papers to you as soon as they are completed.

> Good Bye My own dear wife
> God bless you
> John

July 2^{d} [1864]

My Dear Husband.

Will you excuse me if I write you a little with a pencil? I am so disappointed to-night. I thought you would write me from N.Y. and I thought I would certainly hear last night or to-night—naughty boy not to write your little wife. I am almost anxious about you, but mean to think you safe—perhaps the vessel left sooner than you expected.

Sabbath Eve—Please excuse this pencil scribbling. I thought I would destroy it and commence anew but I remember that you think anything once written to you your property, so here it is. Come to your little wife to-night, please? She wants you so much. I wonder if you miss me as much as I do you: its very lonely without you my soldier husband—and the months that must pass before you come back ever so long. fortunately I've not been left alone any for Greenleaf came Wednesday night—and my Aunt Noodman is with us too. if I could see you only one evening more I would be very happy. I dont feel as if I said good-bye at all. 'Tis a little past 9 o'clock and I have but just risen from prayer, our prayer. Will God spare you to come back to me. I'm so afraid but I've given you into His keeping and I trust Him.

Attended church to-day and listened to a sermon from Mr. Chase, Ophelia's friend. I think 'twill prove a serious friendship—she was here with him. I walked home with Clarinda[52] after prayer-meeting and we sat in the parlor by ourselves and talked until 'twas so dark that I was almost afraid to go home alone—only two months more and I wont need to go home alone any more, will I? I know I am writing a very foolish love letter to-night and I dont approve of them you know but I love [you] so much. I never loved you as well before in my life I think as these days since you went away. my love seems different—warmer, truer. the questions which you have sometimes asked me I can now answer, fully, truly—yes. I wonder where you are while I am writing—perhaps you have arrived at Hilton Head. I shall hope to receive a letter to-morrow from you written at N.Y. and if I dont get one then must reconcile myself to waiting two weeks or more I suppose until you can send a letter back from Beaufort. I think I've been a very naughty Christian these weeks past—the earth love has almost driven from my heart the thought of God. Pray for

---

[52] Emma's aunt Clarinda Spaulding, Dastine Spaulding's wife.

me dear that I may serve God faithfully, that he may bless us both and make us his own children. I mustn't sit up longer. I kiss you good-night.

Truly, only. Your own loving wife—
Emma

————

P.M.   Washington
Jul 31   DC

Headquarters 8th Me Vols
2d Brig 2d Div 18th Army Corps
In the field near Petersburgh
July 29th 1864

My Darling Wife

I am at last with my Regiment I arrived last eve "at the front" and it is not so bad a place after all. The men are cheerful and contented, but those who are to return in September look forward to that time with pleasure, I find. I am well and much, very much more pleasantly situated than I expected. I am in command of the Regiment and my reception was so cordial by officers and men that I already feel at home in this Regt where I have not been on duty for twenty months. How changable [*sic*] the fortunes of men and mine in particular. In this Regiment where I was in arrest four months and from which I came near being discharged in disgrace I am the commanding officer. And if nothing unforeseen prevents I will cause Rust to be discharged. Thus the tables turn. I wish I could see my pet today but I cannot. In five weeks if the Lord will I will be with you How soon the time will come and how I long for it to come.

I shall have no trouble on account of my trip home and if I had remained until Monday it would have been as well. For I could not get transportation until Tuesday But we can not see into the future and do not know what is for the best.

I have not time to write more tonight for I must go on duty on picket in a short time. I will write to you when I return.

With much love
and a thousand kisses
John

8th Me Vols
Near Petersburg Va
Aug 5th 1864

My <u>Darling</u> Wife

It is but two days since I wrote you but it seems a week to me and I will write this morning. The day I wrote to you but after the letter was sent I received three letters from you. . . . I was <u>delighted</u>. You are more dear to me now than ever before. I am so happy to think that you are my wife my own darling little wife. I love you as I want to love my wife and it makes me <u>so</u> <u>happy</u> to know that you love me warmly. Our future life is to be <u>happy so</u> <u>happy</u>—the Lord willing—

The letter from your sister is not in the letters you sent to Beaufort. . . . I should have said that I did not see anything in them that looked like a mention of your sister but as I had to guess at much of what you wrote It might have been there. I used to think that you wrote as badly as it was possible but since you are married you beat yourself in bad writing. I did wrong I fear in marrying a wife who writes so badly. My father and mother write poorly and so do all of their children and what will become of ours(?)

But you need not give up writing because you do not write well. . . . It makes me happy to have you tell me that I am dear to you. Yes if you were to write every day I should want you to say the same thing over and over again. Never fear that you shall say too much or say it too often. Oh how I love my darling wife to have me so good [*sic*] and one who loves me so much is very sweet to me. I wish we could be together. I wish you could be with me. In thirty three days I trust we will. The longer I am married and the more I think of it the more my judgment approves And the happier I am. I have never for <u>an instant</u> regretted the step.

My last visit home was the happiest I have ever had. I anticipated much happiness and my anticipations were more than realized.

Yes my little wife does satisfy me "<u>fully truly</u>"—

I think you had better let Poney stay out of doors as much as possible even if he can not feed out. It will be much better for him. Yes I shall ride with you often after I return.

Yes my darling your face will always be pleasant to me and the more we are together the happier I shall be.

You may send for the daily Tribune also send for the Atlantic. Send for the Tribune six months and for the Atlantic one year. For the Tribune direct to
New York Tribune
New York City and send four dollars—
Have it sent to your address. Direct them to send the <u>Daily</u> Tribune.

I am well and enjoy myself as well as could be expected. . . . I sleep in my clothes only pulling off my boots for I am but a half mile from the rebel line and may be called up at any time of night when I should have but a moment to get ready for action. It is a luxury to stay here for we are here but half the time the other half we are at "the front" and about two hundred yards from the enemy in some places not more than thirty feet—only think of being so near to the enemy that you can speak to him and throw dirt at him and if you put your head above the breast work get a bullet through it. I suppose you can hardly think that it is safe to be there and yet it is as safe as a half mile away if one is careful. Care is required. You may be sure that I shall be careful. I do not think we shall have another fight until more men are added to the army and that will be after my term of service expires. It is dangerous for us to attack the enemy and equally dangerous for them to attack us.

I told you of the part I took in the fight of last Saturday ie—no part. Our Division was in reserve but the other Brigades went into the fight ours was in reserve. Such you see is my luck I have always been a lucky boy.

Direct
8th Maine Vols
2d Div 18 Army Corps

Of course send some of the money I left.
I find that some of the old men of my Company have been killed and but two wounded. But very few men have been killed in the Regt.

Good bye darling Write often
Remember [me] to your family
With warm love and kisses
John

———

8th Maine Vols
In camp near Petersburg
Aug 12 1864

My Darling Wife

I have written you since I received any letter but I know you must be anxious about me and I will write often. I am well and have as yet no narrow escapes to speak of. Some men are wounded and some killed but in nearly every case carelessness is the cause. It is singular to see how careless men will be when their lives depend upon it. They learn to disregard danger and life I think I speak to men almost every day who are careless. My company have been very careful and I think none have been killed or wounded carelessly. I need not tell you that I have been and shall be careful.

The Maj has arrived and assumed command of the Regt I am glad For it is so long since I have been with the Regt and commanded troops that I had much rather some other man would assume the responsibility I am again in command of my company.

The Regt is "In the trenches" I was yesterday Division Officer of the Day and am today in camp. I shall go to the trenches tonight and come out tomorrow night. We have two days on duty and two off.

Twenty six days more and I am free. I shall be more than glad. I want to live with my pet, to enjoy her society to have her love in a word to be <u>happy</u> Shall it not be so? I know it will. I love you darling and want so much to see you I can hardly wait three weeks. Only think three weeks more. Have you received the Atlantic and Tribune?

Good Bye Darling
God Bless You
With warm love and kisses
John

8th Maine Vols
Near Petersburg Va
Aug 21st 1864

My Darling

I have not written to you for several days but I think of you all of the time. I have but sixteen days longer to stay. I expect to leave here the morning of

Sept 7ᵗʰ and go directly to Augusta. I wish you to take for me my best military coat, pants and a white vest a fine shirt and a pair of socks also my patent leather boots. I think you had better hire a horse and carriage and meet me in Augusta at the Stanly House. Perhaps Alice would like to go with you if not one of the Warren boys will go unless Greenleaf can go with you. But you can tell what is best. Alice you know was in Augusta when I left three years ago.

My health is good but we have rough duty. If you should see your <u>liege lord</u> I fear you would be horror stricken and I doubt if you would own him. It has rained every day for the past seven days and you may depend that the ground is muddy enough. My feet are wet every day and my boots all the time covered with mud and indeed I am mud from head to foot. Nevertheless I am still the same. We have been in the trenches ten days in thirteen. Have now had two days rest and last night the Regt went again. I was Brigade officer of the day and had a chance to remain in camp last night and today. I go tonight and shall have a delightful bed. My rubber coat spread on the ground to lay on and my overcoat for a covering. Some different from my pet, how would she fancy such a life. I love you darling today more than all. Never more. If it were not for you I do think I would remain in the army. I never felt more patriotism. Are our people cowards? Do they mean to give up the best government the world ever saw because they have not patriotism enough to fight? I sometimes fear so. Officers who have lately come from the North say that the people are desponding that many are willing to have peace at any price. If so I do not wish to be a Northerner. I would a hundred times rather be a Southerner. Oh! For a nation of brave men! for a people ready to sacrifice every thing but honor! A Southern faction have rebelled and fight—we are ten to one; they are brave and make up for a bad cause by valor and shall we like great cowes [*sic*] bellow and give up? God forbid!

I love you my darling oh so much. I am looking forward to a life of happiness but if we loose [*sic*] our national honor I assure you it will mar any happiness. Have I given three years of my life for nothing? and the most important part of my life too. Have we lost thousands of lives for nothing? Are we after all a cowardly nation. I have my fears. I believe God directs our affairs but will he aid us if we prove after all to be cowards? This army has suffered and lost severely but the offices and men are hopeful they say if the people at home will give us a victory at the polls⁵³ we will conquer a peace. They are more troubled about that than about the rebels.

---

⁵³ President Abraham Lincoln's reelection to a second term was in jeopardy.

Genl Grant has been displaying most splendid strategy for a few days past. . . . You see I was a poor prophet when I told you that I thought we should have no more fighting. Whether our corps will be engaged before my time expires is more than I can tell, but Grant will work his army again to its utmost until Lee gets himself into a position too strong to assault. Then Grant will rest and study again so it appears now. If the Northern people support him he will finally succeed of this I feel confident.

But I suppose my pet does not care to have me write so much war now for love.

Your letter directed to Beaufort in which was the letter from your sister has been received at last. . . . I was delighted to receive it. Indeed your letters have a charm that never grows old. The love messages are often repeated but are every time more sweet. One kiss is as good as another but you can witness that I am never satisfied with a single one. just so with expressions of love when I am absent from you. They are to the mind what kisses are to the senses. I shall live for you and you for me will you not? Your love is very sweet to me and I am so glad that mine is to you. I shall love you so much and always I trust. May nothing arise to mar our happiness. In a little more than two weeks . . . we will be together again. . . . We will then enjoy our honeymoon will we not?

P.M. Our time for prayer arrived . . . and I left every thing for a moment to call upon our Father to bless us. About this time my pet far away is doing the same. Will not God bless us?

Oh yes! I will be very very attentive. Indeed you are and shall be my all. Will you be pleased to have it so? . . . Good night darling God bless you

With warm love and kisses from your husband

P.S. I will telegraph to you when I arrive in New York on my way home. Take my money with you when you go to meet me.

J. E.

———

8th Maine Vols
Near Petersburg Va
Aug 24th 1864

My Darling

I received a letter from you commenced on the 13th two days ago. Your letters are very dear to me like your own little self and it seems that they are more dear as the time approaches for me to come to you again. I can not now count the time by weeks but must by days. Thirteen days more and I shall have served my country three years. I am anxious as the time approaches. As yet I have not been in but one battle since I joined this army and did not take an active part in that. This corps has had I think a harder chance than any in this army. I suppose it was owing to the fact that Genl Smith[54] who commanded was one of the best fighters and always anxious for a fight—for a like reason I think at present it will not be actively engaged unless all are, for Genl Ord[55] the present commander I do not think is considered equal to either of the other corps commanders. But we do not know what a day may bring forth. If we go I trust I may do my duty and not disgrace myself or friends and that my life may be spared. God forbid that I shall fail to obey all orders. If I die I trust I may not disgrace my friends or my children (?) But darling the Fates have not decreed that we should part at present.

As soon as I arrived at the Regiment I wrote a communication to the Sec of War[56] informing him that Col Rust of this Regiment had been absent from his Regt since the day it was ordered to march to the front and asked that he might be dismissed. Today the order from the Sec of War has been received dismissing him and at length we are rid of that villain, and he who did all in his power to disgrace me has himself been disgraced by my effort. Of course I am pleased. Now I am ready to come home to my darling wife she who loves me so dearly and whom I love with all the warmth of true love. I shall be so happy when I can again press you to my bosom "fold you in my arms and press head to head and lip to lip"(?). I feel that I am one of the most fortunate men alive in having such a darling wife. God bless her and may care and trouble be removed from her path. You ask do I ever wonder whether our united lives will make one harmonious whole; whether we will live in and for each other? I thought of it much before we were married but never now for I have no doubt. I have known so many unhappy matches that I thought well before I was engaged after that never. Our tastes in so many respects are alike and we are always so ready to yield to each other that we will always be happy. I think of you so often wherever I may be; whether in the trenches sleeping on the ground with the sky about me and the bullets whistling over my head and

---

[54] Brigade Commander Thomas Alfred Smyth of the II Corps made his reputation at the Battle of Cold Harbor in June. He would be made brigadier general on October 1, 1864, and continue to command throughout the Petersburg campaign.

[55] Major General Edward Otho Cresap Ord, Commander of the XVIII Corps.

[56] Secretary of War, Edwin McMasters Stanton.

shells bursting from a score of guns or whether I am in camp where I have a little better situation My darling wife is ever the same and her memory is always fresh. Do I ever regret that she is my wife. <u>No</u> <u>never</u>. I am too glad to think of such a thing. I am glad you have a girl at last and trust your mother will now rest and improve in health. Do you like to ride poney How does he look? Does he grow poor?

Good Bye my darling two weeks less one day and I go Maineward to see my darling pet and have "some one to love some one to caress"

God bless my darling and preserve her to me these <u>many</u> years.

Give my love to your folks. Tell Mrs Childs that I am very anxious to see her and by no means to leave until I come. Do for my sake help Julie all you can

With warmest love and kisses
John

———

8th Maine Vols
Aug 29th 1864

My Darling Wife

I am well today and love you warmly, truly more than all others my Pet does me and that makes me <u>very very</u> happy. I was never <u>fully</u> satisfied with your writing to me until the last letter was received. Usually there has been several days between the date of your letters and although they were good and delighted me, yet I wanted <u>more</u>. I was not satisfied. I longed so much to hear from you as much as though I had received none. The day before I received the last I had received one and two or three days before that had received one and I was not that night expecting one but I was <u>most happily</u> disappointed. I was delighted. It was one of your best so warm and loving just like your own dear self. I do think I am one of the most fortunate of men, I have for months felt so. But never so fully realized it as now. How happy I shall be only eight days more and I come to you to live with and love you to be happy as man can be. Will you be glad?

The Governor[57] has sent me a major's commission. Shall I accept it? I shall not until I see you and not then if you do not want me to—am I not good? I am excused from duty and am making out my papers.

Good Bye darling
With warmest love and kisses
John

P.S. Did I ask you to carry my black hat with you to Augusta? Please do so. I shall probably arrive in Augusta the 9th or 10th.

J. E.

---

[57] Samuel Cony, governor of Maine, 1864–67; later records showed JEB was commissioned captain on September 5, 1861; registered as major on August 23, 1864; mustered out in October 1864; and recorded as brevetted lieutenant colonel on March 13, 1865 (Adjutant General's Office, March 22, 1867.)

LETTERS: 1865–1867

John Emory Bryant did not take the professional path to a law career in Maine that he once considered. His former commander, General Rufus Saxton, who had recognized JEB's ability and rescued him from military oblivion in the Department of the South, had joined the postwar challenge of winning the peace. In 1865, Saxton headed the Georgia/South Carolina/Florida division of the United States Bureau of Freedmen, Refugees, and Abandoned Lands, popularly known as the Freedmen's Bureau. From his days in the army, John Emory Bryant had accepted and believed the words his friend, Rev. Mansfield French, had written of JEB's work with African Americans: "I think you have a mission to perform for the country and for humanity." Without reluctance, Bryant answered Saxton's call to become bureau agent in Augusta, Georgia.[1]

Thus began the southern odyssey that would determine the features of Emma's life, including long separations from her husband. There are few personal letters to document the hazards of 1865 as the Civil War ended, but Bryant's political papers confirm that in Augusta as in other locales, agents of the bureau were overwhelmed with the multitudinous duties to be accomplished with scant resources as they dealt with the terrible consequences of total war.

Along with generating hostility on the part of native Georgians for his efforts, John Emory Bryant continued to build his reputation as a headstrong radical. Having supported and been identified with the policies of General Saxton to give land to the freed slaves, he quickly found himself afoul of the internal politics of the Freedmen's Bureau. In the fall of 1865, after General Davis Tillson replaced Saxton as head of the bureau in Georgia, Bryant was cut from the bureau rolls. Unwilling to accept termination of the work he considered his mission, in 1866 he turned to other avenues to accomplish his goals, such as using his training in law to serve black clients. Primarily, however, he worked through the Georgia Equal Rights Association (GERA), a political and educational organization for African American males. Recognizing JEB's leadership in founding the

---

[1] See *Carpetbagger of Conscience*, 42–87, for details of JEB's career in the years 1865–67.

association, the freedmen elected JEB its first president; also, he edited the GERA's newspaper, *The Loyal Georgian*. Throughout the year, Bryant's conflict with Tillson over the relationship between the GERA and the Freedmen's Bureau became a nasty personal feud between the two Yankees, both natives of Maine.

John had departed from New York on April 15, 1865. It was not until February 1866 that Emma joined him in Augusta, where she remained until late June. In those five months, the hostility suffered by the Northerners was palpable. Emma's diary recorded some of the incidents she later called the "dark days when I was with you in Augusta."

In the midst of the tumultuous year of 1866, Emma retreated to Earlville, Illinois, the home of her sister Margretta ("Gretta") Browne. Sadly for the Bryants, shortly after her arrival from a lonely and difficult trip, a miscarriage ended Emma's first pregnancy. Safe, however, and welcomed by her family for an extended visit, she would quickly recover her health. Her father also lived with his daughter and son-in-law, as he had since his wife's death in December 1864.

Emma had expected John to visit her in Earlville and that she would then return South with him. John, on the other hand, was busy seeking (successfully) professional standing from the bar in Maine and setting up a law practice in Georgia with an old army friend. When the long-awaited visit never materialized, Emma left Illinois in January 1867 and traveled to New York in the hope of joining her husband there, since he shuttled frequently between New York, Washington, and Augusta. The plan succeeded, but after a warm reunion, Bryant left her in New York, where she stayed for the remainder of the spring. Gretta urged her to return to Illinois for another summer, but Emma refused. Despite other invitations as well, she chose to visit friends and relatives in Farmington, Wells, and Brunswick, Maine, waiting for the signal to move back to Georgia.

But John was deeply embroiled in Reconstruction politics. The Reconstruction Acts passed by Congress in March 1867 had remanded the Southern states to military control, creating an entirely new situation in federal authority. In the fall of 1867, as a delegate in Atlanta to the state constitutional convention mandated by the Reconstruction Acts, JEB played a key role in writing a new constitution and organizing the state's Republican party. John's philosophy, which advocated voting and office-holding rights for African American males, was considered extreme by many Georgians, including some of his own party. Disputes over these issues, as well as the raw politics that produced the slate of party candidates for office, were a harbinger of the factionalism to come. For the time, however, differences were papered over to ensure Republican success. In the spring of 1868, state elections adopted the new constitution and elected a Republican governor and legislature, including John Emory Bryant as a delegate from Richmond County.

Augusta Ga
May 29th 1865

My Darling Pet

I have just come from a meeting of colored people and such a sight! I wish you could have witnessed it. I have never seen anything like it since I have been South. Bishop Pierce of the M.[ethodist] E.[piscopal] Church South first preached and then ordained a colored preacher as a deacon after th[illegible] French preached and in some parts of the discourse he spoke of their freedom and that they were free and it made them happy. After the sermon was over and the benediction pronounced—They could hold in no long but they commenced to sing songs of praise to swing back and forth to jump up clap their hands swing their bodies etc etc. It was a wild thrilling sight I wish you could have seen it. These people are smart They know what freedom is as well as I do and they are as happy as I should be to become free if I had been [illegible]. It does my soul good to witness their joy. They almost consider Mr French and myself their deliverors [*sic*] and wherever we go they all want to shake hands with us. I wish you were with me my darling. I wish you could see this people as they step from slavery into freedom—men are taking their wives and children, families which had been for a long time broken up are united and oh! such happiness.

I am glad I am here.

I love you darling and want so much to see you. I shall count the weeks from [illegible] until you come. . . . God bless us.

With a thousand kisses
John

[Emma's Entries in Printed Diary—Selected Entries]

April [1866]

14—   Anniversary of assasination [*sic*] of Pres. Lincoln

15—   One year ago to-day B. [ryant] left N.Y. for Beaufort

20—   Drank tea with Mrs. DeHarme
       B. came up to tea and passed evening.
       Came home and Capt. Prince Henry and Caesar all sleeping in the
       parlor. Caesar waked, put up his head for me to pat him and in few
       minutes was in a spasm. Jackson put the poor fellow out of misery by
       killing him. Some wicked person has poisoned him.

21—   This morning I buried my poor Caesar in the garden under the fig
       tree. Put him in a box and strewed beautiful flowers over him. I miss
       him to-day as if a child was dead in the house.
       A very violent rain since dinner which flooded our sleeping room.

27—   Propose to strew flowers upon the graves of our brave heroes to-
       morrow. The mayor of the city fears "bad blood may be stirred" by
       so doing and requests that the military forbid and even Gen T. [ill-
       son] discourages—for shame, shame!!

28—   Went this evening to strew flowers upon the graves of our federal
       dead. The colored schools with their teachers formed good portion
       of procession. The mayor with police force met at the cemetery gate
       and refused to allow the procession to pass in whereat we refused to
       pass in ourselves and returned. O. Southern loyalty![2]

29—   Political atmosphere of Augusta somewhat stoney at the present time.

30—   B. was attacked while coming out of Court House this morning, in
       most cowardly and brutal manner. The villain came upon him with
       a club from behind and struck him three blows on his head before he
       was able to turn and defend himself—his life was spared, thanks to
       kind providence.

---

[2] Inspiration for a Southern Memorial Day as distinguished from that for Union soldiers.

May

2—   Colored Picnic to-day—B. went and spoke. Gen. Tilson[3] lasly [*sic*] the Gen spoke. Did not feel able to attend myself—. . . do not feel strong any of the time.

10—   Painted a little—wrote a little—worked a little and felt good deal stronger.
Mrs. DeHarme called this morning, brought me nice bouquet. Mr. Clmen's son brought me magnolia.

11—   Painted for Mrs. Edes. Walked up town to meet B. in the evening.

12—   Painted, made bed—tidied house, cooked and mended beside writing letter to Gussie.

15—   Called on Richard's wife after dinner, from there walked up to the office and came home with B.

19—   Dined very pleasantly with Mrs. DeHarme—rode on their little bay horse—came home in ambulance, bearing bottle porter.

20—   Did not attend church service. Went to Sabbath School. Had one of my crying headaches.

23—   Received letter from Gretta this morning enclosing one from Mr. Browne informing me of the very delicate state of her health and urging me to pass summer with them—nothing in providence preventing will go soon as practicable.

28—   Painted nearly all day. B. stays at house to work in the mornings now. Mrs. DeHarme and Mrs. Smith called this eve. Gen Tilson has forbidden all the members of his staff to associate with Capt. B. on penalty of immediate relief from his staff. Also said should not allow Mrs. T. to call upon me. Strange procedure, but ineffectual I think to accomplish the object which he designs to accomplish.

31—   Called on Teachers this evening—went from there to Springfield church with Mrs. Smith[4] to attend a colored wedding—wedding passed off very prettily.

---

[3] Emma consistently spelled Tillson as "Tilson."
[4] Teacher in school for former slave children, sponsored by the Freedmen's Bureau.

June

1—   Letter from Father this evening. has received my letter speaking of probability of my passing Summer with them.

2—   At home, sewing—cooking etc. B. recieved [*sic*] letter from Benj.[5] last evening informing us he would come this fall and they would wish to board with us.

3—   Attended morning service at our church—from there to Thankful [*sic*]—held short session of Sabbath School, they all went to Springfield with Mr. Russel to hear conference between Gens. Steadman & Fullerton[6] and committee of colored men—house crowded—

5—   B. wrote letter to Gen. T. demanding him to prove or retract charges made against him—
I cut out first one of B's shirts this eve. . . .

6—   Gen. T. makes reply through one of his officers that the two first charges vis—namely deception towards colored people and exorbitant fees he can prove—says he did not assert the others, and threatens that if B. publishes his letter in this week's paper[7] he will suspend paper and arrest him. Colored man came to door, asking if my "pa" was in.

7—   Gen. sent officer to B. to-day ordering him to submit proof sheets to him before issuing his paper. B. demanded order in writing. Gen. T. sent guard this eve to printing office—they will remain through the night and do not know how much longer.

8—   Guard taken away this morning. Paper issued as usual. Capt. A. took paper to Genl. T. then took away guard.

10—   Attended morning Services at our church, Sabbath School at noon—letter from Clarinda this evening.

12—   Home sewing

---

[5] Benjamin Bryant, JEB's brother.

[6] Generals James B. Steedman and Joseph S. Fullerton, emissaries of President Andrew Johnson, gathered evidence concerning the Freedmen's Bureau in the summer of 1866.

[7] *The Loyal Georgian.*

17— Rain prevented us from attending morning services—went to Sabbath School—Mr. Adams, connected with schools for destitute whites in Atlanta was present—brought us home in his carriage. B. Capt. P.[8] and self called on Mrs. Smith and Miss Dowd[9] after dinner—attended prayer meeting at Baptist church—Baptism.

19— Home sewing most of day—went out to look at bonnette [*sic*] before dinner.

20— Went to milliners thence to call on Miss Welch—ladies (?) in the street spoke very insultingly of me after I passed

21— Went to milliners again this morning and called on Richard's wife— read Pilgrim's Progress to her. Saw Dr. Em[10] on Greene St. he did not bow but I thought he knew me—came home and finished writing account of examinations. Mr. B. was refused a glass of soda-water at Gults' this eve—boy telling him that they did not wish his custom longer

22— B. recieved [*sic*] letter from Gen. Howard[11] and Mr. French[12]

24— . . . After dinner went to Catholic vespers. Read to Charity in the evening

25— Made first attempt to frost cake

26— Second anniversary of our marriage—
Mrs. DeHarme dined with us and passed the evening Dr. coming in the ambulance after her as far as the corner and sending Louise here after her.
Mr. Harris from Beaufort—agent of F. Savings Bank[13] also dined with us.
Two years ago my dear mother was with me—

---

[8] Captain Charles H. Prince, friend from Buckfield, Maine; U.S. congressman from Georgia, July 1868–March 1869; postmaster in Augusta, Georgia, 1870–82.

[9] Teacher in the school sponsored by the Freedmen's Bureau.

[10] In 1873, Emma would identify Dr. Em as the doctor who treated her "when I was sick in Augusta."

[11] Brigadier General Oliver Otis Howard, head of the Bureau of Refugees, Freedmen, and Abandoned Lands (Freedmen's Bureau).

[12] Reverend Mansfield French.

[13] Congress chartered the Freedmen's Savings and Trust Company in 1865.

<u>July</u>

4—   "The galorious [*sic*] fourth" as southern press terms it—Colored
       held celebration—Did not go out on account of heat—walked with
       B. and Charles after dinner down by the river bank—afterward
       walked up town and drank glass soda water.

6—   . . . B. brought me letter from Gretta.

12—   Left Augusta and my dear husband this eve en route for Earle.

13—   Arrived in Atlanta and went to National Hotel where passed the
       day—Took evening train for Chattanooga—

14—   Arrived at Chattanooga early this morning having been sick all night
       and took train for Nashville—Detained at Nashville this evening
       quite ill. Went to [illegible] Cloud Hotel.

15—   Passing day very quietly at the hotel—very lonely—
       Passage from Dickens "Remember how strong we are in our <u>happi-
       ness</u>, and how weak he is in his <u>misery</u>"

16—   Took train from Nashville for Louisville.

17—   Arrived at Louisville this morning—went to Louisville Hotel—
       Left in evening train for Indianapolis—ferried across Ohio River in
       evening

18—   Passed day at Bates House Indianapolis—took night train for
       Chicago via Kokomo

19—   Arrived near Chicago this morn—was put off at crossing of
       Burlington & Queens Rd.—took train for Earle and arrived at
       Grettas at noon—

20—   Stupid

22—   Father recieved B's letter this morn [illegible] of my departure

26—   Recv'ed Loyal Georgian—Wrote B.

<u>August</u>

3—   Letter from B. written from Washington
       Company to tea. . . .

7—   Recieved letter from B. dated at N. York

19—   Attended morning Service at Presbyterian and evening at
        Methodist.

———

Earlville Aug. 25th [1866]

My Darling Husband.

Will you forgive if I write a very short letter this morning as have only few
minutes before mail closes. It is Saturday and the week has run off so <u>very</u>
rapidly—have been very busy with sewing and we have had some company
etc. When I heard from you last you were in Philadelphia—Am glad you
were enabled to be there at that time. Am feeling very anxious to know what
the next few months will develope [*sic*] in regard to the affairs of the country—as you are away I get little here but the Johnsonian view[14] which is not
particularly encouraging to me. Still I have an abiding faith in God and the
country and am waiting the results. It is asserted by Chicago Tribune that
Gen. Tilson is to take the place of Gen. Howard in the course of a month.
Should the change occur what will be the effect of it upon our personal fortunes? Can he do more to injure you in that position than in the one which he
now occupies? Will not his time and attentions be given to other matters? We
are having <u>very</u> cool weather, very cold nights and mornings. have worn flan-
nels for some time and portion of the time woolen socks. Wonder how our
friends in Augusta are faring. I have nothing from them but once seen
through Loyal Georgian—suppose it must be very hot and dusty there.

I find myself much invigorated by cool weather—am now much better
than expected I could be. I go out driving considerably and am really gaining
flesh I think. So you expect to find my face quite round and rosy when you
arrive. Please write me very often darling, am hoping to hear to-day from you.
I love you, think of you and dream of you. <u>come</u> <u>Soon</u>. I shall not go home
without you, <u>remember</u> write me when I will have to go in order to go with
you. With many, many kisses and in great Love

Emma

———

[14] At the National Union Convention in Philadelphia, August 1866, President Andrew
Johnson tried to garner support for defeating the Fourteenth Amendment recently passed by
Congress.

August

26—   Attended church service but was faint and obliged to leave

27—   Sick—called Dr Vorberg

28—   In bed

29—   Lay in bed all day

30—   Still in bed

31—   Taken ill last evening and not relieved until near noon of to-day—
        our hopes of an heir blighted—Mrs. Stickel with me all night—
        Mrs. Bigs came to nurse me this morning

September

8—   Sat in rocker a little time this morning for first time—Improving
        rapidly—Mrs. Bigs left to-day and Mrs. Davison came

10—   Rainy—dismal

11—   Sun shows itself spasmodically for first time in many days—Mailed
        letter to B. . . .

12—   . . . Recieved [*sic*] papers from B—walked into kitchen but felt quite
        fatigued—Have sat up and sewed for several days.

13—   Recieved letter from B. written from Phila—Hopes to come in few
        weeks—
        Unpleasant day.

14—   Beautiful morning—Invitation from Mrs. Gammon to tea—quite
        impracticable for me to accept unless taken in my chair. . . .

        Sent letter to B. and recieved one from him—wrote him again after
        dinner in reply to his expression of intention of turning [illegible]

18—   dull again—when will fair weather visit us again—
        Recieved letter from B. this noon, written from N. York 15th inst.

20—   Letter from B. dated N. York 16th inst. Expect him in about two
        weeks.

21—   Beautiful day, warm—sunny. . . .

22—   Another sunny day—blessed life the sunlight. Arrayed myself in lace
        dress and hoops for first time in nearly four weeks—Mrs. Gavly
        here sewing—

———

Earlville Sep. 23$^{\underline{d}}$ 1866
Sabbath P.M.

My Darling Husband

Am feeling lonely this Sabbath day and know no better antidote than to
write you, nothing better save to ask God for the company of His Spirit in my
heart which I do ask for <u>both</u> of us.

It has been beautiful sunshiny day, tho cool. Have been out of doors for
first time—went out in the yard a little this morning and on the [illegible]
after dinner—considered it quite a treat. Have been dressed to-day for the
second time—I mean <u>really</u> dressed with close dress, hoop skirt and all the
etc—had worn loose wrapper for some time before am beginning to feel and
look quite like my former self tho' have little strength for walking yet. Have
felt about as if must have you with me some time during my illness but am
doing nicely now and shall enjoy your visit all the more for being able to go
about as hope I shall be then. Hope I will see you in course of two weeks at
least. What time in Oct are you obliged to <u>appear</u> in Augusta? I learned from
"Loyal Georgian" 15th inst. that Gen Tilson had written Springfield church
and on the occasion he delivered "a short but impressive sermon" quoting
Scripture and [illegible] to a religious life to an extent painfully in contrast
with his own lack of respect for religion and its ministers. You have not yet
answered my question in reply to probability of him receiving Gen Howard's
position. I should be sorry to see the position in the hands of such a man as I
believe Gen Tilson to be. I wish that I might see the time when the public
offices in our country may be filled by men of christian integrity tho' have little hope of such a stride toward the millenium [*sic*] being taken in my day. Do
not my dear husband, in any of your political scheming be induced to take
yourself or encourage in others any step inconsistent with christian dignity of
character. I had rather that we would live poor all our days than you should
do So. Be sure to write often and come Soon as may be. Am [illegible] every
day for a letter from you and impatient for your coming. Please excuse my
writing with pencil. It is less labor for me than to use pen. I do not feel like

writing more to-night will probably add few lines in the morning. May God bless and keep you safely. I pray that <u>neither</u> of us may make the fatal mistake of thinking that we are serving <u>Him</u> while we do only <u>our own wills</u>. "If any man will come after me let him take up his cross and follow me" we can <u>not</u> be his followers without the cross. Good night, darling—

Monday P.M. Did not send this in to-days mail and received this noon letter from you dated 20th, in which you reply at length to my letter in reference to your decision in regard to law—much of your reasoning is formible [*sic*] and we will endeavor to make the best of what <u>must be</u>. tho' I can but <u>hope</u> that the editorship may be temporary, retained only until pecuniary matters are so improved as to enable you to bend your energies to the law. Time and circumstances will perhaps decide the question for you—hope that you may be led to choose that path in which you may be most instrumental for good. Will endeavor to trust God in this as all other matters. Am <u>very anxious</u> for the time when we may be once more together—think it is not well for husband and wife to live very much separate and it <u>certainly</u> is <u>not agreeable</u>. I miss you very much and more than ever since I have been ill. the days pass slowly and the evenings are so <u>lonely</u>. Sister is always busy with baby in the evening and since I have been ill can neither sew nor read then. Shall be <u>very greatly</u> disappointed if do not see you before you go to Augusta, yet would not wish you to incur slightest risk of being late there. If I am with you this winter (As trust I may be, [illegible] will we [illegible] If you <u>would</u> go to Augusta with out coming here <u>please</u> take with you the list of articles enclosed in this and bring me on your return. They are articles which I left at home and shall need this winter. I wrote to Lucy enquiring whether any of the articles were in the trunk and she replied that they were not—therefore they must be in Augusta, and, if you do not know their whereabouts, you can enquire of Charity for I left them for her to take care of. Please <u>be sure</u> not to forget the morning-dress, muff and beaver hat as I shall be in great need of them. Please get them several days before you leave town so that you may be sure of them. I write this particularly in the fear that you may not be able to come [illegible] but certainly earnestly hope that you will come. I would also send love to all our friends there—would like much to see them and to be there with you were it practicable.

Am gaining strength quite rapidly Will try to use all necessary caution. I hope and pray that you may be able to come very soon. May God bless you and keep you safe. Good-night with many kisses.

Your own little wife

September

24— Raining again—Letter from B. dated N. York 20th inst. Writes that he may be unable to come here before going to Augusta. Dyspepsia

29— Gretta and self sent riding this morn—she carried baby and drove— afterward went out on the street—Lovely day—wrote B.

October

3— Lovely Day again—letter from B. dated Boston and informing me that he must go from N. York direct to Augusta—wrote B. in evening—

9— Dull—attempted to paint—cleared off cold middle of day—went out after dinner and wore heavy winter coat

16— Letter from B. written from Augusta—writes that Grand Jury failed to find a bill in the "fraud case" against himself—also that Gen. Tilson is to be mustered out of service 1st. December and now moves his head-quarters to Savannah—Large meeting at Springfield church to welcome him (B.) on his return—

———

Earlville Oct. 19th 1866

My Darling Husband.

Received letter from you yesterday dated 13th inst. and assuring me of your health and prosperity. Am especially glad to know that the sky is more bright in Augusta than when I left there—sincerely trust that your darkest days <u>are</u> over, yet plan to hold myself in readiness to meet them should they come again—do not believe the good of this life entirely dependent upon material prosperity, as I used to do. I believe that faithful performance of our duty will bring a fair share of happiness and content to everyone which nothing else will. May God bless you, my darling husband and help you in <u>all</u> your ways to remember Him. Am glad that Charles is doing so well as you say.

Am very happy that the suit against you has so [illegible] fortunate termi-nation. How about the case for debt—have they yet come off. I enclose in this letter which was forwarded here from Wakeman, received along with it letter from Lucy. . . . She writes also that Susan[15] has returned from Maine and Benj. has bought a small house in Norwalk where they will soon commence housekeeping. Charles is to spend the winter at home—they are still looking for visit from us. I am still improving in health but am much troubled by weakness of the eyes which must be my apology for the brevity of my letters. I haven't turned Democrat yet, as Charles prophecied [*sic*] I would, but I have had two Democratic physicians and have been taking Democratic syrups for several weeks—thinking I am deriving much benefit from them. My Republicanism, or some other ism, is coming out all over my person in the form of large eruptions.

Am trying to get myself in readiness to go to Sycamore to visit my old class-mate Flora Armstrong—wish to go while the pleasant weather continues. Feel very <u>very</u> lonely without you and am waiting anxiously for the time when we will be with each other again, but wish to do all things for the best and am willing to wait until the way shall be opened. Am enjoying my visit much—'tis a great pleasure to be with Gretta but cannot take the place of my husband. Write very often—tell me all that occurs and all about our friends— who of them are there. Baby[16] is growing finely sits in his high chair and has three teeth coming through. Must not write more as my eyes but very weak.

> With many, many loving kisses
> Your little wife. Emma. . . .

————

October

20—   Very lonely this eve—some tears—

————

Earlville Oct 21st 1866

My Darling Husband

Have been thinking much of you this Sabbath day and may not better employ its closing hours than by writing you 'twill do me good, I think, and, I hope afford you pleasure.

————

15 Susan Bryant, Benjamin's wife.
16 Gretta's son O'Neil, sometimes spelled Neale.

I am not exactly growing homesick but miss your love <u>so much</u> <u>more</u> and <u>more</u>. I hope we may not be much longer separated, tho' wish to do what is best for us. I feel quite happy through the day but when evening approaches, I am lonely and uneasy—'tis not that I am enjoying my visit the less but that I miss you more. I am more happily situated here than I could be anywhere else away from you but even the love of father and sister can not fill the place of my husband. Have been unable to attend church services to-day on account of unfavorable weather—have read, thought of you, helped amuse baby etc but the day has seemed long to me. I wonder if sabbath day would <u>ever</u> seem long to us if we were <u>really</u> christians. I often fear that I am not one because I do not love God's services more than I do. I pray God that neither you nor I may be deceived in regard to our own hearts. I wonder where you have been passing this Sabbath day—you have not yet told me where you board. How long do you <u>expect</u> to be detained in Augusta and do you pro- pose coming direct here after leaving there? Do you know how the Sabbath Schools are prospering particularly the Thankful? Was it continued [through] the Summer? I would like to know who has my class—do you see or hear anything of Charity? I would be glad to know if she is comfortably sit- uated. I often think of all our friends there, both black and white, and <u>our</u> <u>enemies</u>, if we have them, I sometimes think of [them] with the hope that they will sometime know us better and dislike us less. I do not feel like writ- ing more to-night—will retire soon have almost learned to dread the night for do not sleep quite well and am so lonely if awake in the night. God's blessing to you my darling, and pleasant dreams.

With Good-Night kisses
Emma

Monday morn—Please inform me if you have received letter containing list of articles which I wish you to bring me from Augusta—please ascertain from Charity if my <u>muff</u> was properly taken care of—also my silver spoons. The light kid gloves which I spoke of I would like sent <u>immediately</u> enclosed in letter if convenient. Charity will know where they are—the gloves were with the things taken from bureau drawer. My health is improving

<u>October</u>

22—   Received letter from B. dated 17. inst. All things prosperous. Also
        letter from Flora Armstrong informing me that they are boarding
        and unable to receive me at present.

26—   Letter from B. The lengthy one of which he had spoken—wrote in
        reply this eve—feel anxious—

———

Earlville Oct. 26th [1866]

My Darling Husband:

I received to-day your "long letter"—I am <u>much</u> pained to tell you that it
is not in father's power to assist you—his property is chiefly in real estate
located here and the remainder is in Maine so that he has little ready money
at command at the present time.

It gives me <u>much unhappiness</u> that you should be distressed for <u>money</u> and
I will cheerfully do anything honorable that lies in my power toward your
relief—will practice all possible economy both in dress and all other matters.
As far as <u>inclination</u> goes, <u>father</u> would be <u>as glad</u> to assist you as Charles'
father-in-law has been to aid him—but if you think a moment you will per-
ceive that the two cases are <u>altogether different</u>. [double underlined]
Firstly—Mr. Atwood is possessed of very much more property than father.
Secondly—Mr. Atwood has no sons and Charles' wife is now his only daughter, whilst father has <u>three</u> children and one of those a son but recently married and needing help perhaps as much as yourself, or nearly as much. Tell
me, do you not <u>see</u> the difference? I think that you imagine father's property
to be more than it really is. He has already done for his daughters more than
<u>most men</u> with his limited means do for their children, and I doubt not would
do still more if in his power.

I can, if necessary, remain here during the winter, altho 'twould be a great
sacrifice to me to remain away from you so long. I miss you more and more
every day and hope and pray for our speedy reunion. I shall be much troubled in regard to your pecuniary affairs until I learn from you that they are
more favorable—shall keep up good courage for the future and pray God
to help you in the midst of all your difficulties. Never conceal from me even
the worst—write me very often and come so soon as practicable. Gretta

wishes you to try to make your arrangements so as to be with us at Thanksgiving and says that if you dont come for me you can not have me— (The latter clause I dont endorse)—I love you and wish to be with—may the Lord keep you.

A loving good-night
Your own little wife

―――――――

Earlville Oct. 29th /66

My Darling Husband.

I am almost ashamed to devote to you only these few minutes in the late evening weary head and mind with the various labours of the day—but have been busy through the day and sewing this eve beside reading a little. I think of you often and look forward longingly to the time when we will be re-united—am wishing that you may come direct to Earlville. Please reply immediately to my last letter, written in answer to your "long letter"—tell whether you have recieved [*sic*] money from the North—am very, very sorry that you should be in such shortened circumstances and regret very much that father is not so situated as to assist you. Do not conceal anything from me but tell me always what your circumstances are.

I am much relieved to know that affairs in Augusta have changed for the better. I think we would be very pleasantly situated were we to be there this winter. Please do not forget the articles which I sent for. I must not write more to-night. I love you darling and hope ere long to be with you. God bless and keep you.

Good-night kisses—
Your loving wife

―――――――

Earlville Nov 1st/ 6 [1866]

My Darling Husband:

Am lonely to-night as almost always am in the evening—miss you very much the time looks long to me before you will be here. Received two letters from to-day—one containing letter from chummie Lewis the other bore the sad tidings of poor Louise Green—altho' I had felt it probable that she had committed suicide still this confirmation is sad indeed. I little thought when I used to sit beside her in painting class, as I have done for weeks at a time, that her earthly cares would have so sudden and [illegible] I can not understand how a person of her religious convictions dare commit the awful sin of going unsummoned into the presence of their maker; my heart has been very sorrowful both for herself and her parents. May God have mercy I would reverently implore. The letter from Chummie Lewis informs me that she is in Boston and may remain there thro' a part of winter. I hope to meet her either there or here before she removes to Kansas.

I feel troubled about Charity[17]—if in power to assist the poor woman, either directly or indirectly, please do not fail to do so. Did you pay her what was due her before leaving Augusta last Summer? The articles which I sent for I do _not_ wish you to _send_ but to bring with you whenever you come. The kid gloves you may _send_ in a letter. Have just read Gen. Tilsons letter in reference to outrages in Henry county, by which I judge that he is more inclined to give the black man justice than formerly. Am very glad if it's so. I am astonished and pained by what you say of difficulty between Mrs. Smith and Miss Dowd. I shall regret exceedingly to lose Mrs. Smith.[18] I valued her society much more than that of any of the other teachers—do you know what the trouble is? Who will supply her place?— I am weary dear and can only reiterate what I have said so many times before that I desire to be with [you] very, _very_ much. May the Lord bless and keep you I shall hope and pray for your coming and am very sorry that [illegible] assist you in pecuniary difficulties. I shall hope for brighter days however and keep good courage for the future. Good night darling and pleasant dreams

> With many kisses—
> Your loving wife—

Is Mrs. DeHarme still at Augusta and will she remain thro' the winter?

---

[17] Charity, now ill, was probably a former African American servant; Emma later wrote, "she _served_ us _faithfully_. . . ."

[18] Mrs. Smith took another teaching position in North Carolina; she called Miss Dowd's charges against her "untruthful."

<u>November</u>

7—   Went to Mendota on noon train—Dr. Woodbridge filled six cavities in my teeth. Mrs. Browne (Calvin's wife) went also—returned on evening train. Saw a woman in reform dress—

10—   Recieved [*sic*] letter from B. dated 6th August—answered B's letter in evening. . . .

———

Earlville Nov. 10th /66

My Darling Husband.

Will devote these closing hours of Saturday night to you. Recieved letter from you to-day telling me that you are safe home from Macon which am very glad to know—am hoping that things are changed for the better since last Summer. Shall certainly be very thankful if the time ever comes when we can live in Georgia in same security of life as in N. England.

Am glad for Charles and Eunice Ann that they are again united—hope that the same may be said of us ere many months—please remember me to both of them. Is their baby pretty—should like to see it. Twill be very pleasant for us to board with them besides being much less expensive than housekeeping. Am very much disappointed that Mrs. Smith does not return—have you learned anything of the nature or cause of the difficulty between herself and Miss Dowd? You have not yet answered my query whether Dr. DeHarme and wife are still there—much love to her if she is there—also regard to Dr. Is Richard's wife still living? I have heard nothing of her since I left Augusta.

I do not think it best for you to <u>send</u> my things to me but take them along with you when you come—the cost of express on them would be heavy, would it not? beside I shall not need them <u>immediately</u>. How long will you probably remain away from Augusta? Am always glad to recieve the Loyal Georgian and peruse its columns with more interest than while at home.

Will not write more to-night. I wish you pleasant dreams and wish too that I might dream in your arms to-night. May the Lord bless you. With love kisses,

Good-night
Emma

November

11—   Attended Presbyterian service in morning and Baptist in evening—
         Baby quite ill—walked to Dr. Badgley's with Gretta.

13—   Sewing for Gretta

14—   Finished Gretta's dress

16—   Finished bead trimming—Letter from B. Went to prayer-meeting

17—   Letter from B. informing me of death of Richards wife—it occurred
         in the Summer—Am very sorry that I neglected to call to say good-by
         to her—let it be a warning to me that I do not neglect my duty to the
         sick and the poor—Charles' wife and baby have arrived at Augusta

18—   Home all day—not well

21—   Went to Mendota—purchased travelling dress—poplin—
         Father met me at depot when I returned—rainy and dark–

23—   Letter from B. from Augusta. . . .

———

Earlville Nov 25th '66

My Darling Husband:

'Tis Sabbath eve have gone to my chamber preparatory to retiring and will close the day by writing you, if tis only to tell you that I love you and ardently desire to be with you. Have attended two church services to-day— Presbyterian and Baptist. Had most excellent sermon this morning text taken from last chap. of Rev[elation]. Christ's invitation to Sinners to come to Him—"And the Spirit and the bride say, Come. And let him that heareth say, Come. And let him that is atheist, come: and whosoever will, let him take the water of life freely.["] It is such a full and free offer of Salvation—but the Saviour gives us no encouragement that he will Save those who do not <u>come</u>. <u>Have you</u>, my darling husband, given your heart to Christ and devoted your life to his service? do you look to his atoning blood for Salvation? <u>do not</u> be decieved [*sic*]—there is not power in your own morality to save your soul— seek prayerfully and honestly and pray for your own Salvation and mine—<u>do not</u> set this aside with arguments as you do my words when I speak to you on

the same subject. Do not, I beg of you, seek your soul's sal[va]tion less anxiously than you are seeking the treasures of this earth.

I wish to be with you very, <u>very</u> much. I love you and miss you every day—
may the time that you are detained be brief—may God bless and keep you
safe—write every day or two—With good-night kisses

Emma

Monday Morn—I have sent the package of things for Charity. addressed to
Capt. Prince—if they arrive before your departure please inform me. To the
list of articles which I wish you to bring me I will add a white flannel under-
skirt. It I packed with my other woolens at Longs I think—all my woolen
clothing and furs should be there. It is a drizzly rainy day and the broad
streets a dreary waste of black mud—you can form no conception of Illinois
mud until you see it—not its <u>quantity</u> but its quality.

Bye-bye—Emma

Love to Mrs. Prince—Charles too. Please remember me to Misses Dowd
and Harme—would like to see them all

<u>November</u>

30—   Sent letter to B. and Alice White—too late for evening mail

---

Earlville Dec. 2^d 66

My Darling Husband:

It is Sabbath day—clear, cold and sunshiny—such a day as we so often
have in Maine. Do not think I would like this climate as well as that of N.
England.

Have not been out to church on account of indisposition of Gretta—nothing serious I hope—. . . .

I wish that could be with you this Sabbath day or better still, that you were
here with me—before many Sabbaths more have passed trust that we shall be
reunited. I miss you every day but at evening and on Sabbath days. I wonder
where you are passing the day and how. . . .

A young man accidentally shot himself here to-day while loading his gun to go hunting—was killed instantly. It seems strange that these dreadful accidents do not prove a warning to others both to respect God's day and to be also ready for the coming of the son of man.

It seems almost trite for me to tell you what I have told you so many times that I love and miss you, but I do and none the less as the time lengthens since I left you. I am not homesick exactly or unhappy, but there is something lacking from my daily life that used to sweeten it and lighten its cares. "It is not good for man to be alone" a wise God has said and it is true vice-versa. Do you think that you will be here as early as Christmas? Wish that you might but will be patient.

Bye-bye
Emma

———

December

4—   Pleasant day—finished travelling dress this evening . . . cleaned bottom part of trunk

8—   Letter from B. prepares to leave for Washington to-day—hopes to reach here N. Years if not at Christmas—

11—   Very cold—Second anniversary of our dear mother's death. In the short two years since then a marriage, two births, and two deaths have transpired in our family.

15—   Very cold, windy and snowing. Have mercy on the poor and the wayfarer. Sent letter to B.

16—   Too stormy to go out to church. Went to prayer meeting at Methodist church in evening.

21—   Went out to buy Christmas toys for Birdie

25—   Christmas morning—Gretta presented me with green empress cloth dress pattern. Father had slippers—Mr. Browne dressing gown— Gretta shawl and gloves . . . Wrote B. went to ladies prayer meeting in evening. . . .

29—   Christmas letter from B. written from N.Y.

Earlville Dec. 30th 66

My Darling Husband

Having been wishing you with me this Sabbath morning. I miss you so much and more as the time increases. Do you realize near five months have elapsed since I left Augusta and home?—for it <u>does</u> seem home to me notwithstanding the many unpleasant features of our life then. I often think of them—teachers, pupils—black and white—friend and foe and shall really be glad to see all their faces again. Yes <u>all</u> for I cannot in my heart cherish any unkind feelings towards any and even the faces that looked hostilely to me go to fire up the motive for home and I [illegible] something absent. I sometimes wonder whether the time will <u>ever</u> arrive when we shall be on friendly terms with the Southern people. If it can be, without any concession of principle on our part, I would be glad but it seems scarce probable to me.

I went to church quite alone this morning as I usually do Gretta being obliged to stay at home with Birdie who has not been well for many weeks—shall be so happy when I have my husband to go to church with me once more. We had very good sermon indeed. The subject—Christ the Shepherd and his church the sheep and the illustration drawn from the practice of the shepherds in the Eastern countries. He said there we are informed by modern travellars [sic] in those lands that the shepherd gives to each of his flock a name and that they come to this name thus Christ knows our names, our circumstances our joys and sorrows, all these pertaining to us and has a personal knowledge of and sympathy with us. Have been to evening service since I commenced this. Mr. Eustis preached a Christmas sermon—where he spoke of the cause of gratitude which many of us had in our preservation from sickness and suffering since the last Christmas I began to think of all the blessings of Providence to us since this time last year. It is true we have had trials, but we have been brought out of them, and your life in the midst of imminent danger has been spared. Surrounded by enemies we have been unharmed none of those dear to our hearts have been taken from us and our own health has been spared. I have cause for a thank-offering that I have passed through an illness, often prelude of permanent injury without any apparent detriment to my health—for all these blessings let us make our lives a thank-offering to God. You may be prepared to find me looking stouter and healthier than when I left you—at least people tell me that I have improved wonderfully since I came here. I think I am nearly as well now as any time since we were married. I quite shocked Gretta when I arrived here. She said that I was so much changed since she saw me in Maine, that she would scarce have known me if she had met me accidentally. My coming here has been a great blessing to me physically as well as a pleasure but I am growing <u>very, very</u> weary of the separation from you. I can scarce be thankful enough that I left Augusta <u>when</u> I did and came <u>directly</u> here. If I had waited a few weeks it is not improbable that I should have been unable to travel and if I must be ill anywhere it [is] a privilege to be here with my sister. Am I growing tiresome on the subject? If so excuse me. I pray for you every night—At nine o'clock. Do <u>you pray</u> for me and <u>for</u> yourself at that hour?

. . . I love you darling and long to be with you with warm love kisses

Your own wife

December

31—   Recieved [*sic*] letter from B. written from N. York—he writes very
          cheeringly

Earlville Jan. 11th 67

My Darling Husband:

Recieved [*sic*] to-day your letter dated 7th in which you say hope to be here next week but may not for two or three. You say "dont be impatient." I <u>felt</u> more sick at heart than impatient when I received the letter. I do not blame you, I know that you will come soon as practicable but this weekly expectation and weekly disappointment is wearing to the flesh. I feel like a potatoe [*sic*] that has been frozen and thawed alternately for an indefinite length of time. Will not write more to-day—will write again to-morrow. God bless and keep you and bring you to me soon.

With loving kisses
Your little wife

Earlville Jan. 16th 67

My Darling Husband:

Please excuse a very brief reply to your letter of 12th inst. just recieved [*sic*].
You may think that there is no need for me to write hurried letters but I am
trying to put my wardrobe in condition to leave and am very busy all the time.

I am indeed sorry that you do not expect to come here. I feel much disappointed and so does Gretta but I would not be so childish as to urge you to
come if you must derive injury therefrom. I still look forward to some day
when we will be enabled to visit Illinois together.

Do not come to Wakeman[19] <u>especially</u> on my account (if you would not do
so were it not for me) as I shall not mind taking the journey alone—'twould
be pleasanter to have company but am not afraid to go alone. Gretta bids me
say to you that both she and Mr. Browne are anxious that you come here to
make them a visit. If you do not come for me shall I go by Wakeman or direct
to N. York? I am <u>very glad</u> my darling that you are searching the N.
Testament. May God help you to understand the Scriptures. <u>Be careful</u> not to
trust to any righteousness of your own, but look for Salvation through
Christ's blood alone, then will good works be the fruit which Christ has
enjoined his disciples to bear.

Excuse me if I write hurriedly. I love you darling and wait eagerly to be
with—

With loving kisses
Emma

———

New York Feb. 19th '67

My Darling Husband:

I am writing you to-night, tho' I do not know where to address it, because
I am <u>so lonely</u>. Your empty chair finds me in stately mockery and the coming
days seem long. Wish I might know your whereabouts at the present
moment—perhaps on your way to Buffaloe [*sic*]. I left Mattawan[20] this morning at 7 o'clock (or thereabouts) and arrived in town about 10 o'clock A.M. I

---

[19] Wakeman, Ohio, home of JEB's sister Lucy.
[20] Matawan, New Jersey.

went to Mattawan Thursday according to intention, notwithstanding the very disagreeable weather—have passed the time since then very pleasantly with Alice.[21] The School does not seem much like Kents Hill—the scholars being nearly all day scholars and much less proficient than our Kents Hillites. Don't think Alice quite likes [it] there—'tis a funny place—teachers divided against each other and all uniting in hating the principal and his wife.

Alice and myself drank tea at the Baptist minister's yesterday. Found your letter on my return here, also received one at Mattawan last night—will not try to tell you how glad I am to hear from you—please write every day or two, if 'tis but a few lines.

Your posters are here, also the bill for the same from printers. Did you make any arrangement about the payment or tell them that you would be away for several days? If not they may think that you do not propose paying. I mention it for fear that you may have forgotten it. There is a room upstairs vacated and I expect to move into it to-morrow—it is the room occupied by the English lady and husband—the price is twenty five dollars per week instead of twenty as you thought. Shall not know where to send this until hear from you again. I love you darling and miss you very very much. May God bless you with the presence of His Spirit—do not neglect to seek Him.

Pray for your little wife and do not forget to love her and write her very often—she wishes she might be in your arms to-night. Pleasant dreams— with loving kisses Good-night—

Friday Eve—Was just upon point of sitting down to write as the dinner bell rings—will write a few lines notwithstanding dinner just to tell you that I love you dearly and am O! so lonely! have heard nothing from you since Tuesday—shall be much disappointed if I do not hear to-night. I have wondered whether the recent fall of snow has hindered your departure from Washington. Have not been out of the house since I came home from Matawan————

Just at this point I made a large blot on my paper and immediately went down to paper—I mean dinner—I'm so lonely at table without you. Your seat is occupied by a tall, middle-aged [man] whom they call professor and whom I quite like—wonder why I always feel so much more at ease with substantial, middle-aged men than I do with young popinjays, such as most young ladies like?

---

21 Alice White, Emma's best friend.

We had a discussion at table to-day upon women's rights. Mrs. Davis wishes she was a man. I dont—query—Is it because <u>she</u> has a <u>man's</u> place in life to fill, while womanhood has been made sweet to <u>me</u> by the protecting love of my husband?—

Do you think that they <u>really</u> love each other? To change the subject from gossip to the weather. we have had two days snow—Tuesday and Wednesday—and to-day has been fair. think that the fall of snow has been sufficient to impede travel somewhat. I recieved [*sic*] no letter from you to-night and almost fear that you or your letters or both are snow-bound.

I had expected Alice in to-morrow—to remain with me until Monday but fear that the snow will prevent the Stages from running in which case she could not come. I have for you a letter from Charles,[22] also one from Richardson[23]—they came yesterday—will send them with this when I learn your address. I opened and (being interested in Augusta matters) read them. I am encouraged by their contents, but I <u>distrust</u> Richardson a little—he flatters you <u>too much</u>. I fear that he is not entirely <u>sincere</u>, but does it for an object. If so, he is not a <u>real friend</u> or <u>safe counsellor</u>—<u>such friends</u> are often more dangerous than enemies. Charles' letter I like better, tho' I do not <u>rely</u> upon him further than his own interest is in harmony with your success—do you think me faithless? I am not quite so, but more so than I was ten years ago. am determined however never to arrive at the point which some profess to have attained—viz—that there is no real, genuine friendship in the world. I believe there is, and like grains of gold, all the more precious for being rare. Charles, you know, I like and, to a certain extent, trust.

I am moved and quite at home in my new room—hope you will like it. It is not so pleasant as the other but is smaller and I do not feel so <u>lost</u> in it when am alone—beside it has a great abundance of closet room. You can have all the room you like for books and papers.

I have been laying [*sic*] in wait for a mouse this evening. the little fellow has sprung my trap and escaped with the bait once—have baited and set it again and am awaiting the result.

Will not write more to-night—hope to hear from you tomorrow. I never missed you more darling, than now—it seems a long time to wait until you come. If you should send for me shall be delighted to go, but if not will try,

---

[22] Captain Charles Prince.
[23] Captain C. C. Richardson, with whom JEB had established his law firm in Augusta, Georgia.

like a good girl to wait patiently until you come. I pray daily and often for God to bless you. And now Good-night darling—loving kisses—

Saturday Eve—If I begin this evening's letter by saying that I am sick and tired it may not seem cheerful but is nevertheless true. took cold while in Jersey and to-day went away down to the Gen. delivery P.O. on Narran St. after a registered letter both which united have given me a headache. will be quite well again before you return I trust.

The registered letter was from Gretta containing my chain and cross. She and the family sent love to you. She says she misses me very much. There is some pleasure in knowing that one is missed, dont you think so? I was consoled in my loneliness to-day by a letter from your own self—have watched for it for four days past. Am <u>very glad</u> that the future looks so bright to you— remember, darling, to consecrate your ambition as well as other powers unto God. Alice did not come to-day to pass the Sabbath with me as I had hoped— am afraid the day will be a very lonely one—think she must have been prevented by the storm. I shall think of you and wish you with me. sincerely hope that you will not be much longer detained, but will keep as cheery as I can and shall be the happier, perhaps, when I do have you again. Was never before <u>so lonely</u> in your absence as now.

The gentleman that I have spoken of as occupying your seat at table is Prof. Fairchild of Oberlin College. He is receiving a fund to endow the College. I like him more than any of the other gentlemen here. Gretta writes me that Aunt Elisie Bray[24] has written them that Hattie[25] has a fine boy seven months old—isn't it funny? Will probably write you again to-morrow. . . . I shall mail at the same time with this Charles' and Richardson's letter with the Loyal Georgian of last week. Will not attempt to write more to-night as my head feels too badly. Prof. Fairchild will take them out to mail with his own this evening.

I love you darling and would be <u>so happy</u> to lie in your arms to-night. I feel as if when you come, I <u>can not let you</u> go <u>again</u>—but 'tis foolish I know and I will not make a baby of myself. With many loving kisses. My own darling husband—

Bye-bye
Emma

---

24 Probably a sister of Emma's mother, Cynthia Bray Spaulding.
25 JEB's friend Harriet Whitney, now married.

New York Mar. 13th/67

My Darling Husband,

I am now comforting myself that you will very soon be home. Your letter of this morning written on Monday, tells me that you will go to Rochester and from there to me here and I suppose from the telegram that you must have gone to Rochester on Monday or Tuesday. shall be so glad when you are with me again. have been so lonely, most especially at night, altho' miss you at all times. I am pleased with the notice of your lecture, which you sent in letter received to-day. Shall I find one fault, not with that, but with you?

I judge from that, that you gave as one reason for going South, your health, please do not say that again ever. It sounds as if you might have been a feeble, dilapidated man. It seems manly and proper to me that a man should be robust in body and mind. A feeble man strikes the world as rather pitiable than admirable, so please, (for my sake if nothing more) don't say you went South for your health even if that consideration did move you, as it might properly have done.

I have felt the greatest anxiety to judge by hearing and sight of your success in this new field. I have thought of you and prayed for you, darling.

I send you note from Charles and letter from Richardson in which they urge your return to Georgia. Do you think it will be practicable for you to go as soon as they wish? I also send letter from Joseph.

We are solitary and forlorn at the table I can assure you. Have been out on the street for a time to-day, all by myself. I feel more lonely since Alice has left—miss her.

Now, my darling, I am hoping to see you home by last of this week—am so tired living without you—shall be very, very happy.

Pleasant dreams. loving kisses
Your own Emma

––––––––

Farmington [Maine] Oct 10 1867

My darling Husband

I [illegible] from you to-night [illegible] Am homesick [illegible] if [illegible] for you when the night comes. It is so much more lonesome [illegible] now than in summer. Light comes [illegible] and the winds whistle in a lonesome way that makes me wish for husband and love. . . .

I am very glad that you were able to meet Robert Harper's demands am sorry that he should be insolent but he was a friend in time of need and for that we must be grateful.[26] Those were dark days, darling, when I was with you in Augusta, but we have been safely brought through thus far, and will have good courage for the future.

I have realized for a long time that you were struggling under a heavy burden—but if you serve God in all that you do I do believe that you will be helped.

There is company in and my thoughts are somewhat confused in the midst of the general conversation, so am afraid I will be obliged to make my letter brief. Perhaps you will welcome it, tho,' if it is only enough to tell you that I am well and love you and long to be with you again. Shall we be likely to remain any length of time in New York this winter? I am anxious to know whether you will be delegate to convention.[27] I fear stormy times if we have more democratic victories, as I fear we shall—.

Am very glad that the convention is not to be until I can be with you. not that I imagine I should be a valorous protection for you, but if you must be in danger I will feel much easier to be with you. If the Lord will spare our lives to meet again, shall be very, very thankful.

God bless you, darling, and keep you safe. Pleasant dreams

A loving Good-night
Your little wife

———

Wells [Maine] Oct. 27th 1867

My Darling Husband.

I am with Greenleaf and Nancie[28] down on the Sea Shore, with the wild waves breaking on the shore in front of me. It is a grand sight and one to which I am unaccustomed, so that it seems really wonderful to me. I do not wonder that those born and reared near the mighty ocean love it as they do with all its beauty tho' it seems almost like a frightful monster ready to devour.

---

[26] In April 1867, JEB had attempted to borrow $3,000 from Harper Brothers Company on the expectation that he would recommend Harper books in Georgia schools. This may mean that Robert Harper had called in the loan.

[27] Georgia's constitutional convention, mandated by Reconstruction Acts.

[28] Nancy W. Hines Spaulding, Greenleaf's wife.

I came here from Brunswick yesterday (Sat) and this morning we drove out to church two miles and now this afternoon have walked here to the beach—a distance of a mile or more. I would be very, very happy were you here with me—may we very soon be reunited. It is two days since I have written you—the only time that have failed to write in many weeks. The morning I left Farmington I had so much to do in so little time that was obliged to go without writing. I arrived at Brunswick very tired and so deferred writing you until morning and in the morning I had a call to make and so many to talk to me that I did what have not done before this summer—forgot to write you until too late. Forgive me darling 'tis a poor apology to make but I like always to tell the truth. I hope now to have more leisure for writing than have had at Farmington. It is grown quite cold and I think we must return to the house and will finish there.

Evening—Have retraced our steps home, had our tea and are now in a very cozy little parlor. The lamps lighted and nothing lacking to a very cozy and happy evening save a certain man of your [illegible] and age. I am growing very lonely and almost [illegible] without you—shall be very, very glad to turn my steps towards home. I am very impatient to know just when you will come to New York—will try to be very patient and trust that you will come very soon.

Am sleepy and as Greenleaf and Nancie have retired I will do so.

May God bless you, darling. Make you a follower of the Lamb and speedily reunite us. Pleasant dreams. Good-night kisses. Pray for me, dear, that I may be a more faithful christian.

With many loving kisses
Your own little wife

Wells Nov. 1st 1867

My Darling Husband.

I am hoping that you may leave for N.Y. before this has time to reach you but as it is possible you may be delayed will continue to write.

All the family save the old people and myself are gone out to pass the evening. I staid [sic] home because was feeling little tired and beside disliked the cold night air. We have many pleasant days even now but the nights are cold—quite too cold for me to enjoy going out. wish that I didn't feel the cold more than I did when I first knew you. I am growing to dislike our cold northern winters almost as much as you do. Recieved [*sic*] no letter from you to-day shall be quite disappointed if do not get a letter to-morrow (Saturday) to last me over the Sabbath. Am more disappointed to miss my daily letter on Saturday than any other day.

Your election, I presume, closes to-morrow—am anxious to learn the result. It is possible that Nancie and I may go to Buckfield Monday—tho' I do not like to leave Greenleaf so soon. Katie has been keeping house for her father while Nancie is away and now she wants to go home. I think if Mr. Keiner made an effort he might get some one else to keep house for a week or two as Nancie has been with Greenleaf so very little and will be seperated [*sic*] from him all winter. She is disappointed to return so soon and Greenleaf says she shall not go—thinks her father can get along without her as well as he, so can not tell whether we shall go or no. I think however we will not go at present unless Greenleaf is ordered away or I recieve word from you. So you see we are all waiting orders. I am enjoying my visit here but shall welcome any orders to pack and start most joyfully.

If this reaches you before you leave Augusta please bring my heavy shawl with you. I may need it on the way home, the season is so far advanced. As the time draws near for me to go am very impatient. God bless and keep you safe and unite us soon.

With loving kisses
Your own little wife

Wells November 1st [7th?] 1867

My Darling Husband.

I scarcely know whether it is of any use for me to write you longer for if you leave early in next week . . . perhaps you may leave before this arrives—wish that you might for am grown very impatient. I shall continue to write, however, until I feel sure that you are near leaving. I saw by paper yesterday that the polls at Augusta were to be kept open until Saturday evening—fear that this may delay your departure somewhat.

Nancie has some expectations of going home first of next week. presume I shall go where she goes unless she should go to Boston from here which she wishes to do, in which case I should be obliged to go to Buckfield alone and

make preparation for my departure. I recieved three letters from you yesterday . . . two of them containing five dollars each. . . .

I wish that Charles was not such a fair-weather friend. I cannot esteem him
as I would have liked—should be very glad indeed for you to have Benj with
you. If we can have some member of our own immediate families with or near
us it will add greatly to our happiness in our Southern home.

I shall be glad when you are well rid of Richardson,[29] for I do not believe
him to be a man of pure character or great abilities. I am thankful that you
have been enabled to pay off old debts since you returned—trust that ere
many years you may be able to lift the last one from your shoulders. Am very
glad that you have a home once more—will try to make it look and seem
home-like when I reach there. Last evening we (Nancie and self and two
daughters of the people where we board) went out to tea at the camp—
Greenleaf's camp[30]—had a nice time—they have a colored cook who officiated with the usual grace of those individuals. I notice the sudden death of
Gov. Andrews.[31] I wish that one of his last public acts had not been to stul-
tify himself by his license-law argument.

I will not write more. . . . I have still a good days work to finish my pictures and perhaps more. Have to do this finishing part without a pattern as
sent Emma's to her yesterday. I love you and long to be with you. God bless
and keep us.

Lovingly,
Emma

---

[29] Ironically, Richardson would be murdered in February 1868, after a political dispute.
[30] Greenleaf worked with the United States Geodetic Survey.
[31] Former Massachusetts governor John Albion Andrew died suddenly in October 1867.

LETTERS: 1868–1869

At the end of 1867, Emma and John were finally reunited. The absence of surviving letters from the first months of 1868 suggests that they were together through the winter of 1867–68. By July, however, she was writing to him from their home in Augusta with plans to join him in Atlanta. The continuing effort to find suitable boarding arrangements took on added importance because of Emma's second pregnancy, which she wanted to protect at all costs.

In the summer of 1868, John's surprising news was that he was running for a United States Senate seat from Georgia.[1] Since Republican Party leaders in neither Washington nor Atlanta encouraged the effort, his ambition was in vain. More troubling was the developing rift between JEB and the new Republican governor, Rufus Bullock, which resulted in a major division among party leaders and devastated Bryant's expectations for the party and his own future. The fall brought other setbacks. Despite JEB's vigorous efforts in the opposite direction, whites expelled African American legislators from the state assembly, and Georgia Republicans failed to win the state for Ulysses S. Grant in the presidential election.

Emma's letters reflect the continuing turmoil in her husband's affairs at the center of politics in Georgia, as the fight to discredit the governor inevitably brought vicious counterattacks. By March 1869, JEB had been ousted as chairman of the Republican Executive Committee, and he resigned from the legislature. Pushed aside for a time, he sought some stability for his career through the federal position of postmaster in Augusta, Georgia, probably not coincidentally a position held by one of Bullock's strongest supporters.

This nadir of John's political prospects coincided with his wife's time of greatest need. By March 1869, as Emma awaited the birth of their child, John was in Washington, hoping to secure an appointment and finalize his affairs so that he could join her in Atlanta. These poignant letters reflect the birth and death of their only son.

---

[1] See *Carpetbagger of Conscience*, 77–103, for the details of JEB's career in the years 1868–69.

Tilden Ladies' Seminary
West Lebanon, N.H.
March 16th 1868

My Precious Emma:

You don't know how very glad I was for your letter and how much you have been in my mind both before and since its reception. On your birthday I had promised myself I would surely write you, remembering as I did one year ago when you were with me on that anniversary of yours. Many times that Sep Miss Hamilton and I talked of you. How much I enjoyed your visit with me and mine with you. I fully appreciate it <u>now</u> when I am debased from all such privileges of seeing friends and look back [illegible] opportunities of being with you had most all slipped away—that you will stay South the rest of your life visiting the West but leaving Buckfield out almost per force tho' it holds some of your dearest treasures; spot most consecrated and hallowed than all the world beside to you. Darling, when I am there things are not forgotten. Your sainted Mother was dearer to me than almost any friend outside my own family. I never go by the dear old home without a host of dear memories, thronging up and they will bring the tears as they are doing this very minute. You seem so far away—so all alone to me. I shall be so glad when Mr. Bryant can be home with you all the time. But in the present condition of the South it seems to me you can not have that sweet home quiet that you need and crave. I know you may do and probably will [illegible] for you, my darling, just the quiet happiness of your old house without such dreadful fear entering as I know must when Mr. Bryant is being exposed to constant danger. You are not so selfish as I.

Mother wrote me Mr. Bryant's partner was shot at Convention.[2] I don't know [illegible] particulars. Was he a delegate? Was he killed? If I remember aright he was wounded such a way before he went to Augusta. How dreadful! Precious, you need all the fortitude of a Joan of Arc. You know where to go for strength which He has promised to give "sufficiently"—May you and your dear ones be protected "beneath the shadow of His wing."

I, too was bitterly disappointed not to see you the morning you left, but the weather kept me in Thursday of that week. I rode to the Village and saw Greenleaf. . . .

---

[2] C. C. Richardson was killed after a political dispute.

This is a splendid school—very easy teaching for there is a <u>Head</u>, whose word (he only utters a few) is <u>law</u>.—I only teach two and one fourth hours per day for five days in the week and am taking vocal and instrumental lessons, practicing a good bit improving but little; I get discouraged as I never did over any thing else in my life. Prof. Srance is a splendid teacher. I have had a splendid opening to teach in Norwich, four miles from me here, and keep right on with my music but I knew my health would give out so terribly taxed, tho' the money looked tempting. I think now of teaching next year and the following, going to Boston or New York and Mrs. Gelbat, Principal of School at Norwich has partially agreed to go there and teach music two days in the week. To commence week tomorrow; don't know but I'll regret it. But be a diversion—A ride through Hanover Dartmouth College will not be despicable! students are thick as bees about here. ever know any there?—. . . .

> You'll write me ere long again, my own dear Emma!
> With untold love—
> Alice

———

Augusta Ga. July 2$^{\underline{d}}$ 1868

My Darling Husband,

I am almost tempted to call you a naughty husband—two mornings have passed and no letters—not one little word, suppose I must charge all to wise [illegible] and caucusing and keep patient till another morning. I am a little troubled about our rent money. Col Bowles[3] has not yet made his appearance and it is now Thursday P.M. Did you suppose it a <u>certainty</u> that he would bring the money yesterday or was he merely expecting it from Government? You spoke of your resignation before you went away and said you should send it from Atlanta. Mr. Coney was in last evening also the evening before, he has not staid [*sic*] the night however because we did not feel timid enough to need him[4] and if we did not I prefered [*sic*] he should not come because I could not offer him as comfortable room as he has at home. Mrs. Smith has been out the past two evenings and Susan has passed the evening with me—she

---

[3] John Bowles, another anti-Bullock Republican.

[4] Her daughter remembered that when JEB was away, Emma "never went to the door at night without a revolver in her hand and she usually had a guard of colored men in the house."

(Mrs. Smith) is out now and will be out through the early part of the evening. Shall go down to sit with Susan until she returns.

I have had Emily here sewing to-day—shall have her on [illegible] several days if can and shut my eyes to long stiches [*sic*] for do not feel strong enough to sew continuously. I still have ground for future hopes and consequently am careful of myself. . . .

Mrs. Smith leaves to-morrow—presume I will be lonely when she is away, tho' Susan will be with me out of school hours.

I shall be disappointed if do not hear from you to-morrow.

One important item I came near forgetting—I achieved an important victory over the mosquitoes last night. I should say, <u>we</u> achieved for Mrs. Smith mended our old mosquito net and I drew it on the bed and we slept all night in the greatest peace and serenity.

Now, let me have a line from you each day if you can spare the time. I shall be <u>very</u> glad to recieve [*sic*] the word to go to you. God bless you, darling, and keep us very true—

> Bye-bye—
> Your loving wife

I am good deal interested to know whether we have a boarding place and if we have what it is like. Is there white spread on the bed and carpet on the floor

———

Home Saturday P.M. [July 3, 1868?]

My Darling Husband.

Was very, <u>very</u> glad to receive line from you this morning, the first since you left. I have many questions to ask and am not at all satisfied with waiting. You say you are running for the Senate "in earnest." When will that contest be decided? Shall feel good deal of anxiety to learn the result. Are the nominations for the Senate made immediately upon the assembling of the Legislature and will this move make any difference in my going to Atlanta at the time forecast? To try to put many questions in one, can you tell when you will send for me, and is there the <u>least</u> danger that your election to the Senate may necessitate another seperation [*sic*] of weeks and months?

<u>Please take time</u> to answer these questions. Do not think that I am more anxious to be with you than for you to be prospered. I do not believe that I am but I cannot help a little fear that sometimes comes knocking at my heart

that more seperations [*sic*] are in store for us. Please write me very freely about this, whether I am to go to you in a few days, let the matter turn as it may, and whether I must wait until it is decided before going? I send you quite a number of letters, one of them from Hotchkiss with your Life Insurance papers. I am rather surprised that Col. Bowles has kept his engagement no better—he has neither brought the money or made any explanation. Leckie came yesterday for his money and I was obliged to tell him that I expected money which had not come.

He was here again this morning in great trouble saying his note was protested at the bank (which I dont quite believe) and he was in great distress for the money. He wished me to give him a note to the person from whom I expected the money but I did not feel at liberty to do this. . . . I told Leckie I would write you to-day in reference to it. I am afraid Col. Bowles is not quite prompt in business matters. Susan was with me last night to-night I sleep with her.

I feel a bit lonely to-night principally because your letter has aroused the fear that it may not be practicable for me to go to you as soon as I had hoped—if the fear is groundless, please remove it at once. I love you, darling, and think I will be very happy when I am with you.

Am well and still cherish in my heart a little hope of a future blessing to our house—a little light to our home. I pray, darling, that you may be kept from wrong in the midst of political intrigue and that, in this present contest, you may have that success which shall be best for you eventually. I would be happier with my arms around your neck to-night. May it soon be so?— With loving kisses.

Your own wife

Home, Sabbath P.M.
[July 5, 1868]

My Darling Husband,

Have been quite alone save Major since I came home from S. School. he comes in and puts those great fore paws of his up in my lap and lays his black head down on them as if desirous to show his affection and sympathy. I do miss you to-day, darling, very very much. I have been feeling quite happy all the week until yesterday with the thought that I was so soon to go to you, but yesterday and to-day I have wanted you very, very much. I almost feared that my yesterday's letter with its questions as to how your present course would affect my going speedily to you might seem selfish, but I will not be so. I will be a brave little wife even though your advancement should cause us still further seperation [*sic*] but O, I pray it may not! I need to be with you—my life is incomplete and barren without your life and your society. If we can be together I believe it will be better for the souls of both of us. May God bless us, my dear husband, first of all, and above all with the baptism of His Spirit.

Shall I be with you before another Sunday night?

If you are elected to the Senate will you be obliged to go direct to Washington and if you do shall I be left home or can you take me with you? Please answer these questions immediately if you have not already done so. I love you, darling, and would be <u>so glad</u> to have you with me to-day.

Last night I passed at the Mission House with Susan. This morning went to Sabbath School, went in a rain and came home in a burning sun. Only Mr. Corrin and myself there of the adult teachers. I think Mr. Corrin will make an excellent Superintendent.

The peonies I was disappointed in getting. I bought two Friday and decided upon others but they were at another store and I came home to meet an engagement thinking I would get the other two yesterday—but yesterday the store was closed. I told the children the reason that I had not the peonies for them to-day and that I would carry or send them next Sunday. We had but very few out to-day. I presume on account of the rain. and now my dear, I have told you of my lonely Sabbath, how have you passed the day? Shall I not hear from you in the morning? . . .

God bless you, darling, and shed abroad the love of Christ in your heart— prosper you and fit you to do to His glory whatever work is laid upon you and may He very soon restore us to each other.

> Bye-bye, Darling
> Your Loving Wife

———

Augusta Monday July 6, 1868

My Darling Husband.

I am very anxious to know the result of your senatorial contest. Have not had a word of information in regard to it, save the line in your one letter, I have imagined the nominations might possibly be made to-day. Now that you have decided to run "in earnest" am of course anxious for your success.

Cant you spare just five minutes to write me a line? remember it is a whole week to-night since you left me and only one little letter. Was much disappointed when mail came this morning that there was no letter from you. but am brightening up again and looking for to-morrow morning's mail to bring me tidings from you and perhaps the senatorial nominations.

I enclose a letter from Perham which came this morning.

Don't you think it rather dishonorable in Col Bowles to neither bring me that money or give me any explanation?

Leckie was here again this morning before the mail came and said he would call round again to learn if I heard anything from you in reference to it.

When Mrs. Smith left me she charged me a very cordial good-bye to you which I have forgotten to transmit until now—have been more lonely since she left.

I go down to sleep with Susan to-night—she was with me last night. God bless you, darling, and reunite us soon.

You do not know how it will lighten my heart if I have a letter saying I am to go to you some time this week or first of next, tho' I desire to do that which is necessary and best for you. I am well and shall be happy, I believe, when am with you.

Bye Bye, Darling
Your loving wife.

Tell Charles his nightstand is here. What shall I do with it also a black-handled knife—is that his?

––––––––

Augusta July 9th /68
Thursday P.M.

My Darling Husband.

I will not try to tell you how much good your two letters recieved [*sic*] this morning did a sore spot in my heart that has been there some days, and, not least, the assurance that you will send for me in a day or two. I shall be so glad to go. I must spare only a few moments for writing because have so many things to do before you send for me.

Col. Bowles called this morning and asked me to send Leckie round to his office if he (Col Bowles) did not come here with the money before Leckie came. Leckie was here, or rather his son, this morning and was to come again this P.M. Leckie wishes to know whether you wish to retain this rent another year at the same price—he asked me several days ago but I forgot to mention it.

And now a word of my own finances. The money which you left me for housekeeping, personal and travelling expenses has not proved sufficient. You see I have had a fortnight, is nearly that, housekeeping, part of the time with company, beside wood to buy and all the other little items, beside that <u>my health</u> at the present is such that it is not safe for me to overexert myself greatly and I am obliged to hire some one to sew for me, then there will be about two dollars more to pay to Sarah when I leave.

If you can not conveniently send me money I think it probable that I can borrow of Susan and return the money from Atlanta. Shall try to do this at any rate if you send before you have time to recieve [*sic*] this. I think I would prefer to go on night train if can. What I hoped when you were here I have little doubt of now. I only fear the same disaster as befell me two years ago—shall try to be very careful. I am very desirous to be with you. I think I never so much before felt the <u>need</u> of you as now. Am almost low-spirited to be away from you. About the money I hope that ten dollars will pay my bills here and travelling expenses with what I have with me.

> And now must say a hasty good-bye.
> With loving kisses,
> Your loving wife—

Augusta July 11th /68

My Darling Husband.

I have already sent to the office one letter for you this P.M. but have since then received yours of yesterday, much to my pleasure.

If I followed my inclinations I should start immediately but I cannot feel that it is right to start on a journey Saturday night which one knows will encroach upon Sunday. I have decided to let my views of right control my desire to be with you and will go on Monday, providence permitting. The money I can get of Susan. I would start on Monday morning were it not for two reasons the more important one is that in in [*sic*] the morning I have the sickness peculiar to my situation and I fear that this combined with the heat would give me a very uncomfortable day, a lesser reason is that I have still several pieces of sewing which it is really necessary to finish before going.

This latter reason I should set aside and go to-night could I feel it right to travel on the Sabbath. Please do not think that I am lacking in desire to be with you for I have been looking forward to it with exceedingly pleasant anticipation and the time looks long between now and Monday night. If by any possibility I should decide to start on Monday morning I will telegraph you at the National—if I do <u>not</u> telegraph you may expect to find me there on Tuesday morning. Am pleased to learn that you have so pleasant a boarding place.

I am anticipating a very pleasant summer. I shall go to pass to-night with Susan as she expects company from Macon so that she cannot leave to come here. I must not spend the time to write more. With the blessing of God we will soon be together. For a little time

Good bye,
Your loving wife

Atlanta Oct 8th "/68

My Darling Husband.

I am safely housed at Col. Spauldings[5] and only wish that I was sure of your being as safe. I feel strongly confident that the Lord will care for you and bring you safe home to me tho' I know that sometimes He allows his people to suffer martyrdom in a good cause, but I have never felt that you were to lose your life in this cause but were to live to work through it. God bless you darling, make you a good soldier of the Lord and your country and bring you safe back to me.

The night you left I slept alone quite unintentionally on my part I assure you. I went round to sleep with Miss Welch and learned to my dismay that she had gone to Augusta. Peach [illegible] cleared up and she returned home. Wended my way back rather slowly and sadly <u>but</u> thought I could do no better than to lay myself away in bed with the hope that weariness and sleepiness would make me oblivious till morning—had rather a wakeful night of it however so that did not care to try it again. Came up here late evening and am having very pleasant visit—will remain here until Saturday night—probably possibly longer so that my letters had best come in Mr. Spaulding's care. Am

---

5 Volney Spalding, born in New York, and his second wife, Mary Kellogg Ramsdell, lived in Atlanta. Though he spelled his name differently from Emma's family, he was probably a cousin. Colonel Spalding would become JEB's close business associate in the 1880s.

feeling very well since I came here—much better than at the Hotel. Eat [*sic*] a solitary dinner there yesterday and missed my husband very much.

I have learned as yet nothing definite in regard to our boarding here. Mrs. Spauldings talks as if she would like to have us here if they can plan about room—she has some expectation that her sister will come down and I think is waiting to hear from her before she decides. Pauline wants us to come and I am inclined to think that they will take us.

I shall hope to hear from you to-morrow, certainly, be sure to telegraph should anything ill befal [*sic*] you. Be careful as you can consistently with your duty. Once more God bless you—I kiss you warmly, lovingly

Your own loving wife

————

Atlanta Dec. 12th /68

My Darling Husband:

It is near bed-time of another Sabbath evening—believe all the other members of the household have retired. Can I hope or expect that you will be home before another Sabbath? Should be <u>so glad</u> to think so but do not dare set my heart on it.

I have wondered how you were passing the day and whether you were in the midst of association fit for the day or surrounded by scheming politicians, not christian politicians.

It seems a long time since you left and long to be [illegible] a letter from you—hope very soon to hear from you. I went to our church this morning—we had a stranger in the pulpit who but poorly filled Mr. Lee's place, I thought, Mr. Lee was also there.

After church I yielded to my feelings of dread to returning to my lonely room and went to Mission House, walked nearly there with Mrs. Lee—met with cordial welcome from the inmates of the home—remained to dinner and afternoon service and then returned home just before dark.

Instead of preaching this afternoon at the Mission chapel, they had communion service. Mr. Lance's remarks seemed very appropriate and full of the gospel spirit. I joined with them in communion, the first time that I have ever done so out of my own church, but have decided that a mere church usage is not binding upon me when my own conscience does not approve it. I met a man there by the name of Chase who said that he met you in N.Y. two years ago. He is superintendent of education in Florida.

And now my darling husband, I will close my letter, write a bit in my diary pray for you, your success and safe return and retire, hoping before very long to have you with me.

> God bless and keep you—
> Pleasant dreams—
> Loving good-night kisses
> Emma

————

> Atlanta Mar. 10th /69
> Wednesday morn

My Darling Husband

Another night without you come and gone.

Seems a little lonely when am wakeful and fidgetty to have no husband in bed with me, but feel as if it will not be many days before will have a little remembrance of him to share my bed. Do not feel as if my sickness can will [*sic*] be delayed longer than Easter-day or Sunday—hope not sincerely. Recieved [*sic*] invitations yesterday to Judge Erskine's[6] to-morrow evening. Shall return our regrets to-day, mentioning your absence from town.

Hope I may not be sick at such a time as to prevent Mr. & Mrs. Sherman[7] from attending.

Mr. Sherman is sick to-day but has just been sent for to go to Senate to vote and Mrs. Sherman is flying round getting him ready and altogether I haven't very collected ideas.

I walked up to Mrs. Spaulding's yesterday morning, but do not expect to get so far from home again at present. Your gold pen I put in the top of your trunk. The case by itself and the pen in little pen box. I also put in box of blue pens. I imagine you are this morning in Washington—trust you will be entirely successful. Does the reinstatement of Blodgett[8] forebode any ill to you, or does it simply give him his back pay and government an opportunity to displace him?

————

[6] John Erskine, district court judge in Atlanta.
[7] Georgia senator Josiah Sherman, Vermont carpetbagger, and his wife, with whom Emma boarded on the outskirts of Atlanta.
[8] Foster Blodgett, JEB's political nemesis, was a close associate of Governor Rufus Bullock; former mayor and postmaster in Augusta.

I shall hope to hear from you by Saturday. God bless you, darling, and keep you safe. Shall be so very glad to see you home again.

> With Loving kisses
> Emma

———

> Thursday P.M. [March 11, 1869]

My Darling Husband,

Have time for only a word to-day as must send out by Mrs. Sherman.

Walked out this morning, called on Mrs. Walker.

Am feeling same as for past few days, scarce as well as when you left, or rather, think I feel little more as if might be sick some time—hope it will not be much longer delayed.

Shall be so glad to be able to send you word that it is safely through. I dread it without you, must confess—should feel so much better if could have you with [me], still do not regret that you went when you did and will try to keep up courage and bear it bravely.

Poor Mr. Sherman is groaning with rheumatism and has been for day or two. God bless you, darling and keep you safe. I love you and would be so happy if could have you with me.

> With loving kisses—
> Emma

———

> Atlanta Mar. 12th /69
> Tuesday morn [Friday?]

My Darling Husband.

Although I have so little of interest to write, will not neglect you for single day while am able because I know the simple assurance that I am well will be worth something to you—shall be more glad, however, when some one else can write you that the crisis is safely past and you have a nice baby, as I think will be ere long.

We have such a lovely day—just a little cool with a bright sun, went out walking and not feeling like walking long distance, went into an open field and sat down for long time on the roots of a tree—it was so lovely and the air so fresh and sweet that almost dreaded to come back into the house. Mrs. Sherman is visiting the Senate this morning and I am at home alone for a little while.

They went last evening to the reception of Judge Erskine's, remaining till about 11 o'clock. Mrs. Rice was with me, and her husband failing to come for her, passed the night with me.

I am very comfortably situated here and only lack your presence to make me very comfortable and happy. As the time approaches for my illness and I feel that it must be close at hand, I can not help a little dread of passing through it without you. But I trust that God will help us and spare to you the life of both wife and baby. The thought of dying with you away would be very hard to me. But away with such thoughts. I expect to be carried safely through and to be almost well again before your return. I am anxious for your success in Washington. May God take all our affairs into His own hands.

God bless you abundantly, darling, and reunite us again on earth, if it may be. I kiss you many times, warm, loving kisses,

> Bye-bye Darling,
> Your own loving wife
> God keep us true in <u>life</u> and <u>death</u>.

Mr. Sherman has just told me astounding news of the Dicksons, the one that boarded at Mr. Spaulding's and her brother, the U.S. Marshall. They were reported in Court to-day as having absconded. It came to me with a real shock, and I think must to you. Mr. Sherman has had it hinted to me that sum was a defaultion [*sic*] of large amount.

———

> Atlanta Mar. 13th /69
> Saturday P.M.

My Darling Husband

Had hoped to hear from you by to-day but Mr. Sherman came in and tells me no mail for me, so must wait until to-morrow.

I feel as if I may be sick before that time—indeed, begin to feel rather impatient for the struggle to be over.

We are having lovely day—almost like summer—Pauline came in to see me this morning. Wish you could be with me to-night and to-morrow. God bless you, darling, and reunite us soon as may be.

> With loving kisses
> Your own loving wife
> Emma

————

Atlanta Mar. 14th /69

My Darling Husband.

Another Sunday has come and I am still out of my bed, would scarce have believed last Sabbath that I should be. Would be so glad to have you with me but can only wish that you may have the blessing of God's spirit in your heart where you are, and be restored to me ere many weeks have passed. . . .

Shall be very glad, I think, when the time comes for us to take our wee one and go home, if God spares us all to that time. Am well as could expect, save cold that makes me feel stupid, and contented as can be without you. Mrs. Sherman is very kind and I am as much at home here as can be away from my own home. Mr. S. and Lily are much more kind and pleasant than when I boarded with them.

Do you remember the Vermont family by the name of Moses that we met on the cars the first time we came South? There is a family by that name very near us and Mrs. Moses told Miss Brett (who sews for me) that she should call on me—they are northern people and I think must be the same.

I fear may be unable to get this in the office this morning for Mr. Sherman is just going to church. Will try however to get the girl to take it before mail closes. God bless you darling, Keep us in his love and reunite us speedily as may be. with warm kisses—

> Your loving wife

Monday P.M. I didn't send this yesterday as intended and thought I would surely hear from you to-day—but Mr. Sherman has just come in and brings me no letter. Am very anxious to hear from you. I am still quite well tho' with some symptoms of sickness very soon.

Mr. & Mrs. Spaulding called to see me last evening—had a very pleasant call from them. They say that Mr. Dickson appeared in a very distressed state of mind when he left and for some time before.

God bless you, darling, and reunite us speedily.

Emma

————

Atlanta Tuesday Mar. 23 [1869]

My Darling Husband.

Our little baby still lingers with us and O that you might see it. I almost feel as if I cannot have it, that our little darling, our first-born, perhaps only child, shall be lain in the grave without you looking upon its sweet little face—it is a world of comfort to me to have him lie here in bed beside me and I want his papa to see him—O so much.

Last night he was very sick and seemed in danger of convulsions—he has had the same symptoms to-day too, not as severe, but seems a little better now. I have sent no word to your folks of the birth, because they were not expecting it and so would not be anxious about me, and I felt that it could only be sad news to them at the best. Had he been a well baby, should have had them informed immediately. Mr. Sherman encloses you a letter from Lucy.

Greenleaf and father have been informed of the birth but do not know the sad feature of it. I wish if you feel like it you would write Greenleaf and tell him. I will write to Earlville when I am able.

God help you, darling—help both of us in this terrible disappointment and deal gently with the little dear child that he has permitted to come into this world to suffer—

he opens his bright blue eyes on me now as I write.

God bring you home in season to see him if it may be.

I never wanted you more, darling, never but to cling to you closer, I think, than now—

With warmest kisses,
Your loving wife

When our darling is taken from me I feel that must have him carried to Augusta to be buried. I cannot think of leaving him here.

Atlanta Apr. 2<u>d</u> [1869]
Friday P.M.

My Darling Husband.

I have not written you for several days because a letter from you first of the week gave me hope that I should see you home to-morrow morning—but Mr. Spaulding came in this morning and told me that he had a telegram from you sent yesterday from which I suppose you cannot have started on Thursday as you intended. I had eight dollars from Mr. Spaulding this morning—had not needed it until now very much, but was just out.

I <u>am</u> very much disappointed that I cannot hope to see you to-morrow, as I fear I cannot. but will try to keep up courage and wait until next week. I trust, if you are not much longer delayed you may have the dear privilege of seeing your darling baby. I kiss him many times for his papa and pray God that you be enabled to see him alive. He continued to seem comparatively free from pain but very weak. The tumor is much reduced in size—think it is now scarce one quarter as large as when it was fullest for days after his birth. It is badly ulcerated and the Dr. says it is not possible that the child can live—but people do live in spite of Dr's and I cannot help feeling that the Dr. may be mistaken in this and that nature itself may heal him. I do not myself feel certain that it has any connection with the spine. The convulsive symptoms have almost or entirely disappeared and it discharges daily, sometimes large amounts, while the Dr. did not expect him to live after the first breaking and discharge.

Perhaps this is more a mothers clinging to her baby than any reasonable hope but it is all in God's hands and he does not willingly afflict us. I sat up in my chair a little yesterday and again to-day—am doing quite well and hope to be almost strong again in a few days. I shall be so glad to see you home once more. I trust you may leave W-[ashington] before this letter has time to reach you but will send it lest you should be delayed and feel anxious about us.

God bless you darling and bring you safe home to us very, <u>very</u> soon if it may be. I must not try my eyes to write longer.

With warmest kisses
Your own loving wife.

Saturday Morning—Mr. Sherman was away and had no opportunity to mail this. Baby darling is not as well today—seems weaker and sicker [illegible] the Lord make you to hasten [illegible] to see him. I love you darling [illegible] will not try to tell you how [good it] will be to see you home.

Emma

———

Atlanta Apr. 18<u>th</u> /69
Sunday P.M.

My Darling Husband.

Your letter rec'd this morning tells me that you will be detained till to-morrow night, perhaps longer—am sorry that such necessity has arisen and sorry, too, for Col. Bowles if he is innocent of the charges brought against him.

I think that am growing stronger—am dressed to-day—went out to breakfast and will go out to dinner. The day is lonely and I can but think longingly of the little babe that would have made all the days so short and cheery—but he, I believe is with his Savior and God has other work on earth for me to do. I often find myself conjecturing what that work shall be—whether the blessed work of rearing other children of our own flesh (tho none could quite fill the void it seems to me left by our first-born darling) or some other work which I have not looked forward to or desired. He only knows. God help us both.

I love you darling, and am <u>very</u> sorry to be without you, God unite us soon. I am called to dinner and must close as wish this taken out after dinner.

I am so sorry that my poor Major is sick—it seems as if there is a fatality about any pet I try to raise. Can't something be done for him. Please give my love to Mrs. Spillam. Am very glad Henry is recovering—it would be a sad blow to them to lose him, I think.

Bye-bye, Darling—
God bless you—
Your loving wife

Dr. & Mrs Hayden returned Saturday.

I feel quite sure that the charges against Col. Bowles as regards yourself must be untrue, are they not?

Hope On Hope Ever
May 2, 1869

Col. J. E. Bryant
Dear Sir,

I rec'd your note of the 23^d ult, yesterday evening, on my plantation. In reply to its contents, I would state that you can place the remains of your infant, as you request, provided Mrs. Bryant will see that the beauty of the place is not all marred & that when you remove the body to another place, she will see that the flowers now growing there are replaced by others, if it is necessary to disturb them, in order to dig another grave. Perhaps as good a spot as any would be by the side of Lizzy Shermans' grave. If this is any accommodation to you, I shall be amply recompenced [sic] by any additional attempt either of you may make, to beautify & adorn the resting place of my beloved wifes' remains.[9] The deep & extreme poverty I am at present plunged in, prevents me from doing more than I have done to render the spot worthy of the resting place of so fair & beautiful a form as now lies there. I am happy to be able to confer this favor upon you & Mrs. Bryant; and desire to express my sympathy further in the disappointment it must necessarily be to her to have her first-born, as I suppose, snatched from her arms of love, & consigned to the silent tomb. But doubtless its germ of soul, has ere this, been transplanted to our Saviours' heavenly gardens—where under the skillful culture of the divine gardiner [sic] it will yet become a beautiful flower destined to bloom forever in the paradise of God. I expect to leave for the North in a few days, to see if I can do anything to promote the common cause we are all engaged in. My address for the next 6 mos. will be 25 Gardner St. Springfield Mass.

Yours truly,
C. Stearns

---

[9] Charles Stearns, northern planter and also a Georgia carpetbagger, had been saddened by the death of his wife, Etta.

LETTERS: 1870–1871

In 1869, John attempted to recoup his political influence from Augusta, the same locus as his initial federal post with the Freedmen's Bureau. Along with the postmaster position, which he assumed on July 21, 1869, he initiated the publication of his second newspaper effort, *The Georgia Republican*. Optimistically, Bryant asserted that the new paper would serve to unite Republicans to his version of the cause. JEB used his new patronage power to appoint African American males and he organized new social/political groups for them.[1]

The respite was temporary, however, for Bryant was inevitably drawn back into the political vortex by the actions of Georgia's governor. In an attempt to prolong his administration, Bullock engineered a so-called "Third Reconstruction" of Georgia, which drew bipartisan dismay. JEB, having withdrawn his previous resignation from the legislature, was again on hand in Atlanta in January 1870—in the midst of shifting coalitions and contradictory strategies.

At the national level, Congress and the president were tiring of the "Georgia Question." Reconstruction policy was disintegrating state by state as Republican carpetbag administrations lost their local constituencies as well as support in Washington. Bryant was among the Republicans seeking to reclaim the moral high ground, claiming that he had "done as much as I can do" for the party in purging Bullock's questionable schemes. But Democrats, acknowledging few differences in the Republican factions, closed ranks and regained power.

It is unclear whether Emma ever moved to Augusta in 1869 after the death of her firstborn. The Bryants may have resided together in Atlanta for a time, perhaps until mid-1871. In the fall of 1872, she would note that they had been living separately for almost a year. This suggests that when John returned to Augusta in the summer of 1871, Emma had moved to the outskirts of Atlanta, where she again boarded with the Shermans, this time to await the birth of their second child. Concerned for her health and safety, John was, nevertheless, absorbed by the climax of his ongoing skirmish

---

[1] See *Carpetbagger of Conscience*, 103–17, for details of JEB's career in the years 1870–71.

with the governor. Thus, he corresponded with his wife from Augusta. To JEB's relief, Bullock fled the state in October 1871.

With her husband absent as before, Emma gave birth to their daughter Emma Alice on November 16, 1871. From Earlville, Gretta Spaulding Browne reflected the relief that the family felt for a safe delivery. From Maine, the mother of Alice White, Emma's dear "chummie" at Kents Hill, wrote to wistfully remember the baby's namesake, who had died recently. Written years later, the autobiography of Emma Alice (or Alice, as she came to be called) described the circumstances of the birth.

Earlville Ill June 7 1871

Dear Daughter [2]

I received a letter from you a few days ago by your writing have a hope that you are improving slowly. If you get along through the warm weather you will get up again. My health is good this season so far I am at work all the time. We have 65 acres of Corn growing and it requires a good deal of work to take care of it. We had a heavy shower last Thursday rain and hail that cut our corn to pieces badly and it has ben [sic] showering most every day since which makes it bad taking care of it—the weeds grow faster than we can get them out. We are having a great quantity of Fruit this season wish you was here to enjoy it with us—we have more than we can use. Our strawberrys are the best there is in town shall have a great quantity of raspberrys and cherrys Currants goosbeerys and plums and pears and grapes if there is nothing to destroy them. Margarett[a] will write you soon. Mr Brown[e] thinks of going to Maine next month if he does I think he will take Neal with him. I hope you will be able to come and stay with us next season. I think it would be better for your health to come here through the warm weather—the children are getting along finely. I think you would enjoy them very much now the boy gets a whipping most every day for running of [sic] and getting into the mud and water he is easy to go to the Creek fishing. I go with him some times they dont allow him to go alone for fear he will get in and drowned, we feell verry anxious abut [sic] you and hope to hear from you often. Greenleaf I expect is at Buckfield now. Dont know how long he will stop there. Give my love to Mr Bryant tell him I

---

[2] Emma's father spelled too many words incorrectly to mark even first occurrences. All spellings original.

should be verry glad to see him you mustuns [*sic*] careful of yourself as possible and try to regain your health again—much love to you

Yours Truly
Father

————

[letterhead]
Georgia Legislature,
House of Representatives,
Augusta Ga, Oct 22, 1871

My Darling Wife,

I find that I am not obliged to be in Atlanta as soon as I expected, and shall therefore not go until Wednesday or Thursday night. Shall probably reach there Friday morning and remain until Sunday night and go to Washington the first of next week.

I reached here safely this morning made my bed and had a good sleep after I reached here. I have been busy putting my things to rights and am quite pleasantly settled as much so as can be without a wife.

I have not seen the Capt. or Susan but shall this eve. I learn that Susan is better.

I love you darling warmly truly and kiss you,
Y.[our] H.[usband]

————

Augusta Ga. Nov 9th 1871

My Darling Wife

I reached here safely yesterday morning. Called on Susan and Mrs. Ritter yesterday and brought Spottie home with me. She slept at the office with me last night. Appeared to be very glad to see me.

I shall leave here Saturday night for Atlanta.

I feel anxious for you darling and want to be with you.

With warmest love and kisses
From Y. H.

Earlville Leu Salle A.
Illinois Nov 21 /71

My darling Sister,

The good tidings of your safe delivery, of the advent of a <u>nice plump baby girl</u> is just recieved [*sic*] & I hasten to offer congratulations to both parents. Thanks to Brother B. for his promptness in informing us—'tis a great relief to me, especially to hear that you are comfortable & Baby well. May a merciful Providence speedily restore you to health & strength & speed the darling babe in health. Wish I could kiss the darling—love it even now—'twill seem like my own. Now dear listen be extremely careful of yourself the little one will require all the strength you can command. Shall anticipate <u>solid comfort</u> with you & Baby next summer.

The children were delighted when I told them Auntie had a little Baby girl & that she was their little cousin. Neilly says tell Auntie to come up here & bring her little girl & he will try & kiss her.

Kittie would like to see you all particularly Uncle Bryant—& little Bell. How sorry your Husband could not have been with you in your sickness— there seems a futility about it—if he leaves you 'tis sure to happen just that time. Is your nurse with you? Is she good & efficient—Will not ask particulars until you are up & able to write.

B.[rowne] sends congratulations also twould be remembered to Mr. & Mrs. Sherman & sends thanks for their politeness to his wife & little girl. My regards to them all—would like the privilege of returning hospitality.

Am working very hard since my return. Kittie has not get [*sic*] entirely over her cough. Father was much pleased to hear of the birth of a little grand-daughter.

Had our first snow last night—about ½ inch Mr. Higgins says they have had 21. inches.

'Tis mail time must close—get some time to write just a line often.

Good bye
aff. M[argaretta] J[ane] Browne

Buckfield Dec 15th 1871

My Dear Emma—

I have been meditating for several hours this evening, we have long evenings here, the duty I owe womankind in general is the duty of writing to many several of the sex. I believe you are the most honored one among them. None of them can boast of a daughter and if they could, I know could not be as bright, cunning, pretty, as wonderful as your little Alice. I think the best wish I can wish her is that she may be loved by everyone as our Alice was. I would so like to see the little one, my Alice's first namesake. Emma, I was so thankful Louise's baby was a boy so she would not name it Alice, but I am just as glad yours can have her name for I know she would be pleased. I thank Cap. Bryant very much for taking the trouble to let us know of the little stranger and of your welfare. If you would only move a little nearer me, I would take care of the baby half of the time while it is a dear little baby but when it gets to be two or three years old I shall not promise.

I never knew much about but one baby and he was so nice, it seems to me I should never want to do without one. How I used to wish that some-body would leave a nice boy baby on our steps and I do not know that I wish so now.

Charlie Prince is here now as I suppose you knew. He got here the next day after Mrs. Atwood was buried. The conductor was so drunk he kept the telegram until Monday. I was on my way home from Bangor that night and did not get to Buckfield until midnight. Just escaped traveling Sunday. We have got the best managed railroad in the country. Martin says it is time to go to bed so I shall have to cut my epistle short. He sends very much love to you and your little daughter as also does father. And now good night and pleasant dreams and kiss baby in the morning from her

Aunt Frans

———

Washington DC. Dec 19 1871

My Darling Wife

I am most ready to leave for home. Shall probably leave Thursday morning and reach Atlanta Saturday morning.

The Senate today decided that Blodgett is not entitled to a seat and Mr. Norwod[3] was sworn in.

I think Col. Atkins[4] will be appointed Collector of Customs of Savannah within a few days.

I love you darling and shall be glad to be home again. Kiss little Emma often for me.

> With warmest love and kisses
> From
> Y. H.

[From Alice Bryant's autobiography (typescript)]

... I think I was about nine years old when we lived in the upstairs apartment of a farm house in the country, some distance from Atlanta, Georgia. We had lived there before as it was at the Sherman's apartment that I was born. It was before the house was completly [*sic*] finished. I greatly embarassed [*sic*] my mother once when she was shopping in Atlanta by telling the gentleman clerk that I was born in a room that had a curtain hung up instead of a door to the room.

The family who lived there were named Sherman. This house was infested with ants, and they believed it was due to the fact that it was built over an ant hill. The soldiers had camped on that spot during the Civil War. Whenever we went to Atlanta we walked a long distance through the woods to the street-car. . . .

---

[3] JEB was successful in blocking Blodgett's confirmation as United States senator from Georgia; Thomas Manson Norwood, elected as a Democrat, was seated instead. Norwood served until March 1877.

[4] James Atkins, Georgia-born Republican, served in the state legislature 1868–70; he was JEB's political ally for the time being.

LETTERS: 1872–1873

In 1872, John Emory Bryant probably expected a return to the executive structure of Georgia's Republican Party after having accomplished his two political goals. He had been instrumental both in unseating Governor Bullock and in aborting Foster Blodgett's attempt to secure a Senate seat from the state. Not surprisingly, however, the bruising struggle had left the field strewn with political enemies. As the Republicans attempted to regroup, JEB kept a low profile by continuing his law practice in Augusta. He did feel, nevertheless, that his service to the party justified a patronage position to bolster his livelihood and enable him to support his growing family. By May 1872, he had secured the post of deputy collector of customs in Savannah.[1]

Letters during the year reflect the joys of parenting for both Emma and John, as well as the hazards of rearing a healthy child in that setting. Apparently, John visited his wife and new baby frequently but continued to maintain a separate residence in Augusta, and then Savannah, while Emma stayed with the Shermans in Atlanta until September. Even in the face of continued danger faced by the unwelcome Yankees, Emma was growing more self-sufficient as well as courageous; she was also more tolerant of her husband's unpredictable schedule. Faced with the national presidential election in the fall of 1872, JEB was embroiled in the futile effort to hold together a Republican coalition. The ability of the party to effect change in the state by political means was quickly ebbing.

If the personal correspondence between John and Emma reflected his professional life during 1872–73, it is not apparent in the existing letters. Instead, in the spring of 1873, Emma was planning extended visits: to Illinois to see her sister and father, and to Ohio to let John's mother and sister Lucy enjoy the new addition. With the travel also came opportunities outside the beleaguered South. She would consult with a physician in Cleveland regarding Emma Alice's development; and, she would visit various artists in Chicago, a reflection of her renewed interest in painting.

---

[1] See *Carpetbagger of Conscience*, 118–28, for the details of JEB's career in the years 1872–73.

Even more important, Emma planned to see the doctor her sister-in-law Lucy recommended for treating her longstanding affliction with some troublesome (and unnamed) uterine disease, apparently exacerbated by the recent birth of her child. In 1873, the exchange of letters between Emma in Cleveland and John in Savannah provide a significant window on both the strains on their marriage relationship and the growing strength of Emma's character.[2]

———

[letterhead] Office of J. E. Bryant,
Attorney at Law,
Corner Jackson and Greene Streets,
Augusta, Ga., Jan. 24th 1872

My Darling,

I am anxious to know how you and the baby are tonight. I wish I could be with you but here I am in my office all alone.

This has been a day of triumph for me. I managed my first case in court and gained it. The Judge appointed me to defend a colored man charged with stealing. It was apparantly [sic] a strong case against him but I succeed[ed] in making a defense strong enough to satisfy the jury that the man was not guilty and they returned a virdict [sic] accordingly. It was very fortunate for me that I gained my first case. It shows that I can practice law here with some hope of success. It gives me new courage, and I shall continue the struggle with more confidence in ultimate success.

I told Mr. Sherman that I thought he had better engage a girl he found in Atlanta in case you did not get a wet nurse but I have concluded not to do so but if you do not get a wet nurse to send the nurse from here of whom I spoke to you about. The more I see of her the better I like her. She has never brought a baby up on a bottle but Mrs. Lee of this city with whom her daughter is nursing a young baby is bringing it up on the bottle and it

———

[2] This exchange in 1873 has elicited additional interest in Emma's letters. See Shan Holt, "The Anatomy of a Marriage: Letters of Emma Spaulding Bryant, 1873," *Signs: Journal of Women in Culture and Society,* vol. 17, no. 1 (Autumn 1991), 187–204. Ms. Holt uses Emma's case for an interesting discussion of the nineteenth-century debate over medical treatment for women. While the author includes a few inaccuracies ("Earl" is not Emma's brother; Mrs. Sherman not Mr. Sherman assisted Emma), the article is useful in analyzing the conflict between Emma and John from the perspective of current feminist theory.

is doing well. She has never milked a goat but has milked cows and says she can learn to milk goats and is willing to take care of them. If you do not have a wet nurse I shall certainly send this one and you had better get a goat at once.

> With warmest love and kisses for you and baby
> From
> Y. H.

———

> [letterhead] Office of J. E. Bryant,
> Attorney at Law,
> Corner Jackson and Greene Streets,
> Augusta, Ga., Feb 13th 1872

My Darling Wife:

I wish I could see you and our little darling Emma tonight; but I cannot, and must write, and send kisses. Tell me how she is. How about her head is it any better. I talked with Mr. Sherman about letting Henry take the horse and go with you for a goat. He was willing. Tell me all about the goat. You had better ask where you get it about the feed for it.

I went yesterday to look for the oilcloth rug but could find none. Can you tell me where it was put. It is not in the chest.

I love you darling and every day think how pleasant it will be if we can have a home of our own next winter. I shall try hard to have it so and feel sure that I shall succeed. My business prospects here continue good.

May God bless you darling, and if for the best, spare our little Emma to us.

> With warmest love and kisses for you both
> From Y. H.

P.S. Tell Julia that I saw her girl this morning and gave her the letter. She has the prospect of a place but it is not yet certain where she will go. Long told me there were three places she could have but did not know whether she would want either. We will get her a good place if her mother does not.

> J.E.B.

[letterhead] Office of J. E. Bryant,
Attorney at Law,
Corner Jackson and Greene Streets,
Augusta, Ga., Feb 15th 1872

My darling

I received a letter from you yesterday morning and one this morning. Now that you are doing better in writing I will do as well.

I am glad that the nurse proves to be all that I expected. It relieves you so much and will be such a help to our little darling who I do hope is to be spared to us.

Tell Julia that Nellie has the offer of a <u>very good</u> place. Old Mrs. Turpin who lives about two miles from town wants a servant simply to wait on her to sleep in her room and travel with her. She is a wealthy lady whose husband is dead and she spends much of her time visiting her friends. She wants Nellie and offers her six dollars per month. Long got the place for her. He and his wife think it is a <u>first rate</u> place. Nellie is to give Mrs. Turpin an answer on Monday. I send today two letters to Julie your care. They were handed to me by her daughter.

I love you darling—Wish we could be together but must wait a few months when I hope we can have a pleasant house by ourselves here.

Kiss the little darling often for me. With warmest love and kisses for you both
From
Y. H.

Tell me all about the baby every day about the goat etc etc

———

[letterhead] Office of J. E. Bryant,
Attorney at Law,
Corner Jackson and Greene Streets,
Augusta, Ga., Feb 16th 1872

My Darling

Yours of the 14th came this morning. I hope you are unnecessarily alarmed about our Little Emma. I do hope she is to be spared to us. I am working hard to prepare a house where we can enjoy ourselves next winter and it will be sad if we cannot have our little darling with us.

I love you both darling very much. May God bless you.

I am very much encouraged in regard to my business. Think I will have a good business here. I called last eve at Bro. Rodgers. He is not very well. Her health is good.

> With warmest love and kisses for you and baby
> From
> Y. H.

———

> [letterhead] Office of J. E. Bryant,
> Attorney at Law,
> Corner Jackson and Greene Streets,
> Augusta, Ga., Feb 17 1872

My Darling

I will write a few lines just to say that I am well and love you.

I have been very busy today preparing a case to be argued on Monday. That has kept me so constantly employed that I have had no time to write.

I did not hear from you this morning hope you and our little darling are well.

> With warmest love for you and baby and many kisses
> From
> Y. H.

———

> [letterhead] Office of J. E. Bryant,
> Attorney at Law,
> Corner Jackson and Greene Streets,
> Augusta, Ga., Feb 18 1872

My Darling,

Yours of the 15th came last night and of the 16th this morning.

So it seems I am charged with sending valentines to Lucy and Bell, and by my wife too! and worse than all with attempting to counterfeit my handwriting and failing! Is not that a good cause for divorce! Do you think I would do such a thing?

I think of you and our little darling often, and particularly at night, when I miss you more than at any other time. I pray that God may spare her to us, if it is for the best. He knows.

I will attend to the errand for Julia tomorrow. It will be a joke if your goat does not give milk. I do not think you had better give the baby its milk without putting in some water, at first, at least. I am glad Julia is so good a nurse and trust she may be willing to remain with you.

Susan is having some trouble about teaching. She is afraid to go before the Superintendent to be examined. The other teachers have been examined and have secured a certificate but she is afraid. There has been some talk of discontinuing her school but the Captain has taken the matter in hand and I think she will go to be examined and will undoubtedly get a certificate. She is so sensitive I pity her.

> With warmest love and kisses for you and baby
> From
> Y. H.

————

> [letterhead] Office of J. E. Bryant,
> Attorney at Law,
> Corner Jackson and Greene Streets,
> Augusta, Ga., Feb 19 1872

My Darling

Got no letter from you this morning am anxious about our little darling and hope she is improving. How about the goat does she give down her milk yet.

I am quite well and hard at work at law; attended to a case of the Ordinarys [*sic*] today.

I love you darling and shall be glad when I can see you again.

Kiss our little darling often for me.

> With warmest love and kisses
> for you and little Emma
> From
> Y. H.

[letterhead] Office of J. E. Bryant,
Attorney at Law,
Corner Jackson and Greene Streets,
Augusta, Ga., Feb 20th 1872

My Darling;

I received this morning yours of the 18th. I do hope our darling may be spared to us. You had better do the best you can with the goat until I go to Atlanta unless she refuses entirely to give milk. I will find out what is the trouble.

It appears that Mrs. Rodgers was one who has been making arrangements to send the girls to school at Boston. Nellie went yesterday to see her and she reports that Mrs. Rodgers said there was some trouble about sending them and Nellie has given up the idea of trying to go. She went yesterday to see Mrs. Turpin and made arrangements to commence work there Thursday. Long and his wife think she has a very good place.

My prospects for business here continue very good. I feel that by next winter I shall have a home for you and our little Emma. May God spare her to us.

With warmest love and kisses
From
Y. H.

———

[letterhead] Office of J. E. Bryant,
Attorney at Law,
Corner Jackson and Greene Streets,
Augusta, Ga., Feb 21st 1872

My Darling;

Yours of the 19th came this morning. I write every day. I have sent two Tribunes which you must have received before this.

Bro Rodgers was in this morning and I asked him about the girls going North. He says several Methodist ministers have written for colored girls to come into their families to do some work and have the privilege of going to school. He has already sent two or three girls and thinks that perhaps Nellie might get a chance if she wished. Would her mother be willing for her to go if she could get a good chance?

Nellie was in the office this morning. She is well and will go to Mrs Turpins Thursday. She thinks it is a good place and she will like [it].

I am glad that our little darling is better and hope that she may continue to improve. Perhaps it may be best for you not to go West on babys account. We will think of that matter and decide hereafter.

I will send you money tomorrow.

I love you darling and shall be glad when I can be with you again.

> With warmest love and kisses for you and baby
> From
> Y. H.

————

Augusta Ga Feb 22 1872

My Darling:

Yours of Tuesday evening came this morning. I can hardly express my joy in learning that our little darling is improving. I shall look forward to my next visit with much pleasure for I expect my little Emma will be able to play with her papa.

We are now having very pleasant weather. I am hard at work. Have something to do every day or rather I should say have new business every day. I have already a large amount of business on hand.

> I love you darling and send warm kisses to you and baby
> Y. H.

P.S. I send enclosed five dollars

————

[letterhead] Custom House, Savannah, Ga.,
COLLECTOR'S OFFICE,
May 14th 1872

My darling:

I heard nothing from you yesterday or today.

I wrote thus far and was interrupted by callers. In the meantime the Atlanta mail has arrived, and a letter comes from you; yours of Sunday I am glad to hear. Am disappointed, if do not get one every day. I am so glad to hear from you in regard to our little Emma. I so much wish that we could be together, but should not dare to have you here and could not get a living in Atlanta, thus we are kept apart.

All you say of our little one is very interesting to me. I do feel thankful to God that he has blessed us. I feel that our little one will be very sweet as she grows up.

I send you ten dollars in this [illegible] P.O. money order. I will send more as soon as possible. This will supply immediate wants. As soon as this is received please write me fully about money matters. Make an estimate of what you will need next month for expenses, and what to pay what you owe. Please do not forget this, as I hope to send you the money the first of next month, including $25 for clothing as you wrote me a few days since.

> I love you darling warmly truly, and
> send warmest kisses for you and baby.
> Y. H.

————

[written in JEB's hand] About money

Atlanta May 16. /72

My Darling,

I have just received yours of 14th, but think now that I must lay aside my writing and trust to having time in the morning to answer. A good-night-kiss for you from baby and mama.

Morning—I received the P.O. order for $10. and will pay Mrs. S. the $6.00 that I borrowed yesterday which leaves me only $4, and washing bill to be paid out of that beside little more than a dollar a week for Loeflundes [*sic*] Food. I use not as much of that as formerly.

You ask particularly about money needed for next month. First of all—can I conveniently have any more this month. You remember that I put off paying bills last month with the understanding that they were to be paid first of this month—my milk bill, especially, I am mortified about. I have paid nothing since I began and it amts. to $8.00 or more already and I am anxious to pay up and pay for my tickets when I buy them or as soon as they are used.

The last of the month comes nurse's bill. I dont wish to annoy you about money this month, but you ask for particular and full information of my needs and I do need and desire, if possible, to pay up back bills this month, according to the promises that I have made.

For myself I will wait as long as necessary. You ask my running expenses for each month. Nurses wages, baby's food and our washing will amt. each month to $20.

With Loving Kisses Emma

[written in JEB's hand] About money

Atlanta May 18, /72

My Darling

Will try to write a little this morning while I keep the flies off baby. We cannot leave her for a moment without danger of waking from the flies. If I do not get my nets from Augusta very soon I must buy here.

I have been thinking of the estimate that I made for my own wardrobe and fear that $25. will not enable me to do as you wish from the fact that I must have my sewing done and am in need of common articles of clothing. I can make that amt. lower [illegible] for the present and use more whenever it is convenient for you to send it. Please answer me whether I must wait until next month for money for baby's sewing and my bills now due. I wish to know and will make my arrangements accordingly. Am hurrying now to get the sewing that must be done ready to send out in order that I may give more attention to regaining my strength.

Night before last Rev and Gen. Van Wyke (I dont know how to spell their names) with their wives and the baby and nurse called. Old Mrs. Van Wyke had been out riding with them and became too much fatigued to call. They inquired after you. Gen. and his wife go North next Tuesday. I enclose in this Capt's letter and a bill from the Harper Bro's that came yesterday. Must go now for our darling's milk. She seems well—Is a fine baby—so her mama thinks—wish you could be with her to enjoy her day by day. I think I have a very faithful nurse. She keeps the baby much out of doors.

Bye, Darling,
Emma

Atlanta June 22, 1872

My Hubbie Dear—

I am just prepared for bed and trying under disadvantages to write a word. Went out to town today with Susan and brought her home with me. She designs to stay two or three weeks in Atlanta so you will probably see her. Should baby darling be well when you come I feel that we may all enjoy it. I hope that our darling is a little better to-night. She has had fewer passages this afternoon than usual. She has fretted a good deal and refuses to have her gums touched. If she cuts one or two teeth soon think that will relieve her trouble at least for a time. I can not help being anxious about her for teething is a critical season and [illegible] often proves fatal even during teething, but I do think that God will spare her to us. Have you been at Macon within two or three weeks? I heard of you there but concluded it must be some mistake.

Write me when you go to church tomorrow and if you have so identified yourself with any church as to be a regular attendant upon the prayer meetings. I shall enjoy it so much if we can go together when I go to Savannah.

A loving good-night.

Sabbath P.M. Went to the college to church this morning, but owing to Mr. Sherman's tardiness were so late as to miss the sermon—went from there to Methodist S. School.

Wish you could see baby now as she lies on the bed heels up in the air and engaged in the admiration of her crimson sock. I hope our darling is a little better tho' her passages are far from being reduced to as few as they should be.

You seem far away from me, darling. Do you realize that it is coming round to a year since we were seperated [sic]? I almost fear we may become inured to Such a way of living. Should our hearts ever stray from each other it would be a worse calamity than seperation or death, but I think that cloud shall never come into our lives, but rather a daily coming nearer together in heart and soon, I hope, an actual enjoyment of each other's society day by day. . . .

Lucy is in and says tell you she has just been talking to your baby and she seems to understand every word she says. Says she thinks she is a right nice baby, but won't tell you so. She has a long lingo to tell, but I won't send it. Mrs. Eggleston told me to-day that the older Mrs. Van Wyck has been very dangerously ill but is now better. Her son's wife is [illegible] and she [is] alone save her son, I suppose. I think I will go to see her tomorrow if baby is sufficiently well for me to leave her. Dr. Fuller[3] enquired for you to-day—also Mr. Kimball.[4] Dr. Fuller's family are to move into the building in which the Theological Institute is held. Am very glad for they will then be within more neighborly distance. Sister Lee was at church—will remain here for the summer. I am quite surprised to learn that Thomas[5] baby is so big. I feel rejoiced to hear of an improvement in Beth's health—it will be a great encouragement to both of them. I have faith that she may make quite a woman yet if she has any strength of body to give cheerfulness to her mind. She is certainly hard working and disposed to help Thomas all in her power. I do hope that Thomas will be prospered. I think that a little prosperity now would do good to both of them in mind and body. When you come will you not remain over the Sabbath and attend church if baby is sufficiently well for us to leave her. I hope to be able to go part of the time to commencement exercises this week. Shall not leave however if I think baby needs me. Melinda is sufficiently better to go to Dr. Clevelands to spend a week.

Have you thought that next Wed. is our eighth anniversary? Wish you could be here then. I receive the Journal regularly I think. Remember me to Robinson if he is there.

———

Atlanta June 27, 1872

My Darling.

Rec'd yours of 24th yesterday morning. It would have been extremely pleasant for us to be together on yesterday, but I think we have both learned to receive disappointments or deprivations more quietly than I at least would once have done. Baby dear has been worse yesterday evening and last night. I think it possible that I have not done well in feeding her, aside from her milk, for last two days, altho' it was by Dr's advice.

---

[3] Erasmus Q. Fuller, editor of *Atlanta Methodist Advocate*, would become a close associate of JEB.

[4] Hannibal Ingalls Kimball, native of Maine who came to Georgia in 1867; entrepreneur and railroad executive; Bullock associate.

[5] JEB's brother, Thomas Bryant.

If she has as many discharges to-day will send for him to-morrow or go and see him. I am sorry that you think there is any danger in going alone from here to the West End, for it is the only independent mode of getting out that I have. I dont like much better than gentlemen do to feel cramped and prevented from going so short distance as from here to town, if I have strength to carry me. Rather than give up this independent mode of going and coming I think I will arm myself. I am naturally cowardly about long walk but I have just succeeded in attaining to a comfortable degree of courage when my good husband must needs frighten me out of it all, just as he used about travelling alone.

> Must not write more.
> Bye darling and may God keep us.
> Emma

————

Atlanta July 9, 1872

My Darling

I missed writing you this morning because of two bundles of work that I was forced to get ready to send and to-night I have promised to retire very early. Mrs. Sherman is not well and I must be in bed early or lose my treatment. Baby darling is sleeping—seems quite well but is occasionally fretful on account of her teeth I think. We have had company nearly all day—Miss Williams among the rest. I have arranged to take baby to see Dr. D'Avigny this week Friday if I can. Mrs. Chase thinks she would prefer his judgement to Dr. Cleveland's as to the condition of her back. I do trust that it is coming all right and yet feel that we ought to know. We may have cause to reflect if we do not. Susan goes to spend Friday with Miss Williams and I shall try to go, too, and take the baby with me and Miss Williams will go with me to see the Dr.

Miss Foote who is visiting in town was here yesterday. There is some prospect that Mrs. Ware and the little wee baby may be here to-day. Expect Susan will go home Friday night.

> With loving kisses
> Bye Darling—
> Emma

Atlanta July 15, 1872

My Darling

My last letter was broken off by Mr. Shermans departure for town and this
seems likely to be the same. I think that I mentioned that I went to see Dr.
D'Avigny with baby.

I was much pleased with what he said of her and very glad that I took her
to him. He says the spine is right save a slight tendency to curvature which
must make us careful of her.

The actual curvature which he found there in her babyhood had disappeared. Said I might tell you that she was doing as well as any body could ask
for a baby to do. Said she was sufficiently plump for a Southern climate—he
especially mentioned as a favorable symptom the absence of anything like languor in her appearance.

Must wash baby

With loving kisses
Emma

———

Atlanta July 15, 1872

My Darling.

From your letter receiv'd to-night I think you did not go to Augusta as I
thought you would. Have you received my letter sent there? Baby darling
continues quite well but is worrying now because she is sleepy and too much
excited by a ride that she had little time ago to sleep.

I let Allwilda go with her on the street cars to town and back because I
thought the ride might be good for her, but I must discontinue taking her out
among many people just at night. She becomes too much excited to sleep
invariably. Saw brother and Sister Lee. Brother Lee inquired for you—
indeed both did I think. Brother Lee has made overtures to the African
church to unite with him in the theological School, paying one teacher—

I broke off here last night and was so busy getting self and baby ready to go
out that had no time to finish till now. I am passing the day with Mrs. Vanwyck
and her son tells me that the mare goes from here this P.M. I have our darling
along—she seems well and happy—so sweet and good always when I take her
out, hasn't fretted save when Allwilda was getting her to sleep. As I told you

she had a ride on the street car last night. We have unfavorable weather of late for taking her out, for we are obliged to go between the showers.

The mail has just gone from here and I have missed it am very sorry indeed. Did you receive the letter sent to Augusta? I rarely fail to write you and yet you often say you have no letter from me. Baby has still a little of her diarrhoea but I hope nothing more than naturally accompanies teething. there are no more signs of teeth now than when you were here.

The time is flying until we will be with you in Savannah. God granted [*sic*] that we may be spared and united in health and happiness. I do feel that we have great cause to "bless the Lord" that he has spared our little one and prospered her so much.

> God bless and keep you, bye, darling
> Emma

———

> Atlanta, July 19, 1872
> Friday morning

My Darling.

I have time for but a bit this morning as have much before me to be done. Baby dear is not quite as well—is very restless at night, but I hope some of her teeth will soon be through. Aside from the difficulties accompanying teething I think she is very well.

I heard by way of Susan that Mr Smith was expected in.

Saturday Morn. Did not send you any letter yesterday morning for did not know where to send and am no better informed this morning.

If this finds you in Augusta please look up my jelly glasses and my glass-top fruit jars and have them packed to send me with the dictionary and saddle I wish to make a little jelly (remembering my husband's fondness for it) and to put up a few jars of fruit. We may be very glad of them if we are at a boarding house next winter. Bear in mind that it is the jars with glass tops and metal screws that I want and see that the rubbers are with the jars. I think Susan can tell you something about them. I believe they are packed somewhere with our things.

I have cautioned the nurse about riding baby rapidly and I go myself with her whenever I can. She has not ridden very much since you were here, for

Allwilda was ill for a few days, so much so that I dont not [*sic*] want her to go out with baby, and the carriage was several days in town on account of our being caught there in a rain storm.

Have not time for more now. I fear that our darling may have another real attack of illness before her teeth are through she is very restless at night now and has considerable diarrhoea.

Last night I woke and seeing her slipped down towards the foot of the bed attempted to place her up higher but after an ineffectual effort, discovered that I had her by the heels, she had thrown herself over all the covering with her face towards the foot of the bed.

She would stand by holding on things I think if I dared let her—but the Dr. cautioned about allowing her to put much weight on her spine at present so I dont dare encourage her.

> and now Good bye darling,
> Emma

———————

Atlanta July 27 1872

My Darling,

I was absolutely prevented from writing in morn to send you a letter yesterday—was preparing work to send out and in the morning in a hurry to get baby to the street car for her ride. I feel that they are beneficial to her and I make an especial effort to get out with her early. She enjoys the rides very much, but is uneasy and difficult to keep in the arms—wants to be on the floor, on the car seat and all about. Is tired of being little baby and wants to get about herself. You'll find when we go to Savannah that your little baby is merged into a mischievous little girl I expect.

She is a great pleasure and comfort now and quite well, tho' still has some diarrhoea. . . .

> Bye, bye Darling
> Emma

Seeley[6] is here from Savannah

———————

[6] Isaac Seeley, native of New York, Republican delegate to Georgia constitutional convention.

Atlanta July 28 1872

My Darling

This Sabbath night I had promised myself to write you more at leisure and enjoy it as do not usually but have been absolutely prevented until I am tired and sleepy. I am sorry always to write you in haste but my day is filled so very full of little, little and yet necessary things. . . .

Monday night. Last night Mrs. S. sent me off to bed and this morning I hurried to go the street cars again. I will try to make sure of a letter to you early in the day tho' my days are very busy—am trying to get my sewing done now in anticipation of keeping no nurse next winter. . . .

Then my mornings have been devoted to taking baby to town and back on street car—you ought to see how much she enjoys her street car ride—she has grown to be a real little witch tho' and hard to hold in the lap, for she wants to be all about—looking out of the car window, then this way and that and on the seat and on the floor, too, if she could.

She is nearly well of her second diarrhoea attack—as well as I can expect her to be in teething. When she is not on the bed to sleep we have to hedge her in all ways. She has already had four tumbles since you were here two from the bed and two in the chair. Hope it will not occur again but she is something like an eel to keep in place. The talking I fear you must wait for for a long time yet. She hasn't any more idea of creeping than when you were here, but she dont like to sit long in the arms—wants to be on the floor if she feels well.

In your last you speak of a boarding place—what will you pay there and what accommodations can we have? Have you decided what time we shall go? I have found that it would not be best to take baby before 1st of Nov if we are to go sooner I must, if convenient, get my blk. silk in little more than a month in order to have it made. I think I shall send to Stewarts for it and also for any other dress goods that I am obliged to have for next winter, I hope not to need very much beside the blk. silk. It is time for me to wash baby for I am finishing this Sunday morning.

God bless and keep you darling
Bye, Bye—
Emma

P.S. Capt. brought saddle and dictionary but the former is so utterly ruined by moths that it is useless to think of sitting it. We have thrown it away by neglect, and I hope in future to see that articles of value are taken better care of, I will save the leather work and if our little one ever has a pony it is possible it may be of use to her.

Please dont spell gums with a b. I do not think it would be wise to lance baby's gums unless there is more need than now appears

———

Atlanta
July [line drawn through July] Aug. 1 1872

My Darling,

August has taken me by surprise as you will guess from the erasure at the head of the page. Instead of writing you last night I devoted the few minutes leisure that I had from preparing a line to send out, to sketching Mr. Sherman as he sat on the back porch paring peaches by lamplight. The whole family save myself were out there. Bell and a little colored girl that is here sitting in the same chair. It made a graphic picture, but I had time to sketch only one figure and was very doubtful of my ability to do that.

I met with much better success than I expected. It is my first attempt at making a figure sketch from life and I begin to feel that with time and work I might do considerable with my brushes. I used to think that original [illegible] on work from nature were quite past my abilities. I have begun to finish the little watermelon piece, my first attempt in the fruit line perhaps you remember, but have found only a few hours to work on it. I attempted to introduce a bunch of blackberries but the berries are so nearly gone that must draw largely upon memory to paint them.

Then my husband feels, too, that it is not good for us to live separated. I am glad, very glad that you do feel it.

Now that August has come there will not be a very long time before we hope to be again together. I shall crowd my part of it, if can come so full of work that it will not lag I hope. I wish you could be with baby now. She is frolicsome and well and just right to enjoy—sits alone well, prefers lying on the floor to being tended in the arms—has now a good many small boils on her face and head. I think they are a benefit to her and consequently cannot feel sorry to see them—no teeth through yet. You would find it a difficult matter to sleep with us now for baby looks upon the whole bed as hers and when I wake I am more apt to find her in the center of the bed head towards the foot than where she belongs. I have not time for more. You shall see the sketch of Mr. Sherman when you come. And now with loving kisses,

Bye, Bye—Emma—

P.S. The advent of Harper each week is a real pleasure. I have partially read that long story "A Woman's Vengeance." It shows a good knowledge of character. Do you read it?

Are my fruit jars where anyone can get them?

———

Atlanta
Aug 3, 1872

My Darling,

I am wondering now why I do not hear from you in these last two days. I cannot help some anxiety since I have heard of the riot, altho' I am told that no one was seriously hurt. If do not hear from you by to-night or to-morrow I shall be really anxious.

I hear that Seeley received a number of bullets in his clothing—did his usual coolness desert him? I imagine not. . . .

I begin this morning to take board for Allwilda from Mrs. Megna's. I should scarcely have thought but to change from here, had it not been that she is sometimes unavoidably or accidentally a little late at table and thereby causes a good deal of fretting on Mrs. Sherman's part. She was out with the baby yesterday morning and came back late. Mrs. S. said a good deal about the inconvenience to her and on thinking the matter over I made up my mind that I might as well save half her board money as to keep her and have so much fretting. Mrs. Megna boards here for $12. per month—a little more than I had to pay for my colored nurse, but as Mrs. Megna says, "A white lady is a white lady and must be treated like a white lady." I shall have the board to pay each week so you will need to calculate for that. I am ashamed to say that before I had an opportunity to see Dr. Cleveland I used so much money for my own use that I had not enough left to pay him but shall attend to it just as soon as I receive the 15. and the money from this month and will tell him that you left money for him first of the month (July) as you had promised, for I dont like you to be thought careless of your promises. I have needed to spend more money than I thought in order to put my wardrobe in such order as you wished, but I shall thereby have occasion to spend very little next summer in clothing for myself.

Baby seems very well indeed—good as a baby can be—is at the present moment on the floor playing with a bottle that has rolled beyond her reach. has just succeeded in capturing it—showed a little disposition to creep. If papa was here he would take solid comfort with her. She is full of fun and very active. . . . And now, darling, I must say good by.

> May God bless you and keep you darling, With loving kisses
> Emma

———

Atlanta Aug 4th 1872
Sabbath Evening

My Darling.

Another of the months that keep us from each other is well begun. Did not a busy mind and busy hands make my time fly fast, it would look long to me until the time for us to go to you. My anxiety was relieved by a few lines from you yesterday. . . . Baby has worried a good deal to-day—caused I think by her teeth and the boils on her face.

She is now sleeping and I must soon put myself beside her. I was quite interested by an account of the order of Jesuits that I read in Watchman & Reflection to-day. It gave a more careful account of Jesuitism than I had ever read before. The article was in connection with some notice of their recent expulsion from Germany by Bismarck. If you have not seen a similar article I will lay aside the paper until you come. Their expulsion seems to me almost too much like the catholic measures towards protestants and others differing from them, and yet I doubt not they are a great injury and danger to the state.

I went to Christian church this morning and to Meth. [odist] to S. [unday] S. [chool]

The christian minister had a good deal of sound to him but I did not pick out much else. Dr. Fuller preaches at Meth. I have not heard him yet save a few words to-day. They had communion there to-day and I took a step that I have meditated for some time—I partook of communion.

I am not entirely certain that I did right but my own conscience is not committed to close [d] communion and I decided to-day that I would go according to my own feelings and say nothing if nothing is said to me. If I receive a rebuke from our church I will then consider what is right to do next. Did it seem to you that I have done right to follow my individual conscience in opposition to the custom of my church? Are you situated at any church yourself yet? and, do you attend class or prayer meetings? Do make an effort to do that regularly for your own soul will I fear, become lean if you neglect Christ privilege.

Next winter looks in the distance very happy to me. I trust we will not be disappointed. . . .

> Pleasant dreams, darling. I want to be with you.
> May God spare us thus and reunite when we expect.
> With Loving Kisses
> Emma

P.S. The boarding out of nurse raised a burr with the mistress of the house and I thought it better to take her back here than to pack and leave.

I had an amicable talk with Mr. S. and have become so accustomed to squalls in the other quarter that I just wait for them to blow over and say nothing.[7]

Atlanta Aug. 25, 1872
Sabbath Evening.

My Darling.

I want to write you a little to-night but have a back ache and must go to bed soon. "To be or not to be" is still the question.

Our darling has been quite sick for two days owing to combined effects, I think, of teething, boils and a severe cold. Last night and the night before slept comparatively little.

Hope I may be able to announce some improvement in her to-morrow—wish you could help us to care for and assure her. She makes a sick, distressed or worrisome sound most of the time.

Mr. S. and I have been discussing the dog question, he takes the sternly practical view of it i.e. time spent in making a dog happy is wasted—should be devoted to human beings. I answered him by telling him that the heart that was tender towards dumb creatures was proportionably [sic] so towards humans—and I believe that it is true.

---

[7] Apparently, Mrs. Sherman's temperament was unpredictable. Alice described her as "a woman of very high temper and at times was unbalanced mentally."

If our darling lives to grow up I hope she will love the domestic animals and pets generally and her mama will not tell her that the little time spent of them is wasted (or her papa either will he?) I am sorely afraid I should be disposed to quarrel with the [illegible] type of man.

> I must to bed. God keep you darling
> and make me a more loving wife.

Monday morn. Baby passed a comfortable night and I was much surprised and disappointed to find her very sick this morning. Her cold has settled upon her lungs and if she cannot be relieved soon I shall send for the Dr. I hope she is now a little better than an hour ago.

I am using hot applications to the chest and remedies that I have.

> Bye Darling Pray for our little one. I know you do—
> Emma

———

Atlanta Aug. 29, 1872

My Darling.

I am able this morning to relieve your apprehension regarding myself. I do feel quite relieved myself I can assure you, altho' our fear did not render me unhappy.

Baby is a little better I hope tho' she coughed a good deal this morning.

I have her in my arms and must be excused from writing more.

The time is quite near now when I hope to be with you.

God bless and keep you, darling.

> With loving kisses
> Emma

———

Atlanta Sep. 16, 1872

My Darling.

Our poor Melinda has gone. I went around this morning to see her and found her body only waiting for its burial. She will be buried to-morrow from the chapel of the Stokes school. I shall go over in the morning to avoid heat of the sun at noon. The funeral will be at 3 P.M.

Mrs. Grant was engaged to spend the day with us to-morrow and I felt obliged to see her or send a word to her this evening. So I took the horse out from Mr. Sherman to-night and then after failing to find [illegible] town went out to the house [illegible] engagement to Wednesday and by that time it was near dark and I was at the other end of the city, but I believe providence helped me for as I was watching for the cemetery car I saw Mr. Chase and he brought me home.

To speak a word of my going to Savannah. Have you business that will take you up here at that time?

I have already mentioned that I wish to spend a few days in Augusta and I think I had but if I can, go there on next week, Friday.

I can hire a woman here to pack my furniture and a man to take it to town and have it sent to you when I start for Augusta so that you can have it all unpacked and everything ready except the carpet when I arrive. I appreciate your thoughtfulness in waiting for me to select a carpet as I would like to do it myself. If there is any doubt about your having money to buy a new carpet at once, perhaps I had better have this one thoroughly cleaned and take it down to use for a time.

I think I can also go from Augusta alone unless you are obliged to come up and thereby have the money to pay for what I need here. I have two months wages to pay nurse, two months milk bill to pay and articles for self and baby that must be bought before going. I can much easier hire help to pack and then go alone than go without this sewing so please plan to send me as much extra money as your fare would be, and let me go alone unless you are obliged to come up.

Lovingly.
Emma

––––––

Wakeman June 26, 1873

My Darling.

I went so far as to date this last night but weariness overcame me. Baby has taken one of her restless fits and troubles me good deal about going to sleep. Presume it will be only transient however—her face is grown nearly smooth.

She has had encounters with the hen and the cat in which she came off somewhat scratched. Saturday morning took her down to play with Mrs. Leren's youngest.

I have rec'd letter from sister since I came here. She hurries me to go there, or rather expresses the hurry she feels to see me, but does not wish me to curtail my visit here.

You ask about the money I shall require before leaving here. The fare from here to Chicago exclusive of sleeping cars and fare to Earlville is $10. or in that vicinity. I would like $25. or $30. for all my expenses if convenient, if not I must do with less.

Lucy sends much love. She and I go to visit Mary[8] next week. I shall have an ambrotype of baby taken at Norwich when I go to Mary's if I can possibly spare the money, which latter looks rather doubtful. If cannot have it taken then will if possible before I go to Ill. The shoes which I bought for baby few days before I left home are completely worn out—were scarce good for anything.

I have great deal to do to-day and must ask you to excuse a short letter.

Rec'd Harper this week—

I presume that you have ere this been entertained by my note to Col Atkins. I was scarce ever so alarmed about you when away as then.

Lovingly
Emma

Baby kissed her hand for papa

————

Wakeman June 28 1873
Saturday Morning

My Darling,

I have time for only few lines this morning. Lucy goes into Cleveland this morning to see her physician. [She] will return to-night and Monday night we expect to go to see Mary.

Baby is well, full of life and fun. I think her teeth are troubling her a little. Her grandmother often refers to her likeness to her father in regard to activity & dont think her quite as mischievous as you used to be tho' she does perpetrate some daring deeds.

Some time ago I made a pitcher of lemonade and sat it on the middle of the dining table to soak the lemon fully before pouring out. Baby had watched the operation impatiently and being left alone in the room decided to help herself

---

[8] Mary E. Bryant, another of JEB's sisters.

so when her aunt Lucy went into the room a few minutes after she saw her on the middle of the table spoon in hand stirring the lemonade.

A day or two since when I dressed her in the morning I couldn't find her shoes and enquired of mother and Lucy if they had seen them, soon baby came bringing the shoes to me—she had heard me enquiring and understood what was wanted. I had thought of our marriage anniversary just before it but when the day came was so engrossed with my work that allowed it to pass, or rather did not remember until this morning. I am very sorry and hope you treated me better. Love to Mrs. Atkins—I intend to write her soon—but since I was a little refreshed from my journey have been extremely busy. I must not write more.

> God bless you, darling. I dreamed last night of being with you—
> With loving kisses
> Emma

[letter has been marked with red crayon or pen as indicated]

Cleveland
July 25, 1873

My Darling,

Do you query how it happen that I am writing you from this place?

I had not time to write the day before I left Wakeman.

Yesterday morning Lucy and I came here and brought baby with us. We took baby hoping to get her picture and also to have the Drs. examine her back and one of her legs that mother thought was not straight. He said the legs were all right and that there is between the shoulders the least bit of spinal curvature, but he says it is not enough to call for any treatments—will do her not harm and will probably be outgrown.

Our attempt to get baby's picture entirely failed. I tried to get a large photograph. She was afraid as soon as they began to push the camera toward her and we could do nothing with her.

I am very sorry and still more so because I think we shall be unable to get one at present for I think she will be afraid and cry.

I shall not again take her out of town to try it.

Now I must give a little explanation of my prolonged stay here. I came here to consult Lucy's Dr. Saunders for my-self. He made an examination and told me that there was ulceration and that it had been of long standing. He also thought that if I remained here for a few days that he could help me sufficiently so that I could treat myself through the summer without further medical aid.

So after consulting with Lucy I decided to remain until Monday (I came on Thursday), and possibly a day or two longer and sent baby home with Lucy. I felt very unwilling to do it and yet on looking the whole matter over it seemed best. He tells me that he sees no reason why I should not become entirely well and strong, but that the ulceration left to itself will gradually debilitate me. He found me a boarding place at the Private Homeopathic Hospital near by his office. It is a very pleasant spot but few boarders chiefly ladies and a pleasant matron. I have a large room on the first floor, board only $6.00 per week. Please tell me when you write what you think of my decision. This expense will make me rather short of money but I decided to risk it. If this reaches you in season you can, if convenient, add a little to what I rent for, if not I will manage with what I have.

It will of course prevent me from having any picture of myself taken, but if the actual wife can thereby grow strong I do not think you will complain. Address my letter to Wakeman as formerly as I shall return there first on middle of the week. I do hope much from my treatment and shall do all in my power toward recovery. I had a very [X marked here] pleasant ride this morning through the city with Dr. Saunders. I went to his office for treatment [underline added in red] and after it he invited me to go with him while he went to visit his patients. I so seldom take a drive in other than some stupid public conveyance that it was quite a treat for me.

It was very odd to be without baby last night and I don't think I slept as well as I would have done with her. It is not yet 11.30 A.M. and yet the day seems already to have been long though I have been to the office and to drive. I go to the Dr's office for treatment between 8 and 9 [underline added in red] in the morning and about [X marked here] 8 at night. I wish you were with me, darling and I do very much hope to be quite well and strong when you see me at Christmas. Please destroy this letter because I do not think it wise to keep letters that speak of disease of a private nature.

And now goodbye, Darling. May God keep us.
Emma

[letter has been marked with red crayon or pen as indicated]

Cleveland July 30, 1873

[X marked here] My Dear Hubbie! [X marked here]

I think I promised to enclose Lucy's letter in my last but did not will put it in this letter as it gives full account of baby.

I had a letter this morning from Lucy in which she says that baby is doing finely—sitting in the rocking chair singing as happy as [a] child can be. She sleeps in our bed quite alone, Lucy sleeping in the next room.

This will be the last letter written from here as I leave here to-night.

Shall sleep with our darling to-night, D.V.[9] They are not expecting me until to-morrow night so I shall take them quite by surprise.

I visited a lady's studio yesterday, that of Miss Ransom perhaps I mentioned it to you. She is a portrait painter, has made it a profession for twenty years she told me. She recommended me to an artist in Chicago where instruction would be valuable, I do not know if I have mentioned to you that if I can see the way to do it, I am desirous to paint with a good artist for a short time this summer—it has been in my mind for a long time. I intend, if possible, to stop in Chicago a day when I go out.

Miss Ransom gave me some suggestions in regard to color that I think may be valuable. She had in her studio an immense full length portrait of Sen. Thomas recently painted.

I think I will go to the Dr.'s office now to get medicine and instructions before leaving. The husband of one of the patients came this morning making me wish mine here, too.

Now I think of it I want to tell you of a Syringe that I wish you to get and use for your cataracts (you needn't use it for "weakness") It is marked on the Rubber bag which contains the water Fountain Syringe—manufactured by Fairbanks & co. 121 court Street, Boston Mass. If you cannot find it in Savannah a druggist will probably send for it for you. There are directions how to use it for cataracts. I like it very much, Be sure to try it.

I think I will call this letter finished and take it with me and post when I reach Wakeman.

Bye Darling
Emma

---

9 Deus Volente, God willing.

[letter has been marked with red crayon or pen as indicated]

Wakeman

July 31, 1873

[X marked here] My Darling Hubbie [X marked here]

Allow me to suggest that correspondence by telegraph is both public and expensive.

I feel that there must have been some terrible earthquake in your mind or at least a severe shock of some kind to produce two such peremptory telegrams as we have been in receipt of. Did you think that terrible and unknown danger threatened to engulf me in the homeopathic hospital, or that I should be suddenly cut off by cholera?

I was utterly confounded on reaching home last night to find a telegram from you awaiting me (I had left before the arrival of Lucy's word in Cleveland) and still again astonished by a fresh telegram to-day notwithstanding Lucy's telegram to you that she would send for me.

I am strongly inclined to be vexed but will try to suspend judgement until I receive your explanation.

I feel in better courage in regard to my own health than have done for years—courage that I may recover real strength such as I used to have. If I have had ulceration all these years as I cannot doubt from the testimony of two skillful physicians like Dr. Saunders and Dr. Fitch of Maine, I think that it is quite wonderful that I have preserved as much strength as I have.

I think that the strength of constitution that has enabled me to bear its draining efforts so long, will if it is cured, give me my old strength and health again.

I bought from Cleveland medicine with directions how to care for myself by aid of which the Dr. thinks I may be able to recover without further treatment from a physician. If I could have had as skillful medical assistance soon after I was married I fully believe that I might have escaped all these years of increasing debility. If I am well when you go to Earl next Christmas I shall be a proud little wife. Baby has been slightly ill with diarrhoea but I do not think it will prove serious. I bought some medicine from Dr. Saunders for bowel complaints anticipating that she might have an attack because there is just now a great deal of that disease among children. [I] should have been quite anxious about her if I had had her in Cleveland with me, there was a great deal of cholera infantum among children there.

If she is well and my money reaches here in season I design to leave here on the 9th, which will be Saturday remain with my cousin at Swanton until Tuesday and reach Chicago on Sunday night.

If sister meets me there and my funds hold out I wish to remain in Chicago until Wed. night in order to look about among the artists. Mr. Irving is waiting for my letter and I must close hastily.

Did you receive a letter from me urging you to get nasal douche like one which I have.

With loving kisses,
Emma.

Baby sends kiss.

————

[letter marked with red crayon or pen as indicated]

Wakeman
Aug. 1st, 1873

My Darling

I am still further hurt and worried by your telegram sent to Cleveland and forwarded to me from there to-day. If my treasury was a full one I should certainly leave baby with her auntie and go straight to Savannah for an explanation.

As it is I must wait the tardy coming of a letter.

The first two telegrams have surprised and slightly vexed me. This one addressed directly to me has made me really unhappy. If you are unhappy too, I am sorry. Will await your explanation as patiently as possible.

Baby still has a slight diarrhoea but I do not think that with the care that she will receive it will prove anything serious—may follow her for some weeks as it did last summer. In the past week I have received just two letters from you. I think your letters may have been delayed.

Do you receive my letters regularly?

I write nearly every day—

I may not write again until I receive an explanation of the telegrams which I trust will be very soon.

If baby is worse will write every day, may do so in any case.

[X marked here] If you had any possible objections to my making the trip to Cleveland why did you not make them known when I asked your opinion upon the matter some weeks (I think) ago? [X marked here] Your mother felt as I did that it was necessary for me to have the advice of some skillful physician in regard to my health and approved of my plan to consult Dr. Saunders. As I have before written you I believe that I have received substantial benefit thereby. I have not time to write more now and scarce feel like it if I had the time. I most heartily wish that I could be with you now if only for the space of one hour.

Bye, Darling—
Emma

Aug. 2 9 A.M.

I love you a little this morning notwithstanding all your abuse by telegraph—are you willing to be forgiven?

Baby is no worse and I have written to the Dr. for especial instruction in regard to her so I think you have no occasion to be unusually anxious about her. We can scarce expect her to go through this month without some little sickness. I do feel that God will spare her to us.

Did it not occur to you that I must be about leaving Cleveland when you sent your telegram? I had written you that I should return on Monday or at the very farthest on Thursday. I did return on Wed. the very day that your despatches [*sic*] were dated.

I intended to write sister to-day telling her that I expect to leave here on the 9th, and asking her to meet me in Chicago on the following Tuesday (or Wed. morning) Expect to pass the interval between Sat and Tues. with my cousins. Shall be greatly disappointed if do not receive my money order in season as I feel that I have already made a long visit here and that sister and father are growing impatient.

———

[letter marked with red crayon or pen as indicated]

Wakeman Aug. 3, 1873

My Darling Husband.

I am keeping my resolution not to write just as I am apt to keep such resolutions—viz—writing every day.

I received a letter from you yesterday written on last Sabbath—a week to-day.

Am glad to think of you as attending church regularly. Have not been to church to-day as did not care to take baby and did not feel very well myself—only tired and not quite strong. Beside my local treatment I have medicine from the Dr. for the debility accompanied by the local disease. I hope to be quite strong when you see me at Christmas.

Mary and husband came last night to make us a little visit before my departure.

They left this afternoon. They seem very happy together and Mary's health which was a good deal injured by teaching is nearly recovered. Baby has no diarrhoea to-day.

Her eruption is troubling her a good deal now. The Dr. gave me some medicine that he said would cure it but I have not given it yet because was treating her for the diarrhoea. She seems well and vigorous and is a veritable witch. She embraces every opportunity of gaining access to her grandmothers sugar bowl to pilfer sugar—apparently feels an "all gone feeling in her stomach" as her grandmother says that her father used to.

It is almost as cool as fall to-day—wonder whether you are suffering from the heat. I had a postal card from Louise Allen the other day saying that she wrote me months ago and had recieved [sic] no response. I wonder why it is that I lose so many letters? Baby attempts to say many new words and I think will talk like a blackbird by winter.

Lucy is already dreading for me to take her away. Do not feel like writing more—shall look for that important letter, heralded by so many telegrams, on Sunday—day after to-morrow. Seriously, I am at a loss to know what to think and have felt really unhappy. [X marked here] I do not like to think that you would be so unreasonable as to object to my recieving needed medical treatment from a physician under whose care your sister has been for nearly three years. [X marked here] But will try to say nothing and think nothing until I recieve an explanation of your extraordinary course.

I think I have never more ardently desired to annihilate the space between us than since the receipt of your telegrams on Wed. Thurs. and Friday. The bells are ringing for evening service, the late sun is shining brightly and the world seems beautiful. I feel an involuntary sympathy with it.

> With a true love kiss—
> Emma

10 P.M. Everybody but me is in bed and I shall be shortly, but I am so lonesome as to be almost low spirited, or else so low spirited as to be lonesome. It doesn't much [matter] the sensation is the same. Pleasant dreams to you.

[Fragments of letter from August 1873, as noted below]

[first fragment (mistakenly dated later by JEB as Aug 19); ESB adds comments to portions of an earlier JEB letter]

I have by mistake burned the sheet which I wished to enclose to you, speaking of the husband as absolute head over the wife using the parallel of church, government, nation, companies etc. It was apparently a very conclusive and satisfactory argument to you at the time, but I wished to give you the pleasure of re-reading it with the other paragraphs.

I have only to say in reply—if you value my love—if you wish to retain any respect—if you desire to remain my ideal of what is manly and noble and true, never use such words or sentiments to me again by letter or by word.

You degrade yourself by them, and would degrade me if I received them.

This sheet is my full, final answer to your letter by express. I will do anything, everything in my power for your happiness my darling husband and, if I could, perhaps I would believe (for your happiness) black to be white, and a lie to be the truth, but unfortunately I can't. There are women so constituted that they can. But I am not thus constituted as you must have learned before we were married, so please do not urge impossibilities.

[JEB's handwriting.] **If I had been enabled to carry out my purposes our family would have been disgraced for ever it is true; but little Alice would grow up, if she was permitted to live, with the iron driven deep into her soul, but even that was better than for me to go through life broken in spirit.**

Please read the above very carefully and tell me if you are not shocked at the spirit of utter selfishness that pervades it. Remember that Our leader, Christ, died that the guilty might live. You would have thought it better to destroy the happiness of all your family and that of the baby dearer than self to you than that your spirit should be broken—to let the innocent suffer that you might gratify hate and revenge. Please, dear husband, take in the whole horribleness of this thing that you may see what an evil spirit you have permitted to creep into your heart and that you may seize him and throw him out so completely that he shall never dare lay wait to ensnare you again.

[JEB's hand] **Let me tell you where your course will lead, if I consent; sooner or later to free love; just as in civil affairs the same tendency leads to the commune, so in domestic affairs the freedom of the wife leads to free love.**[10]

Where does the "freedom" of the husband lead to? "Is it not a poor rule that will not work both ways" (I quote from your last letter).

[second fragment]

In all my life I have never been grossly insulted until now—and that <u>by my husband</u>.

Do not dare to write me again, or expect ever to receive another line from me until you can assure me of your <u>unlimited</u> <u>confidence</u> in me and feel <u>sincerely repentant</u> for the terrible things you have said to me.

I have never lived with you on other terms than those of the most perfect <u>love</u> and <u>trust</u> and <u>equality</u>.

I <u>never</u> <u>intend</u> <u>to live</u> <u>with</u> <u>you</u> <u>on other</u> <u>terms</u>. I love you and I hope to be your true wife for time and eternity but I cannot—(God helping me) <u>will</u> <u>not</u> cast my womanhood from me. I trust you <u>fully</u> in spite of circumstances if need be. I will receive nothing less in return.

Emma

———

[letter marked with red crayon or pen as indicated]

Wakeman
Aug. 7, 1873

My Darling Husband.

I wish to add something to what I sent in Lucy's letter yesterday (I retract nothing of it).

———

[10] Victoria Woodhull, who was outspoken regarding women's rights, was charged with advocating "free love," as were utopian communities with unconventional marriage arrangements. Woodhull's visibility in 1872 as a candidate for president was fairly recent to this exchange, as was her role in exposing the sexual affair of prominent minister Henry Ward Beecher. All added to the publicity Elizabeth Cady Stanton, Susan B. Anthony, Lucy Stone, and others had brought to women's issues.

First of all, I want to tell you that from the very depths of my heart I grieve that you have been and are so distressed. Even my woman's indignation at the unspeakably dreadful things that you have written to me is overborne by my sorrow for you, and my desire to help you out of your distress.

Have you forgotten the old saying that "Whom the Gods wish to destroy they first make mad."?

[X marked here] You are "mad" both angry and insane. [X marked here] And beware that you do not thereby destroy the happiness of both of us!

Do you imagine that I could ever lay my head upon your breast again without the fullest recall of every sentiment and insinuation of your letters of the past week? without the assurance of your full unreserved confidence in me?

If you think that I could or would you have not learned to know me in these nine years of our wedded life.

Now, my darling, in true honest love let me [X marked here] remind you of the confidence I have had in you, and the confidence (or lack of it) that you have returned me for it. [X marked here]

[X marked here] In all your social relations with ladies I have always trusted you fully—[X marked here] have never allowed circumstances which even seemed suspicious to make me doubt your honor—have been ready to believe that I was mistaken, that circumstances lied—[X marked here] anything but to believe you false.

If I even had doubts of any lady the fact that she was a trusted friend of yours has been sufficient for me to battle against those doubts and refuse to entertain them. Whenever you venture to visit any lady—to be with her alone at night or under any circumstances without first "consulting me" I do not reproach you with lack of obedience or falsity to your duties as a husband. There should be no chains in love (these pertain to slavery instead).

I expect and wish you to exercise your own judgement when away from me. I grant you "the same right to do as you please" not as a "single person" has, but as a married woman has.

[X marked here] I never wrote you in more sincere honest love than I write this letter. [X marked here]

Now look at the other side. Since I married you I have never felt other than repulsion at the thought of a kiss or caress of any kind from any man but you, unless it be my immediate family or yours.

Have never had that feeling toward any man but himself that would make his kiss pleasant to me.

From the present time till now not only my acts but the thoughts of my heart have been open to your inspection.

[X marked here] Now, for the medical question.

When I was sick in Augusta you did not scruple to send old Dr. Em in to see me with the expectation that he would treat me for uterine difficulties which of course presupposed the "examination" (of which you have such a disturbed idea) you were in the house at the time and I really wished you with me and yet you did not come in. You left me in my room alone—"a bed" in the room—expecting an examination—and Dr. Em I would quite as soon suspect of licentiousness as Dr. Saunders, of <u>indelicacy</u> with his patients <u>much</u> <u>sooner</u>. I have been informed by a woman who had employed Dr. Em and who has been with him in other cases that he is sometimes a very vulgar old fellow with his patients. The only cases in which my <u>person was ever exposed</u> in the <u>least</u> <u>degree</u> to the gaze of any man but you were—slightly in Portland when Dr. Fitch examined me with the speculum (which Dr. Saunders does not use), and at the birth of our first baby when a Dr. of <u>your</u> <u>selection</u> raised the clothes in applying the cloths to me after birth (as Mrs. Sherman tells me) I was in that condition that I did not realize it and was not able to defend myself, as, Thank God! I now am.

Still again when I went with you and baby to consult a strange physician in Savannah, after we received directions regarding baby you took baby out for a walk and left me alone with a strange physician in his office (in a much more retired spot than Dr. Saunders office is) to consult him about uterine difficulties when the natural expectation always is that a physician will wish to make an examination when there are such difficulties, as otherwise he cannot tell what treatment the case requires. After all these things do you wonder that I supposed you had lost your old objection to my being <u>alone</u> with a physician for consultation or treatment on uterine difficulties? It had so far made me forget your former scruples that the thought of them never even entered my mind. [X marked here]

Now we come to going to Dr. Saunders. For ten years or more I have suffered from this weakness, to your distress as well as mine.[11] Lucy has been under Dr. Saunders treatment for the same difficulties, only much more serious ones, for three years—she recommends him to me. I have found no physician in the South to whose skill I could trust. Mrs. Sherman has treated

---

[11] Clearly, Emma's medical condition predated her marriage, making it highly unlikely that it resulted from venereal disease contracted from her husband, as Holt suspected. See her *"The Anatomy of a Marriage."*

me, helping but not curing me and not able to tell me why I do not fully recover. [X marked here] I go to Dr. Saunders and by making an examination, by inserting the finger in the vagina (which is what I meant by saying that his treatment is like Mrs. Shermans [X marked here] i.e. that neither of them use the speculum, which is attended with something of pain and exposure) he tells me that there is ulceration of long standing, that it is gradually weakening me (as I have so long realized) that it will be comparatively easy to cure and that by a weeks treatment he can alleviate it and give me remedies with which to treat myself.

Lucy had not the funds to enable her to remain with me, but she would take baby home and take care of her.

On thinking over my funds I concluded I had barely enough to take me through the weeks treatment. If I waited I should not incur the expense of going again. If I went to Earl I could not have treatment short of Chicago when it would be alone with a strange physician, for my sister could not leave her family to go with me and would consider it the greatest absurdity, if she could.

I remained supposing that my husband would be delighted to hear that there was so good a purpose of my being restored to sound health. [X marked here] The Dr. gave not more indication of sensual feeling or of thinking that he was doing anything indelicate than he would if he had been treating my face [red underline] or my hand. [X marked here]

[X marked here] If he had shown passion, [red underline] do you think so meanly of me as to believe that I could not and would not instantly have repulsed him and left for home? Why have you sought to humiliate your wife and injure yourself by such dreadful suspicions as you have cast upon me. [X marked here] I was safe both because I could have detected the design of a passionate man in this very beginning and defended myself, and because no physician of the character and standing of Dr. Saunders or indeed of any standing in the medical fraternity would compromise himself by offering insult to his patient, much less by overcoming them by brute force. [X marked here]

I am not safer walking the crowded street than I was in the Dr's office.

[X marked here] Do you think that I have no love of my own virtue, no pride, no temper or will of my own that you fancied me so helpless in his hands? [X marked here] The matter of going at bet. 7 & 8 o'clock in the evening is a mere bugaboo. I asked him if it would be as well for me to go in the afternoon and when he gave me the reason why it would not I readily see the reasonableness of it. [X marked here] It was precisely this—he inserted a small piece of medicated sponge between the lip of the uterus and the rectum, the sponge to keep the uterus in position and the medicine upon it to ease the ulceration, he inserted one in the morning which I was to retain through the day till after tea when I withdrew it used my syringe and went to the office between 7 & 8 P.M. and had a fresh one put in which was to remain till the next morning. He had no office hour later than four, 4 P.M. until evening and that would have permitted the morning sponge to remain too short a time and the evening too long a time.

He treated me twice a day simply because I could remain so short a time.

His manner of treatment was perfectly delicate and such as all women afflicted with such disease and wishing to recover must receive at the hands of some male physician until there are sufficient educated female physicians to supersede the males.

[X marked here] I consider treatment at a physician's office if it is situated like Dr. Saunders as safe and therefore better than at a lady's home.

It is not customary among ladies to have anyone with them when treated. I know that Clarinda told me years ago when she was under Dr. Fitch's care that she would not have any one but the Dr. present (that it added to her mortification) Other ladies have told me the same thing.

My [X marked here] character has been and is above suspicion [red underline] and you would pity me if you knew how humiliated I feel to even explain to you. [X marked here] I resolved that I would not, but hoping to restore you from your present state of insanity I have done it—and I have written very fully meaning it to be the only and final vindication of my character on my part.

In regard to going out to church on Sunday night the Dr. had left the office when we returned and after waiting some little time for him Charlie took me home and I missed treatment altogether for that night. To sum up—I have applied to a physician of skill and standing—well known to sister Lucy for more than three years—and have received medical treatment precisely the same as thousands of pure women have done and are doing and [X marked here] my husband repays my full trust in him by torturing [red underline] himself with the vilest suspicions [red underline] of me—even inclined to the opinion that I am "ruined" or, at the very least, injured—panic! [X marked here]

[X marked here] Taunts me with leaving my baby [red underline] for a few days in care of her grandma and aunty! [red slash here] morally raises the lash over me and says now will you obey? Will you be my inferior, my obedient child?—To this I answer Never [double underline]. I will be your true, loving wife your companion and equal in every and the fullest sense—the mother of your children. Nothing <u>less</u> and nothing <u>else</u>.[12]

[X marked here] With a true love kiss for <u>my</u> <u>husband</u>—the man whom I married and have been happy with all these years—not the <u>debased imagination</u> [red underline] which has addressed these terrible letters to me. I am [X marked here]

Your loving wife—
Emma

Aug. 7—At night—

I have just received yours of last Saturday and Sunday and am more and more deeply wounded—

[X marked here] What am I to suppose—that you believe me ruined by my one <u>voluntary</u> [red underline] act, or that if I had been in any manner insulted by brute <u>force</u> [red underline] you would lose your love for me and put me from you—which of the two terrible meanings must I put upon your words?

Are you my husband, or are you some false spirit entered into him?

Have you never thought that if my ruin had been compared or attempted, I was as utterly wretched as you could possibly be? and yet you have not one word of love for me—of pity for me—your arms stretch out towards me, not in love, but in reproach and anger. To the wife who [X marked here] has never in all her married life received from any other man than you the lightest token of love or passion you can address these <u>selfish</u> <u>unloving</u> <u>insulting</u> words that you have written me. I cannot realize it. I am <u>stupified</u> [*sic*] by it. You do not even call our baby by my name—and yet you profess at the worst to fear that I have only been a helpless victim in the hands of a bad man. This utter lack of love for me—this perfection of selfishness is harder for me to bear than your insulting suspicions have been. Did you ever <u>really</u> <u>love</u> me, or did you only hold me as a possession tributary to your pleasure to be cast aside if you became displeased with it?

If it were <u>possible</u> for you to do so I should <u>entreat</u> <u>you</u> to <u>come</u> <u>to</u> me immediately. Do you realize how <u>cruelly</u> you <u>have</u> <u>stabbed</u> me?—Through all these terrible suspicions which you have entertained of me I have never been so heartbroken as I am to-night. To think that if I had been in any way injured my hus-

---

[12] The motto of *Revolution*, Elizabeth Cady Stanton and Susan B. Anthony's feminist journal, published January 1868–March 1870, was "Principle, not policy—Justice, not favors—Men their rights and nothing more—Women their rights and nothing less."

band would push me from him, reproaching me for the misery to himself without one single thought of <u>my</u> utter wretchedness. Through all these terrible things that you have written me I have never lost my love—never ceased to be sorry that you were in distress, but I have watched in vain for a <u>single</u> <u>unselfish</u> <u>loving</u> thought toward me. It <u>is</u> <u>not</u> <u>you</u>—<u>it</u> <u>is</u> <u>not</u> <u>like</u> <u>you</u>—write and tell me that some madness has possessed you and that you in your own proper self never wrote such things. If it were in my power I think I should start for Savannah to-morrow leaving baby here. I want to see you face to face.

Aug 8, A.M. I have sent to Earlville for my letter. If I receive that on Monday or Tuesday I shall probably go to Earl on Wednesday—or rather leave here on Wed. morning—reach Swanton beyond Toledo about noon stop the night with my cousins there and go on to Chicago by the next forenoon train. I shall expect sister to meet me in Chicago.

In my present state of mind I would much prefer to go without stopping but I had before this terrible occurrence written to my cousin that I would visit her; and she writes me that she has lost her only sister and her brother (an only one) is dying with consumption. Her mother is already dead, too, and she feels very lonely and depends much on [my] seeing her.

If my own heart is heavy I will not refuse to comfort another if in my powers.

<u>Our</u> baby is well—has improved much since she came here in size, strength and talking.

Mother has received yours of 4th. I probably shall wait a week or two longer instead of going to Earl on Wed.

———

[letter marked with red crayon or pen as indicated]

Wakeman
Aug. 16–1873

My Darling Husband.

I received yours of last Monday this (Sat.) morning. Had feared you might not write each day waiting for a reply to your letter. Now that my husband can write me love-letters like his own self, they can not come too often.

By the tone of both your letters—Sun. and Mon.—I think you almost feel that I am not ready to forgive the harsh words you wrote me. Indeed, I am, my darling husband—the assurance that you love and trust me as of yore wipes out the impression of all the terrible letters that you wrote before this last two. I have forgiven all, and if you really fully love me and trust me and cast out the [X marked here] suspicion and <u>bitterness</u> [red underline] that was in your heart [X marked here] when you wrote those letters, then there is no difference between us to settle—no need to talk of seperation [*sic*].

If we love and trust each other fully there can be no ground between us— is it true darling?

[X marked here] The letter written under two dates and times was partially destroyed for the reason that I wrote something at night which in the morning I thought best (not to conceal from you altogether) but to tell you when I saw you—lest you may think it worse than it was will tell you now.

I had been quite isolated since I left you from the society of any man who was in the least sparkling or vivacious in his manner, so seldom either since I left or before had any rides, that I enjoyed the Dr's society (the little that I had of it) and enjoyed the rides—you know how much company and surroundings exhilarate me: and so, as I said, I have enjoyed the Dr. (tho' not in a lackadaisical manner at all) and the <u>slight attention</u> that he had shown me—and it was precisely these that I had written you and told you that I felt half vexed with myself that I should find zest and relish in the society of any man away from you.

That is what I have done that was wrong if anything was—for that "I am willing to be forgiven." Perhaps my husband can recall pleasant hours spent in the society of some lady friend and not <u>consider my misdemeanor a very grave one</u>. [X marked here]

My stay at his office was usually very brief unless I had to wait for him— my stay in the consultation was usually about 5 min. I should judge.

Let me enlighten you on the matter of going to the office in the evening as you may feel glad to know. You fancied me alone after dark—it was a grave mistake. I went before dark and returned just at dusk and had scarce a square to go.

[X marked here] In objection to going in the evening I told the Dr. I was timid in being out after dark and he told me that I should not be left to <u>return alone</u> [red underline] if it was dark. The first night his colored office man took me home in the Dr's buggy. another night it was raining but not dark and the Dr. walked to the gate with me himself. another time he sent his man home with me but I finally protested again at his doing [that].

I feel more unwilling to be away from you till Christmas than I did before this trouble. I heartily desire to return with you. We are expecting company and I must lay aside writing to help a little.

I want to tell you again <u>how</u> happy I am to receive messages of love from you. Mother and Lucy rec'd letters yesterday—last night. Mother wishes to answer immediately but has company to provide for to-day and expect some one for her to-morrow—will write as soon as possible. She is very tender toward her dear boy if she [illegible] think he was happy towards his wife.

Baby darling gave me a sweet kiss and a hug to send to papa. She is growing very interesting since you saw her.

Yes I will "permit you to come see her"—

May God bless you, darling, and make us happier in each other than we have ever been before.

Bye darling—
Emma

––––––––

Wakeman
Aug. 19, 1873
Tuesday morning—

My Darling Husband.

I went to the train this morning intending to go to Swanton to-day stop there to-night and go direct to Earl to-morrow but my plans have been again frustrated. Just before starting I rec'd a note from cousin and in it she said that her children had had the scarlet fever one of them being sick with it a week ago when she expected me but that they were entirely well now and I need not fear to go. I was in a great dilemma about going but on thinking the matter over decided to go and make my visit at the home of one of the other relations where I could see my cousin instead of at her own home. but on the way to the depot I began to wonder what sister would think about it and thought that she would perhaps feel uneasy about it if I did go, and so very reluctantly gave it up. I feel very badly in disappointing my cousin for her husband came out to meet me a week ago and will come again to-day. I did not feel that there was any real danger or I would not, of course, have decided to carry baby, but I did not feel at liberty to do anything which might cause sister any uneasiness even, while I am a guest in her home.

I returned from the depot because the morning train would not only give me a very tiresome ride with baby but would force me to change cars in Chicago between 8 & 9 P.M. o'clock when baby is sleepy and tired, but very likely necessitate my remaining overnight in Chicago.

So I intend now to take the sleeping car here at bet. 4 & 5 this afternoon and will reach Chicago to-morrow morning and probably reach sisters' at noon if not earlier.

I shall hope that we can stop a day at cousins when we return in October. I am very glad, very happy to be "your own darling wife" once more, to know that you love me as warmly as ever.

Now if I am your own darling wife let me ask you one favor. Dont come on in October expecting to talk over all this unhappiness through which we have passed. If we really and truly trust each other and love each other let us trust to that alone to take us safely through the future—a "platform" will be only a source of trouble, and writing is much safer than talking, because I, at least, have carefully considered every word that I have written you and all save the few lines said in Lucy's have been kept over night and reread two or three times to be sure that I wrote nothing that I would ever need to recall, while if you try to talk with me when you come I may say something on the spur of the moment that I do not so fully mean.

In the letters that I have written you I have shown my true self, so I say again, dont let us talk it over. If I think you come with that intention I shall even dread your coming, much as I wish to see you.

Write me please that I shall not be talked over—that we will taboo it as a subject of conversation, shall we not?

I do want to make you happy, my darling, and I mean to try by every means that I do not believe will be an injury to you and me—honestly I do not believe that we shall clash in our views in the future as much as we have done in the past—in any case there is no appeal but mutual love and trust.

I think we can often see whether our arguments are just by the simple experiment of "put yourself in his place."

I think I shall be ready to make any concession which you feel sure you could make if you were wife and I husband—when we differ upon any point suppose we mutually agree to put ourselves (mentally) in each others' place remembering.

———

Earl Aug 21, 1873

My Darling Husband.

I reached here yesterday at noon, as you already are aware as sister telegraphed to that effect last evening. Baby is happy as a bird with the children and they seem very fond of little cousin as they call her. I think you really would be surprised if you could see her, she is so large. I think she has grown a good deal since she left Georgia—and has been in almost perfect health from the time she left the South.

Has some cold now but it does not trouble her very much.

She is very, very sweet and wins the heart of almost every one with whom she comes in contact.

I am sorry, darling, for you to lose these months when she is so very interesting. I do earnestly hope that we will be reunited again early in October, never to be as much seperated [*sic*] again as we have been in the past.

I must write but a few lines for am afraid I shall miss the mail and I must write a line to cousin mother and Lucy of our safe arrival. I gave up going to Swanton, as I think I explained in my letter written at Wakeman day before yesterday.

We left Wakeman about 5 P.M. and reached here at 11 A.M. next day. There has been a fearful railroad accident in this state a few days since.

I must not write more.

Sister wishes to be remembered. Father and all the family enquire after you, God bless and keep you, darling, and show you that your wife's heart is fully, truly yours, even tho' she writes you plain truths—if I did not love you so much perhaps I would not speak so plainly. I left two letters for Lucy to mail when I left Wakeman.

> With loving kisses—
> Bye, Darling
> Emma

LETTERS: 1874–1877

In the years following the crisis of 1873, Emma attempted to create a more normal family existence. The paucity of letters in 1874 argues that the Bryants realized this dream for a time while he held the patronage appointment of assistant collector of customs in Savannah. As had become the pattern, however, John's political endeavors totally absorbed his energies and kept him from extended home life.[1]

John Emory Bryant would rise to the height of his political reputation in Georgia by 1876, but the return of some prestige was again accompanied by opposition and distress. A candidate for Congress in both 1874 and 1876, JEB represented a divided party struggling in an increasingly futile attempt to maintain Republican strength in Georgia. John asked his wife for her assistance in the 1874 campaign, writing when she visited her sister in Illinois. Ever willing, but more realistic than he, she reminded him of the investment in her wardrobe this help would entail. No records show that she joined the effort.

Any hope of success in 1876 was thwarted by the combined vengeance of all of John's prior political enemies, led by Rufus Bullock, who had returned to Georgia to pursue his own rehabilitation. Collectively, these foes derailed Bryant's candidacy, despite the outrage of his supporters locally and in Washington. The following year, yet another investigation resulted in his exoneration, but could not recover the lost congressional seat. Once again chairman of the Republican State Central Committee, Bryant assumed the thankless task of dealing with irreconcilable divisions in the party, including the "lily-whites," who wished to exclude blacks entirely, as well as those advocating Republican fusion with Independent voters. As arbiter between the factions, JEB found himself in an untenable position. Further, his enthusiastic African American supporters held unrealistic expectations of how his term as chair would benefit them, setting the stage for later disappointment.

---

[1] See *Carpetbagger of Conscience*, 129–45, for details of JEB's career in the years 1874–77.

Additional difficulties arose from the disputed national election between Democrat Samuel J. Tilden and opponent Rutherford B. Hayes, not settled until the spring of 1877. Hayes' tarnished victory resulted in a compromised Republican president, whose platform for gaining Southern support and ending Reconstruction would shortly make carpetbaggers like Bryant an anachronism in the South.

One extant mention of family life in Savannah comes from the autobiography written later by Alice. In June 1876, the Bryants celebrated the national centennial with a visit to the grand Centennial Exposition in Philadelphia. Then, with John clearly immersed in his work, Emma and Alice continued on for an extended visit with her brother Greenleaf and his wife Nancy (Nannie). As a United States Coast and Geodetic Surveyor, Greenleaf resided at the time on North Haven Island off the coast of Maine. There, Emma's life was quite remote from her husband's and she missed him dreadfully. The entries in the diary she kept from June to October offer rare insight into the sum of her days as she dealt with the never-ending sewing and the tedium of housework, even as she relished the beauty of her surroundings, seeing with an artist's eye, and seeking time alone to paint.

In October, a change in Greenleaf's circumstance required Emma's departure from his domicile. This necessity, coming at a time of turmoil in John's political life, led to months of uncertainty and frustration. Written from Washington, D.C., where Emma had moved expecting to connect with her husband, her letters in the fall of 1876 reflect not only the national election crisis, but the lonely winter she found there instead of John.[2] Thus strategically placed, nevertheless, she assisted him by meeting with Republican solons, while her anxiety rose in the face of his seeming inability to provide for her. After another desolate Christmas for them both, eventually she returned to the South.

Adding to his woes, JEB's political ambitions for office had conflicted with those of James Atkins, with whom he worked in Savannah. Faced with another impasse, by January 1877 Bryant had resigned his post in the customs house. In April, Emma's letters followed him to the North, where he traveled seeking support for the Republican cause and a new direction for his own career.

---

[2] Curiously, some of the letters from August–December 1876 were misdated as 1867. Best guess: someone, presumably one of the Bryants, tried (after the fact) to affix a date. Internal evidence leaves little doubt of the correct year.

Earl July 5. 74

My Darling.

It is Sabbath eve and most oppressively warm. Tuesday the thermometer stood at 100. and I think it warmer this evening by several degrees.

We are living very quietly here since sister left—expect to be a little lonely before she returns, but there [illegible] been too busy to be lonely. Baby darling I have just rocked to sleep and laid on the parlor floor where I will let her remain till I retire on account of the extreme heat upstairs my room gets the afternoon sun and consequently very hot after a warm day but I prefer it to sleeping below for I think I would be a little timid below as I would be obliged to be alone, father and the girl sleep above, so am not much troubled by timidity. I like being above too because I can sun and ventilate my room there as I choose and below Mr. Browne keeps everything dark and I wouldn't be willing for baby to sleep in such an atmosphere as that creates. I really think that lack of sun indoors has gone to [sic] far towards the great difference between life and death with sisters children. I believe that if I could control, so far as it is controllable the atmosphere in which Neilly lives in-doors and the food that he eats that he would have a fair chance to grow up into a healthy boy unless indeed the error of his rearing thus far is beyond repair. He seems quite delicate and I greatly fear will never grow up to be robust under such a regime and Mr. Browne is still more injuriously indulgent than she.

I hope much from his journey east and if that could be followed by a southern climate in the winter it might work wonders. Father and baby and self went to Pres.[byterian] church this morning—baby did not talk aloud very much but she twitched about until I was ashamed. I doubt if she was quiet for one single minute during the whole service. I think I shall persevere in taking her however for I am very anxious to train her before I return to Savannah.

All my pictures of our next winter's life presuppose housekeeping so please dont forget. I believe that I have been undergoing a deteriorating process ever since we broke up housekeeping for the last time. Such a state of dependence upon the whim and caprices of other people is not healthy soil for mind to expand in. The school teacher—the lawyer and the minister are in a neighboring yard discussing some profound topic with great wisdom. I wish you could hear the wise repartees that our little one makes occasionally—baby waked just here and I left to attend to her.

Speaking of her wise sayings she shows a remarkable likeness to her father in that she is seldom at a loss to give an excuse for any of her misdemeanors.

My great anxiety in regard to her at present is that she is a great runaway and I much fear that she may be run over by horses or otherwise injured if I can't cure her of it. I tie her and sometimes whip also. I would not punish so much for it if I did not fear that her running away might cost her life or a limb. She makes very frequent calls upon Mr. Barnes the Universalist clergyman who lives but a couple doors from us. There is no danger for her to fall in there and I often allow her to go when she asks permission. The methodist church bell has just rung and I have half a mind to go to church either there or among the baptists.

I must close this letter and make arrangements if I go. I shall—find I cannot well leave baby and will relinquish church for to-night. I want to write a few lines to-night or tomorrow to Lucy. I am sorry to find such changes in the weather as we are having. when I reached here it was extremely cold now it is very very warm—so warm and oppressive and dry that I fear hurricanes. I meet Mr. Haight frequently. he enquires after you and expresses a desire to see you. The neighbors are all very kind to baby and pet her a great deal. She seems very well and I have pretty good courage about keeping her well through the summer with God's blessing. I trust much to her present vigor and healthy habits of living. I think this hot and variable weather very dangerous to such children as are allowed to abuse their stomachs daily as many perhaps most children are allowed.

Am sorry that I was so full of work as not even to remember our anniversary days. Thanks to you, darling, that you were more thoughtful than I. We have heard from sister once on her journey—she wrote from Niagara Falls. Will make her first stay in N.Y.

I have had no letter from you in several days and scarcely a postal. Write often if you can—

O. I must tell you baby repeats a prayer after me at night. "Now I lay me down to sleep I pray the Lord my soul to keep"—It sounds very precious to me I assure you. I shall "take off my [illegible] and go to bed with her" to-night. She has had little appetite since we came here and had a little sick turn the other night, sick at her stomach, but I left her to get well without medicine and she seems very well since and has better appetite. It is quite dark and I must close—

> Bye, darling, May God keep us and
> make us better and give us His spirit
> Baby sends kiss—
> Lovingly—
> Emma

Earl Aug. 7, 1874

My Darling.

I have a little time before the mail which will devote to you.

I received letter from you yesterday.

I answered in a previous letter yours in regard to hiring rooms and having meals sent in. I do not know whether in that I made sufficiently prominent my dread of going into a private home simply as a <u>roomer</u>. I have thought of it more since my attempt to that end last winter than I had done then and I should <u>only</u> be willing to do it in order to obtain our board at less rates and that we could only do by taking our meals out, having them sent in would cost much more beside necessitating more room for us. In a boarding house we have certain recognized rights, in a private home those rights might be recognized and they might not.

I fancy I should like at Mrs. [illegible] where those people who boarded at Mrs. Sawyer's used to room, but the rooms <u>especially</u> the bedrooms are dark and unpleasant and I wouldn't consent to go into a dark unventilated bed room on account of the unhealthfulness of it. I feel a good anxiety about this matter and please do not neglect it.

Perhaps you could hire the half of a small house with some acquaintance. I do <u>want</u> to keep house.

A word in regard to money. I have just paid my wash bill and have not enough left to buy soap and starch and sealing and postage for the present month, to say nothing of thread and buttons and other little items that must be had. Hope my calls for money do not annoy you as much as they do me, but the matter stands just here. Last year when I went home I had to hire everything done for me at the last because I did not have funds to buy with in the summer. this causes me much more outlay than having money in season to do with myself. Now another point—dont wait to write to ask me what I want. I can only say that I am <u>very</u> destitute of underclothing, and of fall and winter clothing. I have nothing good, scarce one dress, a cloak and an old velvet hat to make over. Now this is my status and you must send me just what you can spare and when you can spare it and I will do the very best I can. You have some idea yourself of the cost of clothing and of how you desire me to dress and you must balance between your wishes and your abilities according to the best of your judgement.

It only worries me when you write to ask how much I want. I need a great deal because I have had so little in the past, but I am still willing to do with very little if necessary. Baby will need but little—10. perhaps less will fit her out for the whole winter I think.

One thing please keep in mind that you cannot send me money a week or two before I go home and then have me come home with my clothes all made unless I spend a great deal of the money in having sewing done. Now please bear in mind, husband mine, that I am not complaining that I dont consider myself an ill-used woman because I don't have carte blanche for new dresses—not one bit of it—stringency of money has not been (otherwise than through a feeling of your molification [sic]) and I do not believe will ever be any cause of unhappiness to me. I have often thought that these embarrassments through which we have gone together have drawn me closer to you and that the less prosperous you have been the more I have loved you. But as you asked about my needs and necessities I wished you to see exactly how the case stood and I shall be satisfied with whatever you send me, knowing your willingness and desire to gratify all my wishes.

Unless I am to lose my teeth and have false ones I must have them filled before I leave here, but that can be deferred till a week or two before leaving. I can have it done here at about 1/3 the cost in Savannah. I have not written you much purely from the lack of time but I will try hard to do it this week. Baby is well and happy.

Bye darling
Emma

I will agree to almost any plan by which we can live cheaply if it does not sacrifice our health. I believe we can live most cheaply by housekeeping—please burn this or put it where it will be sure not to be seen.

———

Savannah Apr 2 /76

My Darling.

Have heard nothing in several days from you till this morning and dont be hurt if I say that this morning's letter was a great disappointment to me. I have only few minutes in which to write . . . must devote these minutes to expostulation rather than other words that might be pleasanter to us both.

I really fear, darling, that you will alienate your friends here by such course of procedure as the very cheering telegrams which you sent last week with the promise, "details by mail" and then all these days of suspense broken by two letters without one word of details. Fishers[3] letter was almost an insult to waiting, anxious people, in that there was not one grain of information in it—nothing but glittering generalities. It was as exasperating and unsatisfactory as the odors of cooking wafted to the nostrils of a hungry man who is perfectly helpless to possess himself of anything eatable. Please remember that your telegram was such as to amount to an assurance that you had gained what you went for, and that it was something definite and certain—no other interpretation could fairly be put upon it. Now both yourself and Fisher have written since a page each and say you haven't time to explain; surely, if your telegram meant anything you could have told us in half that page something—and if your telegram meant only that you were very hopeful and had encouragement however great, the sending of it was a great mistake. You know, my darling, I am very sensitive for your honor and reputation, and tho' you chide me sometimes because I am not a mere partizan of my husbands (that I can never be) and I shrink painfully from the thought of your friends shrugging their shoulders and saying—that's one of Bryant's telegrams—cant tell how much it means—and it is bound to come to that if you send any word so decided and emphatic as that telegram when there is no fact to base it on that cannot be told in a single page. . . . Now dont understand me, darling, to mean that I am all discouraged and that I feel that your telegram meant nothing—I have not that feeling. I presume that you have great encouragement and I look for your ultimate success, even as I pray for it day by day, but I am convinced by your letter and Fisher's that you have not a decision and definite result such as would justify a general in telegraphing to the nation—"We have won the field"—And if you have not, certainly neither strict trust nor policy could justify your dispatch.

I have been in daily expectation of your boxes being sent up but Porter[4] has been sick and they have been delayed.

In regard to money if you are able to keep your promise in next to the last letter to send me more first (I think) of this month—am not certain now whether you said first—shall do very well. The grocer sent in his bill and I paid 10. on it, had previously paid Susie 5. I have now only 3.00 remaining. Shall not call on Col. Wade[5] for anything unless positively obliged to. If you cannot send me money soon please tell me so at once. I do not like to be in a haze about it. I think if you are unable to send me money it would be much

---

[3] C. O. Fisher, member of Georgia Republican Executive Committee.
[4] David Porter, chairman of Chatham County (Savannah) Republican Party.
[5] Archibald P. Wade, member of Georgia Republican Executive Committee.

better for you to write to Col. Wade yourself to send me something than for me to call on him. Will try to be as prudent as practicable. Emma is waiting to be dressed and I will relieve you from any further "candle"—Emma says tell papa that his little girl is well and sends him a kiss—she says "tell papa to write me a letter and I will answer it." The bigger girl sends a kiss, too, and many of them and a Godspeed to you in your work. I love you, darling, and shall be glad, glad to welcome you home. It is but a dull home to baby and me without you. I have great hopes that you will come home with a commission for some good position. God keep you and speed the day of your coming.

bye darling
Emma

I wrote Mrs. Fairchild[6] not long since, if that has not been rec'd please enquire at the office for that like the others only have 608 12th st. instead the N.W.

Am very sorry that I should have been so careless. I feel almost as if I ought to have made the money last go farther; but I seemed obliged to spend considerable. have been obliged to hire a number of day's works owing to Emma's sickness and my own lack of strength for have not felt well much of the time and do not dare overdo much more. I will try to do my very best to be prudent and keep things straight at the home end of the line trusting to the "sword of the Lord and of Gideon"[7] at Washington.

Emma. . . .

———

Savannah May 10 /76

My Darling.

I have been so hurried with work and with excursions that have scarce had any time to write you. Have not even been able to congratulate you on your election to chairmanship of S.[tate] C.[entral] Com.[mittee] I do congratulate you with all my heart, darling, upon that and all the victory which you gained in the convention. I had quite a minute account of it from Porter also something from Moore.

---

6 Emma would board with the Fairchilds in Washington, D.C.
7 Gideon's rally call of courage and faith for victory, Book of Judges in the Old Testament; Port Royal missionaries were called Gideonites.

Your little girl prays every day that God will give Papa wisdom. She claimed all the kisses in your letter rec'd to-day, believing that her mother had no rights in papa which she was bound to respect.[8] She has been to-day to a picnic with Mrs. Schwarz—came home in gay spirits.

Your letter written on Sat. never reached me. I have not had a line from you since you left home until to-day.

I must close soon or write with my eyes shut. Shall I not see you home last of this week?

It is lonely here I can assure you. Lucy and I are extremely busy with our sewing.

> My love to all the friends.
> Pray for me my darling.
> Bye bye
> Emma

———

[From Alice Bryant's autobiography (typescript)]

[1874?]

When my father and mother were boarding in Savannah, Georgia, and I was a baby my father often walked me to sleep. My mother decided that she must stop that. One night she locked him out of the room while I screamed and screamed, much to my father's embarassment [sic], as they lived in a boarding house and their room was on the first floor, off of the living room.

[1876]

It was from Savannah that my mother and I went to the Centennial Exposition in Philadelphia. . . . After leaving Philadelphia and the Centennial Exposition my mother and I went to Rockland, Maine, where we were going to visit an old school mate, the wife of a minister, on our way to North Haven Island where my Uncle Greenleaf and Aunt Nonnie [sic] lived. He was U.S. Tide Observer and was stationed there for fifteen years, filling out what is called a lunar cycle, after which the recordings of the tides repeat themselves.

---

[8] Emma uses the language of the Supreme Court's Dred Scott ruling (*Scott v. Sandford*, 1857): blacks had "no rights which the white man was bound to respect."

The night we reached Camden I came down with scarlet fever and as there had been some very serious cases previously in Camden my mother's friend was greatly frightened and she and her children went to the home of one of their church members, her husband sleeping down stairs so that we would not be alone in the house.

It was several weeks before it was safe for us to make the all day trip on the little sailing vessel, the "Mayflower," to North Haven Island. . . .

North Haven Island was quite a summer resort then as later. It was there that the Morrow's, Ann Lindburg's [*sic*] parents had a summer home. My uncle lived near one end of the island which was curved in such a way that it was quicker to cross to the part where the church and stores were than to go around by way of land.

I remember with pleasure these boat rides. I also remember picking barnacles off the rocks. . . .

————

[Emma's diary written on notepaper—selected entries]

[North Haven, Maine
June–October 1876]

June 23, Fri. Reached this place (North Haven) yesterday. . . . Baby just recovering from Scarlet fever—seems in no wise injured by the change.

Have been too exhausted and generally demoralized to attempt much of anything to do—have done some desultory reading, two light stories, and numerous anecdotes and short articles, pictures of pernicious life of the sufferings of little children who work in mines etc. I miss B. and especially so because I do not even know where to address a letter to him. Shall write tomorrow addressing probably to Savannah must try to begin to-morrow a more systematic life. Greenleaf went to Rockland to-day, Nannie and I alone to-night.

June 24. Sat. Letter from B. written from Washington Postal from Miss Lowe wrote and sent letter to B. Baby improving.

June 25 Sun. A warm and quiet and peaceful day. none of us went to church on account of Emma's sickness, she is recovering but we thought people might fear contagion from even us. Told Emma some bible stories, wrote B a letter just at night.

June 26 Mon. Day filled up with housework and sewing and some reading. . . .

June 27 Tuesday Have been busy with sewing and household duties, and little desultory reading. . . . Am rather unfavorably impressed by this climate thus far, Wil [*sic*] read my bible and retire, Finished letter to B. to-day and sent to mail

June 29 Thurs. Went to bed very tired with my sewing and failed to write in diary. Baby still confined to house though entirely convalescent. Am not recovered from my fatigue from labor before leaving home and in Emma's illness since.

Have written B. a tame letter. hope it wont seem as stupid to him as it does to me. I resolved some time since to read to Emma daily such portions of bible as she can comprehend but have not carried it well out, shall try now to do so will make a beginning to-night

June [*sic*] Friday June 30 Have begun to-day to read in course to baby. (or rather habitually for shall not read exactly in course) from the bible. Began on the history of Jesus in the first of Mat. [thew] and have had two readings, succeeding I think in interesting her. May I have a genius and grace given me from above to guide her immortal soul. I feel very weak when I think of it.

I sewed yesterday and read a remarkable story of spiritualism, showing heaven <u>nothing but</u> wonder and mystery—no benefit accruing to any one from its revelation. No mail to-day. nothing unusual, unless an unusual fog

Sat. July 1 Have been very busy to-day with household duties and a little sewing. Read to Emma from the bible. . . . her auntie went out by boat and brought home a quantity of pretty pebbles, with which she has been greatly amused. Letter from B. and from Lucy

July 3$^{\underline{d}}$, Monday Have been rather idle to-day, sorted out my colors a bit and looked at book on painting.

July 4, Tuesday Passed a very quiet 4$^{\text{th.}}$ as little Emma's scarlet fever prevented us from going to the neighborhood picnic and a shower even prevented us from taking a little drive. Wrote B. last night I painted a little yesterday on stone the first painting that I have done in many months. Wrote postal to Miss Lowe asking her to send cambric skirt and drawing book.

July 6 Thurs. Have made an attempt to improve or repaint Ella's photo. went over the background to-day quite improving it, I think. We had a heavy gale all night and this morning. went up this morning to look at Camden Mts. They were lovely and the waters of the bay were broken into foam, forming a beautiful veiw [*sic*]

July 7 Friday Went to pick strawberries with Mr. and Mrs. Venice. boated across the water and afterward walked through the field and came home with pails filled. As soon as night-fall approaches I feel such a sense of loneliness and almost of trouble or sorrow—can but wish that could have B. near me and more than all that could feel closer and more loving my Saviour's presence

Mond July 10 Have painted none for some days—

July 15 Sat. Have tried to sew to-day but have spent much of the time out-of-doors with Emma. Went with her and Nannie on a little trip to the woods. Emma had her first ride in a hay rack

July 16. Poor Ben, Greenleaf's gentlest and most valuable horse has hurt his leg badly in the night. he is such a thoroughly good horse that one feels doubly sorry to see him injured. Nannie went to church, I have not been since I went with B. in Phil[adelphia] on the 4th of June.

July 17 Monday Was very busy with sewing. Looking after Emma. a little housework—all the little things that consume a woman's time, as the mouse gnaws a cheese, and leaves me nothing substantial to look back upon. Still I will take it back, mothers ought never to say they are doing nothing or even little if they train the little souls committed to them. God teach me to be faithful to the trust and O! teach me not through loss and sorrow!

July 18, Tuesday A letter from B. to-night. had returned from Florida and was about leaving for Macon to attend a committee meeting. Wonder if the letter has cheered me, since it is I am not near so lonely and so depressed to-night as night fall usually makes me. Have not read to-day—only sewed and but little of that, for have not felt well.

July 20. Thursday Greenleaf went away to spend the day and Nannie baby and self improved the time to go to the woods taking our dinner there picnic fashion. little Emma was greatly delighted by the jaunt though she became quite fatigued. Gathered mosses to carry home with us.

July 21 Friday Very busy all day and sat writing till quite late and then began to fear that baby was croupy and so lay awake till 2, at night watching her. We went on the hill to-night to watch the sunset and found it lovely

July 22 Saturday An unusually busy day, cleaning away the last traces of scarlet fever. sewed a little after dinner. Emma in her prayer to-night asked God to give her children when she was grown up. . . . letter from B. yesterday

July 24 Monday A pleasant day and a sail on the river—the afternoon mostly spent in that and in hunting out a past receipt. during which came upon a receipt for prevention or cure of hydrophobia by the use of elecampane.[9] put the root of it into a pint of new milk (fresh from the cow) and boil it give it to the patient fasting, make him fast after taking it: give a second and third dose on alternate days.

July 30. A lovely day and baby darling was able to gratify her long cherished desire to go to church. The first time she has been since her sickness. My mind is led to-night as it is so many times to think of the management of our darling. to ask myself if I am always judicious, just, tender, God help me! My own strength and wisdom are not sufficient. Will write a few lines to B. then retire

Aug. 4. Friday spent the morning out-of-doors chiefly and afternoon in-door helping Nannie and sewing. Have been thinking to-night for the thousandth time how all these little mean duties of life obscure and shut out the greater ones that look far off tho' they are at our door.

Thinking how we make the grovelling cares and ambition the end and aim of life, instead of striving to hold real, definite, noble views of life and of ourselves as one of the workers in God's army and giving these things their true subordinate place. God help me! Let it not be brought to my charge at the judgement day that while I was deliberating upon some of the minor duties and pleasures of life I let slip an opportunity to save an immortal soul, or even to give a cup of cold water to one of the "little ones."

---

[9] European composite herb with yellow ray flowers.

Let not <u>anything</u> keep me from being all that I can be to the immortal soul given me to rear. Tomorrow is church conference and I have been thinking too whether I might not make Saturday more a day of preparation of heart for Sabbath than I have ever done. Lead me, guide me, more than all strengthen to do what I believe to be right

Aug 5 Saturday Attended church conference. Tried to get good and do duty—hope I succeeded in some little degree but had not so bright a light in my own heart as ought to have. . . .

Aug 10. Thursday. Busy all day making preparations for a little visit to Camden. . . .
    Came home just at night and walked to the Harbour after the mail. Rewarded for my trouble by a letter from B.
    Rec'd a letter from him not long ago saying that Mr. Hillyer has written to invite me to visit them in Washington. Mr. Ritter's people are also there and soon other friends of B's so that I would greatly enjoy a visit there.

Aug. 11. Friday I scarcely imagined anything so lovely as the view on entering Camden or rather approaching it. The distant view of the mountains, and the village at their foot, with the pretty islands in the foreground were a picture to lay away in ones brain for future pleasure as well as to be once drank in and enjoyed. Met Greenleaf at Camden, [illegible] just returning from Boston. After tea . . . a pleasant drive in a part of the town called Rockport.

Aug. 14. Monday Passed to-day in waiting for wind to take us back to N. Haven but no wind came and we remained another night in Camden

Aug 16. Wednesday. Had a quick and slightly rough sail home.

Aug. 17 Thursday Nannie washing and I did housework so that my plans for beggining [sic] painting to-day are thwarted.

Aug. 18. Friday Nannie has planned and we have carried out two sails to-day so painting must be deferred still another day. This afternoon we went . . . to pick pebbles had an enjoyable trip. . . . I took my first lesson in rowing to-day and am much pleased . . . tho' found myself very awkward at it. Have resolved to practice every day if possible. Wrote B. to-night

Aug. 19. Saturday Greenleaf goes to Rockland to hear Blaine[10] speak and I cannot row he will not be on hand to pull me in if I go overboard.

Aug. 21, Monday. Have spent the day in painting a picture for Nannie it being her birthday—nearly finished it and succeeded beyond my anticipation considering the length of time

Aug. 22. Tuesday Finished Nannies picture before dinner, after dinner went with her and Baby to the shore. . . . range of mountains and islands with the expanse of water are very, very lovely. Afterward went out rowing for second time.

Aug 25 Friday Not well, neither painted or rowed. Wrote B. at night. Went with Nannie to call on Mrs. Morton after dinner.

Aug. 28 Monday Very busy painting—a satisfactory day's work on Ella's picture will now lay it aside till reach home

Aug. 29 Tuesday. Have drawn sketched and sewed to-day. Feel very weary to-night
    Letter and paper from B. . . .

Sep 1. Friday Filled up with sketching sewing & housework—Nannie not well.
    Began to enlarge Emma's photograph am making pencil sketch of it and have considerable hope of success tho' have very little time. Have so much to do that know not which way to turn. . . . Wrote letter to B. this morning in regard to time of leaving here etc. Tomorrow conference—

Sep. 2. Saturday Water rough and decided to remain home from conference.

Sep 5. Tuesday First attempt at enlarging photograph. succeeded quite as well as could have hoped—shall attempt to paint portrait of baby from the sketch. . . .

Sep. 6. Wednesday Sketched and painted all the morning sewed after dinner, no rowing

---

[10] James G. Blaine, unsuccessful Republican candidate for president in 1876; the Maine state legislature named him United States senator.

Sep. 18. Monday Am now hurried with preparations to go away. Cut out new wrapper after dinner

Sep. 19 Tuesday Nannie and self did a little washing. After dinner sewed on wrapper. Accounts of yellow fever at Savannah.

Sep 28 Thursday These all have been days very busy with sewing in preparation for leaving Wrote B. sending it this morning in regard to my preparations for journey.

Oct. 1 Sunday Sick with cold all day yesterday and little to-day though approaching convalescence to-night.

A rainy morning followed by sunshine in the afternoon. my own cold and Emma's kept me home from church. Yellow fever still raging severely in Savannah. B. in Augusta. . . .

————

North Haven Aug. 5th /76

My Darling.

It will be scarce more than good-morning that I can say for Emma is sleeping and I must lay down the pen as soon as she wakes.

I wish you could enjoy the refreshing coolness of our mornings here. Have never seen a hot morning since I came here.

We have had good deal of small shipping on the bay of late and the view for a few days past has been lovely. Sometimes the—

P.M. Was interrupted by baby's waking and have been unable to resume since.

Since dinner went across the river to conference meeting, the first meeting of the kind that have seen for years. Baby enjoys the trips very much but isn't particularly quiet in church, says she goes for the ride.

This is mail day again, Saturday, and shall be much disappointed if do not receive a letter from you. Does your position of Chairman of Com. give you the extra work of which you speak? Do politics run high in Savannah now and does it affect your position in the church any? (I have made a mess with my grammar, but pass that by). We are now well into August and, God willing, I will see you before many months, shall soon begin to count it by the weeks. Do you think there will be any objection to my returning in Oct. if you have a healthy season? Do you want wife and baby as soon as that, I think we are sufficiently well trained not to look for much attention from you till after election. I received a postal from Miss Lowe saying that the parcel which I asked you to attend to had been sent. I was very agreeably surprised to see at quarterly meeting Mrs. Bisbee from Camden, one of our old townspeople, and I propose to go to Camden to visit her last of next week, providence permitting. I am anticipating a very pleasant visit both for myself and Emma. She enters into visiting with such a zest that I enjoy taking her out. We expect to go next Friday returning the following Sunday.

I have run off on other topics quite forgetting my attempt to describe some of the beautiful views we have on the bay. One evening this week the water was so smooth that it vividly reminded me of what I have heard called a sea of glass and there were a number of sailing boats and schooners lying there becalmed and the whole view looked like enchantment more than reality. If I had you to enjoy it with me would be very happy in some of these pleasant days.

> Baby is below or she would have some message for papa. With loving kisses
> Bye, Darling
> Emma

Sunday P.M. Have been to church this morning and since dinner reading for my own benefit and Emma's.

Was rejoiced by a letter from you last night, I felt all the while I fretted over your silence that it must be press of business that caused it but I did not realize quite how much burdened you were. May the Lord keep you strong and well and help you to do good work for truth and freedom. Have you an idea that the Hamburg murderers[11] can or will be punished? Emma is in the garden and when I left there she bade me say that she was picking clover for Ben uncle's sick horse. The one whose leg was injured. He is kept in the stable and she makes it part of her daily care usually to pull grass and feed some choice tidbits.

I shall look to hear from you oftener now or at least soon. Do care for your health much as possible. Wonder if you are at church and Sabbath school today. Hope your rush of business will not take you away from your evening

---

[11] Racial incident and murders involving African American militia in Hamburg, South Carolina, beginning July 4, 1876; came to be called the Hamburg Massacre.

meetings. Do your neighborhood meetings continue? Do you see Mr. [illegible] or his family? Do you board at Mrs. Sawyers?

Bye, Darling,
Emma

————

North Haven
Aug. 18 /76

My Darling,

Your letters are so very rare that I have quite given up the thought of letters to reply to, and that with infrequency of our mails is making of me a careless correspondent.

Can only give you now the very fog end of a busy, tired day and am afraid the only sweet thing in my letter will be a kiss that baby entrusted to me before she fell asleep, unless, indeed, one of my own added to it may be pleasant to you after long abstinence.

I am beginning to look forward to the time of my return home and trust it will not be necessary to delay it past the last of October, would like to be home by that time if possible. If a Democratic president should be elected (I <u>don't believe</u> there will) would you think of leaving Savannah and the South?

If so, would it not be well to make an effort to hire our house for the coming year by the month instead of by the year. If a Democrat be elected would you fear sufficient disturbance to render it unsafe to live South, and would we be affected by it sooner than March?

I am now planning to go to Portland to visit Libby Browning about last of Sep. if it should be practicable and should probably spend a fortnight with her and Aunt Minnie. It is my impression now that I shall not go at all to Buckfield. I want to see the friends there but it seems to me that the cons outweigh the pros. Wonder what weather you are having, this evening is really chilly am sitting with a shawl on.

Have been on two boating excursions to-day and taken my first lesson in rowing. I propose to devote a little time to the exercise every morning when weather is suitable. This afternoon we went to a little strip of beach on another part of the island to gather pebbles, it was a very pleasant trip to all but Emma really ran wild. She is looking as strong and well now as I ever saw her.

Have been trying for two days to begin painting and have not yet succeeded—hope to to-morrow. I really must retire at once for am very weary. I hope to hear from you to-morrow, darling. I shall be very, very glad to be home again.

Bye darling,
Emma. . . .

————

North Haven Aug. 20, 1876

My Darling:

Wonder how it will seem to you to be told that I must write briefly because my room is too chilly for me to remain up long! It is quite true, altho' a part of the day was warm. . . . Have thoughts of husband and home many times to-day and am looking almost impatiently for the time to return.

I congratulate you on your nomination. Is there the least hope of an election? Will violence and fraud control Georgia this fall as heretofore?

Emma before going to sleep gave me for you nine kisses counting them as she gave them. I have been reading more of the faith work under Dr. Cullie and the answer to prayers are certainly more wonderful than any thing else of which I have heard.

Lovingly,
Emma

Friday Night—I am shamed that this letter has not been earlier sent. . . . I am trying to paint a very little, have to watch Emma a good deal, sew a little, go out for a few hours with Nannie now and then, help a little of course with the housework and so it comes about that I am hurried as ever, if the days were twice as long I should have none too much time, tho' my health could suffer I fear! Are you out all the time and what kind of a summer have you in Savannah? dry or wet—and healthy or otherwise? . . .

Will you canvas the district and do you anticipate anything like a fair election?

Nannie and Greenleaf are to move from this house and take a much smaller rent the very first of Oct. at least they have hired this place only till then and the owner wishes it for his own use. The only other rent that they may obtain near enough for Greenleaf to attend to his business is the cham-

ber of a neighbor's house and they will have only one sleeping room so that I
will be really obliged to go to Portland the last of Sep. and if I am to go home
last of Oct. (as I greatly desire) that will be none too early. . . . I hear from you
so seldom that I grow a little homesick occasionally. Is election on Nov. 7. and
do the State and National elections come off together? Haven't you found our
home very uncomfortable this summer at night?

Do you think of hiring the house another season? If you do please see that the
awning from the piazza to the kitchen is so well repaired that it will not leak
before you make the entrance. It is useless to attempt getting anything out of him
unless you do it before-hand. He always promises but never does anything.
Have you moved your library into the house, if you do and intend to remain
there another season, please reserve the back room for our sleeping room putting
the library in the front, for I am resolved to have a sunny sleeping room next winter on Emma's account. I must retire soon. I love my husband, and will be glad
and happy to be home again. Emma prays daily, "take us safe home to papa"—

Bye, darling.
Emma

Remember me to Diana and tell her I am glad to hear so good report of the
plants and kitten

Have been out rowing three times

———

North Haven, Aug 27 /67 [1876]

My Darling

It is a lovely Sabbath morning free from fog which often spoils our mornings and just cool enough to be refreshing. Indeed, have just builded [*sic*] a
fire to cheer Emma by, she being still in bed.

She usually sleeps till past breakfast and looks upon it as special good fortune when she can eat her breakfast with the family. I am becoming daily more
attached to the scenery here. If you could enjoy it with me it would be genuine happiness.

I have painted a very small picture for Francis a view of the Camden Mts.
and the water from my chamber window. I did it for her birthday and hurried
it up in a day and a half. But it is nonetheless quite a pretty little thing and
gives me courage to think that I might do something worth doing possibly if
I devoted myself to painting. Perhaps kind fortune will sometime permit it.

Come fly away Savannah and go to church with us this morning, we will go across in boat, and have a gravelly stretch of hill to climb on the other side. Emma enjoys the going and coming so much as to be compensated for the slight degree of quiet that she maintains in church.

She makes the acquaintance of everybody that she meets when [illegible], and, I think, is a universal favorite, her most staunch friend and companion is Mrs. Venill who must be past fifty. She takes her little tin pail and goes every day to visit her and bring in the eggs from the hen house. She takes great pleasure, too, in watching the same lady at her spinning and will stay with by the hour. She is quite ambitious to learn to sew and sometimes is permitted to put her hands on the oars while some one else rows which gives her much satisfaction. Children not very much older than she do now, one of the neighbors allowed her two little children one a year younger than Emma and the other a year or two older to go by themselves for their father a short distance away but far enough to prevent of the drowning of the children if they had capsized, and added to this very few can swim and yet it is seldom that any one is drowned here. Last night Nannie recieved [*sic*] a letter from Lucy she is at Olena with Mary waiting for Benj. and his wife who are expected soon. Do not know whether they will be on their way east or not.

I went to the office with Greenleaf yesterday hoping to receive a letter from you, but came home disappointed.

Unless you are in a hurry to see me home you had best write often for I am growing homesick with every disappointment.

Are you flattered or vexed that I miss your letters? We are so far removed from the excitement of the canvas that we feel only an occasional ripple. Yesterday we had a flag raising near here—at the P.O. Hayes and Wheeler flag.[12] I think baby is waking and I must be ready to care for her. I do want to be with you, darling, at the earliest practicable time. Have you any definite idea when that will be and are you the least bit tired of a bachelor life, or is it rather agreeable than otherwise to be quite far from the trouble of wife and baby?

Lucy wrote me some time ago that her physician thought she made great improvement last winter and she wrote in Nannies letter that she is now better than at any time since her illness two years ago. You say you are "hard at work" but that is all. Please give some more definite ideas. Will you canvass the district or will your work be confined to the cities? Is Capt. P.[rince] doing anything for the cause? . . .

---

12 Republican presidential ticket Rutherford B. Hayes and William A. Wheeler.

Do you think that the feeling in the North in regard to the Hamburg massacre will have any tendency to check such murders South?

... what is your church relation, still agreeable and does your political cause affect it?

Love and kisses
Emma

I don't quite understand whether your Savannah nomination to Congress is conclusive. If so, why the Cong. convention at Macon?[13] A politician's wife ought not to be so ignorant, I know.

I have made so much improvement in the painting of Ella V that I began so long ago that I may have to make a good picture of it. shall lay it by now until my return, as I wish [to] do other painting while I am here. I am feeling encouraged in rowing as I can do better than at first. Have been out only four or five times.

North Haven Sep. 1st 1876

My Darling.

Recieved [*sic*] letter from you last night from which I presume that you are now in Wash. or possibly on your homeward way. Hope a little change from Savannah may be beneficial, 'twill, at least, be pleasant if your trip to Washington is successful.

Is Col. Farrow[14] fearful of being disturbed in his position at Aug. or is he seeking something else? I must make my note brief. . . . Perhaps in your more public duties it seems rather incredible that I <u>can</u> be so hurried, but women's duties are largely of that kind that are noticed only in the omission—they look like nothing if they are done but are disgraceful if they are left undone.

I do heartily hope that you may be successful in this coming campaign if it can be but and [*sic*] God's will. Have you any hope of an election?

I am obliged to say one word more about money. If you cannot send me all I need at once please do not fail to send a portion by middle of Sep. that I may

---

[13] Georgia Republicans held two party conventions in a presidential election year.

[14] Henry P. Farrow, Georgia Republican leader; soon to be replaced by Bryant as state party chairman; tenuous ally of JEB's for present; in future will become his fierce opponent.

receive it and get it cashed before the very last because Greenleaf and Nannie expect to move into very small quarters on the 1st. Oct. so that you see my visit here <u>must</u> end at that time and I shall not make any visit at Rockland unless to pass the night. Do not feel like going there at all and may go by way of Camden instead. In either case must go direct to Boston to Lizzie Bonnys and Uncle Eder where I shall plan to remain ten days or fortnight according to circumstances and then go on to Mary Spaulding's, where I must make up my fall wardrobe if do not have means to do it in Portland. So nearly as I can judge I would rather make a long visit there than anywhere else except at Lizzie Bonny's.

I am sorry in this time of strait and anxiety with you that I cannot be situated as I have been when at Margarite's so that I can wait your convenience until very late if absolutely necessary, but you will, of course, perceive how differently situated I shall be, from the time that I leave here last of Sep. I cannot be without money and must not be unable on that account to leave any of the places where I shall visit whenever it seems desirable. None of them will be <u>homes</u>, as brother's now is, and as Gretta's always has been.

I will be as wise and providant [*sic*], darling, as possible, and I hope it does not pain you as much to be called upon for money now as it does me to call. I shall not go to Buckfield and do not intend to visit any where in Maine save in Portland, both time and money (and other considerations also) will forbid. I shall trust to seeing you in our own home last of Oct. Do you think it best to hire a house for the year till after election? It does not seem so to me.

I should not mind boarding or keeping house in a few rooms and doing my own work through Nov. if necessary, any arrangements that may seem wise to you am willing to enter into. If by any possibility there should be a Democratic triumph in Nov. it might be best for us to live very cheaply in the winter and I would try to do so. But if this necessity does not exist I think we had better keep Diana and try to have Emma out of door as much as possible in order to break up her tendency to a cough. . . . God bless and keep you, darling, and speedily reunite us.

> With true Love kisses
> Emma

an enclosure of as little as one or two dollars in your next would relieve me somewhat. If you sent what you promised Aug. 1 it was lost.

Saw a man belonging to your regt. Turner by name—lives here on the island.

Who wrote biographical sketch of J. E. Bryant in Yulee's paper?[15] Would it not be possible for you to hire the house we now have for six months with the probability or possibility of living [there] for the other six?

————

North Haven Oct. 15th /67 [1876]

My Darling

If you could see the ground white with snow, and hear the wind that howls around my room this Sunday night you would think that we are surely engulfed by winter. The fall of snow is [illegible] and will probably leave us to-morrow but it has been a wonder to Emma and she commissions me <u>to tell papa</u> all about it. She has no recollection of snow and I enjoyed her excitement as she watched the fleecy flakes come down.

Have I told you what an absurd and philosophical speech she made to a young lady who had lost a brother some time ago? We were talking with the lady and also telling Emma how many brothers and sisters she had and when she heard that one was dead she said very coolly "I suppose they are glad to get rid of one if they had so many." The cold weather affects her slightly but she seems aside from a very trifling cold in excellent health and I have high hopes with the Father's blessing of taking her home to papa in good condition.

Have recived [sic] yours in reply to mine of Sep. 29. Thanks. I hope to be in Portland one week from to-morrow—ought to have gone a week or two earlier but it has seemed quite impossible. Please inform me as soon as you form any idea as to the date of my return as it will affect the duration of my visit and I wish to be able to inform the friends in Salem and Wash. of my going in season to receive replies from them.

We are feeling exceedingly anxious about the presidential contest since the loss of Indiana. Isn't the contest, to say the least, very doubtful with Hendricks Gov. of Indiana and Tilden of N.Y.[16] I can not imagine what would become of our country in case of a Democratic victory now, when I think of the South and the poor colored race I feel that such a victory would be a more terrible calamity than the war out of which we have just passed.

————

[15] E. Yulee, African American newspaper editor, JEB supporter.
[16] Democratic presidential ticket, governors Samuel J. Tilden and Thomas A. Hendricks.

Have you any reason for any courage in regard to your own election after the imminent Dem. majority in Georgia?

It is late and cold and must retire. During the day on Sunday I feel that I ought to devote myself largely to Emma's entertainment that the day may have pleasant [illegible] to her and so I find little time even to write you. May the dear God keep you, my hubbie.

Bye Darling,
Emma

Washington Nov. 9. 1867 [1876]
Saturday morning

My Darling,

Will give a part of my Sat morn. to you and then must make the very most of the day in sewing as Emma will amuse herself all day with Mrs. Fairchild's little girl who has holiday to-day.

Have done greater part of my sewing but feel in haste to finish what have remaining and am very anxious to get some real benefit from my stay here. I hope to [find] some free place of instruction in [illegible] by which I may profit.

Have been unable even to write you as often as desired because it has taken every moment almost that I had to spare from calls and visits to put baby's and my own wardrobe into respectable condition. I hope you will be pleased with the arrangement for board which I have made, and indeed, I think you will.

I am for the present in one of the more expensive rooms waiting for my own to be made ready. Mrs. Fairchild said it should cost me no more than the other as long as she had no other occupant for it. We have a dem.[ocratic] memb.[er of] cong.[ress] and his wife here, who are very friendly with baby. The gentleman has promised to take her in on the avenue to-day. Wish you could be enjoying her yourself, darling. It is quite too bad that you should miss so much of her childhood. Your thanksgiving letter received this morning from Salem makes me very sorry that you had so dull a thanksgiving. It almost seems that some of our friends in Savannah should have remembered on that day that you were a lone man without a wife. Have the public schools reopened and are the teachers all back. Did you ever think to ask Miss Lowe about a little seamstress bill that she settled for me (it cannot be very much) and the postage on a parcel that she sent me. Please attend to it for such little things ought not to be neglected—tho very likely she may consider herself more than compensated by rent of Same.

I am afraid our dining room matting and stair carpet is much injured, how do they look? The parlor carpet I suppose is still at the store—can you not arrange to have it left there until we need it? I shall be a little afraid of mice if it should be stored elsewhere.

Have you an idea that we will go to Atlanta next summer? I should be delighted to live there on account of climate.

I intend to go to hear Dr. Parker preach soon. Imagine I shall like him very much. Will go to Metropolitan, too.

Shall probably send Emma to S.[unday] S.[school] with Mrs. Fairchild's children. I asked her what message she would send to you when she gave me a <u>shower</u> of kisses which I <u>herewith</u> pass over to you. She is bearing the cold weather much better than I feared. am not as anxious about her here as would be in a more northern climate. I spent part of yesterday with Mr. Ritter. Have not seen Mr Hillyer's people yet. Thursday visited cong.[ress] and heard Sen. Sargent on the Oregon question.[17] It seems the most bare-faced and wicked thing that N.J. and Oregon should pursue just opposite courses in regard to disqualified electors and both fanning the dem.[ocrats] There ought certainly to be the same construction of the law in all the states. I must close at once—Have not been well for some days but hope to feel better when am once situated—think it is partly traveling and loss of sleep. Will try to write very often now. The slip enclosed in your last is a duplicate of one sent before. I can not imagine why Col. A[tkins] should resort to violence. I am anxious to know what response you receive from Sec. Morrill.[18] Please let me be advised as soon as you hear. Do you ever meet Mr. Atkins?

I am so sorry that things should be made so unpleasant for you at Savannah. Do you ever see the Thompsons? If you do see them please remember me affectionately to them and give them my tenderest sympathies. I shall pray daily for your success and for our speedy reuniting—

Emma

---

[17] Senator Aaron Augustus Sargent (R-CA). In the presidential election, November 7, one disputed electoral vote was in Oregon.

[18] Secretary of the Treasury Lot M. Morrill, from Maine; an investigation of the custom house in Savannah was under way.

Have you been obliged to draw your salary through Atkins and have you recieved [*sic*] all due you? I will send the duplicate slip, rec'd today, to Greenleaf and give him a little account, [illegible] he get it all in Georg. Republican.[19]

————

Washington Nov. 10th /67 [1876]
Sabbath Night.

My Darling.

It is the close of my first Sabbath in Washington, at least, the first for many years—do not feel as happy or as settled as I supposed I should when I reached here. Seem to have a troubled and depressed feeling, but presume it will wear away after a little. can not tell what should give one such a feeling unless it is because of the first letter that I wrote you from here. So, if it has either angered or hurt you, you will have the satisfaction of knowing that I have been less happy in speaking out my grievances than I would have been in burying them in darkness and forgetfulness. The enclosed work of art is, as you will probably surmise, one of Emma's production with her printed autograph, the letter being her first attempts. She did it expressly for you but I dont think she intended it for her own picture altho' the name below might imply that.

We are having for past two days extremely cold weather. Have not learned [how] low the thermometer stands but think it is quite exceptionally cold for this locality.

It is so cold that no part of the house has been really comfortable to-day. and for that reason I did not really dare to go to meeting for holiness this P.M. leaving her home without being here to look after her. Our water pipes all froze last night giving Mr. Fairchild several hours work this morning. I went to church to-day at cong.[regational] because I felt lonely and thought it would be pleasant to sit with the Ritter family—Emma went with me. I saw E. B. French there, inquired who he was because he was such a noticeable man in size and bearing. Is he not a relation of your mothers? Clift,[20] I suppose, goes there to church but did not see him.

I propose to go next Sabbath to Dr. Parker's and, perhaps, habitually till you come when I will go to Metropolitan with you.

————

[19] JEB had reconstituted his newspaper, the Augusta *Loyal Georgian,* as the Savannah *Georgia Republican.*

[20] W. L. Clift, Republican officeholder in the treasury department.

A lady who takes meals here was a member of his church when he was pastor at Calvary and has now followed him to E. Street. The S. Schools are in the morning at all the churches so I shall probably take Emma there to S School instead of sending her with the Fairchild children as I at first designed as the churches are too widely seperated [*sic*] for her to attend school at one and church at another. Mrs. Rheat (the lady of whom I spoke) advises me to put her into the S. S. school at Dr. Parker's now to enable her to take part in the Christmas festival which she says is made very entertaining to the little ones. I may do so, as it would add greatly to a Christmas that may otherwise be a little lonely to her, the only objection is taking her out at night but wrapping her head and ears it might not harm her. She often asks if you will be here Christmas and is scarcely content to take no for an answer, and I am quite unreconciled myself to think that you will not be here that I anticipate rather a lonely day myself because you cannot be here.

On Thursday night—(I think it was) guns were fired in honor of victory of Hayes and on the following night, fired in honor of victory of Tilden. Do you not fear serious trouble before the matter is finally settled?

Do you hear from your mother and Lucy? I have heard from neither in a long time will try to write them soon as practicable. Is it true that Morrie's things were all stolen during the flu epidemic in Savannah? I hope not, for they are ill able to lose them. I heard it from Mrs. Osgood in Boston. Please remember me to them if they are in Savannah. Do you know if they have or anticipate an addition to the family? Is there any fun at all in the city and do you keep well yourself? Please write a line or two every day if possible for if do not hear shall be anxious lest you are sick. Have you resumed your duties at custom House and what report did you receive from Sec. Morrill?

> I must retire at once or fall asleep on my writing—
> Lovingly—
> Emma

————

Washington Dec. 13th /67 [1876]

My Darling

This has been a good day for it began with the bright sunlight and these letters . . . an answer to my five letters from here. The words of explanation tear away "the veil" and make all things right and had they come weeks ago that letter of mine would never have been written.

I cannot make much reply to night as I wished for it ruins my eyes to write by gas without a drop. Mr. Fairchild has promised me a lamp. About money I have written you how much per month our board will be 45, and washing about 5, which later will perhaps be wanted by week, surely by month and I expect the board likewise.

I expect you will have sent me a small sum upon receipt of this, but I shall not replenish my wardrobe until Greenleaf is entirely repaid—it would not be right or honest. I know that he loaned me the money at some inconvenience to himself that he expected it the first of Dec. Nobody could have been kinder to me than he has been and I am anxious that he should be repaid soon as possible.

After that, I shall have a good dress, if I can, costing not more than 25.

I trust that you may be successful as you expect and shall enjoy anything that I can do to help you. Called at Mr. Hillyer's for first time to-day. they seemed very glad to see me and we had some talk of Gov.[ernment] matters. He seemed to think that Col. Atkins had injured himself here by his course— says the party here strongly condemns the bolting of regular party nominations, such as yours was.[21] Would you think it well for me to call on Mrs. Sen. Edmunds[22] (in that problematic future where my wardrobe is rejuvenated?) Receiv'd letter from Lilly to-day saying that she wishes me to call on her friends the Kings of Maryland Sem. (and that she will write them a note introducing me), also that she will write Mrs. Sherman wife of Spk. Blaine's[23] Sec. asking her to call on me. . . . one of Dr. Parker's members boards here, she mentioned me to him and he called on me yesterday but I was unfortunately out. She offered to go with me in [the] evening to return call, and I think I will go. . . .

Mr. Ritter offered to take me into his office and introduce me. I have promised to visit Treasury building some day with Mrs. Fairchild's oldest daughter who expressed desire to go with me there. If I should do so would it be proper or desirable for me to accept Mr. Ritter's offer of introduction to Mr. French? I do not care to do it unless you desire it. Took Emma to the Capitol to-day, also to the Lincoln monument. She has fine opportunities for a child but is scarcely old enough to be advantaged by them. I want to begin a little painting to-morrow if possible. Have planned so much to do

---

[21] James Atkins had joined in the opposition that derailed JEB's candidacy for the House of Representatives.

[22] George Franklin Edmunds, Republican senator from Vermont, 1866–91.

[23] Senator James G. Blaine (R-Me.), former Speaker of the House of Representatives.

that expect the weeks of our seperation [*sic*] will fly, while if I was idly waiting they would drag intolerably. I feel that in no way, perhaps, can I really help you more, than in making good use of these advantages that are now offered me. . . . Mr. Sen. S. Fisher of whom you spoke I think I have never met, who is he. Give me some idea, if you expect me to meet him, please— for it is embarrassing to meet people whom you are expected to know and do not. In regard to calling on Mrs. Edmunds, if her husband is friendly to you I feel quite in favor of it, because she impressed me as a genuine lady, both cultured and sensible and somewhat of an artist I think. . . . I met the elder Mr. Ritter at the capitol to-day. The younger Mr. Ritter I feel quite sure as can count upon as our friend and I presume, the older one, only, I know him less—

> A lovey good night to my darling husband—
> Emma

. . . In rereading your letter I see that you feel that I "distrust" you. Please do not mistake the point of my first letter. It is <u>only this</u>—that you promised and failed to even refer to your promises afterward—that is what puzzled and hurt me—and you sent me not a penny when I wrote you sometimes that so little as a dollar or two would be a relief. Is there any mistake? Have you sent me a penny since I left you in June, or did you fail to receive my letters, or did you write and make an apology, which I never rec'd? some super mistake may have occurred, in which case I humbly beg you pardon—and in any case it is all right now, and we will wipe out every little mark and begin fresh in love and trust, God helping us. The reference to your having sent me nothing at all is that if you have done so, or if you have failed to receive my letters telling my need you may be able to tell me so. I do not refer to it because I am not satisfied and happy in you now. I accept your letter as full explanation and know no trace, even so thin between us now. I only wish that you should see the facts so clearly as to [not] judge me unjustly.

. . . I have referred to the money matter again only in answer to your fear that I was losing confidence in you, I wish to try to make it plain to you how it looked to me and why I was so hurt. It was that when you were unable to keep your promises you did not refer to it by a word of explanation or so much as say "I am sorry" those three words or the slightest explanation would have saved all injured feeling on my part. Please look at it in this light and tell me if you wonder at my feeling.

Washington Dec. 18th [1876]
Monday Night

My Darling

Have just returned from passing the day (or most of it) at Mr. Hillyer's. I received long letter from you this morning and must reply to the money part of it at once as the end of the month is so near. I am much troubled lest you may be unable to send the board money promptly on the last of this month because Mr. Fairchild is peculiarly straitened for money. You seem to suppose very sincerely in the idea that sister Fairchild will take good care of me without realizing that she must have money to enable her to do so. They have rented only part of their rooms and are so much straitened for money that Mr. Fairchild asked me if I thought you could loan him 100, saying he had never before been in such dark and straitened circumstances. I of course told him that you could not and only mention it to show you how dependent they are upon the money due them. He told me that he was depending upon my board bill with others in the house to pay his rent bill first of Jan, my board including washing will be 50. board 45. washing about 5.00, perhaps a dollar less. Shall make washings as small as can and my board bill is small as it can be unless I went into the attic.

I cannot with propriety visit among my friends (as you suggest) now. Mr. Hillyer's people had a room prepared and expected me there but as I came here first they do not now expect me and have removed the furniture from the spare room now into an upper room that they propose to let. They have a spare room on the first floor next to their own which they talk of refurnishing. I have had a thought that if they do refurnish it, it is possible that they might board me a little cheaper than Mrs. Fairchild can, but I have not mentioned it, thinking it might perhaps be no cheaper or that you might not wish me to leave Mrs. Fairchild. If they would board me and board me cheaper than I could board here would you think it best and would you like it when you came? I should not wish to move there if I must move back here when you came. This is a much more central place and on that account better. I had thought of moving only to save something on board. I hope you have written Greenleaf, explaining the reason of your delay in paying him.

Am very glad that the money is sent to Mr. Clapp. I do not think it will be best for you to attempt to make me any christmas gift, some little thing, if only a picture book sent to baby from papa would make her happy.

One of "Aunt Louisa's Series" Robinson Crusoe if you can find it would please her. I think it would have been better in view of your peculiar money stress had I gone direct to Mr. Hillyer's and remained there if they would board me. Mr. Hillyer seems a warm friend of yours. I am invited to attend an [illegible] reception to-morrow night with Henry Hillyer and Mrs. Virgil H—shall go if I can put myself into respectable array for it to-morrow. Must not write more for this gas light ruins my eyes and gives me headache.

I do heartily, earnestly wish you were here—I am lonely and uneasy without you—

I have a mind to be vexed with your somewhat patronizing cautions, as I have not the remotest idea of going out anywhere with any other than old friends of yours or mine nor the least opportunity to do it if I so desired.

If you know how many anxious and sober thoughts I have now-a-days I do not think you would especially fear my doing anything of a <u>frisky nature</u>—but enough of this, I love you husband mine and shall thank God, fervently, I believe when our lives are once more united.

> God keep and sustain you, darling,
> in your many anxieties and trials.
> Emma

Dr. Parker is the one whom you knew in Geo. [rgia] and I will try to enclose his address in this letter.

I heard him preach an excellent sermon sabbath morning on the text "to him that hath shall be given" showing the cumulative nature of all things good and bad, and claiming that we may accomplish almost anything <u>if we will</u>.

I must close with a bright thing of Emma's—she was talking with Mrs. F. about your coming. Mrs. F. told her you might want to see her so much that you couldn't stay away and that you must come sooner than you said, and then told how that you came unexpectedly last time, she turned on Mrs. F and says, "Did papa want to see <u>you</u> so much he couldn't stay away?"

———

Washington Dec. 29th /67 [1876]

My Darling.

Rec'd letter from you this morning written day after Christmas I think. Am so sorry that you did not have a merrie Christmas but I trust that another Christmas season will find you with baby wife and home. I am very glad to know that your trust in God is So Strong and I want to talk with you somewhat more than I have ever done in the past of my own religious life, trust in a few weeks to see you here. the time of our seperation [*sic*] will soon be past, God willing. I write you this morning especially at Mr. Fairchild's request. He is trying very hard to be reinstated, I judge in his old place, at any rate he asks you to send him a letter addressed to Sec. Chandler[24] endorsing him just as strongly as you can. If he is qualified for the place I really hope he may obtain it, for he is very needy. his health poor and was a wounded union soldier which ought not to go for naught.

As he is in haste to end this I will write little more this morning. About change of boarding place I have already written you my own views. I rec'd a letter from Margaretta this morning in which she says would spend a few weeks here with me could she afford it. Should love to see her so much and if we were so situated that it was possible for us to pay her board should urge her to come. She urges me to visit them next summer but I am hoping that a kind providence will permit baby and self to pass next summer with you, though I hope it may be in upper part of Georgia rather than Savannah.

I must close this and hope that it will reach you before you leave for Fla. I shall be delighted to know that you have the titles to the land. When you do please make out the proper legal instrument to secure Greenleaf the the [*sic*] 100 borrowed as it is only just and right that he should be secured therefore.

I have written Lucy and I think she ought not to scold for I put letter in office for her last summer on the very day in which I rec'd her last, and mother has owed me a letter for a year or thereabout and the same is true of Mary. We are having a real winter here, quite unusual for Wash. they tell me. Bye-bye

Emma

Savannah Apr. 15 77
Beach Ins—
Sunday Night

My Darling Hubbie,

In several days I have had no letter from you but I try to attribute it to a delay in mails (not male) and I have been remiss myself in writing because of hurry in my work and now this evening I have defrauded through talking

---

[24] William E. Chandler, chairman of the Republican National Committee; assistant secretary of the treasury.

with Miss Lowe and Mr. Markham. You who love so well to talk yourself on matters in which you feel an interest will probably pardon me, tho' I do look very regretfully at the clock hands which so plainly say bed-time. Mr. Harley had to spoil a good sermon to-day by saying something against our Maine prohibition law[25]—he overtook Emma and self on way home and we had a little talk about it. He needs converting badly and I have faith to believe it will come in the Lord's own good time—he is too good a man to go all his life in the dark. I am hoping, darling, that you will turn your face homewards ere many weeks, perhaps before many days. Emma and I are feeling as if we have been long alone.

She told me to tell papa "if she had a thousand dollars she would give it to see him" I fear her ideas of numbers are rather vague but indeed it would warm our hearts and send our blood tingling through our veins to see you again.

I <u>must, must,</u> [double underline] <u>must</u> [triple underline] to bed—I wish it was to be with you. Now, if that is a disgraceful confession just burn the letter, for I shouldn't like it to be read out before a jury ten years hence.

God bless you, darling. The dear Lord keep you
Lovingly—
Emma

---

[25] In Maine, a 1846 state law prohibited the manufacture or sale of intoxicating beverages.

LETTERS: 1878–1879

As President Hayes presided over the end of Reconstruction, Republicans in Washington sought to bring party structure in line with the new mantra of conciliation. Ignoring the sage advice of seasoned carpetbaggers like JEB, Hayes issued crippling directives that decimated the remaining Republican organization in the South. Faced with leading a state party divided by irreconcilable ideologies and wildly divergent goals, Bryant escaped the local tensions by focusing on his own sputtering career.[1]

Away from Georgia for extended periods, Bryant traveled in the North, shuttling between Washington, New York, Philadelphia, and Providence. His letters began to spin the outline for a new phase of his great crusade to transform the South. Was he a charlatan? a dreamer? a Don Quixote? Or, did he merely seek to avoid drowning in the disillusionment of a failed reformer? It was, in his words, his "last desperate crisis."

Not alone among disheartened erstwhile abolitionists and carpetbaggers, Bryant wandered the lecture circuit seeking a platform and a new strategy for "the Southern question." Fortunately for him, camaraderie among members of the New York Union League eased his plight. While working under the auspices of the Atlanta Republican Publishing Company, his attempts to find "subscribers" afforded hope that his newspaper could be sustained.

Emma, in the role of faithful wife but proceeding with her own character development and independence, pondered as well what the future would hold for them. Left with John's faithful assistant, Volney Spalding (probably her cousin), Emma assisted with the publication of *The Georgia Republican* in Atlanta, acting for a time as John's corresponding secretary. In his letters, her husband raised the expectations of his struggling minions, but John's encouraging words resulted in little monetary support. In July 1879, Spalding's last ominous but unanswered pleas for assistance finally sounded the death knell: "The Paper is suspended." With the finality of that pronouncement, and when it became apparent that John's absence would continue indefinitely, Emma left Atlanta. Taking Alice

---

[1] See *Carpetbagger of Conscience*, 143–50, for details of JEB's career in the years 1878–79.

with her, she traveled again to Earlville, Illinois, beginning what became an extended visit with her aging father and her sister's family.

Many years later, in her autobiography, Alice explained how the woman called "the Countess" began to play a role in the family narrative during this time.

———

Atlanta June 11th /78
Tuesday Morn—

My Darling.

I am writing . . . from Mrs. Eiswald's. I came down last evening to attend . . . teacher's meeting ([illegible]) and . . . came here to pass night— her husband being away so that she like myself is a poor widow. Have had a pleasant visit only that we prolonged our visiting so late into the night that my head feels the worse for it this morning. . . . I am sorry and glad that you have felt the infrequency of my letters, sorry that I could not write oftener and glad that you missed them and wanted them. You say truly we are grown careless and I am quite sure as can reform if both try.

I have thought that if we should substitute in our olden daily [writing and] sending of a letter each to the other . . . perhaps three times per week we would find it very pleasant and more satisfactory than the sending and receiving of letters that are so very brief as yours sometimes are, tho' the few words are often precious words, telling me of your love and trust, and with more than a long letter would be without them. I would still like something additional, something that would bring me more into sympathy with your life day by day.

I am hoping that this absence will soon be terminated and we have you once more with us. Emma often wishes for you and talks of you. I am trying to make the best use of my loneliness. . . . I am not sure whether I have written since Mrs. Sherman's little dinner party last week, (Thurs.) Mrs. Eiswald & Eggleston, Miss Coffin Dr. Fuller and Mr. & Mrs. Jones. It was a pleasant occasion and I regretted that you were not with us. Dr. Fuller and other friends enquire especially after you. . . .

I started on a little mission instead with Mr. Bisbee[2] but was prevented by heavy showers and reached home quite drenched, but comforted myself with

---

[2] R. E. Bisbee, president of Clark University in Atlanta. Clark, established by the Methodist Episcopal Church, was tuition free.

the thought of the great good to the vegetable world as the soil was parched and thirsty. I shall go to the [Georgia] Rep.[ublican] office this morning hoping for another letter from you. I hope that your success will be literal and in hand very soon.

You have already been away three weeks, but I know that you will relieve me from embarrassment soon as possible and consequently keep good courage. Am glad to see the Rep. enlarged. . . .

Lovingly Emma

————

Home June 15th /78

My Darling.

A letter from you last night was very welcome and during the evening I felt hungry for your love.

You must not think that the frequency of my letters is gauged by the warmth of my love. There have been circumstances quite beyond my control to prevent me from writing, and now this morning I must write very briefly to send by Belle for the sun is shining out after two days of rain and I think that Mrs. Bisbee will come and spend the day with me.

Have all my morning's work to do and the morning is now [illegible] spent.

I intended to write you last night and more in the mood of writing than now with all other little [illegible] called down stairs to see company and thus prevented. I feel anxious about the paper but trust that they may have received remittance from you by to-day.

The paper is certainly much improved in appearance and I trust is marching on to success.

Please give my love to our friends in Washington the French's, Dr. Robinson & wife, Clifts, Ritters not forgetting the Fairchilds—should like so much to see them. Remember me also to Mrs. Fuller the Rep.'s wife if she is with him at the boarding house. You say nothing of returning—can you form no idea as yet as to when you will return? I am anxious to know the details of your reception and success but will wait for them till your return as the writing of such things is so unsatisfactory. I do not dare spend more time now lest I may present an unfavorable appearance on Mrs. Bisbees [illegible] if she does come.

May the dear Lord keep you and bring you soon and safe to loving wife and baby—

little Emma is busying herself with printing on slate this morning.

Lovingly
Emma

I rec'd letter containing 1.00 night before last.

———

Washington D.C.
June 19th, 1878

My Darling:

I have not done what I intended and you requested: write some every day. The truth is I am passing through a <u>very</u> important crisis and while I do not forget my wife and little girl I work up to my strength and do not take time to write. I do love you very much and shall have very much to tell you when I return. I am growing in faith and I think spiritually, and gaining I think otherwise.

I send you enclosed two $2 dollar[s]. Please acknowledge the receipt in your next. I hope and expect to send more tomorrow. I realize that I am neglecting you but hope to come to your aid in a day or to [*sic*] and not to leave you in such a fix again. I do feel that I am now passing through the last desperate crisis; but of course may be mistaken God knows what is best. Pray for me my darling. I am doing the best I can.

With warmest love and kisses
Y. H.

———

Atlanta June 20 /78

My Darling.

Belle and Emma and I are just going down town and I had hoped for a quiet half hour to write you before Emma woke but one duty crowding upon another has engrossed the time until now it is near time to start.

I had just a line from you day before yesterday hope to hear again to-day. . . . I have not been able even to go to town and have learned nothing save what I have gotten from Mr. S. through Mrs. Sherman. If possible shall go into the Rep. office this morning and read your letter to Mr. Spaulding. The paper presents a very nice appearance now and I hope and trust that you will be able to sustain it.

I am very anxious to know whether you have any plan in regard to coming home. I have written sister nothing in regard to going West preferring not to do so until I learned whether she had fully decided not to go East. I received a letter from her this week urging me to come to Earl whenever I can and asking if I cannot go this summer. She feels that there will not be many opportunities for me to visit with father—he has just passed his 76th birthday. I cannot bear to think of father's growing old. Gretta's health is poor and she has given up going east in order to go to Quincy Ill. for a time and put herself under the care of Dr. Annie Norton (the same who treated me). Neilly will be left at home and she seems to feel very anxious about him, as indeed I should at his age and surrounded by many bad boys. I suppose she is [*sic*] will go very soon if at all—do not know how long she proposes to remain. I replied to her that my going would depend largely upon whether you would be much away this summer and the placing in the market of excursion tickets. Belle is ready.

> By [*sic*] darling. I love you and want
> to be with you very, very much
> Emma

Friday P.M. I went yesterday—no day before—as I told you, to town with Belle read your long letter to Mr. Spaulding and brought this back with me designing to add more but providence had not smiled on my desires. To-day I have passed pleasantly with Mrs. Bisbee at least since morn.—

. . . I made enquiries regarding your old summer suit and find it can be colored for about 2.75 and they say it will not shrink. If I hear nothing to the contrary from you I think I will leave it to be done. I have not time to write more now as it is approaching night and I must wend my [way] home before dark.

> By darling.
> Emma

> Atlanta June 26 1878
> Wednesday 9. P.M.

My Darling Husband:

It is a warm, sultry night much like its predecessor of fourteen years ago in far away Maine.

How I would love to see to-night (next to you) some of the dear ones we then had near us—My darling mother first and best of all. I almost always associate our marriage with her because her days were so few and feeble after it. You dont know, darling, how my heart cries out after her sometimes. Isnt it a blessed a rapturous thought that we can look forward to an eternity of communion with dear ones gone before and in the presence of God as I firmly believe my mother is. Until recently I did cling to the hope that you would reach home in time to spend this day with me—now I have quite given up planning when you will be home. can only rest myself in the thought of God's care for you and us and the hope of the ultimate benefit to accrue from your trip.

To-day, failing to bring Emma to me by the ringing of the bell, I went to the stable in search of her. . . . I discovered her lying on the [carriage] seat fast asleep her dollies neck ribbon still in her hand and dollie drawn up close to her. This evening she had a treat in going in the wagon to the field after grain and riding back on the load.

. . . Mr. Sherman has been assigned to Jonesboro and is gone all the week coming home only Saturday nights. It seemed very strange for a night or two to have no masculine in the house but we are quite accustomed to it now, cant say I like it though—men are useful creatures. I have always been of that opinion. I shall expect on Sat. or before to receive letter from you written to-day.

Fourteen years ago we looked forward to a very different position from that we are now occupying and would I fear have shrunk from the cramped position in which we have latterly been, but God only knows whether the attainment of our old dreams and aspirations and the absence of these crosses that we have had would have been better for us—perhaps even our blunders and mistakes may be in some way blessed to us—I like to think so, at least. If our faces are set towards the truth, if we long after the beauties of right and true living shall not our ideals be reached in the long years of eternity?

I like to think that you have thoughts especially of wife and baby to-day. . . . I trust that the dear Lord will bring you home . . . keep you . . . and bind us every year in closer and in each others lives, more sympathy for each others needs and more joy in our mutual companionship.

> With loving good-night kisses
> Bye-bye—Emma . . . .

Boston Mass—23 Pinkney St.
June 28th, 1878

My Darling:

I am missing you more and more every day. I feel that it is not well for us to be so much from each other; and I do trust that God may open the way for us to be more together. I <u>think He will</u>. I am stopping with very pleasant people, recommended by Sister Fairchild, and, with a letter of introduction from her, I was taken in—in the good sense—as an old friend. This is pleasant. Please do not make any plans to leave until my plans develop a little more. A few days will probably tell whether I shall be with you most of the summer, or be absent, and then we will decide what to do about going West. Please read my letters to Col. Spalding for business and let me write you family and love letters. I do love you darling very tenderly and warmly; and as I am prospered and the future looks brighter it seems that my love is somehow made more kinder. I can hardly explain or tell why; perhaps it is because the strain upon us is being removed, and I am more my natural self. God is very good to me but I feel how unworthy I am, and how far I fall short of doing my whole duty.

With warmest love and kisses for you and Emma
Y. H.

I have sent you six dollars since I left—two dollars three times. I have only heard from you in regard to the first two dollars sent. Six dollars sent in one month! Tis too bad but I hope to send more in a few days tomorrow [illegible].

———

Home
July 1st, 1878

My Darling Husband:

I have just rec'd yours of 28th from Boston and give it a warm welcome. Am afraid I like love letters as well as I did when I was eighteen and if you stay much longer away shall feel almost as I used when you came home after a years absence in the army.

I am growing hungry for your home coming and trust it may not be long delayed.

Susan is here with me to-night and I took a hurried trip to town quite late in order to send your address to Capt. Prince who leaves for the North in a day or two so that am a good deal fatigued and in need of rest.

Must give you good night kiss and trust to finishing this in the morning.

I received your three letters enclosing money but think you were a little mistaken in amt. Think the first contained only one. The last came exceedingly pat, just in season to relieve especial embarrassment. My faith is usually strong even when the clouds are lowering. I do not know that I have ever seen them darker pecuniarily than in last few weeks but we have been carried through thus far and I trust will be. Have been much distressed at last weeks suspension of paper.

Tuesday morn—Have but a minute before Mrs. Sherman leaves. Have been out to pick berries for breakfast while Emma and Sue still slept, returned basket and now have to get breakfast. I shall do nothing towards going West save to hurry up my sewing and would be obliged to do that whether go or remain. Were it not for father I would choose to remain here, I think, and [illegible] home will be well content in any case.

I do hope you will be prospered and blessed. God keep you darling. I love you and desire you in my heart of hearts.

> Emma is still sleeping. Susan sends love.
> Bye, darling
> Emma

Am extremely glad you have so pleasant boarding place

> [letterhead] Office of
> The Atlanta Republican Publishing Company[3]
> S. S. Ashley, President; V. Spalding, Secretary;
> J. Sherman, Treasurer; J. E. Bryant, Business Manager
> Atlanta, Ga., July 11th 1878

> Col J E Bryant
> Boston, Mass.

Dear Sir

Your telegram saying you have sent by express on the 9th last twenty dollars received yesterday morning. I tried to get Dickson to rec've off on paper

---

[3] Variously called Atlanta Publishing Company or Atlanta Republican Publishing Company, depending on JEB's constituents at the time.

this week by promising him twenty dollars, but he would not do it. So we are obliged to stand still this week. I got Bishop Haven[4] to endorse my note as 15 days for fifty dollars to pay in tomorrow, which note falls due on Saturday. He leaves today, and wants the note taken up before he leaves. I have therefore borrowed to pay it, half to be returned Saturday, the other half on demand. I shall be obliged to use the twenty dollars to help me out this week, unless I find the money in some other way. It is growing monotonous, and were it not for raising money to pay borrowed, I should be idle, but that keeps me busy. I do hope you will complete your arrangements soon, and that they will include material for printing our paper. We are paying Dickson for his type every three months, or four at fartherest [sic]. Then I am provoked that he will not get out our paper this week and take the small chance for balance of cost of this issue. I am not finding fault at the tarttiness [sic] of realizing money. I can fully sympathize with you in your efforts, and the obstacles you have to overcome, and know your whole energies are devoted to the work of raising the means to sustain the Ga. Rep. and that you will succeed I have no misgivings, my only fear is, that your sanguine temperament may not withstand the delay you are subject to. Persistence will win—Be not discouraged at rebuffs, but "Stick."

Yours, truly
V. Spalding

P.S. The Bishop had a party at my house last night of some 40 invited guests amongst whom were Mrs J E Bryant and her friend Miss Hosmer of Augusta for whom the Bishop sent a carriage, you being absent, and consequently unable to render such service. All passed off pleasantly, and the Bishop was greatly elated with the success of the gathering to do him honor.

S.

The Bishop leaves this afternoon for Boston, will stop day or two in N.Y. will be home the forpart [sic] of next week

---

[4] Gilbert Haven, bishop in the Methodist Episcopal Church; supervised the work of the Northern church in the lower and middle South; instrumental in purchasing land for Clark University; advocated integrated schools.

Home July 26th 1878

My Darling,

Have just recieved [*sic*] yours of 22<u>d</u> enclosing 2.00—As I mentioned in previous letter the 5.00 & 10.00 have been rec'd the latter will be appropriated to the payment of Mr. P. on his return unless I should learn that you have already settled it, if you should do so be sure to inform me. You are not necessitated to do it, however, as I can send it myself and not be straitened if you are to return soon, as I hope—shall be much disappointed if do not see you next week.

I have settled all bills here so that there will be no debts on your return save house rent. I fear that after more than two months of wearying and disappointing work you are coming home to very hard work here—having failed of raising what you expected [illegible] I fear will [illegible] great difficulty in rallying the party here. In all your struggles since you came to Georgia I think I am most anxious for success in this, most distressed at thought of failure. I have been haunted by a miserable fear for last two days that [what] I said earnestly in my letter written at the office worried or offended you, but in my heart of hearts I was never truer to you than to-day—never more steadfast in my love, but I am realizing more and more that, even could your family subsist on expectation and prospects, you yourself cannot be using up your energies at the lavish rate of the past few years with no material and pecuniary return—that the time is fast approaching when there must be some element of certainty in our affairs and this has worn upon me with a fright that those only know who watch and wait, and see their husbands slipping under burdens which they cannot help to save, this inability to be a help [to] earn as well as a help [to] save him depressed me and rendered me miserable many times. I can not tell you how hard it has borne upon me in the past few years. So remember, please, that my strictures upon the present management of the paper are born of my extreme desire for its success and my conviction of the surpassing difficulties of the undertaking. I am extremely glad of your brief recreation with the Bishop only that I wish it could have been much longer. Our weather here has been depressing and I have not felt quite well much of the time. I enclose a postal which I rec'd to-day from sister, not knowing what else to answer I have just replied to it that I shall not go.

Yesterday Susan and self with Emma called at Dr. Swign's and Col. Buck's.⁵ Shall try to call upon a few other friends with her before she leaves

---

⁵ Alfred E. Buck, Republican Party official in Georgia, native of Maine.

if weather permits. I find Dr. Fuller's people among the warmest and pleasantest of our friends.

Emma says give papa her love and tell him she wants him to come
home.

Allow me to suggest that instead of bringing presents to her (aside from
candy or some such trifle) you give her the money you would have spent to
add to her savings to be put in savings bank. I do not know but you will think
I am growing shockingly mercenary, but, truly, I dont love money for money's
self any better than of old, but I am anxious to save up for her a little sum that
shall be growing while she grows and be perhaps of great advantage to her
when she is grown.

I must not spend more time. God keep you darling and bring you to
waiting wife and baby very, very soon. I may not write you again before
your return.

I did not send the suit to be colored as I wrote I should, for have felt that
you would be obliged to buy something in its place while away.

> Bye darling. Loving kisses
> Emma

———

> Boston 23 Pinkney St
> July 27th, 1878

My Darling:

I have not heard from you for several days, but hope to get a letter this
morning—The letter has come, that of the 23 acknowledging receipt of five
and ten dollars. I send in this a money order for twenty dollars in your own
name. This will put you out of want I trust. As soon as this is received take
time please to write me here telling me just how this money leaves you, and if
it pays all debts with what has been received how much you have left. Please
do not fail. I do not expect to remain here long enough to receive it, and may
before this is received by you telegraph Col. Spalding to direct my letters to
New York. I shall go there for a few days and then home. I am nearly through
here now; shall probably finish Monday; but I have considerable writing to
attend to and think I will do that here. As soon as letters are answered and
other writing done I shall go to New York.

My letters to Col. Spalding will give you the particulars of my success, and the reason why it is not best to start the paper just now. I have at length gained success. This I will <u>show</u> from time to time.

I love you darling you have been so true to me in all my struggle. May God keep us many years to be happy together. I do not think best to start the paper until September for reasons given in my letter to Col. Spalding, but if my life and health are spared we will start then, and continue with God's blessing.

With warmest kisses
Y. H.

Before you send your letter in answer to this see Col. Spalding and if he has not a telegram to the contrary send here if he has send as directed in that. I sent you two dollars a few days since was it received?

Y. H.

———

Boston 23 Pinkney St
Aug 8 /1878

My Darling:

I hoped to have had a letter from you this morning, but none came. Two came from Col. Spalding with the Georgia Republican out again. I am glad to see it, even if it is but a half-sheet. You have often expressed a desire to do something to aid me. I am glad to say that you have already done very much, but I have concluded that perhaps you can act as you [are my] "confidential private secretary." I must have one, and I do not know how I can do better. When I return we will talk the matter over.

I leave for New York tonight, and shall, unless something entirely unforseen prevents, return home next week. I long to be with you again.

I send enclosed some tin foil taken from a Phonograph. When I return I will explain the matter to you.

With warmest love and kisses.
Y. H.

Astor House New York
Aug. 10th, 1878

My Darling:

I reached this city yesterday, and came temporarily to this house, I go Monday to a private house—No. 28, 11th St. West; near where we boarded when we were here before.

I shall, unless something entirely unforseen prevents, leave for home next week; reaching Atlanta the last of the week, so that I shall, undoubtedly be with you Sunday after next (tomorrow). I can not express the strength of my desire to be with you again. I shall arrange to be as little from you in the future as possible. Let us pray to God that he will open the way for us to be together most of the time. I feel as I have before written that I am now settled down to my life work—As a means of obtaining a living Journalism and lecturing; the latter not for the present and not until I am fully prepared. I have <u>settled</u> the question practically since I came North that with life and health and Gods blessing we can carry the paper through, making a good living for us, and saving some money to pay debts. The crisis was from the time I left Atlanta until I got fairly started in Boston. The paper is to be supported as a business enterprise by subscriptions & advertisements, the subscriptions are to be single ones, and a number taken by one person for free circulation. With the blessing of God I am sure to get enough North for free circulation to meet all deficiency. My work is therefore marked out—a legitimate business for life; one that gives full scope for the display of whatever talents God has given me. The work marked out is what the education of my life has best fitted me for, and as I have before written what I feel God has called me to do.

As I said in my last letter, I think I shall need someone to answer my letters and attend to my mail; and I have thought that perhaps you could do that; this making the work lighter for you, and more profitable for me. Of course we will not attempt to make any change until it is prudent to do so when all house work will be taken from you, and then only unless you fully approve the arrangement, after we have talked matters over.

As near as I can now plan my movements, I shall leave for home next week; and after attending to some necessary business connected with calling a meeting of the State committee and with the paper, I shall return here and remain until the time for the meeting of the State committee. I cannot well say what my movements will be after that.

I want and need the love of my wife very much, and when I return shall feel like having a real lovers meeting. I do not lose my desire for your love, as I grow older. Do not fail to have your full say in regard to business matters. If we do not always agree we shall not most certainly quarrel, if we talk and write to each other in real love. May God keep us and continue our love to the end.

With warmest love and kisses for you and Emma
Y. H.

If you write immediately on receipt of this I shall probably get the letter. Direct care American Missionary Association No. 56 Beade St.

———

[printed slip with date and names written in]
Union League Club[6]
New York <u>Sept 25 1878</u>

The House Committee has the honor of informing
<u>Col. J. E. Bryant</u> that at the request of
<u>Col. Drake DeKay</u> his name has been placed
on the list of visitors admitted to the privileges
of the Club for two weeks.
<u>S T Stanton</u>
House Committee

———

At the Office Sep. 26th /78

My Darling Husband.

I was taken greatly by surprise just now on my way to the office. W. L. Clark[7] met me, gave me a cordial grasp of the hand and, after a little preliminary said his wife wished to see me, that he had just learned that I was at Clark University and that she would call there to see me—also said that his

———

[6] During the Civil War, the Union League provided a vehicle of support for President Lincoln and the entire war effort. After the war, the Union League Club allowed for continued political discussion of Republican principles and strategy in a city club atmosphere.

[7] Editor of *Atlanta Republican*. For a time JEB sought to consolidate their publishing efforts; Clark charged that Bryant was attempting to steal his paper, and the *Georgia Republican* continued separately.

sister Abbie wished to see me and that she and perhaps Miss Ashley would be in his office in about half an hour and requested me to step in to see them. I told him I should be very glad to see his wife, as indeed I would and in regard to the interview with Miss Abbie I requested him to ask her to call on me in your private room here. Had it been his wife I would have gone to her most willingly, but remembering the bitter feeling which Abby [*sic*] is said to have to you I felt that I would prefer to meet her on my own ground.

She may not come, but, in any case, I can only ask to be guided by the Holy spirit that I may say and feel aright. I hope that it is an indication of a better disposition on the part of Mr. Clark and yet I fear by the putting forward of Abby as spokesman that it may be only an attempt to gain some advantage in your absence.

To-day's mail brings a letter from Porter evidently in reply to a proposal for Porter to come into the newspaper—he says if obliged to answer at once it must be <u>no</u> but if your affairs do not require an immediate answer he shall very gladly leave it open for future decision. It is a good letter and most friendly in tone. I think he feels drawn to come here but almost fears to do so financially. I had a mind to write him a few lines myself but concluded it was unnecessary.

Did you receive my letter directed to Mr. F's Washington? I judge by your going to N.Y. that your stay will be prolonged beyond the ten days. Since beginning this I have rec'd yours from Wash. Will read the portion of letter on business to Mr. S. when he comes in.

To-days mail also brings notice of notes against you due Oct 2, & 9, in Merchants and Citizens' Banks—for 50. each. I suppose however that you provided for this before you left or will do so before time expires. Emma keeps well and enjoys her new question—is greatly fascinated with the school and spends hours quietly watching—as they are only known times of quiet aside from her sleep that she has ever had it is quite a marvel to me. I don't like to say anything against your private office but I think it is the nearest to a railroad car in motion of anything professedly stationary that I ever knew.

If Abby does not soon make her appearance I shall return home. I cannot quite make up a mind to call on her—scarcely think it is best for me to do so. Porter writes that a revival is in progress at Wesley church. I am trying to review my letter a little now and with my coming here and my sewing am very busy, have promised to help Mrs. Bisbee with her sewing next week which makes me more than ever hurried.

Have heard nothing of the people that were to occupy our rooms and I reason that they did not decide to take them. Mrs. S's mother sent her draft for traveling expenses since you left. Do not know whether she designs to go North but judge not.

I hope that you may be so blessed as to be soon with us. If you are detained very long do not forget that we are liable for rent of our rooms there until we make a decision. Would it be useful to make any effort to look for rent?

God bless and keep you darling.
Emma

Emma sends love. Abbie has not been in and I am going home now. Mr S. says you did not mention those notes to him but I trust you will be able to meet them in good season. Col S. says his wife is pressing him for money and Dickson threatens to suspend if he doesn't have money at once—it seems to me Dickson is hardly fair not to give you any time.

––––––––

At the Office Sep. 27 /78

My Darling.

I have not really time to write a word to-day for have sent Emma out with Mrs. Sherman and I am very anxious to follow her, have to go out to get some articles that I need.

I have just had a long talk with Mr. Ashly[8] a part of it on the matter I mentioned to you yesterday in regard to W. L. Clark. Mr. Ashly thinks that he asked me to go to see Abby without consultation with her and that that was was [sic] indicated by the fact that she did not come to see me. I am strengthened in that by the fact his paper of yesterday which I have just seen is bitter as ever against you. I am very glad that I did not go to his office to see her. I should have been very humiliatingly placed probably.

I have not time to write more only to say, do let the man alone. His attacks are old and worn out and beneath your notice, and you will surely ruin your paper if you continue to use its columns for replies to him. God keep and prosper you darling. I am feeling a little conscience about the notes and money for Dickson but I am trying to leave it all with the Lord.

Bye bye.
Emma

––––––––

[8] S. S. Ashley, president of Atlanta Republican Publishing Company.

[letterhead]Office of
The Atlanta Republican Publishing Company.
S. S. Ashley, President; V. Spalding, Secretary;
J. Sherman, Treasurer; J. E. Bryant, Business Manager
Atlanta, Ga., Oct. 12 /78

My Darling.

I rec'd this morning your telegram saying 50. sent by express for paper also your money order for 5.00. I have time for only a line now. Mr. Spaulding is much hurt and offended that you send money to me intended for paper, and I myself hardly feel it proper so long as he is business manager. If you have any large sum to send to put in bank that could perhaps be sent to me but sums for immediate use had best be sent to him. When the telegram was sent up to me this morning I sent it directly to him supposing he would at once go to see Dickson and have paper started for Monday but when I came down he said he could not go to Dickson until he had money actually in hand because of the humiliating position in which your actions placed him (these are not his words but the sense of them) After considerable reasoning and persuasion on my part he at last consented to go to see Dickson and try to arrange to have paper started on Monday. I feared all along and am now convinced that it is of no use for me to do more than attend to your private mail and other such incidentals as I can without interfering in his special department it will only work confusion. I cannot blame him really for his feeling in the matter—it is perfectly natural.

The office rent is peremptorily demanded and must be paid Monday or we may be turned out. I am obliged to turn the 5.00 P.O. order received last night to that account and the remainder will have to be taken from the 55. If none comes in from other sources. Peter collected a good deal of money that he did not report, Mr. Spaulding detected it after discharging him.

The goods must wait till I can get money from you. They only gave permission for them to remain this week but I shall ask Peterson to ask them to wait a few days longer till I can hear from you. I am in haste.

Bye. darling
Emma

[letterhead] Office of
The Atlanta Republican Publishing Company.
S. S. Ashley, President; V. Spalding, Secretary;
J. Sherman, Treasurer; J. E. Bryant, Business Manager
Atlanta, Ga., November 4th 1878

Col J E Bryant
New York
Dr Sir

Your two last explanatory letters are received. They give me an insight into your plans and tend to releive [sic] my apprehensions, lest you might be following a mirage, that might vanish in a moment with entire loss of your time and labor. That you are making some headway is surprising under the difficulties you have had to encounter.

It shows conclusively two things, that our cause is not only just, but of vital importance to the Rep. Party, and country as well, and that you possess the force and magnetism to impress our ideas of the Southern question, upon the Northern mind. Push ahead and work out your plans at the North. There is no lack of courage at this end of the line, and the daylight you have let in upon us, inspires us with new hopes, and a confidence that our struggles will, before long, be crowned with success. I telegraphed you Saturday evening, asking whether you could help <u>me</u> this week. My taxes must be paid today or sale will be made tomorrow, and I am more seriously troubled than I would like to express.

12 O'clock PM. I have just made a raise of $100. from our friend Campbell Wallace, as a <u>personal favor</u> for ten days, now send fifty to Frank, so I can draw upon him to meet my engagement with Mr Wallace. Until the debt of fifty is paid, I am debassed [sic] from making any further draft on my brother, as soon as you pay him the fifty, telegraph me. The Major's big heart must not be bruised by failure on my part, or I can never hold up my head again in his presence. I say send fifty to Frank, because it will be easier to raise that, than it will be one hundred, and with that paid, I can carry the hundred a little longer by drawing at a few days sight. I think we had better get out half a sheet weekly at Dickson's if we can raise enough for that, and not attempt a whole sheet, until we see our way clear to do so. Half a sheet is altogether better than none at at [sic] all, we are kept before the public, and in fact nearly as much new matter is contained in a half, as in a whole sheet. Pride revolts, that is all.

I have been out most of the morning looking for money to pay taxes, and breathe freer now, than for many days past. I thought I would write you before I made the effort, but it was no go, I had to stop and do the other thing first, or at least make the effort.

> Write often & freely—All well
> Yours truly
> V Spalding

———

> Atlanta Nov 18 1878.
> Monday morning

My Darling.

I am too tired and sleepy to write this morning but must write business and send Mr. Basch's letter.[9]

Mrs. Sherman was "on the rampage" last night, and Belle went to Mr. Safford's for help at midnight while I held the fort. Anything but a pleasant situation for two little bodies like Belle and me to be all alone with a raving madwoman—though, to tell the truth, I dont think there was much insanity in it; but 'twas none the less dangerous.

We hope to have Aunt Esther here and news came this morning that Alma Herbert, one of Mrs. Sherman's old friends, is to be here Wed. to spend the winter. Belle and I are delighted because she will be a restraint upon her beside being one additional in case of trouble. I feel much relieved by the knowledge that she is to be here so soon. I have felt it necessary for me to remain here until we left the [line illegible]

I enclose note from Mr. Spaulding in regard to rent for South room. I am utterly unable to do anything towards it for tho' I received the 2.00 per letter and the 10. P.O. the first had to go strictly for washing bill and Emma's birthday and the second I collected on Sat. and bought a bag of flour and other necessaries, paid Mrs. Bisbee on board bill and [illegible] milk, and a few other little debts that had accumulated in spite of rigid economy until now I have but little left—not enough to pay the rent and the last I have I dare not spare.

---

[9] Theodore Basch, Republican in Savannah.

I give you this explanation not to frett [*sic*] you, for I do not [illegible] as at all, we have to [illegible] from all actual suffering in your absence and I can say God speed to you in your work, but I speak of this that you may see that it is quite impossible for me to pay the rent and because I wish to suggest the giving up of that room. If you are here permanently I would say nothing about it, but just run over in your mind the number of months that you have kept the room and the very little use you have made of it. Even tho' it is necessary to you (which I do not deny) can you afford to keep it? It looks now as if you will be much of the time for months to come away from here. I can have your things safely packed into your desk and locked up or if there is not sufficient room you could use the small bureau also and I would see that there were locks to make everything secure, then the desk can be put into one of the office rooms and in the brief intervals when you are here surely Peterson and Spaulding can occupy the large room and you can have sole occupancy of the smaller one and lock yourself in when not wishing to be disturbed. I am wearying your patience, perhaps, but I am sorely troubled by the constant outgo of money during this second suspension of paper and troubled than [*sic*] the company should be dunned for rent which it cannot pay. If you have any idea how much longer your stay will be prolonged please tell me. Is there a probability or possibility that you remain for months longer before returning? If so and I should be obliged through Mrs. Sherman's perhaps to go away from her. I have some idea of going West to Gretta tho' I would much prefer not to go till Summer from consideration of health for Emma. Have you any idea of taking us to N.Y. with you this present winter, and how much more would it cost to live there than here? If I cannot be with you I feel that it is best for us to remain right here unless absolutely obliged to flee from Mrs. S. she has been unusually agreeable to me outwardly since my return but I sometimes think it is only a pretense as she shows a strong dislike to me in her ravings. I shall make every effort to keep the peace for my own sake as well as hers and have hopes that I may succeed, but if I fail I know of no place here to go. A hotel or boarding house I would not go to unless I had the money in advance to defray my expenses then and if I had that I should [let] Emma go to my folks, if I could not go to you. I enclose a letter from Jo.[10] I will answer it the best I can and hope you may be so prospered as to be able to do something for him.

---

[10] Joseph Bryant, JEB's cousin.

God keep you, darling, I wish I could do something to help you beside pray and hope and wait. I love you and want to be with you. God help you and bless you with richer blessings.

Emma

Basch hopes to sell furniture soon, if he does I must retain that by me in case of emergency that might force me to leave here.

I sent Basch the desired letter Sat. sent only the letter.

————

New York

Dec 22^d 1878

My Darling Wife:

I do not think you will consider it wrong for me to spend a short time this Sabbath in writing to you. I feel that I have devoted too little time to you since I left, but my love for you has not for a moment grown cold. If I could have done so, I should have been with you long since; necessity however knows no law and I am still here. As hard as it has been for both of us, I, nevertheless, feel that my detention here has been providential. I am still of the opinion that God has called me to the work of political evangelization in the South, and also in the North. The evidence is so strong that I can not doubt. As I have often said, if He has called me to this work, He will take care of me, if I obey Him. You have been able to follow me to some extent through my letters to Col. Spalding, mainly. I have now reached a position that I have for several years expected to reach, but did not see how. I am to go before the public. At length God has opened the way. In recent letters to Col. Spalding I have explained my plans in connection with the Union League of America, not the Union League Club of New York. The former is a secret organization and extends throughout the country, the latter is a club and is confined to New York. At Philadelphia I was called upon to present my views of political work in the South, and my views were unanimously approved. Executive Committees were appointed to organize the South, as I suggested. The com. at Washington of seven members—I am one of them—is to have immediate charge of the work of organization in the South. The com. here, also of seven members, is to have charge of work in the North, and is expected to raise money to do the work in the South. The committee here has unanimously decided to raise money to back me. I have asked for $3000. It has been decided to have a public meeting, and have me address it; and thus raise the money. We are now arranging for that meeting. I expect to leave for home as soon as it is held.

I have been prevented from being with you Christmas, because I could not raise the money in season, as I had hoped to do. It has been decided to raise the money as explained above and therefore I am detained. I must therefore wish you and darling Emma <u>Merry Christmas</u> [double underline] by letter. Make it as merry as possible. I shall return as soon as possible. Do not know when it will be but think immediately after the public meeting here. I shall push that matter as rapidly as possible, but cannot say just when we can reach it. Will keep you informed and telegraph you when I leave.

As mentioned above I believe that God has called me to a work of political evangelization. I have had <u>much</u> light upon this subject since I came here. My stay here has been of <u>great advantage</u> spiritually, I understand my Washington experience as never before. I have had much light upon the subject of holiness, and think I understand where I am spiritually. I shall have very much to say upon this subject and my Christian experiences when I see you.

I had expected to send you more money for Christmas, but have not been able to do so. I shall send you more this week if nothing unforseen prevents. Pray for me my darling that I may know God's will, that I may be prospered and soon returned to you.

In a recent letter you alluded to my debts and suggested prayer as a means of assistance. For many years I have prayed that God would help me and for some time I fasted and prayed one day each week that God would aid me. I feel that He has done so; but I recognize the necessity of continual prayer on this matter. Let us pray unitedly that God will open the way that I may pay all my debts. With warmest love and kisses

Y. H.

———

Home Feb. 12–1879

My Darling Husband.

I went to town Monday and rec'd two letters from you one containing 1.00. I did not write then as I had just given letter to Dr. Fuller who was to leave and did not leave on that day.

You spoke of writing Capt. P.[11] to aid me. I was forced to write to him last week for 5.00 in order to pay some bills which could wait no longer—it came in Mon. morning. I am troubled and distressed when I think that you have been through the same hard times that Emma and I have with the additional weight of your business cares, but I rejoice that in all you have been so helped of God. I can not be other than anxious until I know that you have the money actually in hand and are ready to come home to us. I do lay this burden on the Lord else it would crush my spirits entirely.

Mrs. S. told me last night that she had been told that the stockholders were dissatisfied with you and she said it came from one of the stockholders but would not tell names. I do not attach as much weight to it as I would if she had not always taken a discouraging view. I hope and trust that there is no feeling of dissatisfaction which your successful return will not dissipate. I find myself in such danger of falling asleep over my writing that I must retire very soon. I am so much troubled by the fear that our letters may be tampered with that I write under constraint which is anything but pleasant. I am so hopeful for your home coming next week that I may not write again unless I learn that you are to be longer delayed. God keep and God send you speedily. Good night kisses and pleasant dreams

from the little wife that loves you

————

[letterhead]Clark University,
377 Whitehall Street, Atlanta, Georgia.
Complete Collegiate, Theological and Academic Courses of Study.
Full corps of Competent Instructors, Students of either sex admitted without reference to race or color. Board $10 a month. Incidentals, $1 a month.
Tuition Free. All bills payable in advance.
R. E. Bisbee, A.M., President
Atlanta, Ga. Apr. 15th 1879

My Darling Husband,

I write you with more cheerfulness and courage than last night. I trust Atlanta has seen the last of the Countess. She took the child with her and I learn to-day that she left nothing behind but her debts and that the

————

[11] Charles H. Prince, their friend since Buckfield days, was postmaster in Augusta, Georgia; he would leave Georgia in 1882.

Constitution man rages and threatens to publish her. I called at Mr. Eggleston's to-day and later at Mr. Ashley's—at the latter place I had a very satisfactory call. I do not think that their confidence has been impaired, Mr. Ashley from the first having entertained an unfavorable opinion of her. I think so far as I can learn that she has hung herself here most effectively and I hope that she will not pursue her nefarious schemes elsewhere as far as you are concerned. I learn that at her lecture she had not even a gentleman to introduce her and that she began her lecture by saying that in a city like Atlanta she did suppose she would have a gentleman to introduce her.

I was cheered by a few words from you to-day and hope to hear more at length soon, I ardently hope that that woman wont disturb you in Washington. Be sure in any event to show her no friendship. She has forfeited all claim to your friendship and herself declared war and you will injure yourself if you do not repudiate her at once and entirely. I am <u>positive</u> of this. I do not think you ought to recognize her even by a bow or shake of the hand after the terrible things she has said of you. You cannot in self respect do so and if you do it will be charged to cowardice resulting from some degree of guilt. She had attacked not only your character in money matters but had told me that you were guilty of the gravest licentiousness, pretending even to go into details and offer proof. After such statements as that I think she ought not to claim any further recognition from us in any way.

It is bed time and am weary

God keep you darling.
Loving kisses
Emma

Wed. Morning. How long does it now look as if you will be absent, and what would you think of my going West next week provided I can raise the funds? I shall receive only $20 from Savannah.

Please give me early answer to these questions as many weeks of delay will probably prevent me from going West until summer and perhaps altogether.

I want to do just what is right and best and desire as much to be with you that were it not for father's feeble health and my desire to be with him I should probably give up the journey for this summer

Bye-bye—
Emma

Please burn this at once. love to the Fairchilds. The Co——is fully exposed here I think she can do no further harm here

Home May 11th 1879
Sabbath Night—

My Darling

I have but a few minutes for writing as it is quite bed time. I am disappointed to recieve [*sic*] no letter from you to-day and perhaps you have felt the same feeling as I have of late been remiss in writing. Your last was written from Boston but like the previous one in haste and giving no details. I do hope that you will <u>very</u> <u>soon</u> be successful and return. I have been much disappointed this week in being unable through illness to attend the Bap.[tist] Convention. I went this morning to Sabbath school and morning service. heard a very able and devout sermon. did not learn the name of preacher he preached from Paul's words "for me to live is Christ, to die is gain" his sermon was eminently practical and pressed home upon his hearers the necessity of <u>loving for Christ</u>, working for Christ.

I am trying at odd moments to read the Hist. of the Reformation and am much interested in it.

Please pray urgently and especially my darling husband for a deep thorough work of grace in my heart—that the Savior may fully and truly dwell in my heart, and pray, too, for our little one. I fear that we have yet to pray for the real work of grace in her heart. God knows while I fear I dare not judge. Good night and pleasant dreams. God keep you darling.

Tuesday night—I went down town last evening in [illegible] Mrs. Bisbee thereupon did [illegible] have this to mail [illegible] a few minutes and found there your second letter from Boston. I do hope that you are not mistaken in your expectation of returning soon. If I should tell you how hopeless your effort to build up an influential paper here sometimes seems to me you would surely call me "Little Faith" or "Much Afraid."

God help you, for the undertaking is so enormous for a poor man. I have no lack of sympathy in the work—no doubt of its need, only fear for you that the wheels of progress may roll over you instead of carrying you along. We are almost now at the middle of May and fairly in for the heats of summer tho' thus far we have had little hot weather. I am in better health than a few days ago and Emma is quite well. I rec'd from Basch 18.00 for furniture, 2.00 being deducted from some previous expenses—had hoped to lay that by towards my traveling expenses but shall be obliged to break upon it at once. I was unable to attend any single meeting of the convention which closed yesterday. [I] must do the next best thing by going down town and reading the Convt. Reports at Meth.[odist] Adv.[ocate] office to-morrow or next day. I fear there will be a long gap in my letters as shall probably be unable to mail this until I go down town. Mr. Spaulding told me yesterday that the boy is dismissed. I am very glad but shall be obliged to go oftener to town myself. Scarcely any private letters come now to you, none have being given me for a fortnight or more I think. Under these circumstances will it be necessary for me to go to town as often as every other day unless it should be quite convenient to do so? If necessary I will go. It is now quite bedtime for me. May the dear father help my husband and restore him soon to me.

Bye-By—
Emma

Thurs. Morn. Rec'd a letter from you yesterday in which you speak of having seen John Long[12] and that he cooperates with you. I trust that the Tuesday night meeting was a success and such a success as to bring you home very soon to us. This is a lovely month and I regret for you to lose it for it cannot, I fancy, be as pleasant at the North, certainly not to the sight as we are in the midst of roses.

I am extremely anxious for you to enter upon work in Georgia and almost impatient until you can.

I know that the work is great and you can only go on as God helps. I propose to go to-day to town and to Atlanta University taking the whole day and I must be in haste this morning in order to start before the heat. God keep you darling, Emma sends her love and kisses

Bye bye darling
Emma

————

3 Baglston Place Boston
Aug. 25th 1879

My Darling Wife:

It was my purpose to have written you yesterday but I had no time before church, as I needed to look my Sunday School lesson over more. I did not

---

[12] John D. Long, native of Buckfield, Maine; he would be secretary of the navy in the administration of President William McKinley.

return from church and Sunday School until nearly 2. A friend soon after called to invite me to ride with him, and, as I do not often have such an opportunity I accepted. After my return I had supper, and went to prayer meeting; and when I got to my room again, I was tired enough to go to bed.

I was up in good season this (Monday) morning; have read my morning lesson, had prayer, committed to memory a verse of next Sundays lesson, and am writing to you before breakfast. It is a very pleasant morning, just cool enough to be enjoyable. We have had some warm weather in Boston, but most of the time it has been very comfortable.

I did receive the letter from Geoman forwarded by you.

I wrote this far when the breakfast bell rang, and I put aside writing. Having attended to business in the city, I now return to my letter to you.

I have not said much to you about debts, but for years they have weighed very heavily on me. For weeks at a time I have fasted and prayed each Friday that God would help me to pay them and I have used my best efforts. It is useless to speak of the past except to get lessons of instruction for the future. For reasons which seemed conclusive to me, I have been led to believe that God had led me into my present field of labor, and I feel confident that I shall prosper and pay my debts—You say if I had a fixed salary. You forget that I do have. My salary has been fixed by the company at $125 a month. If I had received my pay for what I have done I could now from the savings pay all I owe Joseph and have money left. But I have not received any pay and, perhaps, you think I will not. As I have before said, if I am doing God's service, He will see that I am paid. I believe He has heard and is answering my prayers to help me pay my debts. Please remember that we own no new debts or but small ones since 1877, and I have paid some of the old ones. True, we have had a hard time, but I have been preparing a new work and a life work. My previous letters and subsequent ones will make this plain. It is a political work but it is politico-missionary. It is as honorable as any other missionary work, and certainly very important. At present, perhaps, Dr. Fuller is the only one in Georgia who fully comprehends the magnitude and importance of the work, and also believes in it; but the time will soon come when we will have many others fully in sympathy with us. As I succeed in raising money and the company is able to pay my salary, we can pay debts, and we will do so. I not only believe that this is God's work, but I believe He is aiding me and I will continue to do so, and I believe that I am and have been pursuing the wisest course open to me after the treachery of Atkins. Against all opposition and treachery I have moved forward, and feel confident of complete success. I believe I am now pursuing a course that will enable me to accomplish more for myself and family and for the course of humanity than I could in any other. But as I have before written you, honor, as well as duty, drive me forward on the line I have marked out. Let us then have brave hearts, and, praying for God's blessing, move forward.

The action of Col. Spalding—and of course I do not blame him so far as I know his course—makes it necessary for you to remain in Atlanta for the present. I am anxious for you to be in the office every day; but I do not want you to do so until I can send you money, so that you can hire some of your work done. Please do not over work. I realize that it is not economy to do so. But for previous years of over-work, I could have accomplished <u>much</u> more the past year than I have. I have been <u>compelled</u> to be careful. It is better to let things go undone than to over-do, unless we can take subsequent rest. Our struggle in the past has been so <u>very</u> great, that over-exertion seemed a <u>necessity</u>. It is so no longer, and <u>must not</u> be, no matter what the necessity seems to be. Please then do not overdo to help me at the office. When I can send you money, then you can help me carry out my plans. This being premised, I will unfold to you my plans.

You say that my plans are large but do not seem to come to anything practicable, or at least that is the way I read what you write, and what is "between the lines." In other words my plans are "glittering generalities." If I did not consider this very important, I would not take time to dwell upon it; but I consider it necessary to do so. You are right in part and wrong in part. My plans are large, but I propose what is entirely practicable, as you will fully understand when you come to understand them fully. The whole matter has been growing in my mind since I started, and no doubt will continue to do so. What I now propose is the organization of the Union League in Georgia. That certainly is practicable <u>for me</u>. It will, I fully understand, be necessary for me to attend to the work in Georgia personally to accomplish very important results; but much can be done by others before I return. It was my purpose to establish the paper before we organized the League. I have been compelled to change, and now we must organize the League before we establish the paper. This I have fully explained in letters to Col. S. All of these letters you should read that you may fully understand my views.

I will not at this time enter into details of what I desire you to do for me. That I will do when I can send you money. I have for some weeks been providing for this time as you know, as I wrote you many weeks ago about going into the office. At this time it is important to give you some insight into my money matters. Previous to my return home last spring I had a very hard time, as you know. We attempted to continue the publication of the paper. I sent all the money I could possibly to Col. Spalding, and frequently had not enough to purchase suitable meals. I was compelled to borrow, and when I returned was indebted to a friend $200. I used the $900 mostly for the paper and my expenses, and trusted to raising money North to meet the $200. Various causes delayed me and the "Countess" matter interfered with my plans. The matter is quite fully explained in my letters to Col. S. I was prevented from working in Washington by the "Countess" matter, as I have explained; and also in New York, and came here. My calculations of returning so soon when I was in Washington were based upon assurances of support there which I believe I could have realized but for the "Countess" trouble.

After my return here my calculations in regard to returning were based upon the result of my first few days labor. In previous letters to Col. Spalding I have shown how I was delayed from day to day until after about three weeks I was fairly started. I had hoped to have a public meeting and raise the money at once. I had reason to believe that such a meeting would be held, but we failed, and finally it was decided that the only practicable way was for me to take a letter from the committee, and by personal interviews with wealthy men raise the money. It was believed that I could do so very soon. I started out under very favorable circumstances, but at once encountered difficulties and have been at work ever since. I have sent Col. Spalding nearly $200; have paid the $200 in New York, and the $40 forced out of me by the boarding matter of the Landsfeldt woman;[13] have sent you money; paid my expenses since I left home, for I had but little more than enough to reach the North when I left, and have about $50 with the committee. I have now experience to guide me in forming an opinion of what I can do. I shall be able to raise some more in Boston now. I expect to go to Providence one week from today, and from there to Philadelphia. I must raise at least $600 before I can return home. I cannot do very much in raising money before the first of September. I think that with my experience I can by the last of September or first of October, raise the money and return home. I fear that I cannot do so sooner. I was anxious to have you with me, for I long for your company, and did intend to send for you as soon as I was fairly started in Philadelphia; but the actions of Col. Spalding [to suspend the paper] may force me to change my plans, as I have already mentioned in this.

---

[13] Countess of Landsfeldt.

My health is very good. I can do more work than when I left home. I am fully confident that I am on the right line, and feel sure of success. I may have a hard struggle until I am fairly started in Philadelphia, the first of September, and I may succeed in Providence next week. I shall send you money as soon as possible. I sent you $3.00 with letters Saturday. That you may understand how difficult it is for me to tell what I can do, this experience is important. I call on a man, explain our work, and he subscribes $50. So far as I know, there is no reason why twenty other men whom I am to call upon, who are worth as much, may not subscribe as much; but perhaps none of the twenty subscribe anything. Again, I call to see, perhaps, ten men in one day, and am not able to have an interview with either because they are either not in or too much engaged to see me and I must call again. It is my faith in the course and my trust in God that give me courage; and what I have accomplished gives me assurance of final success.

This is enough this time I "reckon." I love you darling, and shall be so glad when I can be with you again.

With warmest kisses,
Y. H.

Home Aug. 27th /79
Wed. night

My Darling:

Have just rec'd your brief letter of Sat. the first in a long time and I must confess to equal remission myself—am wicked enough to hope that you have missed my letters as much as I have yours. Susan is here to-day making almost her last visit before leaving—she will go next Tuesday. She regrets much as do I that she has again failed to see you. I felt almost certain when she came that you would be here before she left.

I was obliged to lay by my pen last night and retire as I have been troubled by restlessness at night this week if I do anything to set my brain working at night. It is like Banqou's ghost,[14] it wont down when I tell it. Yesterday was a gala day with Emma as Minnie Fuller came out to visit her. I send enclosed some references of people who have used Dr. W's, Dr. Meyer's catarrh

---

[14] In Shakespeare's *Macbeth*, Lady Macbeth was repeatedly visited by Banquo's ghost.

specific and I wish you would take especial pains when you are again in N.Y. to hunt up some of them and enquire about it. I wish particularly to know how long since they took it and whether they have experienced any ill effects since as well as whether they were cured of the disease.[15] I also send address of agt's who sell it D. B. Dewey & co 46 Day St. N.Y. I am afraid it is no better than other patent medicine still I am attracted by it because I am sure that he has the true theory of the disease itself. My question now is whether it is safe to trust his medicine. Of that I have my fears but I have arrived at the conclusion that we <u>must</u> cure Emma's catarrh in her youth, if we have any expectation of health for her in mature life. I have consulted Dr. Orene and he tells me I might as well try to change the color of her eyes and recommends good diet care etc, and leaving it to nature. I am not willing to accept this for it is just the course which was pursued with me, and I am to this day suffering the results of it. I think that all the ill health I have ever suffered, all the loss of strength and vitality have been due to this one cause and I am utterly unreconciled to allowing Emma to come up with the same poison in her system if it can be eradicated and of this I am convinced that one never <u>outgrows</u> it, it only changes its locality and manifestation. Now can you and will you be certain to make these inquiries? You need not purchase the medicine unless the testimony is overwhelmingly in its favor we can easily order it by mail. Please make especial inquiries also as to Dr. W's, Dr. Meyer himself.

I had a postal from Capt. [Prince] the other day in which he asked me to write him in regard to you. I shall do so this morning but scarce know what to say other than that you are collecting money for general political missionary work in the South and that your object is partially the organization of the Union League here. That is the substance of what I gather from your letters to me and one to Col. S. which I read on Sunday.

I think you will be very glad to know that I have found my old ambrotype tucked away in a trunk. Emma fished it out much to my delight for I am so thin now in my face that I would dread to sit for a picture. Last Sabbath I went to Meth. Church, a rainy morning and very few out, but a good sermon.

Went to dinner at home of one of S. S. scholars afterward and thence to lodge, afterward to University to take a postal to Sue and after taking tea there enjoyed the somewhat unusual pleasure of a ride home. I also spent one day and night there last week, having a ride to town and back in the morning and

---

[15] Alice later wrote that her mother was "far ahead of her time in health and medical problems."

a ride home, was much benefited and refreshed by the rest. You have never written me whether you sent $10 to Mrs. S. please write as I wish to know.

I have planned to accomplish something in sewing to-day and must therefore devote no more time to writing saving just to write a little to Capt. P. I think that a letter from you would be much more satisfactory to him, try to write if you can and allow me to suggest that you do not go back to foundation principles which I think are already understood, but tell briefly what you are doing. Your friends often complain of your failure to write them when ten lines from you would tell what they wish to know, if you would only leave out all preambles, this is the more desirable as the points which you repeat in nearly all of your letters are things which you have said so many times in print and otherwise that your friends are all conversant with them, and the repetition of them will not convince them of their truth, if they are inclined to doubt.

I am not at all doubting the importance of these underlying principles but the frequent repetition of them carries the impression that those to whom you write are ignorant of them and also tires and prejudices them. What they wish to know is the <u>actual progress</u> you are making, the work you are doing. It does no good to tell them that the work is right; ergo it must succeed. Every man feels himself as capable of judging on those points as you, what they ask is, what success <u>have</u> you, not what <u>must</u> you have, <u>ought you</u> to have or do you <u>expect</u> to have, all acknowledge your integrity, singleness of purpose and righteousness of your cause. Therefore you should waste no pen or ink in convincing them of these things, what they <u>do</u> doubt is the coolness and soundness of your judgement. Now you must not think, you <u>ought not</u> to think that I write this to throw cold water on you, to irritate or discourage you. I would hold up your hands, not pull them down, strengthen, not weaken you. The Lord knoweth that my whole heart goes out in fervent prayer for your complete success. I only write this in the hope that it may lead you to <u>condense</u> your letters, throw out everything superfluous and give the necessary facts in such a way as to command respect and attention. Often on reading a letter of seven or eight pages if we were asked at the close what you had written we could sum it all up in these words, the cause is just and it must succeed. That cause being the conversion of the Southern people to a new civilization, now as none of those to whom your letters are addressed doubt these things the frequent repetition of them are a waste of time and tendes [*sic*] to injure where it is so necessary that you should stand high. In other words they are more like an editorial written to set forth principles to the world than the report of the agt. of a society or corporation as to the work done and being done.

I recognize that you have all the work to do while the company gives you only a nominal backing, still the failure of that nominal backing would be disastrous to you in the extreme and so I point out these dangers which are real and not imaginary I am very sure. For myself I can wait and hope and trust, rejoicing in your success and patient I trust in defeat. I am willing to leave the issue with God, and possibly, there is no virtue in that for I know it must be left with Him. You can bear me witness that I have never attempted to draw you out of your chosen line of work, I would not dare, if I could, come between your soul and God but I do desire to see you take every intelligent and right advantage of your position to use all the aids and to lose nothing by shutting your eyes to any of the difficulties of the way. I wonder if you will [illegible] I trust your equanimity will not be disturbed by the enclosed nonsense of Sue's and Emma's.

[illegible] on me now and right you might [say], why I don't condense and give you the gist of my remarks in a few words, as I might have done.

God keep you, darling, and reunite us soon either here or there.

> With loving kisses,
> Emma.

Home Sep. 4th /79

My Darling.

I received last night yours with $10. order enclosed both were most welcome. I hasten to write this morning because I am troubled by something that Mr. Sherman told me last night, viz. that Peterson was at the corner of the streets blowing because he gets no money and saying that you have never sent back a cent since you left last May, that the company is [be]holden for borrowed money and you have sent nothing at all to meet it. Now I am afraid that Col. S. is to blame for this state of affairs for Mr. Sherman tells me that he keeps everything, so far as he knows, to himself showing none of your letters, that you wrote him (Sherman) that Col. S. would show him letters telling what your plans are but that he has not done so. I do not know that Mr. Sherman has asked him to show them but he has seen Spaulding frequently so that he could have shown them if he desired. Mr. Sherman himself was unaware that you had sent Spaulding any money at all until I told him so last night. I do not understand that anything which you write Spaulding is private from the directors, is it? Unless possibly the $40 pitched out of you by the Landsfeldt fraud, is that to be spoken of at all? I see that Mr. Sherman is very much dissatisfied and possibly others may be, he says that altho' he was chosen treasurer no money has ever passed through his hands and still more no account of moneys has ever been rendered to him so that he is kept in absolute ignorance of money transactions, would it not be well for you to write him making a statement of what money you have sent Spaulding this summer.

I shall go to town to-day, see Spaulding, Dr. Fuller and Peterson if I should be so fortunate. I trust that I shall not make any blunder in what I try to do. I would not attempt to say anything, only I feel that Peterson's course is very injurious to you and to the company and that it is induced by ignorance, if the real fact [illegible] which Co. S. is responsible. Peterson has been wonderfully patient and cheerful through all this stage of depression.

I [illegible] upon the principle that there is nothing to conceal (from the directors) in the money matters between you and Col. S. as I am sure there is not. Emma sends love and says you must come home. God keep you, darling

With loving kisses
Emma

———

49 Chestnut St. Providence R.I.
Oct 29 1879

My Darling:

I received yours of Sunday today. My letter to Mrs Sherman sent to her at Chester with $10 enclosed was returned to me today. I forwarded it to her at Atlanta by registered letter. I send enclosed the receipt. Please explain to her. . . .

I go from here Saturday night to New York and from there to Philadelphia. I am nearly ready to return home. I had hoped to raise enough money here to enable me to do so, but have not succeeded, and I do not now expect to. Three hundred dollars more will enable me to return. I have worked down to that. I may raise that in two weeks and it may take me a month. I shall do my best. Please pray that God will help me to return soon. My meeting did not result in raising as much money as I expect[ed] it would. But it placed our cause in excellent shape before the people. It must be constantly borne in mind that I am a pioneer in a new movement—the conversion of Southern whites to American ideas—and I am now sowing seed. You have expressed a fear for the future, I am preparing for the future. My success here gives me more courage than I have had for years. I wish you could have heard my speech Friday night. It was more like my old self than you have seen for some years. I feel very confident as I go forward to Philadelphia. But I now realize that we must grow slowly. I shall keep the company out of debt and go as fast as possible.

I believe my success here, taken in connection with previous experience, makes it certain that I am to have final success. I am now well before the public with our work. The line we are now on will enable us to go forward at small expense and develop the cause, thus enabling me to convince men in the South as well as in the North that I am on the right line. When I have done that I can get all the money we need. It is a great movement and it must take time to fully develop it. At first I put forward the idea of publishing the paper—simply one of the means for accomplishing the object. Now I bring the cause to the front—the building up of a party by the conversion of white men to American ideas. This is a new movement. At present I am the principal advocate. My success in Providence has been in presenting this cause and is in raising money for it. I can undoubtedly do as well throughout the North as I have done here. My success from 1874 to 1878 in reaching the white people of Georgia proves that I am on the right line. I am confident that I am developing a line of policy to settle the Southern question—to protect the lives and rights of the colored people and their white friends and educate the masses in free schools.

You had better make calculations on [illegible] remaining in Georgia this winter. I shall stay there as much as possible.

With warmest love and kisses.
Y. H.

Tell Emma that papa wants to see her and will return as soon as possible. Of course you realize that my plans of returning are changed by my experience as I go forward.

———

[From Alice Bryant's autobiography regarding the Countess]

It was while living at the Sherman's that the "Countess" arrived in Atlanta. My father had met her in New York when he was interested in Missionary work. She claimed to be a daughter of Lola Montes and King Ludwig of Bavaria and lectured on missions. My father believed her story and when she came to Atlanta with her young daughter and asked for his help in procuring a boarding place he introduced her and also introduced her to his friends. . . .

After running up a big board bill and getting credit at a number of stores the "Countess" disappeared.

Unfortunately my father who was in the North at that time had at her request written a very complimentary editorial about her for his newspaper which was published about the time she left.

This was the last my parents heard of the "Countess" until my father attended the trial of "Ann Ophelia Disdebar["] who had cheated a prominent New York lawyer of a great amount of money by selling him fake paintings which were supposed to have been painted by the spirits of the Old Masters. She had led a very checkered career and was undoubtedly the "Countess." She was the daughter of poor but honest parents.

[Alice's autobiography regarding Emma's ideas on medicine]

My mother was far ahead of her time in health and medical problems. Long heavy muslin chemises (called by some, shifts) were worn at the time my mother was in college. She heard of gauze underwear somewhere and immediately bought some. When she went home for vacation some of the neighbors watched her clothes line. They remarked in a shocked tone: "Emma Spaulding does not have a shift to her back."

At that time the "regular" school of medicine gave very strong medicines to which children objected strenuously and they did not believe in using water in case of fevers either internally or externally. My mother combined Homeopathy and Allopathy in her treatment of me.

LETTERS: DECEMBER 1879–JANUARY 1881

After the demise of the *Georgia Republican* in 1879, Emma and Alice lived for more than a year with their Spaulding relatives. This continued one of the longest marital separations for the Bryants, lasting until January 1881 without even brief visits.[1]

At the time John returned South to deal with his state office, he had already expressed uncertainty as to whether he should seek reelection as party chair. His indecision became a moot point, however, as events in Georgia had already passed him by. The 1880 Republican convention saw JEB's African American colleague, William A. Pledger, become the new head of the state party (probably with Bryant's assistance and support). Undeterred, the carpet-bagger continued his shuttle in the North. The latest additional factionalism in Georgia, animus between Southern and Northerner Republicans, was plain evidence that members were scrapping for crumbs as the party struggled to exist in an increasingly Democratic climate.

With Emma in Illinois and John's leadership in Georgia tenuous to non-existent, both wife and husband entered a time of soul-searching. For him, the cities of New York, Philadelphia, and Providence were the backdrop as his quest for a new direction continued—new direction but with the same recognizable vehicle. Supporters in the Georgia Republican Publishing Company were folded into the Southern Advance Association, which Bryant claimed he had first formed in 1877. North Carolina carpet-bagger Albion Tourgée's publication of *A Fool's Errand by One of the Fools* reinforced JEB's faith in his own analysis that two conflicting civilizations continued to exist in America, one in the North and another in the South.

In Illinois, Emma found time to reflect on her own philosophy of life. This period brought a deeper examination and commitment to "the woman issue" and new ways to apply the philosophy of natural rights to her own existence, even bringing her long-held religious beliefs under scrutiny. She also began to mention her association with the national temperance movement.

---

[1] See *Carpetbagger of Conscience*, 151–58, for details of JEB's career in the year 1880.

Dependency weighed heavily on the carpetbagger's wife, now thirty-six years old: dependency on her husband for money, parsimoniously doled out; and dependency on her family for crucial lodging and sustenance. Questioning the prevailing norm that women should not work outside the home but keenly aware of her lack of preparation for a career, she returned to her previous studies in mathematics and bookkeeping. Also, along with the ubiquitous sewing, she found the time to enhance her skills in painting. While her own health was a concern, that of her growing daughter took on primary significance.

The separation dragged on—with the elusive JEB promising more than he could or would deliver, even while relying on Emma to bolster his tarnished reputation and to support his version of reality.

Earl Dec. 11th /79
Thurs. P.M.

My Darling Husband.

I hope that you will receive soon the postal scrawl which I dispatched yesterday to tell you of our safe arrival here, and while sister is napping I will write a brief letter only for my head and body are both tired and I must rest a little, too, before going up town with sister. The object of our trip being a visit to the milliners. Sister is if possible worse than you as regards "worldly pomps and vanities" (that is a methodist quotation in spirit if not in letter) and she has declared war upon my old hat in such vigorous manner that I am forced to yield, the more so, as she proposes that father shall pay for the new one, so much for the outside, now for the inside. Everybody gives me a hearty welcome including neighbors and acquaintances and you know that warms up a body's heart. I found father in comparative health, apparently very glad to see me, Neilly too delighted to go to school yesterday afternoon and all with interested and kindly inquiries after you.

One reason of my weariness to-day perhaps is that instead of retiring early last night I sat up to have my customary tell with Mr. Browne on politics. He and I always agree on general principles better than sister and I, strange to say, but we differ when it comes to application.

Sisters health is not good and she is so much injured by the excitement of such wordy contents that Mr. Browne and I have promised to refrain in future. I think they affect her much as your own political discussions used to do poor mother in sickness. I managed to sleep warm last night in a room where the frost stood on the windows so I have renewed courage for the winter. Emma is happy and full of life has just gone home with a little girl for a play. She finds plenty of playmates and will I think be benefitted. My eyes and head are very tired and I must rest. God keep you, darling, I love you heartily, truly and would be more happy than I could tell you to lie in your arms tonight instead of thinking of you as I must so far away.

God keep you, darling. Please to pray especially for me that in this change from our home life I may not lose in spiritual life as I almost fear I may i.e. if I do not begin these dutties [*sic*] aright.

Bye, darling
Emma

———

1618 Arch St Philadelphia
Feb 1 1880

My Darling Wife:

I feel like having a Sunday chat with you. I have just returned from morning service. It is communion Sunday and I in looking over my Christian life find that I have much strength yet to gain before I can be a perfect Christian. Pray for me my darling that my strength may be increased.

I received a very important letter from Col. Spalding yesterday. It indicates a change in the views of some of my friends. He says that he thinks and mentions others who think that I should be again chairman of the State committee. Did I tell you that I received a letter from Col. Buck a few days since and he informs me that he knows but very few influential Republicans who do do [*sic*] not recognize me as Chairman of the Republican State com. From what he says I am convinced that if there has been a disposition to call an independent State Convention, it has been given up. All now look to the State convention to be called by our committee February 17th to decide party matters. That much I think is settled. Whether I can be again chosen chairman of the State committee or whether it is desirable that I should be are questions I am not now prepared to settle. They are <u>very important</u> and let us make them the subject of earnest prayer.

But important as these questions are the Cause which I advocate is <u>far very</u> [double underlined] <u>very</u> [double underlined] far above them. Laying aside the question of God's call to me to move forward in the development of this work here are the facts. Commencing with my campaign of 1874 I have been deeply impressed with the thoughts that have <u>crowded</u> or have <u>been</u> crowded into my mind in regard to the condition of the Nation. You know what I have done. I came to certain conclusions. So far as I knew when I commenced no other person looked at matters from the same stand point. I have pushed forward until we are preparing to enter upon the campaign of 1880. I have marked out a line of policy and have presented it to the Republicans of Georgia in my address of Jan 20th, a copy of which I have sent you. That I shall follow up by work "in the field"—all I can do. I shall do my best to have the State convention adopt this line of policy as Republicanism, and chose [*sic*] a <u>working</u> State committee to present it to the people of the State, and <u>press</u> it upon their attention. This Cause is infinitely more important than any personal interests I or any other person may have and I shall not allow my personal interests to interfere with the success of this Cause, God helping me.

The Cause as presented in my address is, in my judgement the politic way to put it to the people of the South. The real Cause is, American civilization against the feudal civilization of the South. We are the leaders in Georgia of this great Cause. It is coming to be recognized at the North that this conflict between these two civilizations is not over. Judge Tourgee [*sic*], a Western man who went to North Carolina soon after the war, and has recently returned North has written a book entitled. "A fools errand by one of the fools."[2] I have just read the book and will send it to you in a few days. The story is simple but interesting; the philosophy is the same as I have so often presented in regard to the South; and the remedy he proposes is substantially the same as I propose—the conversion of Southern whites to American ideas. The book is very well written and I think will do our Southern Cause much good. I am of course very much pleased with the book because Judge Tourgee is a very able man and, having studied the Southern question as I have, we have come to almost the same conclusions. The publication of the book will do great good because it will turn the Northern mind to the subject, and will, I think, help to arrest the attention of the Northern people. Of course I am encouraged. There are some things about the book I do not like; but I will not criticize until you have read it to see if you notice the same things. I regard it as in some respects an autobiography. The hero, "Comfort Servosse" is of French origin living in Michigan. He served with Union army and at the

---

2 Albion Winegar Tourgée, *A Fool's Errand, by One of the Fools: A Novel of the South during Reconstruction* (New York: Harper & Brothers, 1879).

close of the war went South with his wife, "Gretta," and little girl "Lily." He fought through Reconstruction as a "Radical, carpet-bagger" and died a few years afterwards of yellow-fever. His daughter married a scion of one of the "first families." But you must read the book to understand the story. I said that "Comfort Servosse" is the hero: his daughter "Lily" is he [*sic*] heroine. She is a noble character. The account of her successful effort to save her father from the Ku Klux, and her night ride is worth the price of the book.

I leave other matters about which I wish to speak to another letter.

> With warmest love and kisses
> Y. H.

> Earl Feb 4th 1880

My Darling.

Your letter of Sunday reached me yesterday. I am so glad to know that prospects in Georgia are brightening both for you personally and the cause which is so dear to us both. I am quite pleased to know that Buck has written. I think it a good sign as he has not been disposed to show his friendship in unfavorable times.

I am very desirous to be with you when you return to Georgia, more so perhaps, than even before and if you were not to go North again so soon should insist upon returning home, but as it is it will be undoubtedly best for me to remain here till you have made another trip north.

Shall be extremely anxious to know the drift and progress of affairs after your return to Atlanta. For yourself personally it seems to me a crisis in your life of no ordinary importance. For your work I know that God will raise up workers and mold events in His own time and way.

I do hope, trust and pray that He will permit you to eat of the fruit of your planting and yet I will try to be content let it result as it may.

Our weather is lovely and I must make this letter very brief in order to treat myself to a few minutes walk. I have neglected out-of-door exercise during the past two weeks and must atone for lost time.

> God keep you darling.
> With loving kisses
> Emma

Earl Feb. 25th 1880

My Darling Husband.

Just a word before bed—I am homesick when I think of you in Atlanta without me.

Have been reading Fool's Errand to-night and for few days past, have reached the Reconstruction period and the opening of Ku Klux brutalities. Thus far I think it wonderfully true to life and memory and am not able to judge so well of his criticisms of reconstruction policy and yet they seem to me just. I find myself very much interested in it. After reading it the other night my mind ran over our own life in the South and your own preservation from a real serious injury. It is often difficult for me to realize that all this blood has been shed because you and our intimate friends have been spared. God be praised for it. I must write very briefly to-night because it is quite bed-time and Emma is not well and I ought to be in bed with her, she is having her first really severe cold.

She sends love and hugs I think to you and complains that you do not write her. I forgot to acknowledge the receipt of the little book that you sent her. She was much pleased with it. Is a good girl and makes considerable progress in reading. . . .

God keep and bless you, darling. I love you and my heart yearns for your companionship.

pleasant dreams & loving kisses
Emma

Thurs morn. Yours of Sunday just rec'd. I am very desirous to be with you now, never more so I think in any of our seperations [*sic*] but recognize the necessity of waiting a little, but hope it may not be many months. I want to speak especially now of our rent at Mr. Sherman's, if we are to move into town it is not best to retain our rent there. The three months for which our rent was to be only 3.00 monthly expires this month. Will it not be well to give up our rent and store our things. . . .

Or it may be best for us if we should return in the summer to continue housekeeping there with some faithful girl to take care of Emma while I am in town. The walk would be no objection if I kept a servant. . . . Mrs. S. might leave my things where they are and use them for the rent if she is so disposed but I should not wish her to allow any one else to use them. If she rented to anyone else I would wish them all packed away see especially that my carpet is properly cared for. I have some fear that the mice may gnaw it if it is packed away unless it is put high up on the shelf in the front closet. It is a lovely day warm as early summer.

Bye darling,
Emma. . . .

———

Earlville Mch. 16th 1880

My Darling Husband.

The days and weeks are passing all too rapidly were it not that they bring nearer the time of our meeting. I go out more or less every day, sew considerable do a little housework and spend considerable time on Emma and these varied employments steal away the hours so rapidly that I am astonished when the night comes. Emma has been out spending the afternoon and I must go for her directly as it is now near her bed time or rather quite that.

She shows much capacity and I am very anxious to direct her exactly right, pray for me that I may be endowed with all these powers that we mothers so much need. To be a parent and especially a mother is a most serious responsibility, and still more so when absence prevents you from giving me any assistance. I change my subject suddenly, who is your choice for President. Blaine as of yore? Mr. Browne told me something to-day that fell upon me like a thunderbolt, viz. that when the Chinese question[3] was up in Congress something more than a year ago, I think, Blaine made a big speech against, quoted that old saying that has been quoted in defense of cruelty and oppression from time immemorial "viz self preservation etc."

I ought to have read the paper so constantly as to be posted in regard to these things but have not. I am greatly shocked and, if this is true, I <u>do not wish to see him President</u>—he is not a fit candidate for the great Republican party who can add his voice to the hue and cry against the rabble. Please if you have Blaine's speech upon that question send it to me. I must leave now and look up Emma.

Bye darling
Emma

———

[3] In 1879, Senator James G. Blaine (R-Me.) had spoken in favor of the Chinese Exclusion Act.

Earl Mch. 28, 1880

My Darling Husband.

The past two days have brought me letters from you written from Savannah and Atlanta.

My heart leaps at the thought that June is only about nine weeks off. I am fearful lest something may transpire to prevent you from coming then but trust not.

Tho' I am enjoying my visit and gaining in health I think it is such a poor lean kind of living without your love, and I am almost discouraged when I remember that almost sixteen years of our married life have passed without any constant living together. Seriously, do you believe it will ever be better? I often fear not. But I wont waste time in grumbling or prognosticating evil.

Monday Morning—I was called off last night to teach Neil chess and he and Emma have been deep in a game this morning. went out last night to prayer meeting. I enjoy and am blessed by the greater privileges of church attendance that I have here, shall miss them when I leave. The baptist pastor here is a man of deep society and spirituality and I enjoy his preaching very much. His wife is a real helpmeet to him—a week ago she led the prayer meeting, by request, in her husband's absence and did it much better I presume than the deacons would have done. I am anxious that you should consider the matter of giving up our rent at Mrs. Shermans unless you are <u>very sure</u> that we shall return there in June. I think it decidedly best to hire some one to take up my carpet and do it up and store our furniture in one room and give up the remainder. If you wish my assistance in the office we shall probably move into town and there is no propriety in paying rent there any longer—remember that the reduction to 3.00 per month ended with Mch. 1st.

We are both too much pressed for money to let these little things go—please answer in your next. What has become of the Florida land?[4] I think much of you darling and my heart longs for you, but I find it almost impossible to write as often as I wish. I have some sick days and am obliged to have some care of my head as I am developing some tendency to headache.

bye darling
God bless and keep you
Emma

love to all friends

---

[4] Charles Prince, Bryant, and perhaps others had tried an unsuccessful investment; Prince handled the details.

Earl Sunday Morning April 18 /80

My Darling,

I am so unusually blessed this morning as to be ready for church a little in advance and will have a bit of talk with you. Have just been reading the April Am.[erican] Mis.[sionary]. . . .

Am glad to see, too, that the A.[merican] M.[issionary] A.[ssociation] proposes to enlarge their Southern work the coming year . . . I am not a bit satisfied with pen and ink talk this morning. I want to see you and be with you. Am a little sick and a good deal babyish—babyish means that I need you. I ought to be ashamed to add to your anxieties by telling you that I am not well. Shall try hard to be well and strong before you reach here.

I have been thinking again this morning about your plan to hire a house in town and I fear it is not wise—unless you are sure to need me at the office or unless your conscience absolutely demands it. I would prefer to remain in the country at present, moving in town would mean <u>for me</u> more housework and less walking—more pecuniary anxiety also. Now the <u>greatest freedom from my uterine weakness</u> that I have had for many years has been since I have been in Atlanta and I can not but attribute it chiefly to my frequent walks to town. I am threatened again with a return of those old difficulties and it is that that gives me the anxiety and depression to which I just confessed. Perhaps I ought to keep it from you in this time of your own anxiety but I feel that it is necessary for you to know it in making plans for the future—doctoring for it is entirely out of the question on account of expense. I shall try to take good care of myself and may throw it off, but I would dread to take upon myself the care that housekeeping in town would bring. . . . I am so sorry, for your difficulty with your own church people. I know it must mar the pleasantness of your church relations. . . .

I long to see you and be with you, darling. The day is entirely past and am just retiring. . . . I want to add to it that I am trusting in the dear Heavenly Father and that I do lay my cares and burdens on the Great Burden-bearer. Perhaps I was trying to carry them myself when I wrote you this morning.

Pray for me darling, not only in things temporal but in things spiritual and pray especially for Fisher, he does not seem at all ancored [*sic*] as yet. I wish you pleasant dreams and send warm loving good night kisses,

Emma

Earl Apr. 20 1880
Tuesday night

My Own Darling

I have been thinking especially of you to-day and of to-morrow as an important crisis, if your convention is held on that day. I only wish I might pray with you to-night as well as for you. May the dear Lord bless you. It is now 10. P.M. and I have robbed you of a half hour in which I should have been writing you, by reading a delicious love [*sic*] love-story. . . .

Wednes night. Emma is safe in bed and I am sitting near her in our chamber and wondering what has been the result of to-day's contest. whether you are enjoying a well earned victory, as I hope, or are [illegible] and possibly disheartened after an unsuccessful struggle. To-morrow I trust will tell me according to the promise of to-day's letter. In none of your political battles have I ever before been as anxious as now, because we are now where we are so illy able to bear disaster. Do not think me unmindful, either, of the work for God and humanity which you hope to do. For it and for ourselves I shall grieve if you are not sustained but in any case I am very thankful that our father above loves us and will care for us when the burden is beyond our strength. I must say one word more in regard to taking a house in town. I am very unwilling that you should obligate yourself to pay even so much as twelve dollars per month and my own opinion is that it is best to remain at Mrs. Sherman's another summer. You speak of the effect upon me of living there. you can not form a correct judgement upon it because I had so much greater troubles to wear upon me than the peculiarities of her disposition. your absence first and most, and next to that my pecuniary anxieties in town these latter will be doubled and trebled, the thought of the rapidly accumulating rent and the greater expenses of our poverty that would necessarily accompany town residence would be much more injurious to me than the trials I had to encounter at Mr. Sherman's unless your own health or convenience absolutely demand the change I feel anxious to take no further responsibility upon us in the way of rent until you are already fully established with some reliable salary or income. During your long absences and in the time of our peculiar straits I have always had this consolation that I had a roof over my head.

If you add to my pecuniary anxieties you will injure me in mind and body. At any rate please leave the houserenting until we return to Georgia.

One thing more if you do rent please avoid a house that is very near the railroad or so situated that Emma would need to cross the railroad in going to School if she should go. I suffer so much anxiety when she has to go alone across railroad tracks. I have never fully recovered, perhaps, from the shock that I experienced when she was brought home to me in Savannah.[5] I wish so much that we could talk over this matter of a house—it is difficult to express ourselves freely and clearly in writing. Even if you are sustained now, as I trust you have been, we have, I believe, many years of privation and labor before us and I fear to assume any added responsibilities in rent until we have money actually in hand, not simply in prospect. When the time comes that you cannot take so long a walk then we must do the best we can in town. I do want to <u>talk</u> over this matter [illegible] to know both sides. One word more in regard to the mistake about chess—I do feel hurt, darling. that knowing my reverence for the sabbath through all these years, you did not at once think that I had made a mistake in dates. I should have thought it of you. we can not afford to misjudge each other darling, when we have loved for so many years. With good-night kisses.

                                                            Bye bye
                                                            Emma

If I could know that you would be always home I would not so much object to the house in town for we could [illegible] I can fix and serve dinners but, with you away I would prefer to be at Mrs. Shermans. . . .

————

[letterhead] Rooms Republican Executive Committee,
State of Georgia.
Executive Committee: J. E. Bryant, Chairman;
Volney Spalding, Secretary; S. A. Darnell; C.O. Fisher;
Geo. S. Thomas; J. F. Long; Jesse A. Holtzclaw; Madison Davis;
Andrew W. Caldwell; John R. Hayes; Archibald P. Wade.
Atlanta, Ga. May 2, 1880

My Darling Wife:

I am again seated in my office for my Sunday chat. I have neglected you for a whole week; neglected you in writing, not otherwise.

————

[5] Alice recounted in her autobiography that in Savannah she was "run over by the street car and two of my toes were cut off and the big [toe] badly injured."

First let me tell you that I have been guilty of a little extravagance. A Mr. Wright has been here during the winter representing a Northern firm who enlarge photographs etc. I have had your picture enlarged and it looks <u>just as</u> you did when that picture was taken. I have that and Emmas photograph in front of me as I write, and it is the next thing to having you both with me, the best I can do now.

I think my church trouble is over. Our educational committee met last Tuesday. Dr. Mitchell was present. I brought up the matter of difficulty, and it finally narrowed itself down to a political difference. He admitted that he had taken sides with W. L. Clarke against me; said he had nothing against my Christian character. This difficulty has done me great good. It has caused the Fuller family and Bro. Winsor to take sides for me so warmly that I have been greatly benefitted. I heard that Mrs. Eiswald and Mrs. Eggleston said that I was an impure man. Bro. Winsor went to them about it and they said that what they did say was that if what "the Countess" said of me was true I was an impure man. It seems that she said to Mr. & Mrs. Eiswald that she was my mistress in New York. I wish you would, <u>as soon</u> <u>as you receive this</u>, write a letter to Bro Winsor and [illegible] to me—Rev. S. A. Winsor—and tell him what the woman told you in regard to that matter, in that famous "interview" in our parlor which ended in prayer. I suggest that you write something like this.—"Mr. Bryant informs me that. the woman calling herself the Countess of Landsfeldt told Mr. & Mrs. Eiswald that she was his mistress in New York"—Then, tell him what she said to you upon that subject. I wish for him to show the letter to Mrs. Eiswald and Mrs. Eggleston.

You seem to question whether my victory at the State Convention was complete. Let me state the matter fully. I have been in a contest for nearly four years with the Atkins-Conley combination.[6] Previous to this convention I formed a combination with Col. Buck, Maj. Smythe, Capt. Prince, Andrew Clark, Col. Wade[7] and others, and we were entirely successful. Upon a test vote we had 180 votes and the Atkins-Conley crowd 69. Nearly the entire delegation to Chicago—22—all my personal friends. The other side are completely overthrown, and Atkins is soon to be removed from the Custom House. He has been so informed by Secretary Sherman[8] who has the

---

[6] James Atkins; John L. Conley, son of Benjamin Conley, Republican governor of Georgia following Bullock.

[7] A. E. Buck; W. H. Smyth, another native of Maine; Charles H. Prince; Andrew Clark, collector of revenue in Georgia; Archibald P. Wade.

[8] John Sherman, secretary of the treasury.

appointment. But I was not chosen Chairman of the State committee and am not a delegate to Chicago. That happened in this way. In forming the combination it was necessary for me to decide upon either going as a delegate to Chicago or being a candidate for Chairman of the State committee. I decided upon the latter. But there has been since the organization of the party a trouble between the white and colored Republicans. Very few white men in our party have fully recognized the manhood of the colored man, and they have not given them a fair share of the patronage. I proposed to settle this conflict; and to that end I offered the following resolution, in the State Convention,

"Resolved that in the distribution of the honors and emoluments at the disposal of Republicans they shall be divided equally as nearly practicable between the white and colored Republicans."

This resolution was amended so as to provide that colored Republicans should receive three fourths of the honors and emoluments. Fourteen colored men and eight white were sent to Chicago. Twenty four colored men and eight whites were put upon the State Committee. After this had been done, I was nominated for Chairman of the State Committee, and it is admitted by friends and enemies that I would have been chosen by a large majority, but I refused to be Chairman under such circumstances.[9] I have gained the most complete triumph that I have won since I came to Georgia, and it is so regarded by my friends who understand all the circumstances.

It is time to prepare for evening service and I must stop although I have much more to write. Will try to do so before next Sunday.

I love you darling, and send warm love and kisses for you and Emma. Y. H.

—————

Earl May 7th 1880
Friday 1 P.M.

My Darling.

I must make my answer to your last very brief for my forenoon has been swallowed up by [illegible] errands and little household duties and two difficult problems in arithmetic and I want to make room for a little bookkeeping this P.M.

—————

[9] William A. Pledger was elected chairman. See Ruth Currie-McDaniel, "Black Power in Georgia: William A. Pledger and the Takeover of the Republican Party."

Neal [*sic*] has a very fine treatise upon book keeping and I feel that it is very essential that I should gain some knowledge of it which I can easily do if can in any way devote the time to it. I have also spent considerable time upon arithmetic partly to assist Neil in difficult problems and partly for my own benefit. I think it is nearly twenty years since I studied it and the circumstances of my life now requiring me to use it I was in danger of losing nearly all knowledge of it.

I have also gathered and analyzed a few specimens of flowers and now the summer is upon us and my summer sewing undone. . . . I wonder if I am detailing these things to unappreciative ears, if you are so engrossed in your own more active life as to feel little interest in these things which necessarily make up so much of the substance of mine? I am so exacting as to hope not for we wives are much in need of receiving as well as ready to give sympathy and interest. And now after this long prologue I must plunge "in medis res" and reply to your request to write Mr. Windsor [*sic*] a letter in regard to our interview with the Countess in our parlor. I am <u>very unwilling</u> to write such a letter, because I feel very certain that <u>it would be injurious to you</u> for me to do so. I can not give you all the reasons by letter for thinking so, but I am thoroughly convinced that the less you say of that matter the better. I have the <u>most perfect</u> and <u>complete confidence</u> that, in no sense, were you then, or at any other time, untrue to me, that in all your intercourse with the Countess you did nothing unbecoming a christian and a gentleman—both Bro. Windsor and Mrs. Eiswald <u>must know</u> this by my actions and by my statements in conversation with them. Mrs. Eiswald you say remarked that <u>if</u> the Countess told the truth you were so & so. Now Mrs. Eiswald has detected the Countess in the most flagrant and unprovoked lies, has put money under lock and key lest she might prove a common thief, and has loaned her underclothes which she wore away and never returned beside her knowledge that she borrowed money in Atlanta and went away leaving that and her bills unpaid. Now if she chooses to take the word of such a woman as against that of a brother church member who has sustained a blameless reputation heretofore before the world and in his own church nothing remains to be done and the writing of any letter by me would be not only useless but quite beneath my own dignity and yours.

If you have promised Bro. Windsor any such letter as you request of me you can read him what I have written in regard to the matter thus far if you choose, beginning where I have made the parallel strokes of the pen on the preceding page.

I hope you will not feel hurt by my refusal to write the letter that you request. I feel that my love and trust in you in all those days of your trial, while they were no greater than you deserved, still were such as to entitle my advice or wishes (whichever you chose to call it) to have weight now, and I say <u>please</u> talk no more of that affair, or at least make no further explanation than you have already done. You remember that was your own decision, at the time, and I am perfectly convinced of the wisdom of it.

Her character is such that if left to herself she will be confounded, but when you attempt to explain and make written statements you give your opinion an opportunity to injure you. I think from what you write that your troubles in the church are working out quite as well as can be expected, when Dr. Mitchell acknowledged that his dislike to you was not on account of your personal character that was an entire vindication of you as far as the church are [*sic*] concerned and I am very much pleased at such an outcome of it. As for the other, if Mrs. Eiswald and Mrs. Eggleston choose to gossip about you I know of no way to prevent it and only one way of making it comparatively harmless viz. take no notice of it. I am extremely sorry that these private matters have come up to add to all your other anxiety and care. but the dear Father knows and will not permit you to be burdened above that you can bear. I am inclined to think that you did well to decline chairmanship under the circumstances but I am sorry that could not have been foreseen in order to prevent you from surrendering the place of delegate.

I feel anxious that you should come as a delegate but shall trust that it will be all for the best. You have not yet answered my question if you will come to the convention at all. I am very anxious to know and anxious to know whether I will go away when you do. I feel that I have already made as long visit as is proper and am somewhat anxious not to remain very long after June 1. . . .

I am sorry not to write you oftener . . . I find myself almost utterly incapacitated from using my eyes after lamplight. . . .

> Bye darling.
> Loving kisses
> Emma. . . .

Earl May 13th 1880

My Darling.

A bit of this early morning hour must be devoted to you. . . . I have almost defrauded you of letters of late but I find my sewing presses me exceedingly and my old difficulties are threatening me and I know no way to avoid them unless by spending considerable time in the open air.

Rec'd yesterday your long Sunday letter and a short one containing Lucy's wedding card. . . . I hope that marriage [illegible] bring her as much real happiness and as little sorrow as it has to us.

I am more than glad that you feel your present situation so favorable. God grant that the road be smoother for you than it has been for the two years past. Had I not felt a close and firmer faith in God than I used these years would have been very dark to me. . . . I am placing very strong dependence now upon seeing you June.1st. and counting the weeks which seperate [*sic*] us from that time.

If you do not reach Chicago before June 1st, will you come here before the convention? as hurried as I am to see you I would rather wait till after the convention if in that way you can remain longer. Even if I go with you when you leave I still wish you to remain as long as you can. I have refrained hitherto from mentioning my pecuniary necessities . . . but it has occurred to me that you might be able to enclose a trifle weekly in your letters when your means do not admit of sending any large sum. I am already somewhat indebted to sister and do not wish to borrow more, and beside she has herself been somewhat cramped for money since I came here. Times have been very close with Mr. Browne for the last year or two—he says it is impossible for him to support his family here and he proposes to go away somewhere this month. They have from time to time added to the farm so that they are some 3000. in debt for that, so that all that comes from the farm is swallowed up by it again. . . .

I have felt the need of economy so much that I have done my own ironings since I came here [illegible] for a few weeks, my own washings and my uterine difficulties may be in some degree owing to this; at any rate, I shall not run the risk of doing either, now that the warm weather is upon us. . . .

I am glad that Clark, Buck and Smythe are working in harmony with you, but fear [illegible] enthusiastic when you denominated them "fast friends" still I think that their friendship is an augury that your star is in the ascendent. I do not think them the men to espouse your cause unless they believe it on the road to success. altho I regret the necessity for relinquishing chairmanship [of the] committee I do not see that you could well have done otherwise. . . .

Bye darling.
Emma

Earl June 1st 1880

My Own Darling Husband.

Yesterday morning brought me a great disappointment which you can doubtless measure by your own. I have seldom felt a disappointment more keenly and yet I dare not repine at this or any of the privations our dear Father permits to come to me for he has sustained and succored us wonderfully in these two or three years past. . . . I wish you, please, to make especial prayer for me, in regard to my own christian life, that I may know God's teachings to me, and obey them. . . .

I shall be heartily thankful if you are ever able to settle down where I can be with you. Sister was much disappointed not to see you here and Neilly scolded a good deal, Alice too, took it quite to heart. Please write me often as possible. I shall be impatient to know of any turn of the wheel that will bring us together. When I do go from here I am very anxious to plan so as to visit in Aurora and Chicago, so please do not expect me to go on so short notice as I usually do. . . . I rec'd the 1.00 in last letter also 2.00 in previous and have just spent them in a summer hat, the first since the centennial. I have just finished it (made it myself) and it is pronounced very pretty and I think it so myself.

I have not told you that sister has given me the materials for a new black dress, bunting trimmed with silk—have nearly finished it. Father gave me 3.00, too, and so, little by little, I am trying to put my wardrobe into a tidy and respectable condition—it has been so long neglected. . . . Alice enjoys her school very much but I have almost felt that her nervousness is increased since she went to school—shall not send her any more to school for some years to come, I think. I fully believe that I can bring her up to my ideal of womanhood, both physically and mentally more nearly by home education until she is nearly grown. She enjoys the companionship of children here very much and at school picks up the bad and good together as we must expect. She has formed a fast friendship with Miss Whaley a young lady of twenty or more . . . the attachment appears to be mutual, and is very agreeable to me as she is a very amiable young lady. Alice promises to grow up into a lovely womanhood and yet I have an almost constant anxiety regarding her like most mothers I suppose. . . . I shall be delighted when the proper time comes for me to go to you. Your society will be as grateful as sunshine to the birds and flowers, meanwhile, I shall make time short as possible by being very busy on my own work and sisters. She is unable to use her eye[s] for any sewing at all and I am anxious to assist her as much as previously. . . . With loving kisses

Emma

————

Earl June 19th / 80

My Darling Husband.

Would that this beautiful morning might bring you to me bodily instead of these vain longings for you and unsatisfactory use of ink. . . . Your last letter was a long one and spoke somewhat fully of your hopes and plans. Now that the paper is no longer published I have often feared that there might be a lack of definition in the expenditure of money which might cause you trouble, we have I think spoken of this before and it troubles me often now. I have felt that so large a proportion of it has gone into expenses instead of into any direct work of enlightenment among the people. But as I cannot myself do your work I will try to be sparing of criticism, and pray God to bless you and give you wisdom as well as faith and energy in the Lord's work. I have often felt strengthened by that passage in James, "if any of you lack wisdom let him ask of God"—I hope you may be successful in obtaining a government position, not because I wish to see you again in government employ but because we are in such absolute need of the money. and if you do get such a position I beg of you, first and foremost, to devote a portion every month to the payment of debts. I do not believe that otherwise you can be blessed of God. In no respect are my convictions of duty stronger than in this. Yesterday I had a very pleasant call from Bro. Lee, he came expecting to see you. . . . We talked politics a little and your work and I gave him the article from the Ph.[iladelphia] News which you enclosed in your last. Bro. Lee, as you know, is one of the friends to whom I am much attached.

This is Sat. and I am invited out to tea with a party of young people, by which invitation I feel quite flattered, having been so long dropped from the young people's ranks. Laura was so complimentary as to say that she thought me about as young as any of them but really I think the secret of her leaning towards me is my sentiment upon the woman question. Last night—I was at a church festival and must get time for a nap to-day or am afraid I will not be able to make myself agreeable to the youthful element this evening. Alice gone [*sic*] with me to tea. She is well and happy.

With loving kisses from my heart of hearts.
Emma

Earl July 19, 1880

My Darling Husband,

. . . I wonder if you are as hungry to see me to-night as I am to see you. It is
only half a life away from you. Am afraid I am a little blue to-night. Alice is not
very well . . . tho' not really sick. . . . Alice's legs are covered with sores that discharge like boils and many other children have similar boils. . . . On Sat. last she
jumped off the fence and struck her bare heel on the width of an iron rake making quite a wound and I have been intensely anxious about her but she seems
to be doing extremely well now. . . . She is in the main a very good girl and obedient but does some things out from my sight that she would not in, as I well
remember I did myself. . . . I long to be with you darling, to be in your arms
and in your heart and your daily life. God grant it soon. With loving kisses

Emma

[Emma adds a note on a page she began on July 14.]

I will not try to tell you the pleasure that your Monday's letter . . . gave me—
nor the pain that I felt in knowing of the straits of which you speak . . . but I
thank God, darling that in every trouble you cling close to the Saviour, that you
keep your faith in God and humanity. I [can] think of no temporal privation
that would be so great a calamity to either of us as the possession of that species
of philosophy which turns all of God's creation into gall and bitterness.

The portion of this letter which I wrote some days ago and of necessity
kept until now I found that I had left below and must therefore write now on
another sheet.

I like the Bishop's article and am rejoiced in the work of Mrs. Watson, in
one thing at least (and many other[s] I may add) we have, I think, quite
agreed viz. that the Marietta st. church needed to work among the Southern
people and I am very ready to say God speed to the work now inaugurated.[10]
In the close of your letter you express your hope and belief . . . that our future
is to be brighter than our past has been. When I remember how fast time is
gaining on us and how heavily loaded you are and, in all human probability
must be for many, many years, I dare not rest my happiness on the hope of
brighter days, but, rather thank God that we have each other and the dear
child that He has given us and take our pleasure day by day. . . . I find that all

---

[10] The effort was to target poor white children for education.

my life has been occupied in anticipations of the future which anticipations are in most things quite unfulfilled and I am trying to school myself to live more for to-day and less for to-morrow, my greatest longing now, in temporal matters, is that we three may be constantly together and that you may be blessed in your present work with of course that wonderful blessing of health which we so seldom remember to thank God for. I send enclosed a letter from Alice which I doubt not will be more important to you than my own as it is almost her first attempt to write a letter in writing text. I have not written you, perhaps, that she has begun to take music lessons. [Miss Whaley] giving her lessons gratuitously.

Mendota Aug. 2$\underline{d}$ /80
Monday Mornig [*sic*]

My Darling,

... I have been here since Thursday last enjoying a very pleasant visit with Mr. & Mrs. Lee. They enquire very cordially for you. ... They are very pleasantly situated here and Bro. Lee seems to be very active and useful, but his health is very poor so that I think work, even for the Master must be often very burdensome. Alice was much pleased with her letters from papa but quite scolded because I insisted upon her reading it herself. She made a long work of it and required a good deal of help, but did better than I expected. If she makes the requisite effort she will very soon write and read writing.

Thanks for the 2.00 enclosed. Thus far I am obliged to use everything as fast as rec'd for washing and small bills. It will be necessary for me to spend quite a little sum in shoes and hose when you are able to send it. ... I am constantly distressed with the fear that owing to your own pecuniary necessities you will be unable to make such direct application of funds collected to the designed objects as shall satisfy the givers. I do not mean that your services do not deserve recompense, but that the society in Atlanta under whose auspices you work being unable to pay you any salary so much of what you collect necessarily goes for our support and your travelling expenses, but as I cannot remedy this I suppose it is quite useless for me to knit my brows over it or add to the wrinkles already envading [*sic*] my face. God keep you and help you out of all those places that look so dark to me. I am interested in what you write of Dr. Fulton's work and bid him Godspeed, tho' I have not been quite prepossessed in favor of the man in the past. You know that I always feel just a grain of indignation toward any man who presumes to [de]fine woman's sphere for her as Dr. Fulton has done in the past. My lip always curls a little when I think of that part of his history.

I propose to return to Earl to-day wind and weather permitting. [I] begin to feel that I ought to be there to resume my bookkeeping and sewing as I have still much to do in both departments and I am looking forward to being with you in a very few weeks. I want to write a line now to Lucy or your mother so will say good bye to you.

Lovingly
Emma

Tuesday morning

Returned from Mendota yesterday—hope to hear from you again very soon.

————

Earl Aug. 4. 1880

My Darling.

Yours written on Sunday reached me to-day but have time to-night for scarcely more than good night and pleasant dreams. Have just finished a shirt for Father and I find that my eyes and head suffer if I use the former much at night. I am glad that you feel so strong and confident in your work and trust that your confidence is well founded. Indeed I feel myself a good deal of confidence that you will be blessed in the work that you are doing. I sometimes think that you are in danger of somewhat overestimating the coincidences or providences of your life. I think it is quite right that we should be encouraged and our faith strengthened by them and yet they may not be as wonderful as they seem to us and are not sure evidence that we are in the way of duty.

God grant that you are in the way of duty and if you are we can surely trust fully in God, knowing that He will give us that which is good for us. The Lord has blessed you spiritually [illegible] the last few years and I can say from the depths of my heart "bless His holy name" even tho' our pathway has been hedged about with many difficulties.

Alice is growing rapidly and is now quite well. . . . I cant say that she develops a very industrious disposition yet and she is not at all proficient in sewing. I doubt if she will gain her livelihood by manual labor if there is any other way open.

Taken all in all she bears a remarkable likeness to her father mentally as well physically, in her little habits she reminds me so much more of you than myself. I can trace scarce a resemblance to myself, but I presume that she will imbibe from me by training and association sufficient to create in time some slight likeness between us.[11] She is a dear child, remarkably free from ill temper and making many warm friends. She and Neilly live very harmoniously, considering that both are only children, they are really very fond of each other.

> And now I must retire at once. . . .
> With loving kisses
> Bye darling
> Emma

———

Earl Aug. 8th 1880

My Darling.

God has given us such a big and beautiful Sabbath morning that it seems as if all hearts ought to break forth with the words of David, "Bless the Lord O, my Soul and all that is within me, bless his holy name." It is near church time. Alice is studying her S.S. lesson, or, judging by the sound, worshiping in song. I dont think her singing is always in tune but I am determined she shall have the comfort of singing tune or no tune and dont allow any one to discourage her. Within the last few years it has been a great deprivation to me to be unable to join in the singing during worship. I have almost imagined that it was to some degree responsible for the loss of a high degree of enthusiasm and enjoyment in my religious life. I wonder where you worship to-day and if your heart has already turned towards wife and child as mine towards you. Your presence not only with me but close beside me in the house of God has always added much to my happiness therein. It seems to me that in the house of God especially is the place where families should be together before God and that a part of the blessing is lost when they worship apart or scattered in different portions of the house. God grant that in our repeated and long continued separation the family closeness of feeling may not be weakened.

———

[11] Alice later said, "I think my mother was the most conscientious and truthful person I have ever known in my life. Uncompromising in her beliefs, she made every sacrifice to carry out the things she felt were right and yet she never sharply criticized others who felt differently. She did give advice where she felt it was necessary. . . . She was the stuff that martyrs are made of."

Monday morning I am inclined to complain a little because your letters have fallen off to one a week, possibly I have been as remiss myself, shall I not hear at least twice a week the remainder of my absence from you?

I am reading just now a book which I am very desirous for you to read, at least one chapter of it, if you care to read no more. It is "Studies in the Creator's Work" by George D. Boardman, he is the son of the missionary Boardman and himself a Baptist minister.

The particular chapter which I wish you to read is entitled "Genesis of Woman" and I ask you to read it because it reconciles St. Pauls charges to women, which almost all mankind quotes against our equality in the family and before the law, with St. Paul's other assertion that in "Christ Jesus there is neither male nor female, but both are one in Him."

I ask you to read it <u>carefully</u> and <u>thoughtfully</u> because, while you have proved yourself a true christian and true husband by <u>respecting</u> my views, you have still <u>believed</u> them to be incorrect and unsanctioned by God's word. You can undoubtedly borrow this this [*sic*] book from baptist S.S. or private library or even take it from some public library and I particularly wish you to read this chapter at least, and I think you will be pleased and benefitted by the whole. He takes just as advanced ground as I have ever taken or ask any one to take, and is one of the few male writers whose ideas of women I can read without feeling my blood boil with honest indignation and my lip curl with contempt, perhaps you think that I speak strongly. My darling, if you ever have revealed to you as has been revealed to me day by day and year by year the connection between sin and social disorder and wickedness and the disbelief of womans equality with man you will feel as strongly as I do. I verily believe that no woman who fails to assert and maintain in her own family that position of equality with her husband is at all fit to bring up a son, perhaps I should omit the word <u>assert</u> because it is always unfortunate when the woman needs to assert that which she should simply <u>use</u> as her <u>natural</u> inheritance without any dispute or need of assertion.

It is only the unwillingness to grant woman's true power that brings into woman's rights that element of sharpness which is so discordant and unwomanly. God grant that our own little daughter shall never need to <u>assert</u> her rights in her own household, that she shall never rear a son who shall consider woman inferior to man—she bids fair now to grow up to a noble womanhood.

With loving kisses.
Emma

. . . September will soon be here—are you able to make any definite plans as to our return to Georgia? sincerely trust that I will not need to remain North until after the presidential election as I have almost always done. I shall not go from here to your folks until I have means to purchase my ticket through and make them a brief visit—on the way. I did not write your mother the other day but will do so very soon.

———

Earl Aug. 14, 1880

My Darling Husband.

A bit of this lovely morning shall be devoted to you even tho' something else suffer in consequence.

To-morrow August will be half gone and I am wondering whether early September will see a renewal of our home-life in Atlanta. Have you any definite plan of operations and of where you will be between now and the November election? Is what you say of being with us in a few weeks founded on anything but your desires? The desire to be sure is the most important thing but it may not have power to bring us together nevertheless. I am very anxious to be settled with you in Atlanta in Sep. if possible because I begin to be haunted with a fear that I may be left here till after the election and I shall be very unwilling either to be away from you so long or to be away from you at that time.

Of course I hear little but democracy here and it has given me a good deal of fear that we may be defeated at the polls through the solid South made so only by intimidation and fraud. I went last night to the baptist church to hear a colored minister lecture and night before to hear him preach. He was only an average man but told them some truths in regard to the Ku Klux and the negro exodus, but there were few to hear and I presume comparatively few that would have believed if they had heard.

I am not discontented here and I find myself leading a busy and useful life but I feel that we have been apart much too long and I am grown very hungry for the dear home life and your companionship which is the brightness of that life. God grant that it be not very long in coming. I shall hope to hear from you at least two or three times each week during the remainder of my absence from you. Alice is well and happy and usually good. I am encouraged to see indications that she is coming up in the path that leads towards true womanhood. I have great reason to be thankful that God has helped me to be firm in such things as I have required of her . . . [and] have been able to establish . . . in her mind . . . some idea of law human and divine. I see daily cause for rejoicing that I have pursued this course, without it she with her abundant spirit and pushing, somewhat dominant disposition would control me and lead both me and herself a hard life. I am beginning to feel anxiety in regard to her education. . . . I believe her capable of becoming a noble woman, one to attain any station where providence may place her. I must try to do a little bookeeping [*sic*] this morning and so must say good bye to you now.

> With loving kisses
> Bye, darling
> Emma

———

Earl Sep. 20th 1880

My Darling.

To-days mail brought yours of the 16th with 5.00 enclosed, both money and letter found a ready welcome. I am hoping that very soon you will be able to return to Atlanta taking us with you, aside from my own great desire to be with you I am anxious to take Alice to a warmer climate she has contracted a cold which causes her to cough every night and is quite as much troubled with ague as she was at home. Indeed I never saw her in so poor health for the same length of time. . . .

I wonder if you are aware that in this letter which you write as an answer to my own upon our pecuniary situation you have not answered a single question (save in regard to Fla. lands). You must realize that it does not affect the question at all whether you were better or worse off some years ago. Is it not possible, my darling, for you to answer me a plain question or two without going back into the past or dealing in generalities. I will try this <u>once again</u> and if you go around it and behind it and over it as you did in your last I shall content myself in ignorance as best I can, but remember, husband mine, that in thus dealing with my questions you are increasing my anxiety and diminishing my faith in your ultimate success, and you know, darling, how great is the need that we work together and believe together, as well as pray together.

What definite plans have you for making an immediate or very early <u>beginning</u> of paying your debts, especially Jo[seph]'s and the Ga. debt?— how can money be earned in your present work for more than the support of your family and that in the same economical fashion of for [*sic*] the past years? If you have anything definite and tangible in your own mind you can surely communicate it to me, and, if not, please say that you have not, that I may know on just what to depend. Alice is in bed and asleep but she breathes badly and I am haunted with a fear as I have often been that I may sacrifice her life to our coming here. I cannot tell you how much I dread the autumn months in the north—here especially they always seem unhealthy to me. Can I depend upon being settled with you in Georgia early next month? I should be very happy if could depend upon it. I wish so very much that I could assist you by some labor of my own perhaps this providence may open the way, which now looks so hedged up to me. I love you darling and long to be with you. Please do not think that I am thoughtless of you over anxiety and labor. I know that you are very heavily burdened,—God help you, darling, bye, bye.

When I say you go over around and behind my questions I do not for a moment mean to convey the idea that you are insincere or content to deceive me. I know that it is only the general and large view which you take of it, but nevertheless a very unsatisfactory one to me. What I need is an <u>answer</u> that is definite and confined to the question.

When I am anxious regarding Alice I am so overburdened and troubled that I cannot be over careful of my words and you must not be over critical. While I believe that I am not unsubmissive to God's will, even in regard to our child, I cannot express to you the terror and grief and anxiety that surges over me when she is sick. It is best that you do not feel it in just in [*sic*] the same manner and degree that I do because you would be quite unfit for your special manly duties in life if you did. I am troubled both for her and for you and for our future. God help us.

Bye darling.

Earl Sep. 29th 1880

My Darling Husband.

Your telegram and letter both from Boston arrived to-day and should have written you this morning immediately on receipt of telegram but had a little painting still to finish and did not dare leave it but I might not finish it in season to dry before the wedding. The bride and her family are intimate friends of sisters and mine and we are consequently a good deal interested in said wedding, but I am afraid there is to be a curious and unfortunate circumstance in connection with it, viz. no bridegroom. He is a lawyer in some city west of here and the bride wrote him the day fixed upon for the wedding and gave out her invitations without waiting to hear from him, and up to this time she has received no intimation that he has received her letter naming the day or that he will be here on time. The wedding is fixed for to-morrow night. . . .

Is not it a sorry dilemma for a young lady? So much for the wedding, now a word to our own affairs, the letter rec'd to-day and one previously are a little more definite than the first as to your business matters and expectations. I have some serious fear in connection with your present work but seeing that your confidence is strong I shall hope that my fears are groundless, as they may be, and forbear to trouble you with them. I find it difficult, too, to discuss these matters by letter as I almost invariably find myself more or less misunderstood. . . .

As regards my own health there is nothing alarming. Alice's cough is less troublesome . . . but she complains of headache again to-night. She says give her love to papa and tell him I want to go home. I shall begin at once to make such preparations as I can for going home. The money (2.00) in to-days letter was very acceptable, especially so, as I can do little towards preparing to go home without money, if you can send something more soon it will help materially towards preparing for our early departure. I wish if possible to make all my preparations before you send the money for my fare or at least before you are ready to say come. I am very glad that you are meeting with good success in your speech making and can say God speed you—and speed you, too, in the direction of home, please write as often as possible.

I must write no more for am sitting in a cold room and fear I am taking cold.

Bye, bye darling.
Emma

Earl Oct. 8, 1880

My Darling Husband.

I have just come up stairs with Alice and she says "Send my love and tell him to come some night when I am asleep and pull my tooth." I made an unsuccessful attempt to pull it to-night and I am afraid weakened her confidence in my dental skill. . . .

You dont write me as often as you used before we were married, I think, but in sober truth, I need quite as much wooing as I did then and appreciate it fully as much.

We have had quite a little romance here.

The young lady whose wedding was deferred last week because the bridegroom did not make his appearance, rec'd a telegram yesterday to go to her intended immediately. He is near Sioux City Iowa lying dangerously [ill], unable to write even as the letter rec'd on same day as the telegram was written by the landlady. I was at her house all yesterday evening helping her to pack her things as she left this morning at 11 A.M. They are to be married immediately on her arrival if he is alive, her own health is in a miserable state and I feel very anxious for both. I feel a little anxious about yourself, too, when the whole week passes without a letter. . . . God keep you, darling. I pray with all my heart that our home life may be soon renewed,

Bye, darling
Emma

P.S. When you send money it is quite necessary that I should know how much I can depend upon aside from the money to go home with. perhaps I am asking, tho' what is not in your power to do.

I am now entirely out of money with Drs. bill unpaid, washing bill unpaid and in need of things both for self, as the money that should have gone for those was necessarily devoted to other things. And if possible Alice's 10. must be paid her and put into her grandpa's hands for his note on interest, she is depending on it and will be quite discouraged about saving money if she does not have it. . . .

How does the result of the election in Atlanta please you? Do you consider Colquitt[12] any improvement upon Norwood? perhaps that is not correctly phrased but you understand my meaning.

I enclose an article from the Chi. [ago] Times of to-day. Is not their view of Colquitt more favorable than facts warrant? Yours of 6th with 2.00 enclosed just rec'd this (Sat) morning. also news. slip referring to you in complimentary terms, which of course is a pleasure to me. . . .

---

[12] Alfred H. Colquitt, Democratic governor of Georgia; would serve in United States Senate 1883–94.

[Oct. 15, 1880?]

My Darling Husband.

Yesterday brought yours enclosing experience of "N.Y." in the South and to-day your replies to question concerning Fla. Lands. I have already written to Charles concerning it.

If the wish of the minister's wife was only another way of wishing for suffrage I doubt not it will be realized if she lives a few years longer.[13] I am glad to know that you are successful in speaking but am very anxious for the time when we will return to [illegible] your work there begins or be taken up again when you dropped [illegible]

Shall we return before the election which is near at hand? I am [illegible] my sewing because I hope that the time of home going is so near at hand. Alice and I have severe cold and she has a troublesome enlargement of the tonsils which troubles me exceedingly. I am not aware that she had it before coming here. I must not spend more time in writing now as have apron to finish for Alice to wear to school in the morning, she sends love and seems quite well saving the severe cold and enlargement of tonsils.

With loving kisses
Bye, darling
Emma

————

Earl Oct. 29, 1880

My Darling.

Your letter rec'd this morning tho' most welcome brings me disappointment, because our home going is longer deferred. Tho I <u>do</u> trust all in our Father's hands, I am still very anxious to be home on Alice's account. She has never recovered from the cold which she contracted some two months ago by wading in the brook after the cold weather began, and her tonsils are enlarged and inflamed. It is now a very unhealthy season of the year and diphtheria is pervading very seriously in some places, altho' it has not reached here as yet. Mendota where Bro. Lee lives, usually a very healthy place, has diphtheria in a malignant form I am told this morning. I consider this an unhealthy place

---

[13] Alice later wrote of her mother, "She was a woman's suffragist when the movement was very unpopular."

for children in the fall of the year and our whole past year has been unfavorable and abnormal. While I am ready to do and work and sacrifice with you in your work I am not ready to risk the life of our child. I have always protested against remaining north at this season of the year and have always been obliged to do it. I am not blaming you, my darling, for the past or asking more than you can do for the present, but this I ask, that, if possible, you will send me money at once, $100, if you can, if not less, so that I may have it in my power to go home even without you if Alice's health or any epidemic here makes it absolutely necessary. and, if you can by return mail please send me one or two dollars as I am seriously hindered in my preparation for lack of even a small sum. I cannot express to you save as your own heart may tell you with what a desperate hold I cling to our only child or how my heart sinks at any danger that menaces her. and yet I do not believe that I am holding her with an unsanctified love, remember that I have not the public work to fill heart and soul that you have. Knowing all this, I am sure that you will at once, if possible, provide me the means of returning home should that be necessary. Now one other [illegible], in your next please tell me <u>explicitly</u> what remaining until after election means. does it mean an indefinite stay prolonged perhaps till Christmas or past? and secondly is our return to the south an absolute certainty?—it is very necessary that I should have direct and full answer to these questions. To put them in a little different form if I go to Georgia next week or the week after how soon can you meet me there, and is there an absolute certainty that our home will continue to be in the South? . . .
[no signature in copy]

———

Earl Nov. 18th 1880
Thursday Morning

My Darling.

I must write very briefly this morning for have spent nearly all the morning running out to attend to little matters that could not well be neglected and it is now near mail time. I am heartily glad of the prospect of being with [you] even for the comparatively brief time you mention, till after Jan. but wish it might be longer. When you planned for us to be home together on thanksgiving I think you did not take into account what I have before mentioned that any homeward trip will of necessity occupy about ten days on account of stopping in Aurora and Chicago.

In all my visits here I have never been outside of Earlville save for the time that I have spent in Mendota, and I am unwilling to go home this time without spending some time in Chicago. It may be many years before another so favorable opportunity occurs, as I have friends who give me an urgent invitation to visit them there and I shall incur no extra expense in so doing. Aside from the pleasure of stopping there it is really a necessity for me to do so as I wish to visit some works of art and examine the hand painting upon satin opportunities for which I do not have in Georgia so please in all your calculations bear this in mind that I cannot fly as soon as the money reaches me, but you may be sure I shall make all practicable haste.

Alice's birthday on Tuesday passed off very pleasantly for her, she had a little girl to tea . . . and I gave her some candy and a small joosted [*sic*] ware doll with which she was delighted and her Auntie gave her the material for a cashmere dress and I am just now especially hurried because I wish if possible to make it up this week as next week begins the housework, so . . . I am hurrying in order to be with you the sooner. I shall make the greatest effort to be ready to start as soon as I receive funds from you so that there may be no more delay than the time consumed in the journey and visits. I shall probably not stop more than a day and night in Aurora but in Chicago I am obliged to have several days. The friends I will visit in Aurora are people whom I value highly and have promised a visit ever since I came here.

I love you darling and shall be happier with you than anywhere else.

> God keep and bless you darling
> With loving kisses
> Emma

When you speak of thanksgiving do you mean five week[s] from to-day, which is thanksgiving here?

————

Earl Dec. 21, 1880

My Darling

I dreamed last night of you, as I often do, but my dreams of late are not so pleasant as they always used to be, there seems of late to be some element of trouble when I dream of you, but it may be born of my disappointment in the deferred home-going and reunion.

Can you now fix upon the time of your return to Atlanta with any thing like certainty? I have a dismal fear that your absence may still be prolonged through weeks and months. I hope tho' that my fears are only idle and unfounded. I shall in any event, if funds reach me, return to Atlanta directly after Christmas unless some entirely unforseen providence shall prevent. Alice is much better in health than she [was] some weeks ago, but diptheria [*sic*] is prevailing in different portions of the state and I shall feel safer when I have her fairly out of the country. I must spend only a few minutes in writing this morning for I have a little painting on satin to do before Christmas and only four days now remaining and our housework leaves us very little time for anything else. I shall do very little for Christmas, some trifle for Alice and a little to others to whom I am under special obligations. I have paid Alice the 10. loaned me last year when I came here with 1. int.[erest] making 11. which she has put in her grandpa's hands taking her note at .08% I felt that this was important to be done and shall be obliged to be very prudent about Christmas gifts in consequence.

I am growing extremely tired of absence from you and feel fears sometimes that these long continued absences will weaken the bonds that have always held our hearts and lives so closely together. Does this fear ever trouble you, husband mine?

God keep you, darling and reunite us <u>very soon</u>
Emma

Earl Dec. 25, 1880

My Darling.

I wish you Merry Christmas and only wish that I could do it in person. I feel very sure that you have felt this Christmas disappointment as well as I. I did feel very sure that we would, at the the [*sic*] very farthest be together on Christmas day. Do you realize that this is the second Christmas since we have seen each other and the third in succession that we have not passed together.

I little thought on last Christmas that another Christmas would come before I should return to you. Our Christmas has passed off pleasantly to the children, ergo pleasantly to us. They are just now winding up the day's festivities by a candy pull in the kitchen with a young man who has spent the day with them. O'Neil received a sett [*sic*] of chess-men a present from Alice, and they spent the morning playing chess.

Alice, for a little girl, plays quite a game. I am distressed by what you write me of Farrow's course,[14] even if your answer is ever so conclusive I fear that his attack will be a serious injury to you, but I must leave it in God's hands. As I have received no telegram from you yet I judge that you did not leave for Atlanta as you intended.

We wished for your presence at the dinner table to-day and I wondered where you might be. If you answer this before I see you tell me where and how you passed your Christmas, pleasantly or otherwise?

I must leave now to prepare Alice for bed. I long to be with you, darling, and am only made more impatient by such fresh delay. May the dear Father very soon reunite us

Bye darling.

Emma

Earl Dec. 30, 1880

My Darling.

Yours of Sunday and O'Neils book arrived yesterday by same mail, and he wishes me to return his thanks for book. The letter which fell to my share I enjoyed, and none the less because it falls under the head of love letters, a taste for which I have never outgrown.

I regret deeply that your return home is again postponed and still more the opposition from Georgia which causes it. I am sometimes almost discouraged when this opposition breaks out in addition to all the other obstacles in your path, but I can heartily thank God that none of these things make you lose faith in God or render you sour and misanthropic. These would be to me much worse afflictions than any disasters which could befall us. I am very glad to know that you passed so pleasant Christmas.

I must make my chat very brief this morning for I have a little painting on hand which I could not refuse to do, as the lady who asked has shown me favors which place me under obligations to her. I am also obliged to make a waterproof for Alice to travel in as it is so cold that I dare not trust to her cloak alone in traveling. I had hoped to save a portion of the money already sent for

---

[14] Henry P. Farrow, Georgia Republican, attorney general in the Bullock administration and longtime party rival to JEB, would turn on him with vengeance in the coming year.

some shopping in Chicago but fear I will not be able, as small debts, money paid to Alice and necessary articles for her and self together with washing and Christmas have nearly eaten it up. All are small bills save the debt to Alice, but have aggregated considerable. The fifty yet to come I shall not dare to break shall reserve that for the journey home. I have still sufficient to buy the waterproof for Alice and such other little items as are needed to start me off. I shall be obliged to take an extra [illegible] by freight or express as my possessions have accumulated and sister proposes to give me a nice little jar of butter and some fruit but the money is running straight away from me. with a hurried kiss.

bye, bye
Emma

P.S. If you have an opportunity I wish you would make inquiries about Mr Pray's family in my name. He had two brothers doing business in Boston they kept carpet store under the name of Pray Bros.

Earl Jan. 11th 1881

My Darling Husband.

I am grown homesick for a letter from you and dont even dare scold about it for have kept you unenlightened as to my whereabouts. Shall look very soon tho' for a reply to my last, directing you to write here until you learn that I have left, could I be certain that you would be in Atlanta as early as the last week in this month I should start next week, unless prevented by sickness. Thus far it has been impossible to go as there has been sickness in the house ever since receipt of money, first O'Neil, and, as he recovered, father. Father has been sick with very severe cold, so sick that I have been up to care for him for past two nights and am feeling almost ill myself now with watching and a cold. Father is better to-day and I hope for a fair nights sleep. The lateness of the hour and my own weariness admonish me that I must retire. Alice has been out to a small party of four to-day and is invited to a larger one to-morrow night. She doesn't go to school but is making fair progress in her studies, at home.

I love you, darling, and long to be with
[you]. bye bye. with loving kisses.
Emma

Wed. Morn—Your letter of 8th came like the sunshine, both because I had been so many days without news and because it promises an early return to Atlanta.

If father continues to improve I think sister and I will start on Wed. or Thurs. of next week, in which case I could leave Chicago on Monday, reaching Atlanta on Wed. the 26th. I so hope that we can arrange to arrive there at same time. In regard to money I hope that you have already sent it to me, as I wrote you some days ago to direct to me here until you knew that I had left.

If you have not, and can send me something on receipt of this, send it to me by P.O. order at Chicago. . . . My blood flows quicker at the thought of seeing you soon. I trust that the thought may be soon realized.

I scarce think it best for you to incur the expense of telegraphing when you start unless you should start sooner than you now indicate, but write me at Chicago as late as the 19th or 20th. . . .

Bye-bye
With loving kisses
Emma

LETTERS: 1881–1883

Even with Emma's return to Atlanta, domestic stability proved illusory. While the early letters of the years 1881–83 reveal some months together, this period chronicles the same pattern of separation, another defining round in the relationship between husband and wife, and the continuing instability of John's career.[1]

Politically, Bryant's influence in Georgia politics was at another low. Having been cleared of the charges raised in the 1876 election smear, he now faced another frontal attack on his character. In 1881, his longtime opponent, Georgia politician Henry Farrow, followed the carpetbagger to Rhode Island and to the pages of the *Providence Journal*. There he blasted JEB's efforts to raise funds as a "political missionary" under the banner of the Southern Advance Association.

Emma herself questioned the tactics of her husband and the "salary" he drew from his solicitations, money also meted out for her meager life with Alice. For him, the society of the Union League cushioned his efforts, while his reports from northern cities and locales such as the seaside resort of Ocean Grove in New Jersey send images of a life vastly different from her indigent existence in Atlanta.

Confronting criticism was not a new thing for John Emory Bryant. While recognizing the questionable nature of his methods, he still defended the new phase of his mission as God's work. And he was not alone in seeking ways to confront the rising tide of oppression against African Americans and Republican idealism of the Reconstruction era. Acknowledging the current ineffectual political front, along with other former abolitionists and carpetbaggers, JEB returned to education as the most promising avenue for change.

Seeking to eradicate the roots of prejudice, now the goal would be re-education, beginning with the castoffs from mainstream society in the South: the Southern Advance would focus on schools for poor white children. In Atlanta, JEB found an ally in Erasmus Q. Fuller, Methodist minister and controversial editor of the *Atlanta Methodist Advocate*. Fuller and

---

[1] See *Carpetbagger of Conscience*, 158–72, for details of JEB's career in the years 1881–83.

Bryant joined forces, employing the missionary zeal formerly seen in political organization but now directed to schools. The source for funding became the Methodist Episcopal Church, which already claimed an honorable missionary effort to educate former slaves. In 1881, Bryant became a lay delegate to the Methodist General Conference, where he served on the State of the Church Committee as well as the Freedmen's Aid Society Committee. From that vantage, he successfully redirected a portion of church monies to the schools for white children designated by his Southern Advance Association. JEB would continue to attend the General Conferences meetings throughout the 1880s.

All the activities of her husband impinged on the choices before Emma, as did her fragile health. There was the ongoing dilemma of domicile—where would she live? And the new matter—what work would she do? And the ever-present question of control—who would decide? The correspondence of these years again revealed the strong, determined woman glimpsed in the 1870s but with an added dimension. Emma was still dependent on her husband and ever committed to his causes (even when she questioned his methods or judgment), but she remained determined that no one—not even John—would possess her will.

———

Home Aug. 19ᵗʰ 1881

My Darling.

Yesterday brought your letter from Augusta enclosing 5.00 and also a letter for yourself which I send with this. I am sorry you could do no better in Augusta but trust you will not be seriously inconvenienced thereby. I shall be obliged to pay out at least half what you sent me at once. . . . I shall be obliged to pay Mrs. Sherman something because they are very close for money—the milk bill will have to run. I give you these details, not because I like to write them or to trouble you with them, indeed I am always a little vexed with myself when I remind you of these little annoyances and yet it seems somewhat necessary that you should know first our status. . . . I will not try to tell you the sense of desolation that I felt when Emma and I returned on Tuesday and that I have felt ever since, especially at night. I think I have not felt your absence so much before in years. Your long stay home this summer has quite spoiled me for living alone. Yesterday I made the day a full one if not a bright one by canning peaches for ourselves and the day before by helping Mrs. Sherman to prepare peaches for canning. To-day I make grape cordial (or unfermented wine) for Emma and that will end my fruit business for a few days at least, shall then take some rest.

Night—Emma is in bed and asleep whither I must soon follow. I find myself very tired to-night and quite in need of rest to prepare me for the morrows duties.

Have read a little to-day, as hope to every day in the coming six weeks, am reading "A Century of Dishonor"[2] and feel almost ashamed of being an American citizen (I believe even women are citizens) when I read the record of my country's shameful dealings with the Indian. I trust that it will not be followed by the dreadful retribution which baptized this land in blood before slavery was destroyed. Please write me just how you are prospered and how situated. I feel some anxiety but you may have left with an inadequate supply of money for your own needs. It is a great relief to me in these anxious time[s] to remember that our Saviour has said "your Father <u>knoweth</u> that you have need of all these things"—God bless you richly and abundantly, my darling husband.

> With loving kisses
> Emma

Atlanta Aug. 23, 1881

My Darling.

I had hoped to write you at the office on Sunday but did not remain there long enough to do so. Emma and I went to Marietta St. and I found it very forlorn occupying a seat all by ourselves.

It was quarterly meeting, as you remember I presume, and ~~we~~ were honored with the presence of no less than six ministers. The one who preached bore a striking resemblance in manner and elocution to our meek yellow pussy cat, but gave us a very good sermon. I remained to the communion service but am not certain that I was as much benefitted thereby as I ought to have been, for I was forcibly empressed [*sic*] at the very beginning of the ordinance that the methodist ministry (theoretically at least) are not members of the church but a <u>priesthood over</u> the <u>church</u>. The six ministers collected at the altar and

---

[2] Helen Hunt Jackson, *A Century of Dishonor: The Early Crusade for Indian Reform* (New York: Harper & Brothers, 1881).

had communion by themselves going through with the whole ceremony including prayer and after this was concluded the church was invited to the second table. I do not presume that there is any essential difference in feeling between Meth. pastors and others and I suppose that the form is a relic of Romanism which is retained only in form not in spirit, but nevertheless it jarred upon me considerably.[3] Did it ever impress you in a like manner?

I tried to divest myself of these thoughts but find that as my mind recurs to the communion season these impressions are the prominent ones. I did not have an opportunity to speak with either Mr. or Mrs. Cook. . . . Saw Bro. Jones and delivered your message. . . . They are to have a Sunday School concert at Marietta week from Sunday night. We went in just before the Sabbath School closed and Mr. Spencer was acting as Supt. The school looked quite full and prosperous.

You must enjoy your Sabbath feasts of good things for yourself and me, too. and treasure up some of the tit-bits [sic] to write me. I have thus had but little of the rest that I promised myself because of the fruit and to-day I have pears to put up. Emma bids me send her love to papa and tell him she has to pare pears for mama to-day. She says when will you subscribe for St. Nicholas?

The weather is lovely this morning clear and bright and making us forget that we are in the midst of dog days. Bye bye [no signature]

Home Aug. 28th "/81

My Darling Husband.

I am at the close of the most stormy and boisterous sabbath that I have known in all my residence here—nearly all last night the wind blew fiercly [sic] and in the morning it continued with now and then a bit of rain, but should have gone out to church notwithstanding the weather, if had not been so tired and weak that did not dare to, having had Mrs. Cochran here housecleaning yesterday and gone with the children to the temperance party last night. . . .

I was much shocked last night to learn of the sudden death of Bro. Churchill and was doubly anxious to go into town to-day thinking that his funeral would be some time during the day. He was at church (3d Baptist) on

---

[3] Emma continued her membership in the Baptist Church, while JEB remained a Methodist.

Friday night and passed away so suddenly that no one reached him until he was dead, the cause is said to be heart disease. I know that he has been quite out of health for two or three years past. I feel almost as if I had lost a dear personal friend. There are very few people in Atlanta whose death I would feel so much. Emma like the other children loved him very much. He has labored in the infant class, among the juvenile templars and in the Y.M.C.A. and I know of no one else here whose death will be so much of a loss to the children and young people. When death comes so suddenly it is delightful to think that the one called is fully ripe and ready for the Master's summons. "Watch therefore, for ye know not what hour your Lord doth come" Do pray for me, darling, You know my own individual doubts and fears and anxieties. Unless the Lord enriches my daily life with His own presence and blessing 'twill be but a bare and poor one in three months of your absence, and I must not say in your absence alone, for all my life will be unsatisfactory and poor without the blessing and presence of Christ.

But even with spiritual blessings and with the companionship of our darling child who is so precious to me I am so very human, that life is very incomplete to me without you, and I hug to my heart the pleasing delusion(?) that life seperated [*sic*] from wife and child is alike unsatisfactory to you.

Ever since we were married we have looked forward to some golden Eldorado where we should be able to live habitually together. I hope that we may live long enough to realize our dreams in this respect. I wonder if the elements have been unpropitious with you to-day. I would so much enjoy being with you on Sabbath would like to visit Wanamaker's Sabbath School exceedingly. I am distressed to learn that the presidents condition is considered almost hopeless, at least that is what Col. S. tells me.[4] I think it must be almost more terrible to his wife and family than a fatal termination at the first. I do not mean that these weeks which he has been spared to them are not of priceless value, but that the raising of their hope almost to assurance makes the present blow only the more crushing. For the nation I believe that the result will be much less disastrous than immediate death would have been.

Of last nights party and of money I will speak to-morrow. I slept but little last night owing to late hours and various disturbances and I must retire at once to make up for lost time if possible. God bless you, my darling and bring

---

[4] Charles J. Guiteau shot President James A. Garfield in the back on July 2, 1881; Garfield died on September 19, 1881. Vice President Chester A. Arthur became president.

you speedily to me. Emma intended to write but deferred it till it was too late, may write to-morrow. She sends love.

> With loving kisses,
> Emma

Tuesday morn. I had no opportunity to send that to town yesterday but will send by Mrs. S. this morning. Emma is still sleeping. I have tried (but quite in vain) to keep my promise of resting since you left. for the past two nights, or three rather, cats storm and wind has seriously interfered with my sleep and I am suffering the effects. I have made fresh resolutions this morning to make health a primary object, I do want you to find me a little fresher when you next return than you did the last time. I have begun a course of gymnastic exercises with Emma which I hope may do something to counteract her stooping tendencies. I took Emma and Mary to the temperance party Sat. night which I suppose is one of the causes of my present exhaustion. I had been superintending the cleaning of the parlor and was quite exhausted when just as night [came] Mrs. Sherman told us that Mr. S. would take us to the party. I knew that it was suicidal for me to go but had not the heart to disappoint the children. They had a very pleasant time. . . .

I promised to speak of money rec'd. I have rec'd all I think that you have sent. 5.00 from Augusta and 1. & 5. & 5. at different times since the last in your letter of the 24th. They came just in good season and were most welcome. The last enables me to pay Molly, make all straight with Mrs. Sherman and leave a little balance to do our marketing for the present. Do you expect to send money to Dr. Ossen or shall I do it out of funds sent me? I wish to know that there may be no mistake made. Emma promises to write you soon and sends love. . . . God bless and keep you, darling,

> With true love kisses
> Emma

> Home Oct. 13th 1881

My Darling.

I am just going into town with Mrs. S. and have scarce time for a word. Emma is not very well but am doing all I can for her and trust that she will improve. Shall leave her with Mollie Cochran this morning.

I am anxious for your home coming and trust that it will not be delayed. I had only time for these few words before Mrs. S. called at the Office I find yours of the 7th & 9th with a promise of another to be sent on Sunday which may rec' on or upon leaving for home.

You speak of my health I cannot get up strength. I most unfortunately took two cathartic pills last week. I intended to take one only but took two by Mrs. Shermans advice and they have left me very weak. If my finances will permit I shall have help while you are home. I trust that you were thoroughly successful in your address on Monday night and I have some hope, much hope I may say, that you may succeed in obtaining government office, should you decide to apply.

I am often troubled in regard to it. I dont know whether I ought to say it, but I almost feel of late as if my life depends upon a different situation financially—perhaps it is not so. At any rate I must not talk more now for they are calling me to go. I love you darling and long for your return

With loving kisses
Emma

Did you recv'e Brusk's letter

[letterhead] The Southern Advance Association,
(Formerly The Atlanta Republican Publishing Co.)
Office, Corner Pryor and Hunter Streets,
Atlanta, Ga. [marked through]
Philadelphia, Pa.
Officers: E. Q. Fuller, President; J. E. Bryant, Business Manager;
V. Spalding, Sec'y & Asst. B.M.; A. B. Jonas, Treasurer.
Directors: E. Q. Fuller, E. C. Wade, V. Spalding, C. O. Fisher,
S. A. Darnell, W. W. Brown, J. Sherman, J. E. Bryant.
Oct 20th 1881

My Darling Wife.

I received this morning yours of Sunday night; Monday night, and Tuesday, acknowledging the receipt of money—$2, $5, and $5. I sent you $5 more on the 19th.

I saw Mrs. Watson again on Tuesday night. She speaks of you with warmest terms of friendship. I think she is having a hard time.

As I write your picture and Emma's are before me on the table, their usual place. Emma's is pronounced a very handsome picture by all who see it. I shall be glad to see the one you have and compare them. I regret to hear of the feeble condition of your father, hope he may regain his usual strength.

I was really troubled because I did not hear from you. Please send me a letter more frequently even if it is but a few lines. I am glad that you are to have your dinners with Mrs. Sherman. I think it will perhaps be better for us to board as soon as we are able, as it will be cheaper than keeping house in town and will save your strength; providing we can find a proper place, one that will be agreeable.

I have written to Joseph.

I am glad to have another Methodist in the family even if it is a cat.[5]

I am making important headway now with our work, of which I will write in my next.

> With warmest love and kisses.
> Y. H.

Home Oct. 23$^{\underline{d}}$ 1881

My Darling,

I had intended to write you but have been hindered till my fire is entirely out and I dare not sit long as am but partially recovered from severe cold. Emma has just retired and I am feeling some solicitude lest she may have another attack of sickness having had them on two alternate nights . . . have been very careful of her food to-day. . . . It is Sabbath night—I went to church this morning with Mrs. S. and Mary, leaving Emma home with grandma. We went to hear Dr. Bowman at Liberal Hall, near the Baptist church. I supposed him to be a Universalist but was disappointed to find him a spiritualist and infidel. So far as I can judge from his utterances, he derided vicarious atonement and a "personal God" and made no reference to Christ otherwise than in his denial of the atonement—he expressed himself in a few words upon these points and announced the topic of his lecture (he did not call it a sermon) "The astronomical view of the creation," and the lecture itself was really very interesting. I dare not sit to write longer as it is growing cool. I long to have you with us, darling, and begin to count the days. I promise myself not more than one more Sabbath before your coming. Thanks for the

---

[5] Alice named her cat John Wesley, for the founder of Methodism.

little slip in recent letter, altho' it seemed almost sacrilege to bring the little, loving looks and words of the home life before the public, it is nevertheless a pretty picture and pleasant to look upon. Did it remind you of the days when a certain other "tutor" loved his "girl pupil"? I must confess that my thoughts flew back and over an interval of almost twenty years. But bye by darling—good night and pleasant dreams

Wed. P.M. I have sorely neglected you this week. I am trying to make the most of my time in sewing while I board with Mrs. S. which will probably be only this week. . . . My letters are but evidence of my love for you and desire for your presence. I am now at the office but find nothing from—_____. Saw Bro. Cook a few minutes. Have a postal from Prince saying he will come up next month and enquiring your address. I do not believe I have ever replied to your birthday letter in which you say that you are most forty. how long before it will be most fifty, I shall have to say at my next birthday that I am "most forty"—Emma is home and I am running to get to her which must excuse my haste.

Bye darling.
Emma

———

28 W. 11th St New York
April 23^d 1882

My Darling Wife:

Another Sabbath has come and I am here in New York and not in Atlanta. This morning I went to hear Mr. Beecher.[6] I reached the church about fifteen minutes before ten when but few persons had arrived. The usher told me that I would find the best seat in the house in the upper gallery—the second—so I went away up near the roof and got a front seat. I could hear Mr. Beecher perfectly—every word. It was a grand sight to look down upon the multitude below on the first floor and first gallery which extended completely around the house. The second gallery extended only across the end of the church opposite the pulpit or platform. Back of the platform were the organ and the

---

6 Henry Ward Beecher, still minister of the Plymouth Congregational Church, Brooklyn, New York, having survived his sexual affair and scandal exposed by Victoria Woodhull in the early 1870s.

singers—a quartet and a large chorus. The entire congregation sang and the sound came rolling up grandly. If you and Emma should be in New York at any time with me I should want to go and hear Beecher, if he is then at home and take a seat in the same place.

At night I went to hear Dr. Newman but he was sick and did not preach.

Tuesday:

I commenced this Sunday night, and will finish this morning—

I have not yet been here long enough to tell what I can do. I shall do the best I can and then go to Washington for an office. I hope to get one that will enable me to continue my work but shall get one at any rate if possible—one that will enable me to provide for my family and pay something on my debts.

> With warmest love and kisses
> Y. H.

———

> 28 West 11th St New York
> May 5th 1882

My Darling Wife:

I have written you I think since I received your last but I write again to answer some questions that I have not previously answered.

I think I have told you that I hope to be home June 1st. I cannot now say just how long I shall then be home that will depend upon how well I do here in the next two weeks, or how soon I succeed in Washington. I shall take steps to get either an office or something else that we may be together.

I am troubled about your sickness although I have not said much about it for I have struggled so hard to aid you and be at home that I have talked of that and nothing else much.

I think you had better go forward and have Emma baptised without regard to my movements—be governed by circumstances. If you are able to go with her and the weather is fit and she can be—if the arrangements at the Church are satisfactory. I think you had better not wait for me.

I did receive Emma's letter and will answer Sunday.

I have sent her March St Nicholas and have April and May which I will send.

I send enclosed one dollar. In a few days I shall have more to send you enough to releive [*sic*] you of embarrassment. Will send as soon as possible. I am certainly gaining here but must have the endorsement of the Union League before I reach money. That I hope to get in a few days. I have written Col. Spalding quite fully on this point.

With warmest love and kisses for you
and Emma
Y. H.

Marietta Sep. 13th /82
Wednesday Night—

My Darling Husband.

I did not give up seeing you again until I rec'd your letter this morning, and even then I thought it just possible you might miss this morning['s] train and come this way. I went to the three o'clock train to-day thinking it barely possible you might be on it. Suppose you are now well on your way to Washington. . . . I rec'd your letter of yesterday with 5.00 enclosed. . . .

Was very glad to hear from Sister. O'Neil has just gone away to school and she, of course, is feeling lonely and anxious. I am uneasy about her. Her lungs are troubling her very much and she is fearful that she cannot winter in Ill[inois]. I think she ought to come here but do not know whether she will feel that she can leave father. They have sold their corn but have not delivered it yet.

Monday night being windy I did not ride, instead Emma and I called on Mrs. Cole, were very cordially received. . . . Yesterday I was out-of-doors nearly all day. Walked to Mrs. Spilman's in the morning—remained to dinner and rode down with him after dinner and about 4 o'clock P.M. went riding horseback. Had an easier horse and enjoyed the ride but found that it hurt my back quite as much as before and shall be obliged to give up riding horseback. When I do ride must go in buggy. I think that I am really benefitted by remaining in the open air, in fact my lungs are feeling quite free and natural, my digestion I think is improved.[7] It is 9 o'clock and I must retire at once. I love you very truly, darling, and wish you good night and wish you pleasant dreams

------

[7] Alice later wrote that her mother suffered badly from asthma; Emma's lungs would continue to be a source of health problems.

Thurs. morn. I intended to mail this yesterday. . . . Mrs. Gober and a relative went out in the morning to a cousin's, four miles from town but as I did not wish to hire horse for all day I waited till after dinner. had a very pleasant ride save that I made a mistake in the road on the last part and drove a mile over a fearful road, so gullied and bad that I couldn't turn round and back out if I desired, but thanks to a gentle horse I went over in safety. It lead [*sic*] to the place where I wished to go, but there was a shorter and smoother road which I ought to have taken. . . . Emma enjoyed it greatly. I mean the ride, in total, not the rough part of it. . . . We are having lovely weather here now. . . . Please write me very often and give me enough of details [to tell me] how you are progressing. I mustnt write more now for the early morning is most favorable for us to be out-of-doors.

> With loving kisses.
> Bye bye
> Emma

———

> Atlanta Dec. 25. 1882
> Christmas Eve

My Darling Husband.

Mr. Palmer came to-night bringing me your two letters and the beautiful present that accompanied them. Many thanks, my darling. It is very handsome and shows excellent taste in selection. I shall wear it with great pleasure.

You remembered my "hint" but forgot or failed to heed my injunction to buy nothing for me this present Christmas. I do not think you ought, and I fear that you inconvenienced yourself to do it, but I shall enjoy it notwithstanding all that, and think of you when I wear it. I am very sorry if the slippers are small—they are the number that you once told me you wore. but if they do not fit be sure to exchange them for there is no comfort in a close slipper. You must thank Emma instead of me for them as my share in them was only trifling. she has been saving up her money for many months to make papa a present. The cards you speak of have not yet arrived. She has gone with the others to a christmas service at Marietta St. She is coughing herself and I would not have sent her out at night had it not been that she had a part in the programme. . . . I have been unable to do for her christmas as I have always done before for had scarce any money to spend. She will learn this year the pleasure of giving to others rather than being herself the chief recipient. I have painted her a picture of her cat that I think is a very fair likeness and that I think will please her very much. I bought her also some trifling little articles and her Aunt Nannie sent her some lace out of which I will fashion her a pretty collar or two, she also has some little gifts from the children and will have the cards from you I trust by to-morrow. I filled her stocking before I sat down . . . and hope she will enjoy it . . . even though it does not represent much money. She has had a new pleasure in going . . . to town to look at the holiday goods and to make her little purchases. . . . Out of material that I had in hand I devised a pretty apron for Miss Coffin and painted a small gilt panel for Mrs. Fuller that I think is very pretty. I do not feel the jaundice symptoms now which leaves me a little more energy. . . . My cough does not disturb me as much at night for the past two or three days. . . .

I shall leave for Thomasville as soon as you are able to provide the funds.[8] My reason for suggesting the country was not a preference for country. I would prefer the town, but I thought that I could get cheaper board in country and I must confess that I shrink from going into a boarding house without one single presentable dress. and I see no way to go unless I go as I am, because a dress cannot be gotten up in a day or two and I have already waited until it is almost too late to go. I have remained here through as bad weather as we can have and must go as soon as I have funds.

But I am afraid that this is not . . . a bright and cheery Christmas letter which I meant. . . . I am very sorry that Col Buck was unable to meet you at Wash. I feared at the time that it might be a serious drawback to you. I am troubled often that you must bear this load of hard work and pecuniary anxiety year after year and I am distressed that my ill health should add another to the burdens with which you are weighted, for the past six years I have so longed to do something by which I could not only care for myself and Emma but help you in your struggle; and instead I am now less helpful to you than ever before since we were married. I do not know whether to call it providential and unavoidable or whether by more courage & resolution I could have broken through the barriers that seemed to forbid me to become a bread winner and have accomplished something before this ill health came upon me and perhaps have avoided the ill health by the very peace of mind that would have probably come with regular occupation.

---

[8] Emma would continue to travel to southern Georgia in the 1880s for health reasons.

However it is I am now where I can only trust it in the Father's hands. . . . Whether I grow worse or better I will try, God helping me, not to sadden any more the atmosphere of my own home. . . .

The other day when I was in the office, Palmer read me a sharp squib against Pledger that he had written for the paper.[9] I suggested that it did not seem to me to be wise to attack Pledger and Col. S.[palding] overhearing it said the same and I think the paragraph was pigeonholed. . . . Was it unnecessary caution on my part? . . . It is growing late and I must prepare for bed. I wish so much that I could be with you darling this christmas night if only for the simple evening. Write me how you spend the Christmas, please, and may the dear Lord bless you abundantly. I shall feel so much farther away from you in Thomasville that I dread to go. you must write me doubly often. . . . Good-night and pleasant dreams, darling.

Monday night—Merry Christmas to you, darling. . . . Emma has had a very happy day. At the breakfast table she rec'd several pretty little presents and was altogether very satisfied and happy. She was delighted with her picture of Kitty, which is pronounced an excellent likeness. We have looked all day for the cards but they have not yet appeared. . . . I must retire now with good night kisses and a hope that you have passed the holiday as pleasantly as we have.

> With loving kisses
> Emma

————

Atlanta Dec. 30 "/82

My Darling,

Your letter was warmly welcomed last night. It is good to hear from you—would be much better to see you. I wonder where you are whilst I write, some where in Washington, striking your best blows I suspect to carry your points. . . . Dr. Fuller told me last night that he had a word with Col. Buck when he started and that he said he was going especially and entirely in your behalf. . . .

---

[9] The "white-only" faction continued to challenge William A. Pledger's leadership of the Georgia Republican Party.

I have to-day carried into execution what I have been thinking of for some days, viz—went to Chamberlain's and bought on credit the material for a blk. cashmere dress and put it in the dressmaker's hands. . . . It is something that I have never done . . . in my married life of nearly twenty yrs. The bill is a little more than fourteen dollars—shall pay it before I leave if can. . . .

Think you will like the dress when done, my material is all good—as I so seldom buy a good dress it seemed the best economy to purchase that. Shall try to leave as soon as rec've funds for am almost afraid that my lungs are badly affected already, tho' hope not. I have had no medical treatment . . . have coughed ever since you left, most of the time much more than at any time while you were here. have recieved [*sic*] some relief from hot fomentations but did not feel the strength to prolong their use. have much hope from the change of climate. It it [*sic*] is time now to prepare for bed. I love you, darling, very warmly and truly may the dear Lord bless you.

With loving kisses
Emma

Sunday Morn. I omitted to acknowledge 5.00 rec'd in letter of 27th. It came just as soon as I had a little borrowed money to pay beside washing bill.

Monday Morn. I wish you a Happy N. Year, darling—and one free from anxieties and difficulties. . . .

An article in my Chautauqua discourses very eloquently on the advantage of disadvantages, to speak less paradoxically, the strength gained by obstacles overcome, in that view you have perhaps much to be thankful for in the past years of toil. Dr. Fuller had not rec'd the money at breakfast time this morning—presume he will do so to-day. I have just returned from Dr. Robertson's. . . . To my great relief he tells me that my lungs are not worse [than] when he examined them before and that I need nothing but change of climate. [He] urges me to make the change as soon as possible and regrets that I could not be gone sooner . . . says that the change will do more for me than he can do . . . he says he sees no reason why I cannot recover my health. I write you thus . . . thinking that it may relieve your anxiety. Emma sends love

With loving kisses
Emma. . . .

Atlanta Jan. 15, 1883

My Darling Husband

Your letter of the 10th from Washington was even more than usually welcome, if that can be, and the money came most opportunely. Emma needed new rubbers, the wash bill was due &c. and I had walked home from town an hour or two before wondering how I should manage, when relief came, just as it always has, when I needed it most, and so I thanked God and took courage. . . .

I went this morning (Sabbath) to hear Dr. Fuller he gave us an excellent talk.

Emma has just retired and bids me tell you that she sends her love and will write soon and wishes you to write her, also that she is doing well in her studies, and I think she is with perhaps the exception of arithmetic. . . . I do not think that the system of teaching arithmetic leads them to think, but rather to fall into certain routines and forms and to depend upon rules. I believe I can give her more real training in arithmetic in a month than she will get in school in a year. The method of teaching is well calculated to bring the whole class up to the same standard, and that a very poor one, and keep them together, which seems to be the great object of the graded school system; but it does not stimulate the really bright minds at all. The teaching in other studies seems to me to be good and thorough. . . . To-day I [had] . . . a letter from your mother and yesterday Emma had a letter from her aunt Nannie and to-day a letter and a beautiful pair of mittens from her auntie Browne. Nannie writes that Greenleaf goes sleigh-riding every day but . . . I presume . . . she is unable to go out in the cold. . . .

Your mother writes that she is quite well and doing all the housework after breakfast to give Lucy her time to sew. Lucy is pretty well for her. Your mother says that if her children knew the good their letters do her they would write more frequently. . . . dear mother her fingers are stiff with the faithful labor for her children. . . . [closing missing]

Monday night—I went down town this P.M. intending to take some steps towards looking for boarding place or rent . . . [but] remembering the notes which will soon be due and my own bill at Chamberlain's and seven dollars at dressmakers I turned about face and decided to take no steps towards changing until I have money in hand. It is necessary to pay my dressmakers bill as soon as practicable, not so much because I need the dress as because I am ashamed to leave it so long at the dressmakers. If I had known that I should remain so long here I would have attempted to make the dress myself, altho' have felt scarcely able. Am thankful to say that am feeling much better now than a few weeks ago.

––––––––

Atlanta Feb. 3$^{\underline{d}}$ 1883

My Darling.

Yours of 31st, with five dollars enclosed was received . . . was most welcome and the money just in season . . . I have found it absolutely necessary to keep fruit for Emma and self, which has added considerably to our incidental expenses. Since the weather has been better and my cough relieved I have begun to go into school again occasionally and find it very essential that I should do so. Emma loves it so much better than study that she is inclined to fritter away her time . . . and she is certainly in danger of falling into the pit which entraps so many bright scholars that flash out brightly in their childhood and never amount to anything as scholars, through lack of study, conscientious application. On the other hand Miss Coffin tells me she should not be anxious about her, thinks it is only the natural love of play and that she will apply herself as she grows older. . . .

Sunday P.M. I began this last evening but did not have time to finish and am suffering with slight headache to-day. . . . Your absence seems long to me to-day and I find myself looking forward wistfully to your return. . . .

Monday noon. I awoke this morning to another rainy day almost every morning is foggy. . . .

In regard to making any change of boarding place I dread to leave here at all, because the family are all so kind and it seems so homelike here, but, for health's sake, I feel that when I can do so I must go to some location that will be healthful and safe to remain in until June or July or possibly all summer, should I be disappointed in going north.[10] I shall however make no change until we can mutually agree upon something. I dread to undertake housekeeping again just now and yet am rather impressed that it may be best.

Mrs. Moser told me recently that she had now nearly decided to rent two or more rooms but wished to give me the first opportunity, before speaking to anyone else. You remember her house is on Whitehall St very near Lutheran

––––––––––––––

[10] Emma boards with the family of JEB's associate Erasmus Q. Fuller.

church—a good situation for health I should think. . . . I really think the best thing will perhaps be to board with her if you will be home soon, as I hope you will. She cooks, I think, much as I should need makes graham bread,[11] uses a good deal of fruit etc. her rooms I think she wishes to leave furnished so there would not be the trouble of unstoring and moving our things. If you are likely to be away two or three months longer and there is pressing need for economy it might be best for me to take two or three rooms and do my own housework. I am quite at sea in the matter because I do not know how we are to be situated financially or when you are to be home and so have nothing certain on which to base a judgement. I suppose you are in Wash[ington] the same condition, but would like your ideas on the subject as soon as practicable. Mrs. Moser is a smart, stirring mistress woman and I imagine will set a good table. She says her house is very cool and comfortable in summer, which would be favorable if I should decide to remain here through the summer. I must not write more now. I fell much behind in my course of reading while I was not well and preparing, as I thought, to go to Thomasville, so that I need now to give a good deal of attention to that. Added to that I try to keep up with the news of the day somewhat and to go out when the weather is at all favorable. I am encouraged and yet anxious in regard to your affairs. Dr. Fuller saw Col. B.[uck] recently and says that he is determined to do everything in power to assist you to an office but does not know just when it will be possible to leave his business here. I long to be with you, darling, God bless and keep you

Emma

Tuesday noon. I delayed mailing this last evening, in order to write you after seeing Mrs. Moser. . . . [She] will not have her rooms vacant probably before Apr. 1st. They will then be thoroughly cleaned—whitewashed etc. and the front one will have down a new matting. She was doubtful whether she could board us this summer but thought she might in winter. If we do not go to housekeeping in a house by ourselves before that time it looks to me as if that would be best thing we could do—we could take fewer rooms (one front room and drawing room) and take our meals at Mrs. Stocer's. She lives near and sets a fine table I am told and would have boarded us or taken us to meals last fall. . . . the rooms at Mrs. Moser's are furnished save kitchen and dining

---

[11] Sylvester Graham, Presbyterian minister and dietary reformer, advocated abstinence from meat, coffee, tea, alcohol, and pastries in favor of fruit, vegetables, whole grain bread, and pure drinking water; he perfected the recipe for graham flour and crackers.

room furniture, and if I tried to do my own work Mrs. Moser would bake my bread for me with hers, think she is a good, motherly woman, who would be pleasant to live with. If you are to be home it would be a pleasanter to have a house by ourselves, keep a servant etc. The greatest drawback would be that we need parlor for furniture, crockery & table linen, (chair would be the only thing absolutely required in furniture perhaps)

If we go there we would not have a parlor, would sit by our bed room as we do in boarding and I presume have the privilege of inviting callers into their parlor. I do not know that it would be worth the trouble of going to housekeeping if I began so late as Apr. if I went north in June. I am [illegible], let me put my ideas in shape. I will write you briefly the several plans and you can form your opinion. . . .

———

Atlanta Feb. 11th /83

My Darling.

I learned from Col [Spalding] to-day that you will be in N. York Tuesday. I hope that it means success in Boston. . . . It is Saturday night and I must make my writing very brief. . . .

Sunday night—The people who havent gone to church have gone to bed and Emma and I must soon follow. We have had another drizzly, muddy day— neither rainy nor fair—Bishop Wiley preached. . . . Miss Coffin and I imagined that when Dr. Rust was praying fervently for the Lord to bless the standard bearers here who were trying to plant the old flag, he was all the while criticizing the small congregation and calling Marietta St. a failure. After service he shook hands with me, inquired after you, and, in his bland and smiling way, began to sympathize with me by calling me a poor widow. I told him I might be a widow but I wasn't a poor widow. I think he is the last man to whom I would like to own up to being disconsolate.[12] Did you rec've a letter from Miss Stokes.[13] She wrote you addressing it to Boston. I had a thought pop into my head in church to-day, tho' I doubt if it is practicable.

———

[12] Possibly John D. Rust, JEB's nemesis in the Eighth Maine.

[13] Miss M. H. Stokes headed the mission school for poor white children JEB and Fuller established in Atlanta with the support of the Methodist Episcopal Church, under the auspices of the Southern Advance Association.

viz—that if I should go to housekeeping before you return and want company Miss Stokes might like to board with me. . . . I would like your ideas as soon as may be as to what arrangements for living we shall make this spring, for when you are able to provide funds for any change I shall not feel willing to wait long for consultation, and if I did so I might lose some eligible place. . . . I can rent by the month, I found when I enquired at real estate offices. I feel that I cannot wait till Apr.1, before making a change unless I am obliged to do so. The meat used here is largely pork and the vegetables, save potatoes, are all cooked with pork. As far as my taste is concerned I can get along and feel more than compensated by the pleasant social relations, but I cannot regain health and strength with such a diet. I should not of course better matters by going into a Southern boarding house and I shall not attempt it.

If I was able I think I should go to Dr. Robertson's till your return. I should not go for treatment but simply for the benefit of the table. [It is] possible I could get a room near and go in for meals, tho' that is doubtful. In that case we could go to Mrs. Moser's, or to housekeeping in a house by ourselves on your return. I think out these different ideas that I may get your thoughts in regard to them and thus be ready to act when I have the means to do so. It is necessary for you to give me your views and then leave me to act according to my best judgement. . . . I shall make no plans that will incur much more expense than I have here, unless you receive an appointment, if you fail in that I must still have a change of diet, but must manage in some way to make it inexpensive. . . .

You need not feel anxious, for I shall make no change till I see my way clear to do so, and am not restless or unhappy I only wish to do best thing when the way opens [no closing]

———

Feb. 21st "/83

[first page damaged]

. . . I called on Misses Packard and Giles recently.[14] Their school is moved to the barracks and is quartered in the hospital building. They are [illegible] living in one of the buildings and have . . . boarding scholars. They have two extra teachers from Mass. and expect a matron from Bangor, Maine. They have shown wonderful energy and have accomplished more than I ever knew

---

[14] Miss S. B. Packard and Miss H. E. Giles, co-principals, Atlanta Baptist Female Seminary.

two women to accomplish before in some time. They have a remarkably fine looking set of pupils. I must give you good-night-kisses and go to call Emma. . . . Good night and pleasant dreams, darling

Sat. Night . . . I am sorry that have been so unusually negligent in writing this week—have not been well for the whole week. My uterine weakness is troubling me, apparently from having walked a little too much a week ago to-day, but back of that I think is the fact that my food does not digest properly. . . . The only hope that I can see at present is proper diet and that is impossible till I can make a change. I think Mrs. F.[uller] does the very best with the means at her command but that food that meets the needs of her family is not good for me, I eat pork or food cooked in pork almost daily from necessity. I feel that it is very deleterious to me and will prevent me from making any gain of strength before the hot days of summer, when I can not expect to do more than hold the fort.

If our circumstances continue cramped I must still have a change of diet, even by getting one or two rooms and doing my own work. In that case I should probably be unable to go to Mrs. Moser's on acc. of too high rent, otherwise that would be better than to be by myself if you were still away and I could not keep a servant. I hope and trust that you will be soon home and that you will be entirely successful in Wash.

I do not see how you can go into the educational work without some salaried position under [the] gov.[ernment] neither does Dr. F. see the way open without that. I shall be only too glad to use my training in teaching to the extent that my body will permit. I do not think on further reflection that what I mentioned in regard to Miss Stokes will be practicable. I will do as you suggest when I am able to walk that far—cannot do it now and have not money to spend in car fare. I am quite out and must hand the next V. to Mrs. F. to finish up last months board. . . .

With loving kisses
Emma

—————

Atlanta Mch. 15th 1883

My Darling.

I rec'd yesterday morning your telegram and this morning your letter enclosing tax card. . . . On the reception of telegram I borrowed money of [illegible] and paid the tax (through Col. S.) yesterday and will enclose your receipt in this. . . . I hear that Col Wade returned from Washington a strong Speer man, does that indicate that Speer will work with the republicans or that Wade hopes to get his influence in his own behalf? the former I hope.[15] I must not write even to you more to-night for am troubled somewhat with sleeplesness [*sic*] of late. . . . the uncertainties of past few weeks have been unfavorable. Do you keep well and strong all the while? have you never felt injury from the overwork of the fall campaign? . . . .

I love you, darling, and hope very soon to be with you. Can you give me any idea as to the latest period to which you may be kept north? And if you fail of marshalship will you then be South or north this summer, please give me an immediate answer to these two questions.[16] I may possibly go to board for a little time with Misses Packard and Giles at the barracks. . . . I should prefer to remain here if I could have a nourishing diet, free from pork and lard, but that is impossible, and it is equally impossible for me to gain strength with my present diet. What do you think of the idea? Please dont see bug-a-boo's where there are none, for this indecision is making my hair gray and my face old. I should, of course, make no plans that could not be changed as soon as you come home. . . .

> With loving kisses
> Bye darling
> Emma

Will do all in my power to forward your educational scheme if you determine to proceed with it. Mrs. Fuller insists that the M.[ethodist] E.[piscopal] people are too poor to go away to a school and that those who can go will be better suited at Ellejay.[17] I do not judge, for do not know enough about the matter. I think, as a rule, her judgement is more accurate than her husband's; but I do not know whether her range of vision is sufficiently broad to make her good authority in this case. . . .

The dear Lord keep you, darling. I love you very warmly, very truly.

> With loving kisses
> Emma

---

[15] Emory Speer, Independent Democrat, with some Republican support was elected to Congress from Georgia's Ninth District in 1878 and 1880, but lost in 1882; appointed federal judge in 1884.

[16] JEB's effort was to secure the post of United States Marshal in Georgia.

[17] JEB and Fuller patterned the school for white children in Atlanta after the one already established by Methodists in Ellijay, Georgia.

Atlanta Mch. 18th /83

My Darling Husband,

The time is long since I talked with you instead of writing. . . . It has been a perfect day, warm enough to hint of spring. . . . There is one point in connection with the barracks . . . since I wrote. If we go there . . . the house next to us is occupied by the family of a saloon keeper and there are several children near Emma's age. . . . Mrs. Fuller told me yesterday that she has discovered that the boys (some of them at least) are very vulgar in their conversation. I am a good deal disturbed by it. . . . [Also] her chief friend at school . . . has her thoughts largely on clothes and the price of them. . . . I must look for Emma's friends among the northern mis.[sionary] element . . . for our child is now at a very impressionable age. . . .

[this fragment written sideways on printed letterhead paper.]

[letterhead] Miss S. B. Packard, Miss H. E. Giles, Principals. Atlanta Baptist Female Seminary, 35 Leonard Street, Atlanta, Ga. _____ 188_

Monday Morn At School—I rec'd yours of 16th just as I left with Emma. I am sorry that you entirely misapprehend my motives and the circumstances connected with my work in this school. I will try to make it clear to you but may fail to do so, in which case you will be able to return me a small portion of the concession which I have always shown you, viz. to be patient and trust when your judgement does not coincide with mine. Let me premise that I have not taken this trifling step, even, without consulting your interests, rather than my own, if there <u>can</u> be such a thing as seperate [*sic*] interests with us. I am not doing this <u>instead of helping you</u>, but because, according to my judgement, it is fitting me to <u>better</u> help you, when the time that I can help you has arrived. It <u>has not yet arrived</u>, for this reason, the work which you specify in your letter I have not strength or vitality to perform. Miss Stokes firstly needs no help from me but friendship and moral support, rather she does not need me to go into her school and take a class, and, if she did, I could not do it in my present physical condition. You who have taught ought to know that it requires a great mental and physical outlay to teach children. When I was seventeen I could have done it, now that time is past—I <u>can not do</u> it and <u>never expect to</u> do it unless I am forced to do it or beg.

Miss Packard asked me to assist in her model school. It is composed of children, cleaner and more docile than Miss Stokes pupils, and is a clean,

light, airy room. I could teach them with one half the injury to my health that
I could Miss Stokes pupils, but I told her at once that I could not do even
that—that to teach any children required an expenditure of vitality that I have
not to give. I am ready in heart and soul to help in your work in such ways as
I can, I cannot teach children or do mission work (save an occasional visit with
Miss Stokes perhaps) for a year or two, or ever, unless I recover my health, my
day for those things has passed. When I went to college I had vitality and to
spare, even when I came to Atlanta I had still a good deal of it. It is gone now
and I cannot make bricks without straw. I have told you what I cannot do. Now
a word of what I can do. I <u>can teach</u> grown girls and boys, who require no discipline, and are eager to learn. I can teach them mathematics, because I have a
natural talent in that direction and a love for it, that will partially counterbal-
ance my lack of experience and normal training. There is little else that I can
teach now, tho' if your white school of a high grade is established I could in
time perhaps teach sewing or painting or some other class tho' my judgement
is that I ought to take mathematics and I must, if possible, have a little preliminary experience in order to gain confidence, if nothing more. This I am having in my present gratuitous work for Miss Packard and having it with almost
no outlay of vitality or strength. I come only three mornings a week and am
already half way here when I leave Emma at Peters St. and after my class I take
the street car home. my class are all grown girls eager to learn and the recitation stimulates my own brain and revives geometry rather than exhausts me. I
am not obliged to have one thought of discipline, or gaining attention, after the
recitation I go to Peters St. by front way and take street car home. added to this
these are live N.E. teachers, understanding normal methods, of which I know
nothing, and if I move here, I intend to visit the classes sufficiently to be myself
instructed. I do not like the methods of public school instruction and can learn
very little in those. Now do you begin to see the motives that lead me into this
work and that it is not squandering my time upon another school when you
need my help, but acquiring confidence and experience here which will enable
me to help you when your school is opened next autumn if you are to have such
a school as you hope in which my services are to be required, this is certainly a
povidence [*sic*] which enables me to work into school life and methods, at forty
years of age and having never taught. Even you would probably find it difficult to teach now with your strength and early experience—how much more so
if you have never taught and had little strength. I am not gaining at all in
strength. there are just two ways of help open to me. The first a <u>good</u> diet. If
that fails a change of climate which will seperate [*sic*] me much longer from

you. It is of great consequence that I try the effect of diet for the month or two of indecision. If I had not to economize I should go to Dr. Robertson, that being out of the question I know of nothing within my means but coming here. I will write more to-day.

Bye darling—
Emma

————

Atlanta Mch. 22 /83

My Darling Husband.

I am in receipt of yours of Mch. 18. from Prov. [idence]

I am hurt and surprised that you should have offered my services to any one without first ascertaining my wishes in the matter. I have informed Miss Stokes this morning that it will be impossible for me to assist her. I think that Miss Coffin would be both surprised and indignant if she knew that you included her name with mine as Miss Stokes informed me.

I have already answered you very clearly and fully, telling you what I can do and what I can not and will not repeat.

I should not think of remaining here at all this summer were it not to be with you, and I must be nursing my strength, instead of spending it, at the present. I am not gaining, but losing if anything, and these differences of judgement, or rather your innocent efforts to judge for me are affecting me very unhappily, altho' I know you do not intend it.

It is not of the least use for you to attempt to judge for me either in this or other things. I think that I can gain in strength even here if you can be with me and we are favorably situated. There are many things that I can do as strength returns but you must expect nothing from me [for] months to come, saving what I have already designated in the way of review of my studies and learning something of methods of teaching from those who know how. Emma is waiting for this. I must close. I love you darling and long to see you. God bless you and return you soon to me.

With loving kisses
Emma

P.S. Perhaps I ought to say that I am in immediate need of money, if only a little, the last having been used to finish up Feb. board bill and now I am feeling anxious about Mchs bill which will so soon be due.

I have not at present enough to pay wash bill due to-day. I prefer house-keeping to boarding in our present situation because in the former I can regulate expenses to means and in the latter a board bill is staring me in the face at close of each month. and even at the worst, if absolutely necessary I can buy groceries on credit which is not worse than board bill.

———

Atlanta Mch. 26th 1883

My Darling.

This morning's post brings your of 21st from Providence. I hoped before I opened it that you had recd (before writing) my letter explaining the teaching for Miss Packard, and the impossibility of entering into school work with Miss Stokes, or mission work.

As your letter is wide of the mark I judge that you have <u>not</u> received my letter upon the subject, tho' it really seems to be time. I hope that it has not miscarried. Your remark that I might get [illegible] outside is a surprising one. It would be entirely impracticable, and injurious more than the trouble that I seek to remedy. In regard to what you say of remaining here on account of children to play with, she would be equally well situated at Barrack's or Mrs. Moser's, especially the former. . . .

The change somewhere I am obliged to make for sake of my health. You seem to entirely forget that when we came here it was to be for a <u>brief</u> time, that I was unwilling to remain even till Jan. 1st. when as expected or would get a house in more healthy location, that I have remained months beyond the time that was set as the farthest time and that to the disadvantage of location is added a disadvantage of diet that neither of us thought of before coming and yet you complacently assure me that you feel perfectly safe about me here. Perhaps you do, I don't feel safe about myself. . . .

Shall not probably make binding arrangement earlier than first of next week and shall probably move some time next week unless I should decide on Mrs. Moser's and should be obliged to wait for the rooms. I think that will be a pleasant place for us. . . .

[placement of this page uncertain]

. . . thought she would have her speak the same piece at close of school. She told me that Mrs. Prather (who has one section of 4th grade at Ma.[rietta] St.[reet]) was a very fine teacher indeed, and one of Dr. Fullers church members who knows her, or knows of her tells me the same thing, and I am naturally very anxious to get Emma into her section; and it looks now as if a kind providence will enable me to do it. . . . On Thurs. of last week I went into Ma. St. school and enquired for 4th grade and was sent into Mrs. Prather's room. . . . To-day as I was going from Bap. [tist] S.S. with Emma I met Mrs. Prather, who I think must be a member of 1st. Bap. who recognized me and stopped to speak and asked if this was the child. I then introduced Emma to her, and she said that she had seen us at church for two or three years, and expressed a desire to have Emma in her room and said that she thought she had a vacancy. I shall consider it quite a providence if I get her into her room, because she is so highly recommended as a teacher, and she has also very winning manners and seemed attracted to Emma. All this will help to counteract the unpleasantness of going into a strange school again. . . .

This removes one difficulty which troubled me a good deal soon after I put her into school viz. a fear that having put her in so far in advance she would always lag behind. . . . I know that anything touching Emma's welfare cannot but be of interest to you, and really you are so much away from us that I fear you will enjoy little of her girlhood, and know little of it unless I do write details. She has fine capabilities and is very affectionate disposition. . . . You must not forget to pray much and often for her, darling, for her very sweetness and attractiveness will be a source of danger to her, and she has to walk a path beset by pitfalls and dangers. . . .

I am hoping that you will be enabled to send me at least sufficient money to move very soon. . . . I shall move just as soon as I get money enough to pay rent and expenses of moving & marketing etc. . . . I will kiss you good night, many kisses and very warm ones, and add to them a wish that they were genuine and not pen and ink ones. Emma sends love.

> Bye darling
> Emma

Every one of these letters called out by your [illegible] since you learned of my geometry class have exhausted my vitality and injured me to an extent that I know you would regret. If you at any time find it necessary, or think it necessary to write in such strains as your recent letters, please to wait for reply before referring to the subject again, you will thus save me much nervous irritation, and forward my recovery to health. I have had reason to fear at some times within past two or three yrs. serious strains or near disease and the tenor of your recent letter is a serious aggravation to such difficulties because they increase my uncertainty and perplexity and irritate me withal. I am not less in love with you and I succeed in time in quieting my nerves but every effort is a frank exhaustion and every attempt to think for me and judge for me, adds fuel to the nervous excitement that threatens me with serious consequences.

You cannot know how unhappily these things affect me, because you do not know how you would feel if <u>you were a woman</u>, with the same mental organization that you now have, try to imagine it.

———

Atlanta Mar. 28th 1883

My Darling Husband.

I have just rec'd yours of 26th from Phil. containing apology for your note from N.Y.

It is a very welcome letter I can assure you and I will show my own appreciation of it by withholding the very indignant reply which I had written (but not mailed) to yours from N.Y.—that came as the culminating stroke of trouble, crowning a series of recent letters which, with the perplexity regarding board etc, had worried me into positive illness and aged me years it seems to me when I look in the glass. I had come to that distracted point that I had resolved not to write you a line further as long as your letters were upon that subject. I did not come to this conclusion so much in anger as because I made myself ill every time that I attempted to answer one of your letters. Even your present letter indicates that you have never rec'd my letter containing full explanation of my work at Miss Packards. I can not enter into full explanations but will speak of a few points.

I do that work only three times per week and for a half hour at a time and when I feel able, (have not been able to go at all this week). The class are [*sic*] composed of grown up pupils, anxious to learn and I have only to explain to them a study which I love myself and am thereby reviewing for first time in many years, you can readily see that the work is not exhausting to me but a pleasure.

On the other hand I could not, under any circumstances, reason no. 1. (teach under Miss Stokes), or no. 2 (teach children of any kind) or no. 3 (teach such children) or no. 4 (teach in such a room) and she herself says that no. 5 she needs no help except some young girl occasionally on a full day, for an hour or two. Here are five reasons any one of them sufficient to prevent me from engaging in this work. If I could have nourishing and suitable diet, feel settled somewhere till June 1ˢᵗ. and you did not excite and distress me (innocently I know) by trying to lay out work for me and by objecting to such plans as I make, it is altogether likely that I shall be able to do more or less general work, in my own way, and guided by my own judgement, as well as in consultation with Dr. Fuller and perhaps some ladies of the church, that will forward your plans. But, at the risk of repitition [*sic*], I feel it necessary to say that you can not plan for me at all at your present distance from me, nor will it even answer for you to <u>ask</u> me to undertake any work this spring or summer. You seem to overlook the point that, whether I believe in the entire feasibility of your plans or not, I am in sympathy with you and shall do what I can, but if you pursue the course that you have for the past few weeks I shall not only be unable to do the least thing for your work but you are likely to find me on your return in May in such a state of nervous prostration and excitement as you never saw me in before, and the result of which I cannot calculate. I think you know me well enough to realize that I am not holding this up to frighten you. I write you of it because it is a serious fact necessary for you to know. Even while I write my hand is unsteady from nervous excitement, the result of the strain upon my nerves of the past few days. . . .

If I should go to the barracks and take a whole tenement I should be perfectly independent of the school and no more connected with the colored work or debarred from the white than I am here.

It is merely a question of where I can most rapidly and cheaply gain my health that I may be able to assist you when the time comes that there is work adapted to me. My location can make no difference in the amount of help I can be to you, unless I should go out to Mr. Sherman's, in which case I should be obliged to say pretty close at home and attend to Emma's education that she might be fitted for the June examinations.

I am going out the first pleasant day, D.V.,[18] to call on some of the ladies of Mar[ietta] St. church, and upon Miss Stokes. In any case, the obvious work for me between now and next Autumn is attend to Emma's development and my own restoration to health, and to reviewing my mathematics and learning the best methods of teaching by watching those who know how to teach and by trying my hand, as I am doing at Miss Packards school. Otherwise I shall be utterly helpless to assist you, if the time comes when you start a seminary.

---

[18] Deus volute ("God willing").

One person can not do all kinds of work and because I am not fitted physically or otherwise to do the work of Miss Stokes or Mrs. Auten you do me grave injustice and fly off on a tangent when you reason that I am helping the colored instead of the whites, Miss Packard instead of you, I am doing nothing of the kind.

I must answer one paragraph in your letter. You say "Please do not trouble yourself about the future, God has wonderfully cared for us thus far, and he will continue to do so if we trust him"

Do you think, husband mine, that God would have thus cared for us in these past years if I had not "troubled" myself by planning and working and economizing? If while you were struggling in the north I had drifted along without exercising my judgement, as you wish me to do now? I trust not.

Another paragraph "Perhaps you will enjoy better health to have something to employ a part of your time out of the usual channel." I can tell you, darling, what will very greatly improve my health. To have my husband remember that God has given me brains and judgement and feeling of responsibility, as well as to himself, and to cease to distress and chafe me by opposing every plan that I make, and by attempting to think for me.

If, at the age of nearly forty, I am still too much of a child to decide when and how our little daughter and myself shall best live in the weeks of your absence, it is certainly pityful [sic], and not only pityful but most unjust, if I am anything but a child. I cheerfully agree to the propriety of your deciding for yourself, and in opposition to my judgement, matters on which the weal or woe of myself and our daughter depend—and it is not wholly my love for you, or because you are husband and I wife, that I can do this. It is because I was born with a respect for the inherent rights of every person, for the right of each person to judge for him or herself what God requires of them, and do you suppose that I grant all this to you, as you know and the Father knows I have, and feel within me none of these rights? If you do fancy this, you know me no better than when we both lay in our cradles. I am in sympathy with you and your work, and I give you the greatest possible proof of my sympathy for both you and it by willingness to help in it without any assured feeling of its success in your life time or mine.—I reserve to myself only this one little right—to judge for myself of my own modes of work of what I can do, and how to do it. I had not any idea of writing one syllable of this when I began but perhaps 'tis best I do for I omitted to acknowledge 5.00 rec'd in yours of 21st.

[no closing]

Atlanta Mch. 30 /83

My Darling,

I can write but a few lines to-night as am tired and not well, have a cough with headache and some fever, hope however that it may pass away in a few days. I planned to-day for the third or fourth time to see Miss Stokes and Miss Ingraham—went out after dinner, but having some business that must be attended to first, was not strong enough to go so far and was glad to take street car and come home. I have seldom had so little strength as I have this spring—Can sometimes walk off quite strong but can never depend on myself. I am sorry to say that my letter to-night must be business. I sent you sometime ago a statement of my pecuniary situation and I know you have done your best, but as you were unable to send sufficeint [sic] to square accounts then I will send another statement, my liabilities being now increased by another month's board bill and the necessities of our spring wardrobe.

I think my only debts now are board, ($30) for Mch. which will be due to-morrow and $5.00 contracted at Chamberlain's shoe store in Feb. I suppose you can scarcely realize in a northern climate that spring is right upon us and changes in our clothing needed.

Emma is especially needy for she has had scarce anything bought her for more than a year, I will go back of that, she has had almost nothing since she came from the north and what she had then I made over from old clothes of sister's & Mr. Browne except a few new articles that sister bought her. For more than a year, worse than that since she returned from the north a fifty ct. hat and a sunbonnet with about fifty ct. worth of trimming comprise all that I have spent on her hats and bonnets. I didnt know till I came to reckon it up that I had been so economical. She ought to have new hat, hose etc by Sunday week, if it is practicable, but I shall buy nothing for her till board bill is paid, for Mrs. Fuller needs the money to buy clothes for her children as well. The boot bill must also be first paid. After that come Emma's necessities and my own.

I have only a little change by me, having been obliged to use the $5. rec'd recently almost as soon as it came.

I am really troubled that you have assumed the responsibility of paying Dr. Fuller a salary from Mch. 1. "sufficient to enable him to live." I am troubled because I fully believe you are promising him what you cannot possibly do, at this unfavorable season of the year, without crippling your missionary work and starving your own family. If you can only carry on your work by paying at this stage sufficient salary to Dr. F. to enable him to piece out the little the church gives, I believe you are basing your work upon an impossibility and might as well stop it. If Dr. Fuller could go into actual school work and create a great and thriving school as Misses P. [ackard] & G. [iles] have done that would be a different matter, but I shall be ill again if I write or think on this. I know you will do as you think best and you need not attempt to give me the reasons, as I do not intend to say any more on the subject and did not intend to say this and all you can say will not relieve me in any degree from the anxiety. I will put it out of mind and, if you answer this you will only injure me by bringing it again to my attention. If my suggestions are worth anything in your mind I think you will heed them, and if not it cannot be helped. One thing I want to mention, I have thought that perhaps one reason that you wished me to remain here was that you somehow counted the $30. that I paid for board as helping them to live. I doubt if they will so consider it, because it is considered very cheap board. Even if it were so, I want to say at the risk of harping on my health to an extent that is disagreeable to myself and I fear to you, that I am by remaining here throwing away the only chance for life that I can see. I am not alarmed or constantly thinking of self as my letter may indicate, but I can not deceive myself, because I know the constitution of my family and I saw my Mother go year by year and month by month, as I am going and never suspected it till she was past help. An entire change of life and freedom from care six months before I was married would have prolonged her many years I am positive. On the board I pay here I can pay $10. rent and keep a servant with probably a little extra for moving. I think I ought to have a whole house unless I can rent with friends. My own judgement is settle [for] the barracks [but] shall not go there against your wishes tho' I think it most important to my recovery. I love you very warmly and truly darling and am sorry that this letter must be all business.

> With loving kisses
> Emma

Emma was pleased with her card and will write to-morrow.

I shall not keep on my mind more than I can help, the matter of Dr. Fuller's salary. I have told you how it looks to me and shall then drop it. . . .

———

Atlanta Apr. 1st. 1883

My Darling Husband:

The weather to-day seems like a very disagreeable April Fool. Instead of the balmy air and sunny skies that we have a right to expect at this time of year we have had a cold rain storm through the morning, and the weather since has been cold and disagreeable and drizzly, as if quite out of humor. The weather and my cold together have kept me a close prisoner.

I am very thankful to be able to say that I am better than yesterday. I hope that there is a decided improvement in condition of my lungs which have been for few days apparently as bad as last winter.

Even Emma did not go out to S.S. or church, should have sent her notwithstanding the weather but she had a cold, which made it necessary to be careful. I think she is improving in her studies. Is perhaps doing as well as I could expect from her backward condition when she went in, still is not doing anything like what she might if she applied herself. At temp.[erance] union this week, one of the ladies who is a Good Templar asked for your place of business, said that she had made an effort to find you, in order to ask your help at some lodge meeting. . . .

By the way, I was a good deal impressed (by an article read to-day) with the fact that human nature controlled by prejudice or self interest is much the same whether north or south. The article was a little incident of anti-slavery agitation and the occurrence was in the girlhood of a writer not yet old, I think hardly if at all past middle age. A delegation of people from Plymouth Mass. went to N.Y. to attend an anti-slavery convention and were so obnoxious on account of their principles that they could not be accommodated at any of the hotels. They attempted to spend the night in the attic of the hall in which they convened (I think), were threatened with a mob and obliged to leave, wandered about the streets of N.Y. were rec'd into boarding house and on being recognized by some one as abolitionists immediatly [sic] ejected, the landlady telling them that it would ruin her business if she kept them. When we remember that we claim the north is at least fifty years in advance of the south in almost every thing, it is certainly not surprising that republicans have met a like treatment here. I have for many years believed that the germs of human nature, the essentials of it I may say, are the same everywhere, and all experience and observation confirm that view. And that is the very point of failure with theories upon the woman question or the relations of the sexes, they forget that, while the sexes are opposites, to some degree, in physique and temperment [sic], they are identical in all the essential elements of human nature, and that whatever would be a galling chain to a man is no less so to a woman.

I have been very unhappily reminded within the past two weeks that your eyes have never yet been opened to that truth. I pray the Dear Lord they may sometime be, and leave it all in His hands.

I think that if you knew the added strength, moral, mental, and physical, that I should derive from it you would at least <u>ask</u> God to enlighten you. I came across a few sentences to-day in which my ideas are so tersely expressed that I shall trespass upon your forbearance sufficiently to quote them, premising it (by way of consolation) with the remark that I will not soon allude to the subject again as I am aware that people are not often converted by personal discussion. If you are ever brought to see woman's rights in the same light as you do man's rights, your wife's rights in the same light in which you look upon your own, it must come from the Lord the same as my own commenced. These are the sentences.

"Each individuals conscience is supreme, irrespective of sex.—

Admit that <u>man's conscience</u> should decide <u>woman's duties</u> and you admit that woman is not an accountable being.

Woman is a better judge than man of what are her needs, of what she is capable, and of what is womanly; and man, <u>in attempting to define woman's sphere, steps out of his own sphere</u>."[19]

These statements seem to me like axioms of mathematics, self evident and unanswerable. I suspect now you will think, if not say, my wife is unfair, she has asked me not to write her anything to agitate her, and yet she talks herself upon the forbidden subject. Granted, but, if you were the prisoner at the bar, pleading for your freedom (as I am) and had no lawyer, I would feel very generous, I think, if I were the opposing counsel. I had no thought of these things in my mind when I began to speak of the anti-slavery incident, but. . . .
[letter incomplete]

———

Atlanta Apr. 3<u>d</u> 1883

My Dear Husband.

I am bewildered, dazed, am I myself, or somebody else? Is it my husband that continues to address me in such language, or are these letters forged? "I do not wish for you to do this, nor to do that. I do not want you to do the other." This is proper language for employer to use to employed, superior to subordinate, parent to child. Your letter is not couched in such language, as any self

---

[19] Emma's quote closely matches the writing of Elizabeth Cady Stanton.

respecting wife can respond to. Is it possible that you seek to take from me, the liberty of individual judgement and action, which I have told you before and tell you now I shall only lay down with my life? Do you realize that what you seek to wrench from me is your own dearest possession and would be defended by you to the death? why cant you realize that it is as dear to me as to you?

That the same influences that have formed your principles have formed mine?

I do not defy you, I know that my happiness and probably my life are in your hands. I am taking rapid strides of late towards that narrow bed where I shall lie very quietly, wherever you put me, and shall not in any way cross you. You are helping to kill me after the same tender hearted and thoughtful manner in which the man cut off his dog's tail a small piece at a time. The dinner bell has rung.

Affectionally, [sic]
Emma

P.S. I will try to spare you all unfavorable reference to my health hereafter, for I know that I have spoken of it frequently of late. I have done it that you might not be ignorant of the unavoidable effect of what you are doing.

That you may be able to judge how strong I am to bear the excitement and distress occasioned by your letters let me tell you what my diet has been from Sunday morn to the present Tuesday morn.

Sund. Morn. Very greasy pancakes, salt mackerel that do not eat at all, rice I think.

Sund. noon. Good dinner of Roast beef

Monday morn. Toasted white bread, eggs fried in lard (eggs in any form were forbidden me by the Boston Dr.) Gingerbread. Monday noon—Boiled fat pork, turnips boiled with same, potatoes that seem greasy perhaps with butter, cannot relish them, rice pudding, much too sweet and of which am never fond, lettuce.

Tuesday morning, pancakes, baker's bread, fried fat pork, oatmeal that I could not eat, because only half cooked. Tues. noon boiled pork, turnips and string beans boiled with pork and therefore ruined for me, lettuce, cheese, and at each meal good white bread, no graham or corn bread. If you will add to this that I am reduced in strength by colds and coughing, wakefulness etc, you will see that if you have determined to force from me an acknowledgment of the husband's divine right of government, you have chosen a most opportune time for it.

But, O, the <u>shame</u> and the <u>humiliation</u> of knowing that, when I am fighting for life with the odds against me, my husband, whom I love so dearly, is willing to hamper me and weight me down by insisting that I shall defer to his judgement as to where and how I shall live in the months of his absence.

When you asked me to marry you, you asked me if I could lie happy in your arms, you did not ask me if I would obey you, if I would yield up to you my individual liberties and right of judgement. You knew me too well to ask such a question, and it is very unfair now to attempt to claim what never belonged to you and was never given you. I challenge you to say that in aught I have been anything but a true, loving wife through these almost twenty years, or that I have ever failed to sacrifice everything but principle to further your plans. And I can say of you that you have never been anything but the dearest and best of husbands save on the few occasions when you have claimed not your own rights, but yours and mine. Can you give me any <u>reason</u> sufficiently weighty to prevent me from going to barracks if I can not find such accomodations [*sic*] elsewhere, as my health demands and my purse will pay? If so, and I receive them in season they will have their full influence with me. As far as diet is concerned Emma is quite as much in need of a change as I. She is growing rapidly and has the strain of school upon her, and shows some indications of spinal weakness, which I have always feared. You can readily imagine that she needs a nourishing diet and can judge whether she gets it from the table which I have given.

I am not attracted to barracks and shall not go there if I can do better, or if can do anything like as well elsewhere. I am go[ing] into a building not owned by school I presume.

————

Atlanta Apr. 5th 1883
Thursday Morning

My Darling Husband

I rec'd your telegram yesterday in regard to money, thanks, it was not necessary for you to telegraph. Dr. Fuller tells me this morning that your talk to Bucher's people was a success of which I am heartily glad.

I have been confined to the house by illness and bad weather since Friday but went out yesterday after dinner to the Real Estate offices, have a good many places to look at, but am unable to form any judgement yet, there are so many limitations to my choice that it renders it very difficult. We can have the little new cottage of Adair's facing the grove at M.S. for 10. per month, (the same that we wanted last autumn or summer) and in the other part of town a perfectly new nice cottage near Fatty Harris[20] at 9. per month. Dr. Fuller thinks that latter would be more convenient if you should come home, but there are two serious objections to both, in the one case we would probably have to pay for Emma's schooling for the spring term, if she did not lose the place entirely, and in the other case she would be thrown into Marietta St. school, which is said to be composed of roughest children in town and has a poor principal. I think that would be worse than taking her out of school. Have you any advice or preference as between these two places? There is one point, having an important bearing on my health which can only be met by going to barracks or taking rooms among strangers, which is hardly practicable. I think I ought to sleep up stairs, instead of ground floor. That and the isolation from all my friends is the objection to the two cottages, otherwise I would like the M.S. cottage. There are two houses near Emma's school, beyond I think, which have not seen. It is necessary, if possible, that I go where she will not need to cross railroad. I have had a cottage in Luckie St. very highly recommended at 15. per month. I fear that I shall be obliged to keep a servant, can you meet expenses if I do? A month ago I could have avoided that expense I think, but now my lungs seem to be in same condition as last winter and I have lost relish for my food and yet am weak and faint and hungry, feel scarcely able to sit up portion of time. I should not mention it except that it is necessary that you should know that my health is such as to demand a larger monthly supply of money than I have called for before, and also necessary that I should know, if you cannot meet my wants, as in that case I must do as I can. If I do not keep a servant shall hardly be able to rent a cottage by itself, but must take rooms or go to barracks when there are two tenements in each building altho' not connected, still it would save me from timidity. It is essential that I have an early answer as to money, and that you do not promise more than you are certain to be able to carry out. I must pay rent in advance, so if anything waits it must be groceries. There will be ½ months rent in April—but there are expenses of moving and wood & coal. I am sorry to trouble you, and sorry that the diet is such as to make it impossible for me to remain here.

Love

Emma

In this call for more money please bear in mind that diet, situation & a untroubled mind are my only Drs, and that I have had neither since you left me.

---

[20] Asa L. Harris, Georgia carpetbagger and businessman, native of Vermont.

Atlanta Apr. 10th /83.

My Darling Husband

    Morning brings two very pleasant things, sunshine and a letter from you. We have had a perfect storm through all of yesterday and my cough is quite troublesome. As soon as I can get settled somewhere I intend to pursue such home treatment as Dr. Robertson may suggest. My washerwoman who will go with me, if I have room for her, will give me such assistance in treatment as I need and I presume I shall find housekeeping better on that occ.[asion] than even good board would be anywhere save at Dr. Robertson's. You suggest my going there. I do not know whether I told you that I wrote him some time ago to ascertain whether he could either give me table board or take me as boarder without treatment and rec'd a negative answer. I tried to think that it was only because he needed all his rooms for patients who would pay full price for treatment and consequently be more profitable, and yet I had a little feeling that it might have something to do with the suspension of the paper etc.

    At any rate I shall consult him soon as to home treatment. I am going out directly to look at houses and shall probably come to some kind of decision soon. I am very sorry, darling, if I have written anything that seemed harsh; indeed, the fear that it might seem so to you has been one aggravation of my trouble. I am very sure that I never used that bad word "tyrant" or "tyrannize." I must remind you of the theory of Dr. Tanner and some other medical theorizers, viz. that the disposition is formed by the kind of food eaten, and I am quite sure that a diet of fried pork and eggs and greasy pancakes is sufficient explanation of a good deal of moral obliquity. I believe that Dr. Tanner and his wife were divorced on account of troubles growing out of his attempt to experiment largely on her in the way of especial diet. As usual my sympathies are with Mrs. Tanner. I am going after dinner, D.V. to look at the house just beyond A. L. Harris. Dr. Fuller thinks that must be a healthful and pleasant locality. Am also going to look at houses in vicinity of Emma's school— those that I spoke of in former letter as in that vicinity prove to be $15. and are not worth it. I do not regret not being able to go to Mrs. Moser's as the little girl who would have been Emma's only mate there shows such unpleasant traits of character that I would not like Emma to be dependent on her for society, is vain and envious. . . . I will write you again this evening, until then good bye with many kisses.

Wed night—I must write but a line for am very weary, altho' have saved myself all I could. I think I have decided on a house, and I do hope that my decision will be for the best, and that you will enjoy it. I have been limited, not only by price and healthful location but by school, there being only two vacancies in the city in fourth grade. . . .

I went to see Dr. Robertson to-day, to get advice for home treatment. The old house of which I speak is really not ill-looking—but does not look fresh and genteel like the other. I have been out to both houses since I wrote this and have decided on the new one. I really think you will be pleased, it is about 15 mts. ride on street car and 5 mts. walk.

Your letter of Sunday makes me very happy, darling. I do not think there will be any difficulty in cooperation when I have any strength and we are able to talk matters instead of write. I can assure you that I have thought of your interests in all that I have done, and I think it will be medicine to me to know that I am making a pleasant home to welcome you to in a few weeks. Please write whether you like my choices. I know you will like the house. I only hesitated about going so far out, I think you can walk it in 25 mts.

———

Atlanta Apr. 16th /83

My Darling,

I must write but a few lines to-night as am quite weary, changing Emma in school and finding a house have been fatigueing [sic]. The distances are so great that I am entrapped into overwalking before I know it. Shall send Emma by street car to Ma.[rietta] school to-morrow. Hope to move by Thursday or Friday at latest. Can do nothing however till I rec've money. Am a little troubled when I remember that I shall owe at that time $45. for board (beside the $4. already paid) $7.50 or thereabouts for rent, must have money to move with and buy wood and provisions and the 1st. of May $15. more for rent. It is the being behind in board and housekeeping expenses coming in advance that make a call for so much money just now. When I am once fairly started in housekeeping I think I will not find it much more expensive than it has been here and I am confident that it will be a great benefit to my health. I am not disappointed that Dr. <u>Robertson</u> (correct spelling) can not receive me. I think the anxiety I should feel in incurring so large bills would retard my recovery and it would leave us all unsettled again when you came because I do not think you would like there even if we could afford the expense. If you are able to provide me with two thirds as much money as it would cost me to board there I believe I can do fully as much for myself as going there would do. I think by having a good girl to rest me and save me from overdoing, and making a complete change of diet with all the fruit that I wish for, I can do for myself more than any physician can do and be greatly improved by your return. You know I have never been able since I came to Atlanta to live in this way or to be free from pecuniary anxiety. And I must confess I cannot see the way clear now to it, but I am trying to trust in the Lord and in you. I only wish I was strong enough to do as I did when we first came here, and be a real help-meet to you, perhaps I will be one of these days. I wish so much that you may get the marshalship. I should then feel that we could pay our debts and that with the burden of debts and pecuniary restriction removed I could grow strong again, while your own heart would grow light and freer from care. I am quite at a loss how to address this.

With loving kisses. Emma is anxiously waiting for your return and often expresses her desire to see papa.

Bye darling
Emma

I think you had best address to 348 Luckie St.

————

Home Apr. 19, 1883
348 Luckie

My Darling Husband.

I will write you a bit [illegible] for am almost too tired to sit up. I have hired hack several times and saved myself . . . but you know that moving is unavoidable hard work.

I was obliged to go to Mr. Shermans yesterday. . . . I was obliged to move everything, (instead of leaving some articles there as I intended) Mr. Sherman having left request for me to do so, as he hoped to rent his rooms. I think it was really best for us, too, I sent the wagon past your office and met them there and left four trunks in the inner room as I have no store room at this house and have and have [sic] four trunks here as it is. . . . Emma and I slept here alone last night with only the cat for guard and now at noon I am sitting in the most disorderly house you ever saw waiting for my girl to come. She has been home to get her own goods moved. Shall not attempt to do anything more myself except as I feel quite able. I was obliged to go to telegraph office this morning and drew my money $50. I also rec'd P.O. for $10 yesterday. . . .

Not expecting money from you so soon and being almost obliged to move I borrowed through Col. S.[palding] $15. of Col. Buck. . . . I repaid the money to Col. Buck this morning and had a short conversation with him in regard to yourself. He says that he is using every effort towards your appointment, and thinks there is ample reason for the removal of the present incumbent. I will try to tell you just how I stand in money matters. My moving has necessarily cost me a little more than if I had been stronger as I have had to hire carriage few times beside furniture wagon. I have paid expenses of moving, our board bill at Mrs. Fullers within five dollars, this months rent and have funds enough I hope to pay current expenses for this month (about $8.) have wood to buy out of this. . . . I owe $5.00 at Chamberlain's for boots bought for E. & self last Feb. . . . I owe nothing but $5. to Mrs. Fuller and $4.50 at grocers. It is quite against my principles to make a grocery debt but I did so because I was owing Mrs. Fuller so large a sum that I felt ought to take pre[cedence] of everything else but moving. I do not think that when I have once caught up with my accounts my bills in housekeeping will be much more than they were in boarding. . . . Thanks for your [illegible] to my needs by sending by telegraph. I am sorry to press my needs upon your attention but the point had come when I seemed obliged to decide in one way or another and having decided to be obliged to act. . . . Emma sends love. I love you very much darling and am looking forward to your homecoming. Direct to me at 348 Luckie

> With loving kisses
> Emma

———

> Home Apr. 22, 1883
> 348 Luckie

My Darling Husband—

I am sorry and ashamed that I delayed mailing my letter acknowledging receipt of money by telegraph and also the P.O. that came at same time. . . .

Our house is pleasant and commodious and the view from the front of the house is much more pleasant than I would have found it in the more central parts of town. I wish you could see the landscape now. Our spring has been extremely backward so that we have now all the delicate tints of the new spring foliage and it is a constant feast to me. Emma is tired to-day and does not feel like going to church and so we shall both remain at home, probably, unless I feel stronger by church time. I think that when I am rested I shall quite enjoy walking in to church on Sunday morning. The church bells are ringing now with a most inviting sound, making me feel as if I could not stay away.

I wonder if you will remember wife and child in your worship to-day. My thoughts are always drawn especially to you when I enter the house of God and bow my head in prayer. I presume that I am not peculiar in this, but that most christians feel most tenderly and closely drawn to the absent dear ones at that time.

To refer to my situation, altho I have the pleasure of the woods and fields close at my door I am in a thickly settled neighborhood and have one neighbor as near as the nearest at Dr. Fuller's. The woman of the house (next door) seems very kind and neighborly sent me in a beautiful bunch of snow balls [white flowers] yesterday. Honeysuckles are in bloom in the woods and the violets dot the ground here and there. I told you that we are in neighborhood of A. L. Harris. Night before last as I came from Ma[rietta]. St. a lady on the porch of a very pretty cottage opposite A. L. Harris' asked if I was not Mrs. Bryant.[21] I did not at first recognize in the matronly individual Louise Harris nee' now Mrs. Kuhn, tho' on a second glance I found her face quite unchanged. The other married daughter Maimee and Mrs. Harris came over and soon after the youngest daughter and Maimee's baby. They all live in the immediate neighborhood. I always feel almost envious when I see mothers and daughters living near each other. . . .
[closing missing]

———

Marietta Aug. 16th 1883

My Darling Husband.

I have been a careless wife this week in not writing you for several days. I rec'd yesterday yours from Ocean Grove,[22] the postal I mean, hoped to rec'v a letter to-day. We are [having] very frequent rains and my lungs are feeling somewhat uncomfortable, tho' am not suffering much with them. Have been

---

[21] Apparently, a former political dispute between JEB and A. L. Harris had been put aside.
[22] Ocean Grove, New Jersey; Methodist Episcopal Church resort and retreat.

quite busy with some sewing that did not finish before leaving home and that wish to do while I am here on acc. of machine, have also the quilt square to paint for ladies in Earl, intend to begin that to-day and after that is finished shall be quite free to recuperate and rest, D.V.

The reading club meets here this evening. Emma hopes to read a selection and anticipates much pleasure in meeting the young people. I am anxious to hear of your success at Ocean Grove.

With loving kisses
Emma

———————

[letterhead] The Southern Advance Association,
Office, corner Pryor and Hunter Streets,
Officers: E. Q. Fuller, President; J. E. Bryant, Corresponding Sec'y;
V. Spalding, Recording Sec'y; C. O. Fisher, Treasurer.
Atlanta, Ga. Aug 21 1883
[Boston, Mass.]

My Darling Wife.

Upon my arrival here on Saturday I found yours of Friday from home and of Sunday from Marietta came to hand. The clothing from Atlanta came in good time. I was glad to receive it.

. . . I had a safe trip to Ocean Grove and a very profitable trip. I did not change my mind about speaking—did not think it best for me to speak—but Dr. Hartzell has invited me to prepare a paper for next year. He is friendly but there is very strong pressure against our white work.[23] I am, however, making headway. I am in a very delicate position and have to manage with great care. Thus far I have every reason to hope for success. I must spend several days in preparing statement of our work for publication. That will take my time for two weeks probably.

I had a pleasant time at Ocean Grove. Reached there Saturday morning and found myself the guest of the Ocean Grove Association so that my expenses at the Grove were paid. Tuesday morning I returned to New York and attended

---

[23] The Methodist Church debated restricting its educational mission work to former slaves and the African American community; some contested support of the schools for poor white children.

to matters there until Friday morning when I again went to Ocean Grove to see about a missionary for Atlanta; returned to New York and took the boat Friday night for Boston arriving Saturday morning and found a room at my old place, No 3 Boylston Place. I was very tired and am just getting rested. Yesterday I went down the bay to Hull, one of the oldest towns in Mass— about a half hours ride on the boat—with Dr. Nichols and dined with him and his intended. Had a very pleasant time. Today is the first day I have done any work since my arrival, although I had yesterday a very important interview with a gentleman it was necessary for me to see in regard to our work.

I will do better in writing to you than since I left and hope to hear from you very frequently. Tell Emma I have commenced to collect cards for her. Write me how your health is, and how you like [your lodging]. I think you will find it was better for your health that you did not come North. I found it quite cool when I arrived. Already we have quite sudden changes.

> With warmest love and kisses for you and Emma.
> Y. H.

————

[letterhead] The Southern Advance Association
Office, corner Pryor and Hunter Streets
Officers: E. Q. Fuller, President; J. E. Bryant, Corresponding Sec'y;
V. Spalding, Recording Sec'y; C. O. Fisher, Treasurer.
Atlanta, Ga. [marked through]
Zions Herald Boston Mass.
Aug. 25th 1883

My Darling Wife:

I received yours of the 19th with a statement of financial needs yesterday. Wednesday I went to Camp-meeting at Asbury Grove—near Boston—and returned Thursday night. Had a pleasant time. Saw James Mears and wife and other friends.

I hope to send you money as you need it. Shall not be much behind if at all.

I fear that I have not written very fully of my movements since I left home. As I have already written I went to Ocean Grove. That is a delightful place. It is on the bank of the Ocean. You look out upon nothing but water and the breakers come rolling in upon the shore in great white capped waves. I went in bathing and had my first experience with breakers that seemed dangerous although I have before been into the surf. I hope that we may be so situated next year that you can go with me to these places by the sea. I can hardly convey to your mind much idea of the looks of the place. At the center of interest although not the center of the grounds is the auditorium. This is a large building open on all sides that will seat from 3000 to 5000 people where public meetings are held. Not far from this, to the North, is a small lake, about a half mile long and a few hundred yards wide. This separates Ocean Grove from Asbury Park. Nearly a mile to the South is another small lake running East and West called Fletcher Lake. These two lakes which run from the ocean back from a half mile to a mile bound Ocean Grove on the North and South. The ocean bounds the place on the East, and a high fence on the West. Within this enclosure is this Methodist cottage city that has a summer population of from 5000 to 20000 and a winter population of a few hundred. The place was bought by an association of Methodists fourteen years ago—or about that time. It is fourteen years since the meetings commenced—and is under their exclusive control. They allow no liquor sold and no places of amusement and dancing is frowned upon and prevented. Across the lake a few hundred yards away at Asbury Park are places of amusement and at the hotels frequent "hops" and I presume liquor is sold. Asbury Park is larger than Ocean Grove and looks more like a city in some parts although both are cottage cities for summer resorts.

Some parts of Ocean Grove are very pretty. From the Auditorium to the Ocean—a few hundred yards—is a broad avenue with wide grass plots and narrow pathways called Ocean Pathway. This gives a very fine view of the ocean from the Auditorium. The cottages are mostly small, some the size of a wall tent, something like ours in Atlanta; others are larger, but only the hotels are large, and they are not large for hotels. There is a plank walk for promenading along the ocean front from near Fletcher lake on the South to the North boundery [sic] of Asbury Park, nearly if not quite two miles. It is wide—about twenty feet, in some places more than that. I walked the length of this promenade Sunday evening and it was crowded with people all the way.

If you and Emma could have been with me I should have been happy. I hope the time will come when we can be together at these places.

Aug 29th

I commenced this on the 25th and am just finishing it. My time has been so taken up with other things that I have neglected to finish. I really will do better no matter what I neglect.

I am delayed in collecting money by the failure to receive our paper. Shall send you some in a few days.—

> With warmest love and kisses for you and Emma
> Y. H.

———

Marietta Sept. 9th 1883

My Darling.

I am lonely when I think how seldom I hear from you or write; it makes you seem further from me than when we write every day or two. I find that I have lost all faculty of letter writing when it is not reciprocated. . . . In our early seperations [*sic*], we either wrote daily or every two or three days, now a week or even longer is not a very unusual interval. I do not blame either you or myself, but I am alarmed, and unwilling to confess, even to myself, that we are becoming accustomed to separation. I must carry it to Jesus and trust Him to save us in some way from so dreadful a result. I have been to church to-day for the first time since I came here. . . . Emma attends sab. [bath] school at Presb. [yterian] church, it being the only practicable one for her to attend. The Meth. being a half mile further and no one to go with her, and the Bap. not being till afternoon. . . . She is quite interested in the Chautauqua Series of books by Pansy. I have considerable difficulty to prevent her from spending a very undue amount of time in story reading. . . .

In a recent letter you express the belief that we shall yet be situated in a pleasant home happier than ever before. I do believe I shall praise the Lord when that time comes. I have experienced an earnest longing, these few years past, for a pleasant, tasteful home where we can enjoy refinement of association of things as well as people and where our daughter may grow up with objects about her by which her life may be enriched. I know that it is absolutely necessary for me to live now just in the bare, literal present and I am trying to do it, realizing that I can make no plans even a month ahead, but I find it a difficult feat to perform. . . . Perhaps this living from day to day and in so uneventful manner is another reason why I have so little to write—but surely your life cannot be so poor and tame and I shall hope for you to enrich my poorer one. . . . But I am hoping for some "golden Eldorado," a future which shall permit you to remain at home or to take us with you. The Lord knoweth when it will come—or whether ever. . . . May the dear Lord bless you and restore you to us again. . . . I suppose that your school is fairly under headway and I hope that it is flourishing. I hear not a word from our friends there and am as ignorant of what is being done as if I were in the Sandwich Islands.[24] Did you recv'e my letter in which I asked you to send some weekly papers?

With true love-kisses
Emma.

———

[letter fragment—difficult to date]

October [1880–1883?]

If that is the best thing to do I will do that. I can never pay my debts that way. That I can alone do in <u>politics</u>. If I cannot that way I do not see how I can. I can do so in politics if we can only go through, and have money to live <u>upon</u>. That is why I suggest that in the last extremely [*sic*] you write your father and lay the matter before him. I know he and Mr. Brown[e] are not in sympathy with my politics, but they are in sympathy with you, and will aid us if by so doing they can help us through. I must get an office that I fully believe I can do, but it may take a little time

There is another reason why I do not like to give up politics. You know how I have been abused. The men who have done so are now in power. To give up now is, I fear, to leave Georgia for in that event I must do so—with a cloud over my name, one that would never be removed. I do not wish to leave it so; on our daughters account so well as our own. If I can go forward, as I am now doing, I can clear up that cloud entirely for there is no truth in the charges. I do not see how I can in any other way.

There is another consideration. I have gained some reputation in politics. I am in the midst of a fight. If I win I shall have a position that I can never hope to gain in any other way. I can win if we can go forward in money matters. Under these circumstances do you not think that your father would advance enough money to you to keep from want and do you not think it best to ask? Upon this may depend my action. I know we do not wish to do that, and you may not think best, but consider it carefully and prayerfully please.

I have thus given as plainly as possible, to be as brief what seems to me to be the situation.

---

[24] Islands of Hawaii.

I have every reason to expect success here. Perhaps I may not raise the $2000 I want but I think I shall raise enough to go forward and not entirely fail. In a letter to Col. Spaulding I give the situation here fully. Please read that letter.

I love you darling and shall push all I can and return as soon as possible.

With warmest kisses
Y. H.

I shall write to Emma soon.

————

Marietta Oct. 13th /83

My Darling Husband.

If I remember correctly this is your birth-day and I must heartily wish you many happy returns of the day. I am obliged to reckon by my own age to know how old you are, and . . . I am puzzled to know how so many years can have flown since we first knew and loved each other and yet the time seems so brief to me. I often think of you as you looked when we were married and the year or two preceeding [*sic*]. I do not think that I ever wish that we were young and at the threshold of life again, but those days, and yourself, as you were then, are like a cherished picture carefully put away among one's treasures. The years that are past have been full of care and struggle to you. God grant that there may be some fruition of your labors before you reach the bottom of the hill.

I am already counting the days to your return but with a good deal of fear of disappointment since the suggestion in a recent letter that you may not come then. We are having very hot weather for past two days and considerable sickness I think. Emma has not been able to study for more than a week, seems to be neither sick or well, plays about and eats well but is unwilling to study or to walk much. I think it springs largely from her age as there is considerable indication of it.

Shall watch her carefully and shall not dare urge her to study till she is able. Dr. Robertson advised me to keep her out of school entirely till her menses were fully settled. I should not be willing to send her to school in this condition even if I was in Atlanta. . . . I have pd. rent for Oct. board (full price) to Oct. 11, and dentists bill and have just enough to defray incidental expenses through the month. You can reckon as easily as I the money I will be obliged to have to get away with and start housekeeping. Send me as liberally as you can please and I shall be as prudent as possible for I realize the absolute necessity of it.

I shall keep my horse hire within $15. if not less. I think I have been benefitted for am certainly stronger. The trimming to my dolman[25] will be rather necessary but shall be governed by what you can do of course.

The family are at dinner and I must close at once. I love you very truly, my darling husband, and am so happy to say that you are just as precious to me as you were twenty years ago. with loving kisses

Bye, darling
Emma

Emma sends love

---

[25] Woman's coat, with sleeves wide at armhole, tight at the wrist.

LETTERS: 1884–1886

The crises of 1883 dissolved into additional separation for the Bryants through the fall and into the early months of 1884. Giving up her hard-earned house on Luckie Street in Atlanta, Emma traveled to the southern part of the state seeking relief for her health problems. John, meanwhile, continued to balance his educational mission interests with political endeavors.[1]

The unrelenting bickering between Georgia Republicans had crystallized into various factions fighting over the meager appointments meted out from Washington. The natives in the Northern-Southern split now stigmatized the "Maine clique," of which Bryant was a part, as illegitimate recipients of Georgia's share of party spoils. Nevertheless, it was the state's carpetbaggers who nurtured the vital Northern political ties. And they continued to feel deserving of reward for their labors in previous decades on behalf of the party.

Ironically, in these years of the mid-1880s, JEB achieved the pinnacle of his success in Georgia. With another Maine native, Alfred E. Buck, now chairman of the state Republican Party, Bryant regained a leadership role as secretary of the party, even as he continued his efforts for the Union League. By the end of the decade he would hold the office of national secretary in the League.

JEB's long-sought patronage position finally materialized for a brief period under the lame-duck presidency of Chester Arthur. Beginning in the summer of 1884 through May 1885, Bryant served as United States Marshal for northern Georgia, the opportunity he had sought to redeem his name and reputation in the state. A scarcity of letters from these years lends credence to Alice's memory in her autobiography that this was a happy time for the family, united at last under one roof.

Other evidence reveals that JEB's service as marshal was unblemished by any corruption or controversy. His high marks in office, and acceptance by the Georgia bar as a result, seemed to grant Bryant a measure of fulfillment in his Southern work. With that exoneration he would make his final departure from the South.

---

[1] See *Carpetbagger of Conscience*, 172–76, for details of JEB's career in the years 1884–86.

Emma now considered her work in the Woman's Christian Temperance Union her own service mission. And as ever, her thoughts for the future were on her daughter. Alice was completing her elementary studies at age fourteen in 1886 and looking to the college education her mother was determined she would have. JEB's opportunity to assist a Methodist university in Tennessee would prove fortuitous.

———

Quitman Jan. 26th /84
Sat. Morning

My Darling.

You have been more than usual in my heart this morning and I long for your society and your love. I do not think it is quite a selfish longing either for I suspect that you need wife and child equal measure. As the worst of winter seems to be nearly over I am looking forward to Spring and reunion with you. From the tenor of your last letter I am hoping that you may rec've your appointment and return to Atlanta before long.

In any case I do not think it will be practicable for us to remain here at all late as we would therby [sic] lose what we have gained through the winter. . . . If it is possible to make arrangements in Albany as cheap as those here we shall leave here in season to spend two or three weeks or more in that place on account of the artesian well water, it is very highly recommended for dyspepsia, kidney, and other troubles. Nannie[2] has a decided kidney trouble and wishes to try the water on that account and I think that my stomach and bowels might be greatly benefitted thereby. I have talked with parties who have been there and they speak very highly of the water.

Monday P.M. . . . We went Sunday morning to Sabbath school and remained to forenoon service. At night we went to Meth. church. One of the prominent members of the baptist church expressed to me sunday morning a good deal of satisfaction at the formation of the W.C.T.U.[3] We have our second meeting to-morrow in the Methodist church. I am hoping <u>so very hard</u> to hear from you today. I expect that you are perhaps at a critical point just now. May the Lord work for you!

———

[2] Nancy Spaulding, Emma's sister-in-law, had joined her in south Georgia for the winter.
[3] Woman's Christian Temperance Union (WCTU), organized in 1874, became the largest national women's movement of the century. It joined several women's reform issues, including suffrage, and became the primary vehicle for Emma's temperance work.

Nannie saw by the paper that Longstreet was to be removed or something to that effect.[4]

If you have not already sent money to pay board bill, please telegraph as soon as you do send it, or telegraph the money if that can be done here. Nannie and Emma have gone walking. . . . we have heard by way of Mr. Goodwin's sister that our kitty John Wesley has shown his appreciation of a good home by remaining very contentedly at Bro. Kents. . . . I love you darling, very warmly, and am looking forward to our meeting with the happiest anticipations.

> With loving kisses
> Emma

————

> Quitman Jan 29, /84
> Tuesday Morn

My Precious Husband

Yours from Phil. telling me that you are unable to send money at present and enclosing note to Mr. Smith came yesterday. I wished you to send the note to Mr. Smith direct and not through me, but I remember that I expressed my wishes in a rather mixed manner and you undoubtedly misunderstood them.

I can scarcely express to you how distressed and anxious I am. On friday of next week we will be in debt for board $69.50 and when you remember that we are utter strangers to Mr. Smith and that I have paid nothing at all since we came here you can perhaps realize my humiliation. Could I have foreseen this I might, perhaps, have overcome my reluctance and attempted to raise a painting class at the very outset. I have not done so, because I have been so entirely without artistic instruction myself that I shrink from attempting to teach others, lest I may make a failure. Added to that Emma was almost without dresses and I was obliged to devote a good deal of time to sewing, and, more than all else, perhaps, all the circumstances of my life since marriage, as well as a strong natural bias, have made it very difficult for me to enter into any money-getting or business scheme, except I had the preparatory training essential to confidence and thoroughness. I say this much in the way of explanation, because I did suggest the possibility of a painting class before I left home.

————

[4] James Longstreet, Confederate general; JEB had protested his appointment as United States Marshal in Georgia in 1881 and had worked for his removal.

Not having done that, I am perfectly helpless to assist you in this crisis. When I kept house and did my own housework in Atlanta I could share pecuniary burdens with you, and found almost a pleasure in my deprivations because I was thereby helping you. But when I left Mr. Shermans I lost all power of such assistance. My father is the only person to whom it would be at all proper to look for help and he is so "land poor" that it is useless for me to apply to him. the last two or three years have been failures with him financially. When I said that Nannie might help me in case of emergency I only meant in trifling loans in case of sickness, or incidental expenses and supposed that you so understood it. She has not money sufficient with her for any further assistance, and she has already paid our washing bills for several weeks. As far as Mr. Griffin[5] is concerned, if he must be applied to, it will be best for you to ask him to send or give the money to me without subjecting me to the mortification of asking him, especially as such a course will be no more onerous to you than the one that you propose. I shall feel very sorry if you are obliged to do this because it would place you under pecuniary obligations to a man of whose honesty in office I have heard doubt (tho' I sincerely hope they are quite unfounded) After thus telling you how utterly helpless I am to assist you I will say that I have done the only thing in my power, or what seemed the least objectionable. I gave your note to Mr. Smith and asked him myself if he could wait a week or two. He was, as he has always been, extremely kind and gentlemanly and will not distress me but he is really inconvenienced. They pay all their bills weekly and expect their boarders to do the same. I think the hotel cannot have made expenses, even, till recently, because of the few patrons and Mr. Smith is only an agent for the widow of Maj. Allen who requires him to run the hotel on what he receives. Under these circumstances, you can readily see that their courtesy and forbearance have already been stretched to the utmost in my care and I feel like a beggar and a fraud. You have always told me that you should not neglect your business and remain on expense in Washington to work for this office. If you do so, are you likely to have God's help and blessing in this matter; and without His blessing of what use are all your efforts? If I had the means to help you in this crisis it would be a pleasure to me to do it. As I have not, and you are so situated (by God's direction, as you believe) that you cannot remain in Washington without running into debt, is it not God's will that you should

---

[5] S. M. Griffin, postmaster in Quitman, Georgia; also proprietor of Quitman Hotel.

attend to your regular business leaving it to one who has all power over the hearts of men to fight your battles for you. May He direct you and bless you.

With loving kisses,
Emma

————

Quitman Feb. 10–84

My Precious Husband.

I am happier to think of you in Atlanta, and I felt so glad to-day to recieve [*sic*] your letter written from there. And I have rejoiced all day in the thought that you are to be with us next Sunday, God willing. I had thought to write you earlier in the day (it is now bed-time) but went this morning to S. School and church and this afternoon to ride and again to-night to church, so that the day has passed quickly. Emma has not been quite well to-day and therefore did not go to church.

We are now having foggy mornings which I fear will be quite unfavorable to health. I am told that the place is subject to fogs in the spring, there is also a good deal of stagnant water about. One of the boarders told me to-day that he thought he should go to Albany soon. If I do not return to Atlanta with you I think it may be well for us to go as far as Albany when you return, but we will talk that all over when you come. I must retire now. I love you, darling. very truly and kiss you a loving good-night.

Monday P.M. I have been thinking of late of Mrs. Wilson's (where Miss Stokes boards) as a boarding place for us. You will perhaps remember that you spoke of it before we left Atlanta, but I had forgotten it till recently. Miss Stokes said that she had one large front room in which she thought she would like boarders and three of us in one room would of course be an object to her.

I think I should prefer it to a place where there are other boarders and the yard is very large and shady and removed from the store and beside the location is very convenient to town and the custom house. I wish you would ascertain before you come whether we can go there. it seems to me it might be the best and cheapest thing we could do. If you do not expect us to return with you, please bring me from Lycetts a round wooden plaque about 11. in. in diameter. I think it will not be much more than .40 or .50 cts. I think.

I have thought several times to speak of my Chautauquan books. I hope you have not bought them for I have now so far dropped behind that I could not profitably take up the course with the expectation of graduating in -86. I will begin afresh at some time in the future. The dinner bell rang some time ago and must cease writing. I rec'd P.O. for 25.—shall collect it after dinner and settle with Mrs. Smith.

With loving kisses Emma

―――――――

Atlanta March 12 1884

My Darling,

I have received your letters here since my return informing me that you did not hear from me while in Washington. I certainly wrote to you from there but I was driven every moment of my time while there and did not write as often as I wanted to. I will try and write at length of my trip there tomorrow and answer some of your questions. It is now nearly twelve at night and I must to bed. I returned in the night Tuesday night. Was obliged to go on a political trip yesterday and returned in the night last night and have been hard at work all day and until now. I telegraphed yesterday that I would send you money today but have been disappointed. Shall send it tomorrow and telegraph it if possible

I love you darling and shall be glad to see you soon. The President told a friend of mine that he should appoint me in two or three weeks. My appointment is certain.

With warmest love and kisses
Y. H.

―――――――

Atlanta Ga. March 14 /84

My Darling:

I regret the delay in sending you money and I will try hard that it shall not occur again. I send enclosed a money order for $50.

In regard to the plans for the future this is the best I can now say. I shall visit you about the first of April, and spend, I hope, a few days, and leave here for Washington about the middle of April to be gone probably until about the middle of June when I expect to return here and remain. I go to Philadelphia the first of May and remain there until the first of June when I go to Chicago to attend the National Convention. I think that the best plan for us to make is for you to remain in Southern Georgia until the last of April and then meet me in Philadelphia. I presume that you can go to Albany soon if you wish although I do not want any more expense than we can help. I shall be hard pushed for money until I get into the marshals office.

The President told a friend of mine that my appointment was only a matter of two or three weeks. I expect it soon after our State convention which will be on the 9th of June. I go to Washington soon after the meeting of the State Convention to look after my appointment and confirmation. I hope to be confirmed before the first of May and be ready to go into the office when I return from the National Convention. I cannot think that there is the <u>least doubt</u> of my appointment by or before the middle of April.

I have been unable to get the painting you wanted but will try to get it tomorrow morning and send to you.

It is perhaps best that I shall explain my delay in writing you lest you may think strange. When I reached Washington I was driven every moment until Sunday with the matters that took me there. The work of the Union League was very exacting upon me as I had an important report to make as the chairman of a very important committee. I reached there Tuesday and pressed into work and did not go to bed any night until about midnight and two nights in succession was working until about one o'clock—writing in my room. The meetings of the League kept me at work Wednesday and Thursday and part of Saturday and political matters pressed me the balance of the time. Sunday morning I went to Church and after church was so tired that I slept until nearly five when I got dinner—the Washington hour—and after dinner called on a Maine Congressman—Seth Milliken[6] an old friend when I was a boy and was detained longer than I expected. Monday I was pressed all day preparing to leave as I did that night. When I reached home it was the same story work <u>work</u>, <u>work</u>. But I wrote you from Washington certainly one letter and I think two. I <u>will</u> try to do better in future. In money matters I have been pushed but am now in a little better circumstances. I hope to send you more in a <u>few</u> days.

I love you very much darling and shall be glad when we can be together all the time. With warmest love and kisses for you and Emma

Y. H.

---

[6] Seth Llewellyn Milliken (1831–97), representative from Maine, 1884–97.

Atlanta March 22 1884

My Darling:

This has been a hard days work. We held our county convention for the election of delegates to the State and Congressional district conventions which, as I wrote you yesterday, are to select delegates to the Republican National Convention that meets at Chicago June 3$\underline{d}$. Our county convention today was the best we have ever held in this county. My friends were successful in all things. I was chosen a delegate to the State and to the Congressional district conventions.

The district convention meets in this city on Tuesday, when I expect to be chosen a delegate to the National Convention. As I wrote you yesterday these are steps taken to make my appointment as Marshal certain as soon as possible.

There is nothing more of interest to say tonight and I am so tired that I will go to bed as soon as possible.

With warmest love and kisses.
Y. H.

———

Atlanta Ga April 14 1884

My Darling Wife:

I had expected that I would reach money today but there have been obstacles in my way that I have not yet overcome. It is however a matter of only a very few days. I am however so anxious for you to come at once that I write [*sic*] Mr. Griffin asking him if he can advance you the money for a few days. If he offers you the money please come at once and if you do telegraph me on what train you leave. You had better leave so as to come directly through. There is no trouble in my matters, only delay. I am constantly gaining.

I love you darling and want to see you very much. If I fail to meet you at the depot come directly to the Grant House on Whitehall St. above Hunter and near the Surprise Store and on the same side of the street.

With warmest kisses for you and Emma
Y. H.

[Alice Bryant's autobiography. In 1884, Alice was almost thirteen when JEB became United States Marshal in Northern Georgia.]

When my father was Marshal in Atlanta, Georgia, I spent hours with him in his offices listening to the men talking politics. I used to go to the barber shop with him and sit on the foot rest of the chair while he was being shaved and when he thought I was too old to go to the barber shop with him as no girls or women went in those days, I was deeply grieved. My mother said that she never heard my father express a regret because I was not a boy. . . .

For a number of years my father was engaged as a lawyer in a claims case before Congress. . . . His fee was conditional on his winning the case. He spent a great amount of money staying in Washington during sessions of Congress, waiting for the case to come up and finally had to give up the case, which was eventually won by the . . . heirs.

I have mentioned the fact that my father was Marshall [*sic*] for the Northern District of Georgia, the best office in Georgia to be given by the President. It was given to him by President Arthur, but at the end of his short term of office Grover Cleveland, the first Democratic President since the war was elected and my father resigned, believing that "to the victor belongs the spoils."

The year I was fourteen my father was still working on the [claims] case and we spent the summer in Washington and Philadelphia. He had also become an agent to collect money for the Grant Memorial University at another time called the U. S. Grant University. He was especially contacting Grand Army Posts throughout the country who contributed to the school because of the name Grant. . . .

———

Quitman Mch. 15th [1886]
Monday Night—

My Darling.

I have been very busy all day with painting and must do some packing before I retire because to-morrow must be devoted also to painting. Shall not be able to finish before leaving but hope to get it in such shape that can finish it after my arrival to Eastman.[7] If the weather continues fair Alice and I may go on a

---

[7] Georgia town about one hundred miles north of Quitman.

trip to Cherry Lake in Fla. on Wed. as a good bye to our southern stay. Should not seek the trip myself just now, tho' I think it will be pleasant and I may get some pretty view that I can take a rough sketch of and improve upon afterward. I go especially if I do go to please Miss Small whose heart seems quite set upon going into Fla. before she returns. We should go by carriage in a large double conveaance [*sic*] similar to our trip to Fla. the first winter that I was here.

I rec'd to-day yours with P.O. enclosed. [I] will draw it to-morrow and settle with Mr. McCall or may possibly leave it til the day of going.

It is possible that I may be unable to write you more than postals from now till I reach Eastman, as I shall be most hurried. I would like to leave here Wed. day after to-morrow if do not take the Fla. trip and if I do must start on Thursday at latest. Shall probably stop one night at Valdosta and reach Eastman Friday or Sat. according to whether make connections by morning train or miss it and am obliged to lay over or take sleeper. There is no certainty that the morning train will make connection they tell me—but as there is a chance I shall probably try it. I wish, too, that this money was to take us to Mch. Do not think I would fear to go even this early but shall abide by your judgement in the matter.

I dare not spend more time in writing now. with loving kisses

Emma

I fear that I shall reach Eastman with so little money as my bill here and the expense of leaving will reduce my funds to about thirteen dollars out of which will come my traveling expenses, and if I am delayed over night, as is quite possible, then will consume nearly all. . . .

––––––––

[letterhead] The Uplands Hotel
Eastman, Georgia.
Is Now Open to the Traveling Public
Under the Management of
Dr. E. S. E. Bryan.

Eastman, Ga. Apr. 7th 1886

My Darling—

I rec'd two letters from you this morning the first in nearly two weeks . . . the mails have been stopped by the flood and the passenger[s] as well. . . .

The passenger[s] detained here left this morning but there are reports that they have got but a short distance from here.

As to money required to reach Atlanta I think 75. will pay our bills here and pay for such articles as we are obliged to have before commencing tho' it will leave me with very little money in hand to meet any unexpected emergency which might arise. I am very anxious to start for Wash. . . . My choice though would be to go to Wash. Apr. 27th especially if the time of your coming to Geo.[rgia] is uncertain. I wish to so arrange as to be with you as much as possible. Please ascertain the fare from Wash. to Chicago and whether they sell round trip tickets etc. . . . I should not think of a trip west this summer or really desire it were it not for father's feeble health. I have written to-day to Chamberlain to send me dress and trimmings which will amt. to little over ten dollars and to charge it till I reach there—do not think he will object. I wish to have it now, both because I need it in Macon, and because there is a dressmaker and milliner here who works cheaply (and people tell me nicely) and who is very kind in giving me suggestions and doing for me many little things which I can not get done in Atlanta so easily or cheaply. About the agency of Grant Mem Univ. if it will be a means of keeping us more together and will not add to your own burdens and anxieties I will favor it.[8] I am exceedingly anxious that the remnant of our lives shall be spent as much as possible together. . . . About money you can calculate how much I will need from Atlanta to Wash. It is a season of the year when we need considerable money for the replenishing of our wardrobes, but, if really necessary, that can be done after we reach Wash. save the few things that must be purchased before the convention. . . . You do not tell me if you have a pleasant boarding place or if you have made any arrangement or plans about our coming. . . .

> With loving kisses
> Emma. . . .

---

[8] In 1886, East Tennessee Wesleyan in Athens, Tennessee, was renamed Grant Memorial University; Alice reported that JEB was "Field and Financial Agent," that is, raised funds for the school; Bryant was a trustee of the university 1886–88.

[Note in Alice's handwriting added across the top of letter.]

I think you might ans. my letter. Alice

Atlanta May 7th 1886

My Darling.

Another letter yesterday still from Wash. reminds me that you can not have received a letter from me since I came here. . . . I will repeat in this what I have previously written to Phil. in regard to going to Wash. While I should have been delighted to go to Wah. could I have gone direct from Macon there, and while I am eager to see you at the earliest possible moment I most decidedly do not wish to go if you are coming here (as you said) last of May or first of June to remain several weeks. My first and greatest reason is that, after all these months of living away from you, I can easier prolong the lonely life for a few weeks more than bear the sharp pain of a second seperation [*sic*] in a few weeks time. There are also minor reasons. one is that it would be most gratifying to Alice and beneficial also, after her fragmentary school life, to be able to finish up the grammar school with her companions as she can do if I remain through June—another that it is a critical time in our [year] and I hope that I may be of some service by remaining—still another that I have been appointed Supt. of a new and most important dept of state work and could in a couple of months inaugurate it and get local supt's at work.[9] I have referred to this at greater length in my Phil. letter written immediately after coming here. I believe that the time is come and the most advanced Christian people are ready for this movement if it is wisely inaugurated. whether God will make use of me or send by another I do not know. I am responsible before Him to make the trial. the issues are with Him. . . .

My opinion is that when I do leave Ga . . . it will be to remain till Alice is old enough to go away from us to college. I think that it is absolutely necessary if Alice is to come up to the standard of womanhood of which she is capable. Last evening I took tea at Bro. Ellington with Mr and Mrs. Arringdale and son. . . . The Arringdales are from Baltimore & Mrs. Arringdale says that it has an almost perfect system of schools with a Meth. College in process of erection that will be second to none in the country. She also thinks that the

---

[9] Work with the Woman's Christian Temperance Union.

moral influences upon young people are excellent. It is possible that may be the place for Alice.

I must close in haste. I long to be with you, darling, and hope to be here or there before long. . . .

With loving kisses
Emma

Emma Francis Spaulding (Bryant), c. 1863. All family photos courtesy of Josephine Zeller Megehee.

John Emory Bryant, c. 1860.

J. E. BRYANT, Chairman.

VOLNEY SPALDING, Secretary.

S. A. Darnell,
C. O. Fisher,
Geo. S. Thomas,
J. F. Long,
Jesse A. Holtzclaw,
Madison Davis,
Andrew W. Caldwell,
John R. Hayes,
Archibald P. Wade.

~ROOMS~

Republican Executive Committee,

STATE OF GEORGIA.

Atlanta, Ga. Feb 14ᵗʰ 187[0]

My Darling Husband.

I am at the Office and have but a moment for I have spent the time talking business with Mr. Pelum until it is near dark. I have rec'd two letters from you with [$10] each enclosed and thank I acknowledge them at the time but I must close now. Your letter rec'd yesterday spoke of the adventure of Captain Lonsdale and threats to telegraph me, no telegram has been rec'd and had there been I think I would have been able too. We have trusted each other too many years to be hasty our confidence thus easily displaced. My anxiety now in regard to your pecuniary concerns from all that I can gather here I fear that a failure there would be disastrous to you here as far as your present connection with the paper is concerned tho' the political field would still be open could you be independent while in the field. but I dare not to say a word of discouragement. only don't let your enthusiasm mislead you. God keep you darling soul and body. I am intensely anxious about our future — crave lay the burden on the great Burden Bearer for I have not strength to carry it.

Portion of letter from Emma Spaulding Bryant to her husband, John Emory Bryant.

Sketches by Emma Spaulding Bryant.

Office at Camp Gaston 1876

Hotel Dennis, Leanna, 1883

Bryant family, c. 1896. From left: John Emory Bryant, daughter Emma Alice Bryant Zeller, granddaughter Miriam Irene Zeller, Emma Spaulding Bryant.

John Emory Bryant, c. 1860.

Zeller family, c. 1922. Seated, from left: Emma Alice Bryant Zeller, Letitia Josephine, Julius Christian Zeller, Margaret Louise; standing, from left: Rachel Elizabeth, Dorothy Spaulding, Alice Caroline, Raymond Bryant, Miriam Irene.

Spaulding–Bryant Descendants

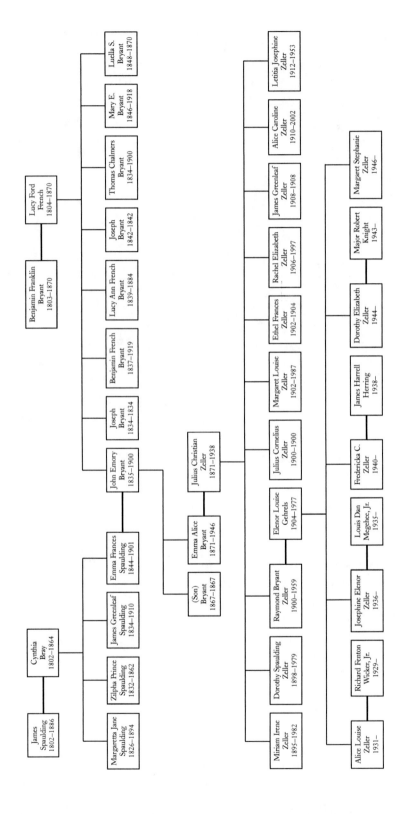

LETTERS: 1887–1890

The success of his last patronage position and restoration of a reputation for integrity brought some closure to John in his Southern venture. Continuing to work for the Republican Party through the National Union League, his primary residence henceforth would be in New York, with ongoing trips to Washington. The educational work of the Southern Advance Association in conjunction with the Methodist Episcopal Church also was centered in the cities as he solicited Northern aid. His connection with a Methodist institution, East Tennessee Wesleyan, which became Grant Memorial University with JEB's support, seemed the ideal transition for the family.[1] In 1886, Emma moved to Athens, Tennessee, expecting that her husband would be on the campus for frequent visits.

The letters of these years show that just the opposite occurred. Attempting the party and educational work of his political mission while at the same time trying to establish some financial stability in business or law, John seemingly could neither adequately support his family in Athens nor bring them to New York. This separation from her husband proved the longest yet for the carpetbagger's wife.

Little suspecting the grinding poverty that awaited her in Tennessee, Emma focused on the task of finding the right college for their daughter. As she expected the stay in Athens to be temporary, she continued to hope that Alice could attend college in the North. The reality was, however, that Grant Memorial University, which targeted children of the surrounding mountain region, provided the only available choice for Alice to continue her studies. These letters reflect Emma's extraordinary determination as she toiled to ensure the educational opportunity necessary for her daughter to realize "noble" adulthood. The experience would only strengthen her allegiance to the growing (though still minority) view that demanded equal rights for women.

---

[1] JEB assisted in garnering support for the school, which he hoped would be aided by a name change to Grant Memorial University. Future name changes would include: 1892, U. S. Grant Memorial University; 1906, Athens School of the University of Chattanooga; 1925, Tennessee Wesleyan College, by which it is still known. See Bill Akins and Genevieve Wiggins, "Keeping the Faith: History of Tennessee Wesleyan College, 1857–2000" (manuscript).

Recognizing that her husband could not be relied on to support his family, much less to meet college expenses, Emma now made good use of her recent efforts at career development. Along with teaching, she found other and varied means of earning income. In addition, she continued to work for the Woman's Christian Temperance Union and with an amazing array of charity efforts through the Methodist church, which she felt were her Christian duty. Both John and Emma readily expressed their reliance on a sustaining faith in God to undergird their lives.

That faith became all the more necessary—along with courage—as Emma struggled to survive under formidable circumstances, and to nurture the bonds of her marriage from such a distance.

———————

Athens Mch. 27th 1887

My Darling.

It is a glorious Sunday morning. [I] will take time for a few lines before I start for Sunday School. The day is perfect and only needs your presence to [sic] me.

Now that the time is crammed down to eight weeks I have good courage and almost look across the intervening time and see you here. Will you not be here as early as eight weeks from yesterday if not earlier? The pear and apple trees are just in bloom—the peach trees are passed their flowering. Alice's throat trouble is the anxiety that mars my content—have been unable thus far to do anything to relieve it. [I] can see not much left to try except change of [illegible] and sleeping on the second floor. Mrs. Marstrom's children have had colds and coughs all winter and spring and have them still. it seems their normal condition.

But I didn't start out this beautiful morning to visit you of our trials or woes to think of them but to count up the bright and beautiful things that are in our lives. It is easy on such a morning as this to believe that the blessed Saviour died to redeem the world and, looking at the world from the outside, to seem really and truly redeemed this morning—bright and clean and free from the stains of Sin.

Among the foremost of our blessings I reckon your fully restored health. I know not how to be thankful enough. and I do so earnestly desire and pray that the remainder of our lives may be passed together in earnest united work for the Master. After so much seperation [sic] clutching our more than twenty years of married life I have great faith that God will permit us to enjoy each other's companionship—in some respect. I think we will know how to appreciate & enjoy it better than ever before, perhaps.

Alice is doing well in her studies and getting gradually into habits of study I hope. Prof Knight told me yesterday that she was very thorough in her Latin and that he could see the beneficial effect of the assistance and training that she received at home. He said that there was a great loss to those pupils who received no inspiration at home. Notwithstanding that the term is passing so pleasantly I am looking eagerly forward to its close.

I recited my first lesson to Prof. Knight yesterday and hope to make good progress in the few weeks that are remaining. We had teachers' meeting here last night and sadly missed our pastor. one of the students will take his place as far as possible in the church. It is nearly Sabbath School time and so good bye with loving kisses

Emma

over

Monday Morn—Our glorious Sunday was diversified by rain before church was out and to-day is cold and damp as a day [illegible] can be. Had a <u>good</u> Sabbath School class enlarged by two transients or rather one visitor and one belonging to another class.

After the temperance lesson we took up the review and I had the privilege of saying a few words on the woman question based upon the fine lesson of the quarter, Gen. 1:26&27v, where the specification immediately following naming show the word to mean both man and woman and the 26th v. showing plainly that dominion was give to "<u>them</u>" not to him alone. Three of the class were married men, and I hope they carry out the doctrine in their own households as heartily as they seemed to concur in it yesterday. I try each Sabbath to get the last issues, and practical point out of the lesson. I feel more especially desirous to do this as a portion of the class are theologians one of them a local preacher and what I say in the case of it only goes through the ear into the heart, they may proclaim upon the housetop. I am not so conceited as to suppose that I can change the opinion of mature men, but where their opinions are already in the right direction the Spirit through my weak words and the application of bible truths may arouse them to greater [illegible] and power—but I haven't time for another word.

with loving kisses
Emma

Athens June 19th 1887
Sabbath Evening

My Darling.

I am through with the active duties for the day and can now treat myself to a few minutes chat with you. We are having exceedingly hot weather but as the ground is dry I am bearing it very well. it is the <u>steaming</u> hot weather that prostrates me most. . . .

After dinner I went to colored Bond of Hope and immediately after to the jail work with the pastor from which I have just returned. I feel blessed in this work but it leaves me little time for other things.

I hope that the day has been a happy and useful one to you and that not many more will pass before we shall be enjoying each others society.

You must be prepared to exercise a little patience after you send for us for as wish to stop over a train or two at Abingdon Va. and at Mt. Lake Park, if we pass those places, as I think we do and yet I am not sure about Mt. Lake Park unless we go through Washington—which I do not presume we do. Please write me about the route etc. A party of eight arrived by the [illegible] o'clock train last night and went on to White Cliff to-day.

Have you ever written Dr. Hagey?[2] If not I would do so. Your friends here frequently enquire for you.

As to our going to Ocean Grove I am hoping that I can do so without injury to myself for I think that Alice would be much benefitted by sea air and bathing. I think that her liver is quite out of order—it is indicated by headache languor and other symptoms. It is quite natural that this should be as when she eats hot biscuits of baking powder and lard three times pr. day and other things to correspond.

I am keeping up very good courage though in the hope of good things soon.

I wish to write Margarette and also to take a little nap in the hope of going to church to-night and so will say good bye with loving kisses and the wish that I may soon give you

bona fide kisses
Emma

---

[2] Methodist minister in Athens.

[Emma's note written on side]

written from Athens on our wedding anniversary June 26, 1887, my first summer in Athens.

Athens June 26th 1887
Sunday P.M.

My Darling:

Do you remember what day this is and have you been thinking of it, or has it passed by like the other Sabbaths of the year? I had greatly hoped to be with you on this anniversary day. twenty three years to-day since we united our lives, thus doubling our joys and dividing our sorrows some author has said.

It has so far proved true with us that we have been very happy in all these years, in spite of all the disappointments that we have experienced in temporal matters. I had looked forward to a house full of happy children and a home to rear them in but I must believe that infinite wisdom and infinite love has given us just what we ought to have, and I do thank him with a full heart for our constant trust in each other and for the unfailing love that has never lost its first warmth and freshness. This anniversary carries me especially back to the day of our marriage because it comes on the Sabbath like that. How rapidly the time has flown since then—almost a quarter of a century since I dropped my name for yours and (girl like and woman like) so merged my life into yours that I came very near having no separate individuality afterward. That would have made me a poorer woman and a poorer mother than I am to-day, so, while I thank the dear Lord for happiness I must thank Him too, for the little unevennesses of the way as well. I do wish most heartily that we could have kept this anniversary together. I hope that you have thought of it to-day. I know, at least, that you have thoughts of wife and daughter and that you keep us close in your heart of hearts. I came across and read one of your old love letters the other day one written not before marriage but afterward from Beaufort in Oct. 1865 a little more than a year after our marriage. I think I enjoyed it as much as on the day of its reception.

I must lay aside this now to finish a letter to Alice and then to retire as am quite fatigued. Sabbath is in some respect my hardest day for the week, as I visit the jail beside going to church & S. [unday] S. [school] and there is no hack running so that I walk in the heat. If you rec've your money on the 2nd as you hope I shall perhaps be with you on Sunday week. I would be very happy to know so.

With loving kisses
Emma

Athens July 4th 1887
5:45 P.M.

My Darling.

Many thanks to you for the telegram just rec'd and to the dear Lord that has enabled you to do this much towards relieving our necessities. It has been all in all a marked day beginning with a good deal of trouble and anxiety pecuniarily but gradually brightening some before the reception of your telegram a few minutes ago. It is not needful to detail the worries and troubles and they would be very insignificant beside your own, but for a little time they seemed heavy, but the Lord helped me and my courage is good. I hope to be able to pay $11.50 living bill out of what I recv'e as well as the $30. on board but can not tell that till I rec've your letter and learn your reasons for the suggestion that I keep 20.

The living includes the two trips to White Cliff which form the larger half of the bill. Mr. & Mrs. Foster are still as considerate and kind as could possibly be expected under the circumstances and I think I could not have been better situated at any other house in Athens. As both you and we are strangers to them it is the more to be appreciated. If she had been such a person as was represented by some I should have been most unhappily situated. I think it would have been even worse if I had remained at Mrs. Marstrom['s] for it would have been a greater hardship to her because she had no other boarders and also because she did not wish to keep boarders through the summer under any circumstances. So I have that drop of sweetness in the trouble that they have not been aggravated by my move in coming here and that no greater hardship or expense has been entailed upon you. Of course if I could have known the first of last May that we were to be delayed here till this time and that you were to be kept waiting for your salary I should have put all my yankee wits to work and saved ourselves some of the hard things we now have to meet, but as that was impossible I can only bow meekly to the rod and ask what lesson the Lord intends to teach me.

I rec'd this morning your note for the bank and went to see Mr. Fisher and learned that he was out of town. he returns to-night and I will see him in the morning. I ascertained that it has not gone to protest.

Alice was to have gone to the Cliff yesterday evening and failed then because there were not enough for a load and this afternoon because so large a load came by train that there was not room for both herself and Mrs.

Helm.[3] They will go to-morrow morning early I expect. She send[s] much love and is anxious to go to you. I am trusting that it will be possible for us to do so very soon. It is growing too dusk to write. may the dear Father keep you safe and bring us both together soon.

Your friends here often enquire for you and our student pastor to-day said some very kind things of myself in my connection with the church and association with the students. I should be very glad to believe that I had been as useful as he intimates. He says that Prof. McLaine [McLain] returns next week. If he is obliged to wait longer for his pay would it not be well for you to write him?

With loving kisses
Emma

My letters I fear are a funny jumble of love and harraning [*sic*] cares. I am much better in health than at last writing. I will relieve any anxiety which I may have caused by reference to my troubles of to-day by saying that it originated in a little bill of less than six dollars and that I borrowed money this morning of Mrs. Marstrom and settled it

Sat. Morn. I am sorry to see that this letter was not mailed yesterday. I had Alice on my mind all day as it was uncertain when she would go and they finally started in the afternoon and being down town when they started I remained there till night and so this was neglected. By that means, however, I met Dr. Spence and arranged about the note, Fisher has been away and I still have it in my possession. Shall leave it with Fisher to-day if he returns and Dr. Spence will go in Monday, sign it and take up the old note. I had a little talk with the Dr. as to your affairs in N.Y. and he speaks very favorably which is, of course, very pleasant to hear.[4] I have just come down town & rec'd money order. Shall pay 30. reserving remainder at least till I rec've your letter and learn your reasons.

As we drove down we passed the son of the prof. at White Cliff who tells me Alice and Mrs. Helm reached there safely last night for which I am very

---

[3] Lucinda Helm, from Macon, Georgia, worked in the Methodist Episcopal Church to expand women's work.

[4] John F. Spence, D.D., was president of the university from 1875 to 1893. JEB and his Southern Advance Association assisted Spence in the effort to gain support for the school in the North.

thankful as I blamed myself last night for having allowed her to start in the afternoon instead of waiting till morning. I am afraid of the mountain roads after the light becomes poor. I must hasten to close this as I want to finish a letter to Alice to be sent by White Cliff mail. I cannot tell you how I long to be with you and for us to emerge from this cramped position. . . .

———

Athens 7/12 1887

My Precious Husband.

Yours of Friday was brought me this morning just as I was about starting for Sunday School. Your daily letters are a great pleasure to me and I have myself written nearly every day this week I think.

I feel the force of your remark "if I could go home to you and Alice." I think many, many times how forlorn that same home-going must be to you— to be met by no kin of welcome, to know that there is no one waiting to whom your coming is joy. I wonder often not only how you bear it but how I can live through it myself so patiently as I have for I can say truly that in all the twenty five years of our married life your coming has never ceased to be a delight to me. your embrace has never failed to thrill me and so our married life has never grown stale and common place but has had for me through all the months and days much of the charm of our courtship. God be thanked for this—it has many times over compensated for any possible lack financially or otherwise. I almost think that it has helped to keep my heart young and responsive to the interests and experiences of our daughter and the young people with whom I am brought in contact. I do not mean their love experiences, necessarily, but their sympathetic, youthful way of looking at all matters which so often raises up a barrier between them and the parents if these parents have outlived the sentiment of their own lives—to put it in plain English have dried up. My writing was interrupted here by sabbath school hour and the whole day since has been occupied by imperative duties with dinner and a brief rest between.

I am strongly inclined to think that we will go to Benton Springs sixteen miles from Cleveland with Prof. Brown and wife from here and the Methoodist [sic] pastor and family from Cleveland. [I] will add a letter to this in the morning as to necessary expense. Should we rec've an invitation from Dr. Carter to visit him we will go there very soon, spend a few days and then go to Benton Springs on our way back. I hope that this has been a happy day to you and that the dear Lord will not only sustain you by his presence but that he will bring some pleasant things to alleviate your loneliness and that not many sabbaths will pass before we see each other. Should we like Benton Springs and it be decided that we could not go north perhaps you could visit us there and we could at last carry out my cherished dream of camping out together.

> With warmest kisses Good night and Pleasant Dreams.
> Emma. . . .

————

Athens July 27th 1887

My Darling Husband.

If you have not already sent me anything written as late as to-day, please write or telegraph at once to me as something occurring last night has left me in that anxious frame of mind that will not be allayed till I know of your health and safety.

I was waked from a sound sleep by Alice who said in a clear, distinct voice "my father is dead" She was talking in her sleep as she often does but she rarely ever speaks so clearly as to be intelligible. When I called out to her "dont say that" she spoke in an indistinct and mumbling tone such as she usually has in sleep. While I do not and did not believe it to be a warning it, of course, made me broad awake and set me to thinking upon the undeniable fact that your death or severe illness was altogether possible in these hot and sickly times. As you may suppose I am uneasy and anxious even more than usual and I have been so before on account of the extreme heat. Be sure to let the people at your boarding house and at the office know my address that they may let me know in case of your illness.

> Lovingly & in haste
> Emma

[Emma's note written on side]

written after a fright in regard to B. through being wakened from sleep by Alice, saying "My father is dead."

Athens Aug. 7th 1887

My Darling.

I can appreciate this evening how lonely you have been this summer—for am alone myself. I have always, too, an anxious feeling when Alice is away from me and presume I should have were she much older than she now is. I am encouraged by Dr. Spence's report to hope that we may be with you in the close of this month. I am as sanguine as ever to look forward to two weeks from to-day as the time when we may possibly be with you but fear it can scarcely be, as that would oblige us to leave here early in next week.

Prof. McLain and family returned to-day and that makes me realize that the beginning of school is not far off—three weeks only, I think.

I suppose you have not as yet thought in reference to Alice's schooling for the coming year. It might be well to make some inquiries as it will probably be nearly time for school to begin when we reach there.[5] If the public schools could meet her needs I think I should prefer them. I am particularly unwilling to put her into a <u>fashionable school</u> such as is likely to be recommended to you. She is wonderfully affected by her surroundings and should be put where good sense and genuine piety are leading elements. next to that I would prefer the mixture of all kinds such as is found in public schools but she might be unable in the latter to pursue those studies required for admission into Wellesly [*sic*]. I wish that you would write at once to Wellesly making application for her there, stating that she will be prepared three years from this coming Sept. Please do so and notify me when you have done it. We have had a delightful day, cool and pleasant and just now a sprinkle of rain is patting upon the leaves of the trees—scarcely enough to be heard elsewhere. I rec'd a postal yesterday from Alice to say that she reached there safely. telegraphic communication is now established between here and the Cliff which will enable to send to her at once on receipt of telegram from you that money has been sent. I hoped to rec've a letter from you last night but was disappointed will undoubtedly find it awaiting me tomorrow morning. I continue to be in better health than a few days ago though do not feel very strong. It has been a very sickly summer here and in the surrounding country and I do not think that there is any foundation in fact for the claim to remarkable healthfulness which has been put forth for Athens. I base this

---

[5] Alice remained in the Preparatory Department of Grant Memorial University as a third-year student 1887–88.

upon the statement of residents as well as upon my own judgement. I do not consider the town proper a good place at all for those troubled with lung or those diseases except as you compare it with the north than which almost any part of the south is better. They are somewhat subject to typhoid fever here every summer, I understand, and throat troubles are more or less prevalent. I do not think the atmosphere at all free from dampness unless it is on this hill. I have taken two very slight colds since I came up here but have been able to keep them off the lungs for which I am very thankful. I am feeling tired this evening and will make an effort to get a nap. I hope that you have passed a pleasant sabbath and that the Lord has been very near and precious to you.

With loving kisses

Emma

I had a long talk with Dr. Hagey the other day. he complains that you never write him unless on business. I tried to explain that you had been much engrossed in business but I think he really feels it. It is rather odd that I feel so much attached to Dr. Hagey with our sentiments on the woman question so antagonistic. but I have great respect and friendship for him and I think that it is mutual. Alice, too, is very intimate there; she and Mollie being very fond of each other. I hear many pleasant things said of Alice here at the hotel chiefly among the ladies. She has formed almost no acquaintance among the gentlemen of the house. The single exception being the young son of Gen. Longstreet, who plays & sings and is a very agreeable young man, has been here but a short time. There is a young widow however about ten yrs. his Senior who engrosses most of his attention so I had no reason to fear a flirtation even had Alice remained here. he is the only society young man that has been here since we came. This filling up the waste places of my sheet is not economy but one of the peculiarities of a woman for which I cannot myself account

––––––

Athens Sep. 4th 1887

Sabbath Eve.

My Darling.

The day is waning—another week begun. I have wondered where you have worshipped to-day and if the day has been pleasant and blessed with the presence of God.

The waiting has been long and weary and only the dear Lord knows when it will cease.

It has been the day for reorganization of the sabbath school classes. I have thus far only one of my old members but hope to have more later on. I do not know whether I wrote you that Bro. Schingler has left us—he is a real loss to the church and school. Bro. Harrison is now filling his place. I have not been able to go out to prayer meeting for some time and miss them. I am anxious to go next Wed. but do not know whether to venture. I think that the school has opened very well and the sabbath school seemed the fullest this morning that I have ever seen it, I thought. Several families have moved into town during the spring and summer that promise to add considerable strength to the church if they remain. The wives, however, in at least two instances, are homesick and I doubt if they become permanent residents. I am very thankful even at this dark stage of our life that you did not carry out your plan of moving library here.[6] I still like the people and the school but do not wish to settle here or have you any more clearly connected with the school than you now are.

I have never been more anxious to bring Alice into contact with the broad christian life that is to be found in some parts of the north than now, never felt so much in haste to do it as now, and yet never, perhaps, has the way seemed so beset with difficulties as now. Still I am trusting the Lord and while I feel very weak in other respects, am strong in the faith that the Lord will not suffer us to endure any unnecessary discipline. It is the one strong support on which I can lean.

I am not anxious for the change because Alice is not doing well. On the contrary she is a good and sweet girl and is developing many strong traits of character. We long to be with you as you do with us. I believe that the anxieties of the present and past few weeks with the present uncertainty has quite unfitted me for letter writing. I hope to be in better mood for writing [illegible]. Alice joins me in sending warmest love.

With loving kisses
Emma

---

[6] JEB left his library in Atlanta, where it was purchased by his political colleague William A. Pledger.

Athens Oct. 18th 1887

My Darling.

Have just returned from the schoolhouse and built up a fire in my grate and now will devote the little remaining time before dark to writing.

This is day no. two in school.[7] When I am out of the school room it seems an odd and an undesirable thing that at past forty I am beginning school teaching, but in the school room I fortunately feel it less and am able to enter heartily into the spirit of my work. If I had sufficient pupils to pay me for the outlay of strength and time I think I should almost enjoy it—even quite enjoy it, if I could see them aroused to habits of thinking and reasoning. As it is, the outlook is not brilliant. I began yesterday with only four pupils which increased to six in the afternoon and to eight to-day. enough more have been promised me to make about fifteen and I hope for that number in the course of two or three weeks. I had hoped to hear from you to-day and may by the evening mail if Alice goes to the office.

We are having a disagreeable rain, though it is shameful in me to call it disagreeable, as it is much needed. You say in your last that three months of anxiety and disappointment have been a strain upon your Christian living. I have thought if it often and have prayed fervently that you might cling close to the Redeemer. I praise His name that you are able to do so. I must say good night with loving kisses for the shadows have already overtaken me.

Lovingly
Emma

———

Athens November 11th 1887
In School

My Darling.

My little school are [sic] having a written examination and I will improve the leisure that it gives me by writing a few words that they may be mailed at noon.

Teacher's meeting last night prevented me from writing.

---

[7] Emma teaches mathematics, possibly in the Preparatory Department of Grant Memorial University.

You do not mention having rec'd any letter from me. I have written at least three addressing them to 27 ½ Hunter St. Would it be better to send them to Mr. Seidells?

So Mrs. Lloyd was expecting you. Give my love to her and the children and remember me warmly to the Seidells'. I felt much anxiety as to the success of the campaign. May the God of battles be with you and all the workers. Have you yet met Miss Stokes or any of our lady workers?

Are they taking as active a part as before? Give my love to any of my friends whom you meet and especially Miss Stokes. Please ask her if the minutes of our last convention are out. I am anxious to have a few copies and will pay for them if she will send them with price.

I rec'd short letter from you this morning which I appreciate as much as I would a longer one under different circumstances.

Lovingly
Emma

————

Athens November 19<u>th</u> 1887

My Darling.

I am sorry to have proved so poor a correspondent this week. my intentions have been of the best but it has been almost impossible to get the time.

I am obliged to look over the lessons that I am to teach before I go into school and that and the school hours consume most of the daylight. then there are some calls to be made upon the sick and upon strangers and I still look after Alice's lessons a little—just now there are some festivities in progress which add to my work. Thanksgiving night there is to be an old fashioned party given here at which the girls dress in costume and that is to be prepared. Alice enjoyed her sixteenth birthday more than she anticipated. That she might not rise in the morning without any gifts at all I bought her a pair of slurr [sic] buttons of which she was greatly in need and with which she was much pleased. I shall be unable to do anything to her new suit until you have gone north again as I wish to devote the time that I can spare to your wardrobe. I am very glad to know that you think so highly of Dr. Hawthorne and I have no doubt that his compliment to yourself was well mented [sic]. I feel anxious for the success of the campaign—a reversal of the last vote would be a serious calamity.

I must content myself with these few hurried lines this morning because there is so much to do and I must go to the dentist about this tooth which is still troubling me.

Please send me some money if convenient. I have just paid Mrs. Harrison my last for board. I can not ask her to wait as she is much shortened and needs it every week. it has been especially so just now as Gertia is going to Powel's Bailey Sem.[inary] to teach music and has to have an outfit for going.

I have written to Bro. Thurman directions for sending the furniture and would like it sent as soon as possible as I need it. I think it would be better to send articles not needed to Bro. Thurman's than to Bro. Ellington because the former is a permanent resident and owns his house I think, the other may move suddenly. the safe and small red bureau and book case might be sent to Bro. Thurman's if he will take charge of them or the safe might be sold with stove etc. What crockery there is you can give away or do as you choose with it. If the "Home" on Prather Street is still in existence give the crockery there unless you wish to dispose of it otherwise. The iron ware will go with the stove and they had best be sold. I don't speak of these things expecting you to have any care about it—but only that you may understand the terms of the directions to Bro. Thurman. There is a small green box, I think, containing some articles that used to belong to mother and sister. I would like these put in the bureau drawers and sent here. I have written Bro. Thurman quite fully. The framed Photos of Alice can be packed in trunk with bureau glass and sent here—the other pictures might be hung on the walls of Bro. Thurman's house. I wish that I could be there to attend to it but the best you can do is to let Bro. Thurman manage. If Chamberlain will keep the parlor carpet for two or three dollars per year please have him do so. I will write Mt. Thurman to ascertain unless you will do so. If he will not send it here to me. The cheap carpeting had best be sold for what it will bring or if it will not bring anything send it here and I will use it or give it away, or if you desire you can give it to Bro. Ellington or Bro. Thurman—which will probably be better than sending it here.

I am sorry to have written you such a hurried scrambling letter. You are much in my thoughts and I am looking eagerly forward to your return.

With loving kisses
Emma

Athens Nov. 26$\underline{th}$ 1887

My Darling.

It was not till to-day that I was able to learn with certainty that it was election day in Atlanta. Mrs. Knight had said that it was to be on next Tuesday
and I had not seen any statement in the paper till to-day. It has been an
exceedingly busy day with me but I have been in heart and mind with you in
the great struggle. Have hoped to receive from you a telegram and yet dread
to hear lest the news should be unfavorable.

With such an array of money and self interest on the other side a victory
for prohibition will be a glorious triumph. I am eager to get some details of
the struggle—shall hope to receive them by word of mouth ere long. I trust
that you will at least be with us before another Saturday night—and perhaps
early next week. I fear that you are quite worn out to-night by your labor.

It has been a very busy week for me and I find myself slightly dilapidated
to-night.

Thursday night was the old fashioned party here which was quite a success. there were between forty and fifty guests the larger number in costume.
Last night the young people from this household were invited to Prof.
McLain's and had such a delightful time that they forgot to consult their
watches and remained rather late. They are invited out again to-night but will
not go. The occasion of these unusual gayities [sic] is the interval between the
fall and winter terms, the latter beginning on Monday next.

I think that my two copies of Horace as well as my Virgil had best be sent
with furniture, but I better include them in my first order to Bro. Thurman.
I am too tired and sleepy to write more to-night. With loving kisses will say
good night.

Sunday P.M. I learned in sabbath school this morning the terrible result in
Atlanta. It is worse than my fears even and I am much disheartened. I feel it
not only as a hard blow to the cause but as a defeat in some measure to yourself, i.e. if it came from or is due to the colored people.[8] I am anxious to get
the details. I suppose that it is money that has done it but it is a hard look for
other cities because if they vote one at a time the money will be concentrated

---

[8] Prohibitionists, with strong support from the WCTU, proposed a statewide ban on the
sale of alcohol, with mixed results county by county; the fight would continue into the twentieth
century. JEB had been expected to influence the African American vote in favor of prohibition.

on each in succession. I hope to learn very soon when you will be here. Are sister Jennie and Miss Sherman there still, and do they come this way on their return?

I should greatly enjoy a little visit from Miss Jennie.

I am very tired this evening and shall be forced to take a little sleep and as my sabbath school lesson must not be left undone it gives me little time for writing.

I want to see you very much indeed, darling, and hope that you will be with me next Saturday and Sunday as well as other days of this week or the following one. We are having unseasonably warm weather quite like summer.

With loving kisses
Emma

If you look forward to our going to New York any time within a year I think it would be well to send here with the furniture my French Grammar and Spanish books. Please bring a quantity of waste papers with you and a pkge of w. closet paper.

————

Athens Tenn. Jan 28 /88

My Darling.

I will seize upon the first minutes after breakfast to answer your last but I may not have another minute at my command to-day. A neighbor who died very suddenly is to be buried this morning and I must attend the funeral and this afternoon some long postponed calls must be made.

This coming week our W.C.T.U. holds its first mother's meeting and it devolves upon me to arrange its program altho' it is possible that Mrs. Wells may be here to address the meeting in which case the responsibility will be shifted from my shoulders till another month. but the preparation has to be made all the same because of the uncertainty of her coming.

The coming week, too, has been fixed upon for Dr. Sallestee to address the men upon the topic of Social Purity.[9] This is at my request, so that the Lord gives me this encouragement in the work, that notwithstanding the feebleness

————

[9] Frances Willard, elected president of WCTU in 1879, expanded its goals beyond temperance; she organized the group into thirty-nine departments for action, one of which was Social Purity.

of it, it has taught the White Class work and literature before the people of the town and now is instrumental in giving them a talk upon the subject by a man well qualified for it.

I have no reason to believe that the work would be known of, at all, here seen by very few people. it is an encouragement to do what we can, trusting to God for faith. I am obliged to close abruptly.

With loving kisses
Emma

———

Athens Apr. 15<u>th</u> 1888

My Darling.

We are having a lovely Sabbath day—bright and clean and sunny. I went to Sabbath school but came home and rested instead of staying to church. hope it was not wicked in me. Have attempted jail service but the jailer was away as he so frequently is.

It is time now, or very nearly, to start for Class meeting after which I will try again to get entrance to the jail. As the days grow warm and I am reminded that summer is near I am longing more than I can tell (perhaps your own heart will tell you) to be with you during the vacation even if we could be with you no longer.

Later—Went to Class which was small but pleasant and afterwards attempted to get into jail but failed again. [I] have the promise of holding a service there on Tuesday after school. To-morrow night I have promised to hold mothers' meeting for the colored union.

I saw Dr. Spence at Prof. M<u>c</u>Lain's yesterday and it seemed pleasant even to speak to some one who had so recently seen you. . . .

Alice sends love and is complaining of my writing because she wants to talk to me. She has been unable to go to church and so has been home alone since she is tired. I want to see you more and more as summer approaches. May the Lord keep us and bring us together.

Lovingly
Emma

Would it be possible for you to obtain the newspaper reports of the Woman's Convention [X marked here] that was held in Wash. in Mar. and send it to me? I intended to ask you to get them at the time but neglected it. The Countess seems likely to be brought to a sudden fall from all her grandeur. It exemplified the adage that when rogues fall out honest people get their dues. I hope that the friends of Mr. March will succeed in protecting him and opening his eyes.

————

Athens May 13. "/88
Sabbath night

My Precious Husband.

I do so long to see you and to be with and the Sabbath days are the hardest of all to be away from you. This has been my first opportunity for reading for a week and have indulged myself in some hours of it and so have crowded my writing into night which I did not intend. Every week day is crowded full and will be till Commencement and even after that but then I shall have my whole time and shall not I hope be obliged to deny myself all reading or recreation as I must do now.

You have been much in my thoughts to-day and I have been thinking, too, of the days of our early married life. I do thank the Heavenly Father that He has permitted us to know what a real, true married life is—that we have not had poverty of love and of happiness; but that our life has been rich in love for each other, and in kindred sympathies and tastes.

Notwithstanding the many disappointments and privations of our life it looks bright and sunny as I look back upon it. We have been very happy in each other and in our precious daughter and to be reunited again would seem a little bit of Paradise.

But I am preparing to be pleasantly surprised rather than grievously disappointed by making my plans for another year away, though I am longing and hoping all the while for the upsetting of those plans by a summons to go to you.

We had a stirring sermon this morning from Dr. Hagey. On one of the morning lessons he read Ezek. 3. 17–22 and the solemn words came to me with even greater power than when I had read them myself.

This afternoon we had class meeting. Sunday night I rarely even go out and have just begun to go to prayer meeting, but hope now to go regularly. Have not been able till to-day to take the time to read the Conference debate you sent—was much interested.

I do not think that the intellectual or moral power of the Convention would be weakened if Frances Willard was a member even to the exclusion of some male member. Seriously speaking I am very glad to see that nearly all the delegates with whom I have any personal acquaintance voted for the reception of these women. I was ashamed of Bro. Boyd. I don't believe that either Thurman or Ellington would have cost that vote. I was glad to see Prof. Crogman's vote recorded on our side.

Please tell Mr. Boyd from me that I hoped better things from him.

The men who have opposed the admission of these women will find I think that they are running in advance of an approaching train which will surely run over them unless they get out of its way. The same leaven which began its work almost nineteen centuries ago and which has emancipated the slaves and has set women beside man in institutions of learning and given her a vote in the Methodist church will not stop the leavening process while more than half the membership of that same church is unrepresented in the General Conference. The only wonder to me is that men of such keen vision as Buckley and Vincent do not discern the signs of the times.

Alice sends love and says tell Papa that I want to see him awfully and want him to send me a new supply of writing paper by Mr. Boyd or whoever comes through here. Did you get the little pkge. that I sent by Mr. Boyd?

> With loving kisses
> Emma

———

Athens June 26$^{\underline{th}}$ /88

My Darling.

I am wondering whether you will write me to-day or to-night and whether you remember that it is our anniversary. I have never known you I think to forget it and shall expect your letter. . . .

I rec'd this P.M. yours of Sunday enclosing 1.00. I fear that you needed it more sorely that we. I am much distressed, darling, that this anniversary day finds you so uncomfortably situated, how I wish that I could, myself, relieve you. I, too, have much faith that your circumstances are to improve in the near future and that this autumn, or, at farthest, early summer will see us united. But if your good fortune is delayed even a few months it will leave both you and us in a very hard place and it is for that reason that I dared not refuse the first situation which offered itself. I am sure that you will not set down my doing so to indifference. I have turned and twisted the matter in every light and have thought and thought what is best to do until there has seemed little refreshment in sleep even, but I am unable in any view to see the way clear for me to depend entirely on your prospects of immediate success. It is still possible that I may not be elected by the Trustees. I long to see you, darling, and look forward to being constantly with you in some pleasant home of our own as to something almost too delightful even to come to pass. . . .

I have not thought as much of money in my life as most people I think but I am beginning to desire it so strongly that I must guard myself or I will give it too high a place in my esteem. If you succeed as well and as soon as you can reasonably expect, will you be able to send for us this autumn and yet begin at once to pay off Joe's debt. So strong are my convictions that we have been allowed to come to poverty and even suffering because of that unpaid debt that I have had very serious thoughts that it was my duty to teach till you are, at least, nearly through with the payment of it. While this is my conviction my feelings are very cowardly and whisper to me that if we continue thus apart death may come between us. nothing else I believe can. . . .

I am so weary of trying to express myself in writing. It is such a lifeless, miserable way of doing. But even this privilege will be diminished if we go to the country where there is not a daily mail. If they are willing to take us I shall go as soon as possible on Alice's account especially and also on my own as the heat and many interruptions prevent me from resting or studying here.

> And now, my precious husband, with warmest, loving kisses I will say good night. . . . Emma

––––––––

Athens June 30$\underline{th}$ "/88

My Darling.

If I can trust what I hear to-day the situation which I expected at Chilhowee has been given to one of the theological Students. Mr. Adams, the principal, has not yet returned but the young man himself told me this afternoon that he had been elected by the board of trustees which met yesterday—he also says that he was at Mr. Buttram's where Dr. Spence's letter was rec'd and that he spoke as if they would not board anyone. I shall probably ascertain that when Mr. Adams returns Monday or Tuesday. I try to think that it is all for the best

and indeed if Alice was well would not mind it. I think that the situation at
Ellijay will be a hard one and have little expectation that I can get it if I desire.

I still think I have a fair chance of the school here but even that is very
uncertain. but I am trusting in God and believe that he will open some way. I
am a little puzzled about the loss of the Chilhowee place but it may be that the
Trustees preferred a male asst. or it may be that Mr. Metcalf, the young man
who has secured it, is one of those who are on Dr. Spence's hands to help and
that he has used his influence for him. I did not ask his influence for myself
for I did not know when I talked with him that the situation was not filled. I
can not help feeling a little depressed and troubled still I am trusting in God
and hoping for good things.

> May the Lord bless you and help you.
> With loving kisses
> Emma

———

Athens Aug. 15$\underline{th}$ /88
Sabbath Night

My Precious Husband.

This week past has been crowded so full . . . it has left no time for writing.
. . . I hope not to be quite so hard pressed this week. . . . I have never before
I think lived from week to week and month to month as entirely as I do now.
I am glad to be able to do it, as I suffer less disappointment thereby than when
I lived in expectation of the things that always just eluded my grasp. My
school is a great help in this direction as it compels me to put my mind each
day upon that days work.

We are having a great deal of rainy weather but I am reasonably sustained in health—last week closed my third month and this street is the
muddiest in town but notwithstanding my walking through the mud so
much and other exposures I have not had a cold in the three months. Were
it not for constant overwork out of school I should be very well indeed. If
you should be prospered or my school increase sufficiently I shall try to
avoid a part of this outside work hereafter. Yesterday I worked all day and
evening and Alice worked afternoon and evening with us correcting examination papers and preparing report cards which we lined and wrote ourselves instead of hiring printed.

New comers continue to come to town and I had planned to call upon some of them, especially the Sallestee's and Cone's yesterday, but was unable to do so for lack of time.

Mr. Sallestee is conducting revival services and proves to be a very able, earnest man.

I went this evening after dinner to Women's Foreign Missionary meeting in which I had been assigned a part, the preparation for which took all the time between it and the morning service. After that I went in the rain to Mr. Hippor's to call on his sister Laura and finding that Mr. Boyd and family lived in the same house called on them also. Mr. Boyd expressed a desire to hear from you or see you before General Conference.

It was very nearly dark when I reached home and with Sabbath school and church my day had been completely filled, giving time for neither writing, reading, or rest. After tea while I sat talking . . . something turning the conversation to the war, gave us some very interesting war reminiscences. [Mrs. Childress] was a young girl living at the time at Kingston Tenn. which was quite a Union stronghold, but the men all went to Kentucky to join the Union Army, leaving their families defenceless. . . . I hope to hear from you to-morrow.

> With loving kisses
> Emma

————

> Athens Sep. 5$\underline{th}$ /88

My Darling.

Lest to-morrow may be crowed as full as to-day and this evening have been I will write you just a bit before I retire.

I am very glad to receive a letter from you nearly every day and to know that all things work well. God has helped us in this hard time by putting it into my dear brother's heart to sent me a small check, $17.$\underline{50}$ which I rec'd day before yesterday. I gave Mrs. H. 10\underline{00}$ and used the remainder with the dollar rec'd from you to-day towards paying small bills, some of which I have been obliged to make in these two months past, and to get a little wood and medicine. We have not suffered save in the anxiety and distress of mind occasioned by the knowledge that Mrs. H. was unable to wait so long for money. I have not given your message as to rewarding her because I am myself doing what I can by assisting her in sewing and have to make a dress for one of the daughters as soon as I finish Mrs. Knight's suit.

I make no charge to Mrs. Harrison for any sewing that I do for her and pay the extra which she charges on board beside. I also helped her about the house somewhat for the two weeks that she was without a servant, but I know that they need the money and fear the arrival of the time when she can no longer wait. but I am trusting in God and thanking Him for this help from brother which came so very seasonably. I have never forgotten that I have much for which to praise God—indeed we have everything almost, except money. So many blessings that we have are beyond all price, so much so that millions would not tempt me to part with them nor could millions buy them for us if we did not have them. And so I do praise God, though I get worried and discouraged sometimes and am a very halting, grumbling pilgrim. Not one of the least of the things to be thankful for is that Alice is a good girl and a good scholar. I do not know how she will measure up with the students in our northern schools but she stands well here and her teachers all speak very favorably of her. One of the girls who is intimate at Prof. Bolton's told her that the Prof. said that she had kept up in mathematics with any of the boys in her classes. She came home quite elated with it to-day and I was not less pleased than she as Prof. Bolton hasn't a very high opinion of the talents of girls of girls [sic] in general in the mathematical line and moreover is not a man given to compliments.

Your letter of Sabbath was appreciated as love letter is always appreciated by a wife of nearly twenty five years standing. The consciousness of your love now is, if possible, more precious than before our marriage. It is common enough for maidens to be loved and wooed but rarer I fear for that love to outlast all the jars and worries of time as I thank God yours has done. "Should we have married could we have foreseen the anxieties and hardships standing in the way." Yes, I think so if we could have foreseen too the precious love that has brightened all the past. I think we have found in each other the things for which we married and for yourself, if you had borne all the hardships of the way without wife and child I think that it would have been much harder than it has.

God help you, darling, and keep you. I think I have not written you that Alice was exposed to diphtheria and being taken down a little more than a week after with a very severe cold gave me a little anxiety.

We went at night to say good bye to Olin Fuller and family and kissed Mrs. Fuller and the children. The little boy had been ill for two days but was

up and out doors. they went back to Atlanta on early morning train and the
Dr. pronounced his illness a bad case of diphtheria said he could not have
saved him if they had been a few hours earlier. It very naturally gave me some
anxiety both for her and Bro. Harrison's children.

Have I written you that Dr. Fuller's daughter Myra—the one we used to
call Minnie is in N.Y. if she has not returned to Chicago which I fear is the
case. She is or was at 86 Fifth Avenue with Sam Dickey. She went to do type
writing at prohibition headquarters. I think the address given is her boarding
place but am not certain. And now darling must say Good-night

With loving kisses
Emma

Sat. Morn. Your second letter containing 1.00 was rec'd this morning. I
paid my last dollar to my wash woman yesterday evening and am very glad
of this aid—may need it for medicine. Alice and I both have severe colds—
have not had such a cold before in more than a year. [At] least I have fought
it from the first appearance and think I will prevent any very serious lung
trouble from it.

————

Athens Oct. 2$\underline{d}$ 1888

My Darling.

I am sorry to have so neglected you for the past few days. Our dear friend,
Dr. Hagey passed over the river on Friday evening and for a day or two before
and the two days following I spent all the time there that was possible. yesterday I expected to have time to write you but I began a letter to Rob. Hagey
who is at Bloomington, Tenn.[10] with Mollie and I was so frequently interrupted that I neither finished that or began yours. Last night Bishop
Fitzgerald spoke at the church and I went to hear him. Alice was introduced
to him at the close of service and he asked if she was your daughter, finding
that he knew you she came for me and I was also introduced.

His talk was very plain but good. As I am much hurried this morning I
will confine myself to some of the details concerning the Dr. . . . Friday morning his physician pronounced the case hopeless. Friday forenoon he had the

————

[10] Possibly Bloomingdale, Tennessee.

members of his theological class in and gave them quite a long talk. I was not present, being home preparing an essay for a W.C.T.U. meeting which had been given out for that day, but which we did not go to at last on account of his condition.

. . . altho I was there so much of the day I did not feel like speaking to him lest I might disturb him. I had a long and very pleasant talk with him some weeks before which it is now a pleasure to me to remember, although in the course of it he became irritated and said some very sharp words and showed more plainly perhaps than I had even seen it the dictatory, tyrannical side of his nature.

But he almost immediately manifested the greatness of his character and the christian humility of spirit which he possessed by asking my pardon so earnestly and heartily that my respect and affection for him was not weakened but increased. When I left he urged me to come often to see them and assured and reassured me that a hearty welcome would always await me. I thought then that I should go very frequently both I liked to go and that he might not feel that I retained any resentment but I have been very busy and burdened with our own cares and do not remember that I saw him at all at least not for any length of time till he was too ill to talk much. I think that he was sincerely attached to all of us for he was fond of Alice and always liked her to go to see him. I have scarcely ever been in since Mollie and Rob. left and they moved into the house near the college that they have not said to me "We have been talking about you and thought you had forgotten us." I have regretted since his sickness and death that I had not gone much more frequently to see them. So it is the little things in life that we fail to do when we could become thorns to prick us afterward. I had hoped for time to write you more of the details but hope that Alice will have time to do so. The funeral was on Sunday morning, memorial service by Theological class on Sunday night and Mrs. Hagey Clarke and Ashley started with the body at 12 Sunday night for Phil. [adelphia] I never had an opportunity to deliver any of your messages sent after his illness except to Mrs. Hagey whom I asked to tell the Dr. He was so ill . . . that I decided not to talk to him at all.

Alice went in to see him and he talked a little to her the last day. Regretted that I did not go into the room with her as I would <u>then</u> probably have been able to say good bye and perhaps had some message for you, but I had a great unwillingness to intrude upon his dying hours as I have so often seen people do. I encouraged Alice to go because I knew that he was fond of her and she had not seen him I think during his illness.

And now, darling, if you do not hear from me again this week do not think I am neglecting you. I have undertaken to make a dress for Mrs. Knight and she wants it for Conference next week. I know my own failing of spending a great deal of time and being hurried at the last and shall be anxious till it is done.

I love you, darling, and long to be with you. I do hope that this may be the last winter away from you.

With loving kisses
Emma

———

Athens Oct. 7th "/88

My Darling.

This Sabbath has been an uncommonly full one and so it comes about that I am overtaken with sleepiness and weariness before I have had time to write you beside my Bond of Hope work to-day and morning service I have been to call on the sick and to-night have had a short address on Social Purity to prepare to be sent by Mrs. Knight to the Holston Conference. I heard a very excellent sermon from Mr. Bachman on the love of God. He far excels any other preacher that I have heard in Athens save a few of them from abroad. I will send just this line in Alice's letter to tell you that I love you and long to see you. Both Alice and I are recovering from our colds for which I am most thankful.

May the Lord keep you,
Most lovingly
Emma

———

Athens Dec. 3^d "/88

My Precious Husband.

Your letter of 29th containing order for five dollars was received this morning. My pleasure in receiving this is damped by the fear that you may have needed it more than we.

This must have been a red letter day for us financially for I rec'd from Greenleaf a letter which also contained five dollars. otherwise it was far from pleasant for it told us that dear Nannie is not likely to live many days longer. poor Greenleaf I can not bear to think of the trouble that he [X marked here] is in. Do pray for him, darling, as you never prayed for him before, for if this grief does not show Christ to him I fear that he will be hardened and despairing—death is such a hard thing to bear and without the Saviour to help is almost unbearable—God help him.

I [X marked here] am quite discouraged about a school for Alice and think that she will remain in college taking only Geometry and Greek. I must make this a shorter letter than I desired for am very tired, having taken an unusual walk to-day on business. [I] am trying to work up my school. fear that the prospect is not very good as far as numbers are concerned. [I] doubt if I can depend on more than from twelve to fifteen while it will be scarcely possible to keep our expenses below twenty dollars per month I fear, but perhaps the Lord will help me beyond my anticipations.

I have [X marked here] not been sustained by such experiences as you speak of and yet we have been relieved just when we seemed unable to bear any more and I give God the praise for it with all my heart. I am very grateful to be free from the paroxysms of coughing but my bronchial tubes are still filled up and give me a great deal of trouble. I must retire at once now as have a good deal of walking to do again to-morrow and all this week probably.

I love you warmly, truly, darling and am hungry and thirsty for the time when we can be together.

> With loving kisses
> Emma

Athens Dec. 6th "/88

My Precious Husband.

I found your very kind letter of the 4th awaiting me when I returned this evening and will reply before retiring. you have ere this learned from my letters that the violent symptoms of my cough are relieved, possibly in answer to your earnest prayers for me. I have never before been relieved without change of climate after once being attacked in this manner. I do not of course mean that I am yet well, but I do mean that the most violent and penetrating form of the cough seems to have left me almost as suddenly as it came—the bronchial tubes are still filled and seldom feel really free and slight causes produce coughing, but I am very much better. . . .

Sunday Night—I have been delayed in finishing this letter by serious causes. . . . I was very busy yesterday with canvassing and calling upon the parents of those pupils whom I hope to secure in my school and when I returned had work that kept me busy till a late bed time.

I can assure you that I appreciate your desire for me to make a change of climate but do not think that it would be wise for me to attempt it till you are fully established in business even if I was in as bad condition as when I first wrote you. To go further South where board would be at least double our present expense here, leaving debts behind us and anxious and uncertain how the bills for the present and future were to be met would be quite too hazardous. these anxieties and that caused by lack of proper clothing would more than neutralize the advantage I fear. happily, I have good ground for hope that I shall recover here if I can be relieved from excessive work and anxiety and have comfortable clothing. these can be obtained for less than half the money that would be required for travelling and paying the increase of board in Atlanta. Thanks to God, I feel quite able now to do some work and think that I can teach without over-tasking myself. It is the excessive work and the strain of mind that has been caused by feeling that I had the whole support of Alice and myself on my hands that have so worn on me. I do not think that I am as capable as many women in those lines of work that bring in money. What few talents I have are in the line of wifehood and motherhood and the general unpaid (in dollars and cents) work of the church and society. it is the necessity for being something that I am so illy adapted to be that has nearly unbalanced me mentally and physically. if I can see that necessity removed I think that I can grow strong and well right here in Athens.

Altho' I can get little financial help here save what I have received from Dr. Spence God has given me so many little helps here that I should feel quite unwilling to take up the same struggle in a new place. First almost, among my blessings here I must count the friendship of the people. I do feel that God's hand has lead [sic] me and that it is through his special blessing that I have been permitted to make a place for myself in the kindness and good will of the people before misfortune overtook us. finances affect our social standing much less here than they would do in a city. our friends who know more or less of our straitened circumstances, as many of course do,

seem only the more kind and friendly. Through church work, temperance
work and occasional work among the sick I have met the lives of many of the
citizens in such a way as has I venture to hope given them a feeling of kindness and respect for me. I do not mean to parade the very little that I have
done for I know that it has been indeed little and far behind my duty neither
have I done it with any thought of such reward. I should despise myself if I
had. I only mention it in thankfulness to God and because it may be a comfort to you in your anxiety and trouble about us and I have written you so
much that is distressing that I do want to give you the bright side of our life
where there is one. Mrs. Cone is a warm and true friend to us and I have not
doubt that she has spoken favorably of us to Prof. and Mrs. Newcome[11]—
from that and other causes Mrs. Newcome feels that she would really like to
have us in the house with them and they kindly offered to keep the room
waiting for us and we have now arranged to go at the low rental for the room
of 2.50 pr. month. Dr. Spence saw Prof. Newcome and arranged about price.
They are cultivated and I think very kindly people so that I am sure we shall
find it pleasant to be with them. Mrs. Cone is like a mother or older sister to
me. She is a very positive woman and likes her own way, I think, but she is
so hearty in her friendship and so warm in her affection that I am greatly
attached to her. I do not know certainly whether I have told you that Dr.
Spaulding, a minister, formerly from Maine, with his wife and daughter are
in town and that they are most cordial and friendly people. I have not yet
called on them or met Mrs. S. but have had several very pleasant meetings
with Mr. S and his daughter. . . .

To-day the funeral service of Mr. Horne, formerly from Maine, were had
at the chapel. It was quite a remarkable circumstance that these clergymen
officiated all of whom had known him in the past, Dr. Spaulding in Maine,
Dr. Sallestee and Prof. Newcome in Maine. I am so sorry for his poor wife, a
gentle, delicate woman who is now left with four children to rear, the youngest
a boy who has I fear more will power than she has. I cannot tell you how sorry
I feel for those whom I see grieving. . . .

Poor, dear Greenleaf I cannot tell you how sorry I am for him. What a desolate Sabbath this must have been for him. I wonder if any other love can be
as great as that of the husband and wife with whom one has lived for many
years and with whom the whole life is so intertwined that the life of either is
maimed and incomplete when they are apart. Alice has gone out to church

---

[11] George T. Newcomb, professor of biblical theology and ecclesiastical history.

and I am looking every minute for her return. She has entered school for the winter term carrying just two studies—Greek and Geometry. I still have a good deal of anxiety about her health but hope that it is improving.

Monday noon—Please excuse if I finish this with pencil as I am writing at Mrs. N's after dinner. Speaking of Alice I am confident that the trouble with her is chiefly with the nervous system and she ought to have plenty of out-of-door exercise and a good time with freedom from care. I cannot however give it to her while we are so poor. A little now in reply to your question as to our needs per week. with the greater economy we may be able to live for a little over or perhaps just about twenty dollars per month or five dollars per week, this for two people is exceedly [sic] low and much less than our expenses have ever been heretofore. I ought to have every minute from now till school begins to get our wardrobe in order, look over text books that I must teach and get settled for the winter, but instead of this I shall be obliged to put in my time trying to earn something and begin school quite unprepared, unless a kind providence enables you to do a good deal, because, of course, I must not settle down to do only what I am able to do while we are owing people who are themselves cramped and troubled for means. I shall try to trust God and not worry but I cannot avoid overwork till we are out of debt and the way clear to meet our weekly expenses. I have bought new boots for Alice and must to-day settle the bill for those she had several months. We are both destitute of many needful articles of clothing and my moving and some housekeeping articles and freight on things from Atlanta that I have sent for will be quite an expense. I have not yet had the two P.O. orders cashed in. I am trying to keep them intact for paying my room rent and moving and settling, but I shall be obliged to break one of them before that time I fear. A stove will cost about five dollars, but I shall pay for it by monthly installments. My canvassing thus far will bring in only 2.50 in cash and pay beside 2.50 more on a debt for books to Prof. Wright.[12] Money is very scarce here and I am not likely to get much for canvassing. I must close now to go out to hunt pupils for my school.

With many loving kisses
Emma

---

[12] William A. Wright, professor of ancient languages and literature.

Athens Dec. 13.$\underline{th}$ "/88

My Darling Husband.

I am constantly sorry that I cannot write you oftener but nearly every letter has to be written at the end of a hard day's work that has extended into the night, for there are household and other duties to be attended to when I return and I am somewhat troubled to sleep unless I retire very early. my work and care run though the night in my mind and I arise unrefreshed in the morning and too late to make a good beginning of the day. Please remember that it is these causes and not carelessness or lack of thought of you that makes me so poor a correspondent. for nearly two weeks now I have been out nearly all day canvassing or soliciting scholars or assisting the bereaved. I have not had I believe a single day at home, Sunday not excepted.

Out of this I have spent only four and one half days in canvassing. It is intensely distasteful to me and requires all the courage I can summon to force myself into it but I almost feel that God has made it the instrument of my recovery from my cough, for I have wonderfully improved and I can attribute it to nothing save the out-of-doors life that this and other causes have forced upon me. I should otherwise have sat close at my sewing and in-doors which I know to be injurious to me. financially I have not done a great deal, only $5.40 in the whole time, but it is more than I could have possibly earned with the needle in the same time and will be a little help to us in this pinch. aside from that I have sold one other book which pays for the outfit that I bought but this pays for school books and brings in no cash. I should only canvass up to Christmas perhaps not as late as that and shall probably do the most of my work to-morrow and next days. I shall move on Monday and that will interfere considerably with my work.

A little of the money has already been paid in and used. I am pretty close pressed to pay for our dinner 2.10 per week, provide breakfast for both and supper for Alice with our other expenses I must pay Mrs. H. as soon as possible for last and this week's board. [I] have paid for the two previous weeks. I am making a hard struggle to avoid slipping any deeper into debt than we already are. my moving will bring quite a little expense and I have not yet dared to spend anything for clothing save boots and rubbers for Alice. I shall be obliged to purchase a stove and quite a number of other articles when I move but I <u>must</u> do this as the partial housekeeping enables us to live considerably cheaper than we could otherwise do. I have thought a good deal of what you said recently of leaving your present business for something that would make immediate return even if only a bare support. I dare not advise you though it has often seemed to me that this might be wisest, altho', of course, I do not know. I think it hardly possible that any school will be sufficient to even meet the daily living expenses of us both, to say nothing of the debts that are so pressing and [illegible]. Alice's nervous system is in a bad condition and if our situation does not enable me to take care of her within a few months I can not tell what may be the result. I shall do the best I can in our present situation and perhaps the good Lord may help her as he has me.

She is taking no school work except two studies, but with our housework she is obliged even with them to study at night though not late.

I thank God from my very heart that he is so sustaining you spiritually. In this he has indeed been good to us. I am very sorry that we shall be unable to send each other Christmas gifts. As I can do nothing for you do not try to send me anything. if you should be able to send anything to Alice do not feel that you must do anything for me. I shall know that it is in your heart. For ourselves we can each write so that our letters will be received on Christmas eve or Christmas day. I thank God that we have not outlived our lover-like days and that a love letter now is as sweet as it was twenty five years ago, neither poverty nor time can rob us of this pleasure and all the wealth of Croecus[13] could not buy it for us.

> And now good-night and pleasant dreams
> With many loving kisses
> Emma

I supposed that you knew that Greenleaf's address was Buckfield. If he should have left there it would be forwarded to him. It might be well to put it in care of Henry Irish. I hope that you will write at once.

———

> Athens Dec. 16th "/88
> Sunday Night

My Darling Husband.

Another of the Sabbaths that are like so many mile stones marking off the months of our absence. . . . Yesterday was a full day—full of work and weariness. I had planned to begin our moving, putting down our carpet and sending one

---

[13] Croesus, king of Lydia in the sixth century, renowned for wealth; spawned the expression "as rich as Croesus."

load of trunks, leaving the actual moving for Monday but when we had once started well along in the afternoon Alice suggested that as it was such a pleasant day we finish it up and so we did but the second load did not start till nearly dark so that by the time that our effects were in such order as to make it possible to retire we were, as you may imagine a tired pair.

When the wind howled outside last night and the rain poured down this morning we felt very thankful though that the deed was done. I am for almost the first time in my life in the South away from my beloved fireplace and grate and living by a stove. Though it [is] very convenient for cooking our breakfast I cant say that I like the air that we are forced to breathe—it is a poor substitute for the good honest oxygen that I have been used to, but Prof. and Mrs. Newcome are the pleasantest of people and I anticipate a very pleasant winter in their house, everybody was very kind when we moved. Prof. Newcome loaned us coal (I could obtain none in town and Mr. Cone's hired man came in to bring kindlings and help us to straighten out our things. We have a lovely view of the mountains from one window and the other faces Mr. Cone's house.

I could be very happy here and in my work if you were with us or if I had a certain[ty] of going to you at some definite time in the near future. As it is I am holding on by faith and trying to praise God for the good things that he has done for us and most especially that our lives are spared and that we are not seperated [sic] from his mercy and love. I enclose in this one of Frances Havergal's poems cut from the last Union Signal.[14] It seems to me to suit our case. I hope that you have already written Greenleaf. I feel great anxiety for him. Please write him to be sure to stop to see you if he passes through New York as he is likely to do.

I am very thankful to know that your hard and spare life is made rich by God's presence—I thank God for it. I have three weeks' more before my school begins—weeks that must be very busy weeks for there is very much that ought to be done and indeed must be.

I am a little dreading the Christmas season as I see no way of doing anything where I wish and feel that I ought, but I shall rest that with the Lord and not fret. May pleasant dreams be yours to-night and good fortune brighten you to-morrow. With loving kisses

                                                                Emma

---

[14] *The Union Signal,* published by the Woman's Temperance Publishing Association in Chicago.

Athens Dec. 21$^{\underline{st}}$ "/88

My Darling.

Your letter containing P.O. order was received to-day. It was not only most welcome financially but gives me hope for your future prosperity to know that you can send us even a little.

What Dr. Spence has loaned me, small sums rec'd from Greenleaf and a little from canvassing have enabled me to move, settle and meet our weekly expenses thus far though I was very nearly out when I received your letter to-day. Were it not for our debts both big and little and the demands for clothing I should feel very hopeful of nearly meeting our expenses after my school begins. but as it is what I shall earn will go but a small way toward it—there are about sixteen dollars at the stores that must be met immediately if possible. My canvassing has netted me or will when all deliveries are made a little less than ten dollars. It seems very little for the labor and unpleasantness but it has helped bridge over the time before school begins and even this small sum has been of great help to us.

Greenleaf sent us an express pkge. containing two dresses and some other things of dear Nannie's. I shall make over one of the dresses for Alice next week. This week beside canvassing and delivery of books I am making a dress for Mrs. Harrison to apply on the debt to her. part of my book money also goes to meet Alice's bill for school books and my rent here. . . .

I have my stove still to pay for; some absolutely indispensable crockery to purchase and fuel for my room and school room to purchase so you see that my needs are insatiable. Still I am very thankful that we are better off than we were a month ago when things seemed so very dark. My health is still quite good and I am enduring my hard work very well though I get very tired.

We find Prof. and Mrs. Newcome very kind indeed and enjoy their society very much. We cannot be too thankful to be with people who are so kind and pleasant. I hope that you are equally fortunate, my darling, and that some good friend will make your Christmas day bright for you. I dreamed last night that I was but a short distance from you and went to you on the train. I rec'd a warm welcome but the unpleasant news that you must leave me in the morning—my feeling of disappointment and meek and hopeless resignation were the most natural features of the dream and quite amused me when I woke.

Alice has been very careless in writing but I hope will make amends in the holiday week, though she will be obliged to keep very busy in helping me with the sewing in order to get a dress made for herself.

> With warmest kisses
> Good Night
> Emma. . . .

————

> Athens Dec. 23$\underline{rd}$ 1888
> Sabbath night

My Darling.

We have had grand weather to-day, clear and bright and bracing. Went to Sabbath School but the church was so cool that did not remain to the morning service and thereby missed the Christmas service—a good one I am told. I don't know that I have written you that Dr. Satterlee of Minneapolis is our pastor. We were without a pastor till a few Sundays ago.

There is considerable feeling on the part of the townspeople (needless it seems to me) against the school taking so prominent a part in the management of the church and for that reason there was some disappointment when it was known that a man identified with the college was to become pastor—he is an interesting preacher—truly and deeply pious I judge and has good social qualities so that I am not disposed to complain.

I hope that you have had a happy Sabbath and I long for the time when our Sabbath days and our week days will be passed together. I am hoping so earnestly that we may go to you in June. Could I know it, the winter would be brighter if not shorter, but I am trying to be patient and to accustom myself to the thought of what I fear must be, namely that I may not see you for the whole winter. once I have been away from you for more than a year and I fear that it will be so again. but one encouragement I do take and that is if we are ever again united and living together we will be less seperated [*sic*] than in the past.

I received a letter from Kate Irish yesterday telling me something of the last of Nannie's life. She said that she was able to walk around among them, tho' feebly, as long as she lived. She says that she was cheerful and ready to go but to Greenleaf it seems very cruel that she has been taken away from him. poor brother, how I pity him—without children, away from sister and without a consciousness of Christ's love to him he is desolate indeed. I have never in my life, I think, been drawn at the holiday season to think so much upon the blessing of having my husband and daughter spared to me as now. though we are so cramped for means and hindered from carrying out any of the plans for gifts that I had made earlier in the year I dare not fret for the thought constantly recurs to me that I have that remaining which is dearer than all else— that death has not come between me and those dearest to me, those whose lives are so interwoven with mine that to take them from me would so maim and mar my life that it could never be the same again. God be thanked that he has spared us to each other. I enclose an article from Miss Havergal that has done me good and may do the same for you. Please return it as it is one of the things that I like to preserve. I must answer Kate's letter to-night lest the many duties of this coming week may leave me no room for it. I fear that this will not reach you till the Christmas day is passed. it should have gone in yesterday's mail but was so busy and so much interrupted that did not even have time to study my sabbath school lesson.

The Sabbath school is to have a Christmas tree to morrow evening. [I] do not know whether I will go out as have taken cold and am trying to throw it off.

I do hope that the dear Lord will bring about a pleasant Christmas for you, darling, at least as pleasant as it can be away from home and wife and daughter. I fear that it will be lonely at the best, but I hope that your Christmas dinner at least will be with friends. I should be very unhappy on that day to think of you dining scantily in some restaurant. We shall be at Mrs. Harrison's as usual and there is to be invited company, Mrs. Knight and others.

I wonder if next Christmas will find us a reunited family in some home or at least like Paul in our own rented house that we can call home—God knows. For ourselves we can have not assurance but that drawn from the past—and that bears the blessed record of uninterrupted love that has made a home of whatever spot we were in together. Looking back over the more than twenty five years since we learned to love each other our mistakes and errors (and they have perhaps been many) are so hidden and softened by the golden rays of the sun of our affection for each other that it is a pleasant life to look back upon despite the many disappointments and the things that we could wish had been different.

Since my head first rested on your breast it has been very sweet to be with you and I wonder sometimes how it is that I get through the weeks and months without you.

Were it not for the society and affection of our precious daughter I fear that it would be a hard life indeed. May the Lord Jesus be very near and precious to you on this Christmas season and may the Heavenly Father permit us to spend the Christmases that shall remain to us on earth in each other's society.

I am hoping as I write that the quarter of a century that has passed since we loved each other looks as pleasant to you as it does to me and that our love for each other seems precious enough to compensate for all the clouds and storms.

With many loving kisses
Emma

————

Grand View [Tennessee] 8/16 1889

My Darling.

I take time this morning for just a line as a picnic is on foot for Piney Falls some two or more miles from here and we will be gone, probably, nearly all day and come home too fatigued for any effort in the way of writing.

It is a delightful morning very cool and clear. a fire in the sitting room is very comfortable.

I have not heard from you in two or three days and am beginning to feel a little impatient. Yesterday I took a long walk with the girls on the unused narrow guage [sic] track that runs up the mountain from Spring City,[15] a station on the Cin.[cinnati] Southern road.

We went over the very high trestle—over one hundred ft. I think and some distance beyond. much of the way the road has been blasted out of the solid rock and the whole distance is over a very rough way. The deep cuts in the road and the glimpse of mountains beyond make some very picturesque views which I would like to transfer to canvass do not know whether I will be able to do so. Should we return to Athens Sep. 1. the time here is brief. I do not think it wise to return to Athens until I can do something towards a school as I would rather remain here than go back there if I cannot earn anything. I think that Alice is as much improved in health as I could expect for the length of time that we have been here. I must make this very brief as I want to do a

————

[15] Grand View and Spring City, Tennessee, approximately twenty to thirty miles northwest of Athens.

little painting if possible before we start. I am trying to finish a picture that I began in Maine when last there and have left all this time unfinished.

How I wish that I could see you this bright morning, my darling. May the Lord keep you and reunite us in his own good time.

I am anxious to know what you think of Alice's photo. I think it a very good likeness indeed.

With warmest kisses—
Emma

I received a letter the other day from Greenleaf in which he says that he has used as a remedy for the slight illness of which he had written previously <u>work</u> in doses of from fifteen to sixteen hours per day and that he is at present feeling well. I am very thankful for the latter but it does seem to me that he incurs a risk by working in the sun and for so may hours per day. Do you not think so? [perpendicular line drawn through last four lines]

He says that he is so sunburned that his face has peeled. He said that most of the time his work had been on shore but a part of the time "<u>in water</u>"—that would indicate that he had been working <u>in</u> the water not from a boat. I fear that he is very careless and shall be glad when he is well away from Sav. because he will not use the caution that ought to be observed in such a climate. He hopes to finish this month but says that he may not do so.

———

Athens 10/6 1889
Sabbath night

My Darling.

It is past bed time and I can write only a wee bit of a letter and I doubt whether you deserve even that. I have been belligerent ever since yesterday morning <u>to think of</u> waiting two or three days without a letter from you and then to receive one full of Brother Thompson and written for the benefit of Dr. Caldwell. I mentally consigned Bro. Thompson to Jericho or some other remote region and felt like literally tossing the letter into the fire.

The quarterly conference was not held on Saturday but I think is expected to be held to-morrow afternoon. Dr. Caldwell is away but is expected home on the noon train to-morrow. I sent the papers to his house yesterday but did not think it necessary to send your letter as the facts seemed to be covered by your letter to Dr. Caldwell.

I have scarcely been at home at all to-day. Went in the morning to Baptist S.S. thence to Meth. church service. [I] accepted invitation from Mrs. McLain to dine—remained there till class time. [I] went to class and on the way home stopped into Mrs. Cobleigh's as we are apt to do whenever there is time and so did not reach home till nearly nightfall and then after a little tea went with Mr. Camp to Cong.[gregational] services at North Athens nearly two miles from here—rode on this latter trip. I do not like so full a Sunday as it leaves no time for reading or study of S.S. lesson. I long for the time where we may go in company to the house of God, but it is a great pleasure to me to know that we are spending the day in His service even though it must be seperately [*sic*].

Diphtheria has been prevailing here for several weeks though in a light form. Dr. Cook's little boy has it now. If it should spread much it is likely to break up the schools, but I am hoping for the best.

I love you warmly and truly darling and hope one of these days to hear from you.

> With loving kisses
> Emma

———

> At Home
> October 6. 89.

My Dearest Papa.

I was very glad to receive the letter you sent. I am always glad to hear from you, it is the next best thing to seeing you. I always loan Mama the money you send, if she needs it.

There are a good many in school this year, more I think than is usual at this time, they seem to be a good class of students too. A great many of the young men are back that were here last year. Saturday I went chestnutting and got my fingers so sore I can scarcely write, so you must not be surprised if this is rather a short letter. We have two chestnut trees right back of the house. I have three studies now so you see I am kept quite busy and I am going to try and make some few things for Xmas.

I want to make Mama an easel scarf—she has wanted one for a long time. I saw a lovely one up at Mr. McLains and Clio said she would show me how to make it. I do not think I will have enough money to buy it though and I thought perhaps we could give it together. You give the money and I do the work. I think it will please her very much. It will not cost more than two dollars, if you think you can't afford it I can give part towards I guess.

Please write me immediately about it, so I can know what to do. I was not able to get her much of anything last year and I would so like to. The scarf will be made of dark green felt and cost 65 cents. Then I intend to make a spider web of silver thread on one end and on the other weave in about four rows of ribbon and finish off the ends with pompoms or brass rings—it will be two yards long and one half yard wide.

I wish I was in the city there are so many remnants of ribbon and such like that are cheap and yet can be made up very prettily in fancy work. I am having excellent health so far and hope it may hold out through the year. Have you a pleasant boarding place? I do hope everything is pleasant for you. How I wish Mama & I could be there. Mama is out to church. Please answer me soon about the Xmas present.

Yours lovingly
Alice

––––––––

Athens Nov. 10. 1889

My Darling.

Though it is six o'clock it is my first opportunity of writing you to-day. I was very tired after morning service and indulged myself in a short nap. After that I had a caller, then went to class-meeting and came home in season for a late dinner which has been only a little time over.

The church (Meth.) is holding revival meetings but I have been unable as yet to attend them. hope to go out once or twice this week.

My work in school and the walk home leave me little strength for night services but I do not know whether it is right for me to entirely absent myself. The distance of our boarding place from the churches is a serious obstacle to going out at night.

I do so long to see you, my precious husband. were it not for Alice's warm affection I dont know how I would bear this seperation [sic] at all. and even with her love and companionship I am often lonely and heart sick for you.

If you should come at Christmas it will be very hard to give you up again. Could we have known for how long our seperation [*sic*] would be I fear that our good-byes would have been sadder even than they were.

With the experience of the past two years I can never feel any certainty of our reunion again until it is actually accomplished, or, at least, rendered certain as human events can be, I earnestly hope that it may not be later than next spring. In one week more our daughter will be eighteen. How quickly the years have passed since she was a little girl. I wonder if she will look and seem changed to you when you see her. Though her health is not firm she is very fleshy and looking as well as when we first came here. While in some respects there is perhaps, as you expressed yourself recently, less cause for anxiety about her than when she was younger, the next few years of her life are likely to decide her whole future. She has gained in judgment and in knowledge of the opposite sex since we came here and has, I believe, good sense and good principles. . . . There is something of sadness in the thoughts that the years are rapidly bearing her to the time when mother cannot decide for her, and cannot shape her future. I can realize now as I could not once my mother's anxiety for her own daughters. it used to seem quite needless to me.

For one thing I can not be too thankful, and that is that I have been able to retain her confidence so that she confides in me much more than most girls do in their mothers. It is a great satisfaction to me and a safeguard to her.

But with all my care and solicitude I can not help a little feeling of sadness in the knowledge that the most I can do for her is to surround her as favorably as possible and leave the rest to the Lord. . . . Were it not that I trust it all in God's hands I should feel great anxiety as to what her surroundings are to be in the next three or four years for with her warm temperament she is very liable to form lasting attachments within that time. I have been anxious to send her to some high grade northern college for that time but it is a serious question whether her health will bear the strain and so with all my desires and anxieties I must just drop it all, taking such care as I can from day to day and leaving the rest to the dear Father in heaven. . . .

And now, my darling I must not impose longer upon my overworked eyes for I have done night work all the past week and much of the time since school began.

> I love you from my heart of hearts and long to see you.
> Emma

New York Nov. 19 / 89

My Darling Wife:

I have again neglected you, not because I was not constantly thinking of you, but because I am working up to the measure of my ability without injury to my health. Sunday I remained at home at night to write you, but was so very tired—last week was a very hard one to me—that I fell asleep in my chair, and so neglected you. I now snatch a few moments to let you know that I am well and love you and am working very hard to spend Christmas with you.

I am being blessed in many ways, but do not yet reach money, although I am expecting every day to do so. I have secured between $11,000 and $12,000 of the stock of the Utility M'f'g Co. which I hope to see worth at least half that amount in cash within six months. God seems to be leading me to large success. I now think I see my way clear to the practice of law. I have given my time to the U. M'f'g Co. only until we placed it in a successful position. I hope soon to be able to give my attention to another matter that promises nearly as much to me as the U. M'f'g Co. My present line of work is a natural development from what I have been doing since I came to New York, and I am being led into the practice of law. I repeat God seems to be leading me to large success. I am hoping, praying and working as hard as I can.

My health is very good; Not a sick day, no cold, no cough, good sleep, and earnest spiritual life.

I am hungry for the love of you and Alice. I do pray that I shall not be long deprived of it.

> With warmest love and kisses for you both
> Y. H.

———

Athens Dec. 21. "/89

My Darling Husband.

I will send in the next mail after this a handkerchief case with a christmas card from Alice enclosed, and the wish that we could do much more. Alice has helped me in the making and the stitches have been put in with loving wishes and a longing desire to see you.

I am in great haste this morning and will write your Christmas letter to-morrow. I send pkge. to-day as I wish to register it and you might not be able to get it on Christmas day.

> With loving kisses
> Emma

————

Athens Jan. 10. 1890

My Darling Husband.

I am really anxious and unhappy over your long silence. I fear that you are ill. If I am sick you know that I am among friends who will not only care for me but inform you if I am in danger; but I have no such assurance for you and can not help anxiety—when there is an unusual interval between your letters. I know no one to whom I can write or telegraph non [*sic*] even the street or number at which you board. does any one where you board know my address, so that they could write me in case of your sudden illness or worse? I think that we are very careless about those things for while we both expect to live many years we have no guarrantee [*sic*] that we shall do so. It is growing dusk and I must make my letter very brief as I have to go out. I come home from school quite tired every night as my school though too small for profit, is still rather hard owing to the fact that I have all grades and another school in the same building is so badly lacking in discipline that it adds a good deal to my labour.

I earnestly hope that this will find you well. Among the possible calamities that may come to us always appears to me that of sickness or death to you. beside this poverty is a light affliction and not worthy to be mentioned. I am anxious on account of the epidemic of influenza that is prevailing in N.Y. and elsewhere and Dr. Akerman tells me that it is often followed by fatal pneumonia. May the dear Lord care for you. Alice sends love.

> With warmest love and kisses
> Emma

[Athens Feb. 4. 1890]
Tuesday Morn—

My Precious Husband,

All the sabbath was so filled with extra duties in addition to the usual ones that I hopped into bed tired out without having written you my usual Sunday letter. Yesterday was a repetition of Sunday and now I have less than five minutes to spare. I had several new scholars yesterday, introducing some troublesome elements into the school that will greatly increase my labours. Pray for me in my work, darling, that I may not only be sustained bodily but that my school may be a success and my application for free school be favorably received if it is best for me to teach it.

I love you darling, very warmly and truly. God bless and keep you. Alice sends love.

Emma

Athens May 28, "/90
Wed. Night

My Darling.

I am too weary and in need of sleep to write much but feel so much like just a word that will scribble in pencil. This has been Commencement Day and everything has passed off well. Alice has just gone out to Junior Sociable which closes up the festivities of Commencement. The girls—and I presume the boys—are getting rather worn as there has been something to take them out every night save Saturday since Friday last. And until Tuesday noon the examinations were in progress also so that it has been an exhausting week. Alice has on the whole kept up remarkably well this year. The grades are not yet given out but I judge from what some of the Prof.s say that she has done very well indeed. The appointments of Faculty will not be made till to-morrow. The board adjourned their meeting here to meet in Chat. [Chattanooga] to-morrow.[16] I have been very busy with sewing this past week and have a hem to be finished to-morrow for Mrs. Ackerman who leaves in the evening so I

---

[16] As noted above, Grant Memorial University would be merged officially with the University of Chattanooga in 1892 and be renamed U. S. Grant Memorial University.

must say Good-night and pleasant dreams. May the dear Lord bring us speedily to each other.

With loving kisses
Emma

————

Athens June 29, "/90

My Precious Husband,

I am in spirit with you this sabbath evening—would that I might be in person. How little we thought that our last good bye was for nearly—perhaps quite three years—possibly more. Do you really expect to see us this summer? I know that you long for it but you have said that you cannot leave your business to come to us. Now is it reasonable, from your own standpoint, to believe that you will be able to pay our debts here and take us to visit you before September?—I would really like to know, aside from your belief that God will do it for you, whether you see good reason for believing that so much will be accomplished in two short months and those the ones most unfavorable for business. I do not ask any of the facts on which you base your belief, but the belief itself. Do you expect to see us this summer? I hope that you will not miss seeing Mrs. Camp. We expect Mr. Camp home early this week but she will possibly remain several weeks longer.

Prof. and Mrs. Brown leave for Minn. Tuesday. This will leave Alice and myself the only occupants save the girl and Mr. Camp. It may be a little long but will be favorable for rest if I get any time for that. Have had none as yet and am feeling the need of it somewhat. The weather of late has been very hot and exhausting and I have felt obliged to keep constantly at work.

I have a little hope that there may yet be an opportunity to take or send Alice a little while to the mountains. It is however very uncertain.

Mr. Henderson called to-day—have not seen him before in some months. he said that he was in N.Y. a week or two since and went into your office but did not find you. [He] will be there again in a week or two. He is a very upright and worthy young man but I think not a christian. Should you have an opportunity please try to speak a word for the Master. . . .

I hope that you have had a good day and I thank the dear Lord that I can always feel in this absence from you that you are living close to him.

With warm and loving kisses.
Emma

Athens Nov. 2. 1890

My Darling Husband.

It has been a bright clear sabbath—one of the days when the air is crisp and cool and all the services of God's house a greater pleasure than under a different atmosphere. I went to the chapel and listened to an excellent sermon from Prof. Rogers, a Presbyterian minister and the Prohibition candidate for congress in Tenn. He is an excellent speaker his ideas clean-cut and his soul on fire with earnestness. there was nothing of a political nature in the sermon which was from the text "By faith the walls of Jericho fell down when they had been compassed about seven days" his theme was faith and his handling of it forcible. It was easy for those knowing his politics to gather his reasons from his sermon and I must say that I could see no flaw in the application which he presumably had in his own mind. And yet there was not a word in the sermon beyond what any earnest christian minister would naturally infer from the text. To-night he preaches upon Bible wines and I shall depart from

Tuesday night. I left at this point to go to church and have not seen a minute since in which to finish.

These are very busy days with me for I had left off taking even one meal with Mrs. Camp after it seemed certain that I should have no school and assumed full housekeeping as well as I could in our cramped quarters. I do not know whether I wrote you that last week I succeeded in obtaining the use of the Academy.[17] I had quite a struggle but the story is too long to tell. I can only say that God helped me through my friends. I opened school yesterday with twenty seven pupils, better than I could have expected under the circumstances. I had decided to return to taking one meal—supper—at Mrs. Camp's but learned to-night that Mrs. C. is unwilling to take us for less than .25 for each per meal this is out of the question for us and an exorbitant charge as board is here. I do not know what I shall do for my strength and time are so taxed by my school and other duties that it [is] impossible for me to attend to all our meals without greatly overtaxing ourselves or myself. Alice ought not to have anything required of her for she scarcely finds time for needed rest as it is. I have much to do to-night and am very tired so must unwillingly say good night. With loving kisses

Emma

---

[17] The Preparatory Department of Grant Memorial University was sometimes called the Academy.

We greatly need the Encyclopedia. If you have not written to Bro. Thurman in regard to it please do so at once if you think it proper for us to have them. If you do not, of course tell us so.

———

Athens Nov. 16. /90

My Precious Husband.

This as you have probably been thinking is the anniversary of the day on which our darling child came to us. A little later than this—nineteen years ago—the pain was forgotten from joy that a child was born unto us. It has been a precious gift growing more so each increasing year and never has she been sweeter to me than now that she is maturing into womanhood and the years are perhaps few before some other home will claim her. or if not that— before she goes out from us to struggle with the world as a bread winner. I would like her to have the strength born of work and independent life and yet I shrink from it for her, but I must leave it all to God for the time has passed by when I can to any great extent shape her life—and this is the more true because of our poverty and inability to do for her.

I feel a great longing to have a home for her next year but dare not think much of it. I am sorry not to have remembered to keep the 11ᵗʰ Nov. with you as you requested, but this past week our church house held revival services and my school has been hard and Alice and I have all our housework to do even washing. we even do the ironing. From the time I can rouse my slumbering energies to activity in the morning till I drop into bed at night there is scarce a moment for rest or thoughts and so the day slipped by much to my regret. It seems just now a struggle to keep our heads above water and my borrowed money and other bills are pressing upon me until I shall be much distressed if I do not get help very soon. I have feared that the financial crash in N.Y. may affect you but hope not. My school if it keeps its present numbers will meet our daily expenses and for that I am most thankful but I must meet other obligations or fall into disgrace.

It is time to start for church.

May God bless you, darling, and keep you. [illegible] that you could be with us.

With loving kisses
Emma

[Athens Dec. 14, 1890?]
Wednesday night

Dearest Papa,

I am ashamed of myself for not writing before, but I have been so busy it has been almost impossible. My studies are very hard this term and I am practising [*sic*] every day for our entertainment the 3rd of January.

I was very glad to get the five dollars and greatly appreciate your kindness in sending it. I was also very much pleased to hear from you although I was quite hurt at the contents. I was not in the least angry, but it did seem hard that when I was trying to the best of my ability to act in a lady like manner. I assure you that the idea of marriage enters my head only when I am obliged to think on it by the receipt of such a letter as your last. As to "friendships" among young gentlemen I have a good many and very pleasant ones too, but as to anything more than friendship I do not plead guilty. The reason I intend to graduate next year is because I want to teach a year or two and then go somewhere else to school. I can get a much better school if I get a diploma from here. Please beg dont mention the subject again, for you have certainly impressed my mind with the fact that I am not to marry for the next hundred years. My dear father are you not aware that nobody wants your "Pashe."[18] I suppose you remember the story. I have got to go to work now and must close. I send much love and will try to write sooner again. Please forgive me and write soon.

Lovingly
Alice

---

[18] Possibly "passion" (obsolete).

LETTERS: 1891–1896

With Alice's graduation and her educational goal achieved, Emma hoped to end her exile in Athens. In the months before their reunion in the fall of 1891, the Bryants struggled to conclude the most prolonged separation of their marriage. Letters from this period were filled with questions concerning the next phase and how their lives would then be structured.

JEB, ever expecting to find the strategy that would bring his family to him, was now convinced that God was leading him to some wealth. Working in stocks, real estate, and law, he sought success in the boom of the Gilded Age. At this point, John revealed more details of his major spiritual experience in 1888, which allowed him once again to reassess his entire life in the light of God's leading and purpose.

Emma, whose strong religious faith had sustained her through the bleak hardship of the Reconstruction years, had some difficulty with John's somewhat self-serving interpretation of her years of deprivation. These letters reveal their latest exchange of contradictory viewpoints, this time regarding the Bible and theology.

Still devoted to her family, however, Emma consented to John's entreaties that they put their differences behind them in Mount Vernon, New York. There they agreed on the expression of their religious faith in a Methodist mission by assisting unfortunates with food, clothing, and lessons in temperance. Life in Mount Vernon allowed Emma more dedicated time to her cause of the Woman's Christian Temperance Union.[1]

Alice, meanwhile, yielded to her father's wish that she postpone marriage and lived for a time with her parents. After considering teaching, instead she found employment as a "society reporter for the newspaper." Then, in January 1895, she married the young man to whom she had first

---

[1] General Directory, Westchester County Woman's Christian Temperance Union, 1896–97, shows Emma as "Mrs. E. S. Bryant of Mt. Vernon, Superintendent of Department of Mothers' Meeting."

been attracted at Grant Memorial University in Athens. Julius Christian Zeller, who had become a Methodist minister, faced all the struggles of a beginning pastorate and held aspirations for more graduate study.

Though she dreaded more separation from her husband, Emma nonetheless traveled twice to Illinois: first, at the death of her dear sister Gretta; and second, to be with Alice for the birth of the first of her nine children (seven of whom lived to adulthood). John remained in New York, finding it impossible to leave the mission and his continuing involvement in Republican causes and state politics.

———

Quitman Jan. 18 "/91

My Darling.

My last day (D.V.) in Quitman draws to a close.

I hope to start on the early train to-morrow and be with Alice Tuesday or Wed. according to time spent in Atlanta.

I am going back with health much improved I think though it will still be weeks perhaps months before I am quite well. Another week here would probably be a great improvement but there is so much prevalence of La. Infs [influenza] that I dare not stay longer even if I was willing to be longer away from Alice.

Weather has been pleasant most of the time since the first day or two. Alice writes me that they have had recently the worst weather of the season. Went to church this morning and heard a good sermon and met several acquaintances.

This afternoon Alice's intimate friend Bessie Tillman has been in to call bringing with her her lover whom I knew as a boy six years ago. I was very favorably impressed with him then and from what I can learn I judge that he has lived a clean life and is fit to aspire to the hand of a pure girl. I think that he is very honestly and thoroughly in love and wish him all success though I think that he is not having an entirely smooth time of it. I tremble for the girls when I think on what a small pivot their lives often turn and I should not simply say the girls for the boys are in equal danger of wrecking their happiness or having it wrecked for them. Did I not believe in God the Father and believe that he cares for our daughter with a love exceeding my own the joy of these years of her girlhood would be sadly clouded by the anxieties for her future. I fully believe that with the right surroundings (perhaps without them) she will make a strong woman intellectually and morally and so sweet willed that she would be a lovely homemaker. So it seems to me and I am glad that there seems no danger of any disposition to take upon herself the care of a home till years shall have developed her into real womanhood. If she is strong enough to teach a year or two I will be glad.

I feel more anxiety of late in regard to your business than for some time before—because I have been too discouraged for anxiety even, but as there seems a little improvement and hope begins to spring up in even so slight a degree delay brings anxiety. I can but feel that if you are on the right line and are not entirely mistaken success must come to you in sufficient measure to meet our expenses by the time my school closes Apr. 1. Unless I should have the public school I shall then be out of employment and I have had so much help from my folks that it will not be decent for me to look for more. May the dear Father forbid that you are following a will-o-the-wisp. May he guide you and bless you in all your undertakings, my darling husband.

Lovingly Emma

Over and over the question comes to me Shall we ever live together again? You seem never to doubt it. It is best that you do not. With you it is faith, and faith to be reasonable must have ground on which to rest and you believe that you have that ground. I know that if God wills it so, we shall be reunited. There I must rest—beyond that I seem to have no power to go. A reasonable expectation of going to you next summer and of your ability to make a home for us would make of me a new woman. I think that I should feel ten years younger for it. Still, God helping me I will not repine at this burden which he has permitted to be laid upon me. I say upon me not because I forget you or think my burden heavier than yours. indeed I often think it harder for you than for me. God help you, darling.

I love you, darling, and long for your society—to feel your arms around me and your lips pressed to mine. It is because my love for you has been so strong and the affinity of feeling has been such a real thing that I dare not interfere in my daughter's love affairs where the object is not unworthy. I feel that she must decide for herself that which no person in the world could have decided for me. Am I wrong in your opinion?

Athens Feb. 17–91

Dearest Papa.

Your very welcome letter was received to-day and I will answer it immediately. I have not written before simply because I have been so busy. I was not angry at anything you had written but do not think I need so many lectures. I think your talks have reference chiefly to Mr. Zeller and really there is no immediate danger. We are both young and would think an engagement very foolish. I do not think that your objections are just though for you have never seen him and can not judge in regard to our acquaintance. I do not think our correspondence is unwise for he is a young man in every way equal to me. I think the wisest thing is to let affairs take care of themselves for he is not one that I would say that in no circumstances I could marry. I have never given him any liberties so you need not be worried on that score. He is a perfect gentleman and one that you would not be shamed of. Do not think by this that I am dead in love with [him] for such is not the case. I like and respect him however and think that at nineteen I am old enough to choose my own friends. I hope and trust you will not think this unkind and disrespectful in me for it was not meant in any such way. I must speak to you now [of] your letters to Mama. She is nearly sick every time she reads one. Then she writes and writes and burns up till she is very nervous. If you want a wife that has any health left I beg that you will not write her long treatises [*sic*] on the Bible. A braver more loving Christian wife no man ever had and it is unkind in you to so worry her. Sometimes she will say with such a pitiful look "am I despondent and dont I have faith?". Papa, darling, dont think me unjust to you. I can bear poverty, heart ache anything but seeing my precious little Mother in trouble. She is working with her feeble strength far beyond her power always thinking, thinking, thinking till I should think her brains would burst and yet cheerful through it all and always longing for a sight of you. Her school is out in less than a month and then I suppose she will do dress making and I dread it for that is worse for her than anything else. I must close now and go to bed and I am very sorry I could not write a better letter, but these things had to be said and I said them. Please write as soon as possible and let me know if you feel hurt at this letter. I have kept still so long that I fear I have said to [*sic*] much now.

Lovingly
Alice

Athens Mch. 1 "/91

My Precious Husband.

You shall not miss your Sunday letter this week. I was much grieved all last week and tried, though vainly, to make good the loss early in the week, but that this letter may not meet the same fate as others I will not touch on the point with which those dealt. . . . I have often some school work to do at night and my eyes have failed rapidly of late so that when I desired to make a fresh attempt to write you I could not either from lack of time or lack of eyesight. I now have some new glasses which I hope will be a help to me. My eyes proved on examination to be of unequal strength and requires [sic] especial fitting. The glasses were delivered yesterday and cost me 3.25 a cost which I could illy afford at this time but there seemed no alternative.

You frequently tell me that I need not fear that you are a fanatic. I have never troubled myself on that score save as your line of reasoning might cause you to be blind to what I believe to be the real cause of your disappointments. In the interpretation of scripture I think that we fully agree but in its application to your case we often disagree because I can not feel that your financial course has been right or wise and God will not bless a wrong thing no matter how sincere it may be or how pious its doer is. I say this, not to call up again a subject on which we disagree—and which I sincerely wish that I might never refer to again—but that you may know exactly where I stand and why I can not always respond to your applications of scripture.

Sometimes I have feared that the strength of my convictions on these points would be a source of unhappiness even if success should crown your effort but to-night I do not feel so. Your words of love bring the same response from my own heart that they did nearly thirty years ago and I know they have in all the intervening years and I know that when we are permitted to come together again our hearts will throb in unison and love will heal all wounds. From my very heart I thank God the Father that this is so & your words of love help and strengthen me more than all else. If I had not known it before the experience of these last sad years would have taught me that love, warm and deep, is the only safe basis for the marriage relation. of course in that is included the truth that love must be founded on respect and sympathetic tastes but it must be much more than that. It is this knowledge and the memory of what this love has been to me that make me unwilling to interfere in Alice's love matters. What their outcome will be only the All-wise and loving Father knows. but I can not see on looking back that I could have done better nor do I believe by the light of the present that intermeddling will help any in the solution of a problem which her heart and head and his own must, under God, work out. were she less a woman or was his character different from what it is I might not reason in this way.

I have made most earnest prayer to God that if it be best that they shall be kept apart he might not come here for the spring term as he has desired to do but saw little hope of doing owing to the ill health which resulted from last year's attack of Grip and his over study during last year. added to the ill health was an unwillingness on the part of his parents for him to come as he returned so ill last year that they felt a natural reluctance to his return. I have prayed earnestly, honestly and I believe in faith. Am I or am I not to accept the answer as from God? If his love was the first which had been offered her I might feel that she was carried away by the mere novelty of it or if there was anything espially [*sic*] captivating in his personal appearance I might charge it to that but neither condition is present. her love has been sought by other young men more mature and in nearly every way more calculated we would think to win her love and yet she has made no return. she values them as friends but feels no warmer sentiment. As for guarding against it you ought to know but the recollection of your own youth that love is almost always aroused before the parents are aware of it. they were both especially attracted to each other before they had been even introduced. if she had been thus far sedulously prevented from receiving any attentions from young men she would have been much more susceptible than she was and have had much less judgment and discretion than she has shown. if I had after a few invitations accepted refused to allow her to go out with him the refusal would have probably precipitated an avowal of her feelings and they would have seen each other daily at school with the same results as now except that I would have no opportunity of seeing him myself or of studying his character and disposition. As it was they saw each other but little alone save as they went out to some entertainment or occasionally to church. We have a caller and I must close.

May the Lord keep you, darling, and grant you in business all that you anticipate.

> I kiss you warmly, darling, and love you with all my heart.
> Emma

Dearest Papa. I received your two magazines and have very much enjoyed reading them.

I know you will be glad when I tell you that I have not written to Ill. for more than a week. P.S. <u>He's</u> here.

————

Athens Mch. 12 "/91

My Darling Husband.

I improve a few minutes before tea time in writing you in reply to three letters recently rec'd. I had grown quite lonely for letters when the first two came.

Am too tired to write a very entertaining letter I fear for I have done what is for me a large wash to-day and am now sitting down for almost the first time since breakfast. I am so unaccustomed to washing that I make hard work of it but am thankful to have the strength to do it at all in this time of need.

I must ask you to excuse these half sheets. they are all that I have and I am entirely out of money and a little in debt—not much of the latter as yet but shall be if not relieved. We take our suppers out. I cook our breakfasts and at noon we eat a very light lunch. I should in this emergency cook all our meals were it not that we are getting our suppers very reasonably and if I once withdraw, I am likely to lose the place or have board advanced as it was once before, and if I have any dressmaking to do the time that it requires to do all my cooking is worth more than the slight advance in cost. I shall be obliged to work very hard at the best as there is a great deal to do to Alices clothes besides what I shall do for others. As stoutly as I had determined to the contrary I am indulging a little hope again in regard to your business so difficult is it to keep even the strongest resolution when your desires point so strongly in an opposite direction. I thank you, my darling, and I thank the Father that you were led to keep back the letter of explanation which you have written and now, my darling, will you, out of your love and forbearance, do still more and spare me from explanation and argument when you come? Perhaps it is a good deal to ask, but in the name of all the suffering which has come into the life of Alice and myself in these years of separation. In the name of the love which we bear each other I ask you to drop these years out of our life so nearly as it can be done and let us take up our life anew remembering only God's goodness and our love for each other. So very painful is the subject that a letter of explanation and sometimes the mere suggestion of it unfits me for the proper discharging of my usual duties for days.

It is utterly useless for you to attempt to combat this feeling for every word increases it. I do not expect you to think my feelings reasonable and do not ask it of you. I only ask you to accept as a fact what you perhaps do not understand or approve just as I must do your own course in these years and let our love for each other cover all and heal every wound as I am sure that it will if we are once together and if we cease to attempt explanations or justifications about this whole matter. I have not been unaware of your religious development and I am very happy in it. I doubt if you, yourself, realize more fully the change from the impetuous, passionate and willful lover to the husband that I feel that you will be if we are permitted to be together again than I do. It is often in my thoughts and makes our separation the more cruel and hard to be borne. God helping me, I hope not to be irresponsive to the warmth and power of your religious life and I hope that nothing in my letters has caused you to feel that I thought lightly of your religious experiences. I have feared sometimes that if you attempted to do the same amount of obligation work as you are now doing there would be no home life for us, as there can be little or none when the husband is out from the house every evening in the week. Except in the warm weather I can go out but little at night. I used to wonder sometimes in Savannah if all of a christian man's duty belonged outside of home—whether the wife and family hadn't a right to a portion of the evenings of the husband and father. what do you think of it, and what is the plan for the home to which you look forward?—Must I stay alone in it, making it for you only a place where you eat and sleep? Do you plan if you have means to come to Commencement or will you save the money toward fitting a home and have us go direct to you after Alice graduates? My heart pleads for you to come, and yet I feel that the money would do a good deal in other ways and so do not dare advise, only to say that I long to be with you and to be with you without more of these fearful separations. I scarce dare think what it would be to be again with you, for if I do the present life becomes very bare by contrast. Were it not for Alice I scarce know how I should bear it.

Alice has gone to chapel to a lecture—am finishing this at night—and I am all by myself and too tired and sleepy I fear to write more.

O, that the Lord would bless you speedily and restore you to us. I love you very truly and warmly, darling, and long to be in your arms.

With warm loving kisses,
Emma

Prof. Brown's sister from Auburn Me. has been visiting here and boarding where we do. She is a very attractive woman and I feel that perhaps you will like to see her as she goes direct from us. She will stop a week or two in Washington and then go to N.Y. to visit her sister Miss Clara B. I gave her your address and she promised to call on you. I send her card with the address at which she will stay in Jersey City and her sisters place of business in the city. The sister is a stenographer.

I do not know whether you care to see the people who go from us to N.Y. and yet there is a feeling in my heart of desire to have them see you.

[perpendicular line drawn through most paragraphs in letter]

———

[letterhead—marked through]
Rooms SOUTHERN ADVANCE ASSOCIATION
27 ½ East Hunter St. EOR. Pryor
Atlanta, Ga.
John E. Bryant, President

New York May 3 1891

My Precious Alice:

I will commence my Sunday letter although it is too late to finish. When you and your mother come I shall arrange my Sunday work to please you, but God has been so good to me that I am giving him all my Sunday—or nearly all. This morning at 9 ½ I was at the church with my morning class, then to preaching service, then to my rooms, and a nap of an hour, then to dinner— we have dinner on Sunday at 1-15; and on other days at 6-15—then to Sunday School, then visiting a sick friend and several of my Sunday School class, then to supper, then to 7 o'clock young peoples praise service, which I usually lead, and did today, there to evening preaching service. Then to Florence Mission, in one of the worst sections of the city, for fallen men and women, where a most wonderful work for Christ is being done, then home at 11 o'clock and writing you. Now to bed and I will finish this later.

Monday May 4

It is a beautiful morning, my precious daughter. We have had delightful weather for a week, and we may expect it most of the time for five or six months. Heretofore since I came North the weather has not made much difference with me. It has all been about the same. Whether pleasant or unpleasant my struggle was so great that I saw but little difference. I knew no real happiness for I was away from you and your mother. But there has come a change. I can now with certainty—with God's continued blessing—expect to see you both in a <u>few</u> weeks or months. Your mother desires to see her sister, and I think it probably best for you both to go there for a short time. When you reach here, it will be in the "height of the season" and there will be so much to see. I think it will be a heaven on earth for all of us, if we only have heaven within, and that can only come from an unconditional surrender to God's will, and perfect faith and trust in him. It will be a new world for all of us. It will be "wonder land," for I have not seen much of it. I have not had the time or the money to "take in" the sights. Now with God's continued blessing we can all take them in together—we three, our little world. I have not dared heretofore to hold out to you this picture which has long been in my mind and heart, but now I consider it safe, safe because I do not think that you will be disappointed.

Tuesday May 19th

Since I wrote the above I have been so very busy, and so constantly busy that I have not had time to add what was in my mind, and now I am taking the time from business as I must to send you $5 which I enclose.

I have had some hope that I could be with you at commencement, for although salary will not permit—I have commissions in addition, and I had hoped to use some of these commissions, or rather to receive enough to enable me to go. I have about given that up, indeed I do not now see any hope but I rejoice in the belief that I am soon to see you.

I have already gained the greatest business success of my life. It is a great triumph for me, but I give God all the praise. I am glad for many reasons, but I think most because it shows to you the reality of trusting in God. You know that from the 11th day of November 1888 until now I have all the time written you that God would certainly carry us through, that He would come to our aid in the nick of time. Now you see that He has done so, but you cannot fully realize how great my triumph is until you come here, and <u>take in</u> the situation.

Remember my darling that you and your mother are my world. I am constantly thinking of you as I struggle, and as I triumph. To you I seek to leave a good name and some money. Therefore do not think strange at my anxiety for your happiness and welfare. But my darling trust God, do not have anxiety about anything. Do not try to do too much. When things do not just suit you, take the matter to Jesus, and <u>rest</u>. You will be happier, and more prosperous by so doing. Do you know how many letters you owe me? I shall expect that you will give me a full account of the commencement.

> With warmest love and kisses.
> From
> Your Father

————

Athens May 3. 1891

My Darling Husband.

   This morning's mail brought me the ever welcome letter from you and a few days ago I rec'd one containing M.O. for five dollars which I have been unable to acknowledge sooner. These are such very busy, hard-working days with me that it is almost impossible for me to crowd in a letter even to you. but perhaps you can be patient with few and hurried letters now that we hope so soon to look into each others eyes and talk face to face. I dare not even yet place full dependence upon this success which seems to be just within your grasp and yet I do depend upon it sufficiently to have a great hope and to thank God from my heart for the help given. If the battle is indeed gained it is just when the need is sore and also an especial blessing that it should come just as Alice finishes her school here and the only reason for remaining here is thus cut off. God has wonderfully sustained me in strength and health since I have been here until within the past six months my power to endure is greatly diminished first by the cough and now by the return of the old weakness. This I attribute to the fact that housework and heavy household labor like washing and ironing have always injured me and quite as much to the other fact that I am now at that time in my life so critical to most women— unlike other women I suffer no pain or other derangement of my health but can not at all depend upon my strength. Even to-night I have been obliged to send word to a meeting under the auspices of the W.C.T.U. which I had promised to attend and possibly preside at that I am unable to go. I have attended two services beside the Sabbath School and when I left the afternoon service felt quite able, as I thought, to go out again but before the arrival of the hour feel the old prostration warning me that I have already gone quite far enough. I greatly regret to go to you with so little strength to bear my share of the burdens and yet I must not forget to thank God that he has sustained me through these years of severe strait when I must work or die. At the best

I shall be under severe strain and at very constant labor till after Commencement but the greater freedom in money matters for which we hope will enable me to hire washing and ironing and to have at least a portion of my meals sent in—this latter is made necessary because I am so crowded with my sewing. I think that if we go to Earl it should be as soon after school closes as possible, probably the following week if I can possibly be ready. About finances I will write you as soon as possible. The money sent last week gave me help just as I greatly needed it and just after writing my letter to you I had rec'd a small sum several weeks due for sewing. this came just as my money was exhausted and at the most welcome time. While this and everything else that happens to me is in the perfectly natural order of events and might come to an infidel just the same I nevertheless feel that altho' they are in accordance with natural law they are also from my Heavenly Father and that he does care for my necessities and that relief is from his hand. While I do not believe that under this dispensation temporal prosperity <u>always</u> accompanies or follows obedience to God or that God's word—on a fair and reasonable interpretation—is pledged in that direction I do receive every blessing that comes into my life as from God and I do try to submit to every evil as from him also— as between God and myself—not as between the doer and myself. Perhaps my wording is a little vague and yet I think that you will understand me and if you do <u>not</u> I am not saying it for discussion.

I do know that some of the most faithful servants of God are left all their life in great poverty and suffering and for this reason it has been impossible for me to believe exactly as you have in regard to a certainty of temporal success for you. but if it comes I shall receive it as from the hand of the Lord as simply and as thankfully as you can do. and while it is withheld I believe that God is giving a blessing even with the withholding though I cannot always recognize it. I am too tired to write much more to-night but may add a little to-morrow on business.

When you are in regular receipt of your salary and it thus becomes certain that we are to go to you I fear that I shall find it difficult not to be very impatient. I rejoice with and for you darling that the long hard night seems so nearly at an end and that you can hope ere the summer is past to be no longer solitary. May the Lord keep and bless you and take us safely to you. I shall never feel quite sure and safe about it until we are in your arms.

With loving kisses
Emma

Dr. Hartsell is here and preaches to-night. Alice went out to church and has not yet returned. I met him this morning he enquired after you and your business and I was glad to be able to reply in a more encouraging manner than I could have done a year ago. He has come here to meet Prof. Sedgwick from the Meth. University at Nashville to look over the new building preparatory to the filling up of four or five depts of the School of Technology which he thinks will be accomplished in a few months. . . . Once more good night and pleasant dreams.

———

Athens May 10 /91

My Darling Husband.

Yours of Friday was given to me at Sabbath School this morning and I find myself already thinking and planning for the reunited life that we hope to enjoy before the summer is over. I had hoped for more time than usual for writing you to-day but am disappointed. I went yesterday on a picnic to Tellico and as there were several miles of walking to be done we came home much fatigued though I bore it better than I expected.[3] The day was lovely and the scenery fine. Neither Alice or I had ever been there and had heard so much about it that we felt unwilling to leave Tenn. without going though in these very busy times I should scarcely have thought it possible for me to go had it not been that Alice was going, the picnic having been planned by some of the young men in school, and I knew that I should be a little uneasy all day if I staid [sic] home as there had been some remarks to the effect that the road was not safe. We had staid home for the same cause several years ago.

Everything passed off safely and pleasantly, the nearest approach to an accident being in a very uncertain belevard [sic] boat in which we crossed and recrossed the river and which upset just after I left it. The Tellico river is one of the few clear pretty streams which I have seen in the South.

I do not know whether I have expressed the satisfaction which I feel in the anticipated residence in Mt. Vernon rather than in the city. I dreaded life in N.Y. city at our time of life with our place there still to make—in a village it will be different. I am also glad to hear you speak of church attendance in the village as it seems to me a very questionable thing to infringe upon the

———

[3] Tellico Plains, Tennessee, approximately twenty miles southeast of Athens.

Sabbath by going into the city to attend church. I must make this letter briefer than I desire because I wish to call upon a friend in feeble health whom I have neglected for months because it has seemed impossible to find the time to call.

I shall feel much encouraged and strengthened in faith if you rec've your salary regularly by the week. We shall also be much in need of the help of it for there has never since we came here been a time when our needs for money seemed so imperative as now, owing to Alice's graduation our preperations [*sic*] to leave and the failure of my own ability to work as hard as formerly. I fear that it may be a couple years before my strength is again fully established, though aside from that I am very well and free from the suffering which so often attacks ladies at this period.

Another thing that causes me some anxiety is the fact that I only rent my rooms from Mrs. P. and she will give up her rent on the 29. of this month and this leaves me liable to be turned out at any time that Mr. C. is able to rent his house to other parties or may desire to have it vacated for painting and repairing. They are very peculiar people and I shall look for no favors from them. To move a few days or weeks before leaving would not only be a good deal of expense but a real hardship which I feel scarcely able to under take. Will you be able to provide us with funds to pay bills here and take the journey west by June 1, if it should be necessary for us to go so soon?—This would probably necessitate some expenditure for help here but it might as well be that as the expense of daily living which must go on while we remain here. I have not time to write more and this is not the day for it but as soon as it is possible for you to tell me just what I can depend upon and to give me your wishes and judgment in regard to moving the best of our household furniture please do so as the time is very limited and if I am to attempt to sell anything here I must know it at once. My own judgment is rather in favor of taking our chamber sett [*sic*] and dining room table.

It is nearly night and I shall miss my call if I do not go at once. Please give your attention as soon as possible to these details and especially to the matter of our leaving here as near June 1. as possible for me to be ready. I am anxious to make a good visit with sister and you can perhaps judge by our own feelings whether I shall be in haste to go to you as soon as you are ready for us.

And now with loving kisses and a God speed in your preparations.

Good-bye
Emma

Earlville June 21. 1891
Sabbath P.M.

My Precious Husband.

As the days go by I am thinking of you and of the home that we hope to have. Until recently I have not permitted myself to look forward to it lest disappointment might possibly be in store for me. Even now my thoughts are shadowy and unreal sometimes, though less so than a few weeks ago. It will be almost like beginning our married life anew, and I fear that we shall be taken for some old couple newly married. Alice would perhaps pass for the first wife's daughter.

But, joking aside, a home together will perhaps come as near happiness as we shall ever attain in this world.

I am feeling more and more that our going had best not be long delayed. After all these years of separation I shall feel that [it] is almost a tempting of providence to remain apart longer than is absolutely necessary.

In my next probably I will give some estimates regarding expense and finance and we will begin to plan towards a time when we can go.

I intend to write your Sister Mary to-day and if practicable will make our plans to go there on our way to N.Y. There is also a cousin in northern Ohio whom I am very anxious to visit if not too far off my line of travel. She is the only one of her family left alive—if indeed she is herself living—and so utterly removed from all her kindred that I know that a visit from us would give her great pleasure.

I find myself almost impatient of visiting in these days—everything but your presence is most unsatisfactory. I have had this feeling strongly for the past two years and fear that I have been a very uninteresting correspondent. To be with you and resume the old life with the added pleasure that I feel there will be in it looks almost too bright for belief. May the dear Lord save us from disappointment.

Alice went to Baptist church this morning and I went with Sister. I would feel a little more at home with my own church with which I have usually worked when here but feel that during this brief visit I ought to go with Sister. by request of Supt. taught a young man's class this morning in the absence of the regular teacher. enjoyed it as well as could with consciousness of imperfect preparation. We have enjoyed a second season of strawberries since coming north and the cherry season has begun. Mr. Browne's trees (cherry) are loaded with fruit.

If I write your sister, look over my Sabbath School lesson and get a little nap before evening service I must make this letter brief. Soon I hope that we shall talk to each other face to face—that I shall see the love light in your eyes and feel your arms about me.

Lovingly
Emma

Sister wishes to be remembered and says tell him we would be glad to see him here, many of the people here have enquired after you

———

[letterhead]
John E. Bryant
38 Broad St.
Room 35

New York, July 21$^{\underline{d}}$, 1891

My Precious Wife:

I am just in receipt of your two letters of July 16 & 18—Thursday & Saturday—which I received upon coming into the office this morning—the New York office, for the Company has an office in New York and one in Mt. Vernon. I spend a part of my time in New York and a part in Mt Vernon. Yesterday I was all day in Mt. Vernon. I shall be in New York today. Most of the time I am or shall hereafter be in Mt. Vernon, but a part of our business has to be attended to in New York, and so we must have a New York office.

I will make it my <u>business</u> to write you now in answer to these letters, although I have other important matters to attend to; but I know by experience that unless I take time from business I shall not write you as carefully as I wish, for when the days business is over, I do not feel like writing careful thoughtful letters.

Now my darling at the start let me say a few things that I think will do us good. God help me to say the right things, and only the right things!

You talk to me as though I was not capable of forming a correct judgement in business matters and needed a guardian, and you are the proper one. Now, my darling, I am not offended. I know you love me, and I am certain I love you very tenderly. I know you do not intend or desire to offend me, and I am not offended. I fully realize that you have much occasion to write thus, because of the mistakes I have made, and the errors of judgement, and hence I write what follows, some of which is repetition.

You will not be able to fully understand me until we are again united but I hope to make myself partly understood. There are two sides to look at—the spiritual and the intellectual. First the spiritual: It is hard perhaps to understand me on this side, but let me tell you what I may say I know to be the truth—some of which, perhaps all, is repetition, but you will pardon me, if I repeat until you come to understand me, for I feel that our happiness very largely depends upon your understanding me spiritually, and if you will do as I do, ask God to show you the truth, and allow the Holy Spirit to lead you, the time will come when we will fully understand each other, and then we will be so happy.

The key to my spiritual life is, as I believe, the effort of God to lead me to do His will, and my determination to have my own way.

In 1852 God told me that he wanted me to preach the gospel, and I told Him I would not. I have heretofore explained the matter fully. Now do not consider this one of my whims. I told Benj. of it when he was here the last spring, and he said our family were always seeing visions. Now, I saw no vision. I heard a voice, or to speak with more care, there came to my spiritual nature a spiritual voice which made itself understood. If the Holy Spirit has ever spoken to you, you know what I mean. If not you cannot understand me, and must take my word. It was the same voice that answered my prayer the 11th day of Nov. 1888; the same voice that called me in 1852 at Kents Hill, when I was called to confess Christ, and would not because I believed if I did I must preach, and I would not because <u>I</u> had determined to be a lawyer; the same voice that did not again speak to me so as to arrest my attention until 1868, when in Atlanta I was told it was my last chance, and if I did not confess Christ I would be lost. It is only within a few months that I have come to clearly understand the matter; or to be more accurate; I have within the last few month[s] come to understand the matter more clearly than ever before. I have come to know more clearly what the witness of the Spirit is, and to know the voice of the Spirit. Now, I repeat, unless you accept as the <u>truth</u> the fact that in 1852, when I was on my way to Kents Hill to school, the Holy Spirit did say to me that I should preach the Gospel, and I did say <u>I will not</u>, you cannot understand me, or the cause of my failures.

I will then start from that point.

God who is all love wanted to save me.

I went to a certain Village to meet a man, in 1858 or 59, on Sunday, to talk with him about temperance, relating to the Sons of Temperance, an organization in which I then took a deep interest. I did not meet him, but I did meet Dr. Child, the itinerant dentist, who was "riding his circuit." He had a Sunday on his hands, and so did I. Neither were Christians, but both prided themselves upon being moralists, and we took a stroll. I can remember as clearly as though it were not a year ago about that day, although all the details are not in my mind.

He found out that I was a school teacher, and I that he was a dentist. He told me of Buckfield, what a beautiful village it was, and that they wanted a high school there in the fall. I can remember how it looked to boyish imagination, for I was a boy in my knowledge of the world. I thought Buckfield was a grand place.

I then and there arranged with Dr. Child to take steps to secure the school in Buckfield. You know the rest.

The day you were baptized you remember I went with you to the water. I think that was the first step I took toward God.

You asked me to pray to God when I was in the army, and to please you, I promised, and that I think was the next step, although I fear I failed sadly in doing as you expected.

In 1865, I went to Augusta Ga., and there the duties imposed upon me were so great—so much beyond my unaided ability—that I threw myself on God in real earnestness, and how he helped me! How many times He saved my life!

In 1868, after 16 years, that dear small voice again came to my spiritual consciousness once, and I confessed Christ. But my self will was not given up, and I fear I was a poor specimen of a Christian. I think you were right when you said, I laid my plans, and asked God to help me.

In 1875 I had that blessed experience in Washington, but I did not fully understand it. There were so many conflicting views, but I did grow in grace. I came to know something of the Holy Spirit.

In 1886 I had lost the witness of the Spirit, and in 1887 I came to New York.

On "Watch night" 1886–87, in Philadelphia, I again fully consecrated myself to God, and the struggle commenced. I cannot if I would, and I would not if I could, describe the experiences until Nov. 11th 1888. It seemed that God was angry with me. It seemed as if Satan was determined to have me. Sometimes I almost doubted the ability of Christ to help me; but I did not let go. Sometimes I thought I had done wrong in leaving the South. Something was wrong, that was certain.

At length Nov 11th, 1888, came. I heard this sermon by Dr. Spence. I went to my room, and talked with God with the simple faith of a little child. God heard and again that "still small voice" spoke to my spiritual consciousness. It was all for you and Alice that I asked, and it was for you and Alice that the answer came, but from that moment, I was a changed Christian. I have told you so much of what has happened since that you have some idea, but I fear, and judge, but a very faint idea of the real situation with me.

The great practical point is that I have been led by the Holy Spirit to some point to make me to know something of what is meant by the indwelling of the Holy Spirit, and of the action of the Holy Spirit that it is no myth, but that Christ was right when He said: "If ye then being evil know how to give good gifts unto your children how much more shall your heavenly Father give the Holy Spirit to them that ask him." [Luke 11:13]

And that Paul knew what he was talking about when said to Timothy:

"That good thing which was committed unto thee keep by the Holy Ghost which dwelleth in us." [2 Timothy 1:14]

In other words, I have come to realize that God, the Holy Ghost, does in point of fact—actually, not figuratively—dwell in the soul of the Christian who has a pure heart, fit for Him to dwell in, and thus we are united with God. The kingdom of heaven is in us. Without holiness no man shall see the Lord.

Now do not be alarmed. I am not so good that I shall blow away, and I am not so wise that I make no mistakes. I do not understand all of the mystery, but I do know that things have happened that seem strange; that I have followed what has seemed to be the leading of the Spirit, and that very remarkable and important results have followed, and all of this has been since Nov 11th 1888. It commenced within three weeks from that time, and I went by invitation to dine with the devotional committee of the Bowery Branch of the Y.M.C.A. Then to Seventh Street M.E. Church. There I met Bro. Wilson. Through him I met Mr. Wilcox. In the early part of December, 1890, I met Bro. Furgeson, and Bro. Belmont. Then the plans were formed that have resulted in the Mt Vernon Suburban Land Company. Now I can see from the 11th day of Nov 1888 until this moment a train of <u>happenings</u> that are closely linked together, that have helped to a final result. I say the Holy Spirit has led. If I am right, He will not now stop; if I continue to seek first the kingdom of God and His righteousness—His holiness.

Now my darling this influences me; but I fear it does not you, save to tremble a little for the soundness of my mind. I have come to have great charity for persons who know nothing of Christ by an experimental knowledge, who think they are insane who are filled with joy at the <u>knowledge</u> of sins forgiven. The knowledge of the indwelling of the Holy Spirit is not more strange, nor of the leading of the Holy Spirit. This whole question of the new birth is strange. It was so to Nicodemus, and it has been ever since. We do not fully understand the mystery but we <u>do know</u> the blessed truth:

"The wind bloweth where it listeth, and we hear the sound thereof, but we cannot tell whence it cometh, and whither it goeth: so is everyone that is born of the Spirit" [John 3:8] Only, my darling, because we do not entirely give up to God, and do not make an unconditional surrender; because we try to hold only God with one hand and the world with the other, our souls are not a fit dwelling place for the Holy Spirit, and we know nothing practically of Him or His work in and for us.[4]

Now my darling I am not discussing the matter with you. I am saying nothing about you or to you except to give you some idea of your husband that you may know him better.

Another practical point is that I have given up my will to God's will. I <u>can</u> now say: Oh Father, if it be possible let this cup pass from me, <u>nevertheless</u> not my will but thine be done. [Mark 14:36] The hard thing sometimes is to know God's will and there comes one of the mysteries of the leading of the Spirit; but <u>knowing</u> His will I try to do it.

From the time I was 17 years old, until since the 11th day of Nov, 1888, I was a boy and man of my own head. You have come nearer to controling [*sic*] me than any one else, save God; but I fear you do not give me the credit of being very obedient to you.

Now I have yielded to God. He does govern me.

This you must consider in now judging me. This I take into consideration in my judgement of business; but I do not ask you to do so. I place the matter upon other grounds entirely in presenting it to you. I put it on hard business grounds leaving God out entirely. But this letter is already very long, and I will leave the business side for another letter.

I sent you yesterday a check for $10.

> With warmest love and kisses for you and Alice
> Y. H.

---

[4] In a similar letter to Alice on February 22, 1891, JEB recounted the leading of the Holy Spirit in his life, with different emphases and events but basically the same. Both letters give November 11, 1888, as the crucial turning point.

[letterhead] John E. Bryant,
38 Broad St.,
Room 35.

New York, July 27 1891

My Precious Wife:

I have commenced a letter regarding my business, which I hoped to finish yesterday, but was so tired and sleepy when the day was over—and I was busy at church from morning until night—that I went to bed and did not write. But I will now write on another line, and finish, and send the other letter later.

In a recent letter you ask, if we cannot give Alice a salary, and have her help about the house. I suggest this. Give her a regular allowance per month, and have her help you and me as we shall all think best. As you will see, when I tell you of my business, I shall need some one to help me, and if Alice is with us, she can help you, and you help me or you can both help me. This is my idea, for Alice to give up all idea of leaving us for a year at least, and then we will consider matters together, and decide what is best. If after consideration, it is best for her to teach, I will not object, but not away from us. I think it best however to delay until we are united. Then you can fully understand the situation with me, and we can the better decide what to do. Now you do not understand, and you can not understand what is best to advise for you do not know how I am situated.

In regard to money matters, I will do as near to what you want as possible. I did promise that $10.^{00} [per] week, but I have asked you to allow me to modify a little. What I have proposed, is that you, Alice, and I shall consider business matters, and act together. I know that is very different from what we have been doing, and from what most husbands and wives do; but you have had some business experience and if Alice lives, as we hope and expect, she will have what property we have when we are gone. If she can feel that she is helping to earn it, will it not be better? and will not the experience do her good? You cannot fully understand the importance of all this until we are united, and you fully understand the nature of my business.

I will try to do as you suggest in your last, send you at least five dollars a week, as I receive it, and consider that the balance of $10 a week is due you. Consider that I owe you that much, and in your next tell me just how much I owe you on that basis up to date. I kept an account in a small diary which I carried in my pocket, and lost. Tell me, and I will keep the account, and when I make my money arrangements will send you a lump sum to cover all due you. Of course my darling I do not expect to confine you to that. What I earn belongs to you and Alice as well as myself. I want you both to so come into my business life, and Christian life, that we can all move on together, led by the dear Spirit, through our united judgements. I realize this is a new departure. But can we not do it? I hope so. Is it not worth trying?

> With warmest love and kisses for you both
> Y. H.

————

Earlville Aug. 10. /91

My Darling.

It has been very difficult in these last few days to devote any time to writing. Saturday we were unusually busy and were out all night watching with the sick. This left us very tired and sleepy on Sabbath and after church and sabbath school I did very little save to rest. To-day is Monday which always brings with it unusual labours and the severe heat of the last few days has rather prostrated our strength. . . . There is now more than one week of Aug. gone leaving but a short time before we must leave if we reach you by the middle of Sep. and visit at all on the way. For myself I would be very willing to go direct from here to you but I am anxious that Alice shall be able to visit in Chicago. we have many friends who would make our visit exceedingly pleasant.

Alice has been feeling somewhat better than when she left Athens but is suffering somewhat with the old spinal trouble. This gives me a good deal of anxiety but I am hoping that favorable surroundings with perhaps medical treatment if that should be necessary will remove it or nearly so. She is very healthy looking but not strong to endure, can not endure nearly as much as I can although she can put forth more strength perhaps for a single effort perhaps than I can.

I am thinking that it may be a good plan for us to undertake the Chautauqua course next year if not so employed as to prevent. I think that Alice will be much better not to drop intellectual work as so many girls do on leaving school, if they do not study a profession. I have wished that she might be drawn to some profession but possibly it is not best. I am trying to live day by day looking unto God the Father. Still I would like to feel that Alice had some life plan in her mind and perhaps she will have after a few months rest. Is there a date fixed when Mr. Wilcox returns from abroad? I think that you said about Sep. 1.

I remember Mr. Ashley very well and am interested in your meeting with his brother. I shall dread to have you identify yourself with even local politics again, altho it may be best. I fear that it will take the little time which business and the church might otherwise leave to your family, but I am determined not to allow fears and anxieties for the future to embitter our lives more than can possibly be avoided and I shall try to leave these questions over which I have no power with God. Where power still remains to me I propose to "Keep my powder dry" as well as to trust God.

I rec'd a very pleasant letter to-day from Fran (White) Austin and Julia written in response to mine after their mother's death. I had hoped to go once more to Buckfield in her life. Do you see or hear anything more of Greenleaf. I have not heard from him in a long time. Is it your plan for us to board while we hunt up a house and furnish? I presume that will be better than renting before we reach there. How many rooms are there in the house at $25. that you have spoken of? I can not feel that we ought to pay one quarter of your whole salary for rent. Please bear it in mind and see if you cannot find a good house of four or five rooms at considerable lower rent than that. By being on the lookout before we go it seems to me quite possible that you might find a suitable house for us at a reasonable rent. I feel quite anxious on this point for I feel that it is a most unwise and unsafe thing for us to burden ourselves with a heavy rent at this time.

With loving kisses
Emma

———

[letterhead] John E. Bryant,
38 Broad St.,
Room 35.

New York, Sept 8th. 1891

My Precious Wife:

We are having beautiful weather. The hot summer weather has nearly gone, and the cool delightful September mornings and evenings have commenced. Life to me never has looked brighter since my early boyhood days. From the time I was 17, where I asked my father to allow me to manage myself, until very recently, I have looked into the future with more or less of anxiety. I am beginning to understand something of what Christ meant when He said: "Come unto me all ye that labor and are heavy laden and I will give you rest." I am beginning to have something of that "<u>Rest</u>." I am trusting God more and more, as I <u>experience</u> the change that has come since I began to <u>rest</u> (as well as I could) upon the <u>promises</u> of God, and particularly that <u>chief of all</u>:

"Seek ye first the kingdom of God and his <u>righteousness</u>, and all these things shall be added unto you."

It has taken some time for me to reach a point where I could day by day see the fulfillment of the promise, although I have seen something for many months; and I have not reached the point where <u>all these things</u>, have been <u>added</u>. For I understand Christ to mean by "<u>all these things</u>" more than simple food, and clothing, and shelter. I understand Him to mean, No good thing will God withhold from them that walk uprightly, <u>if</u> they seek <u>first</u> "the kingdom of God and <u>His righteousness</u>."

I have taken my stand upon the promises. If you and Alice cannot fully agree with me now, "Stand still and see the glory of the Lord."

We will not contend. I will leave the quotations of scripture for you to find, as I press on to demonstrate in this battle of life, that I am correct.

I shall be delayed a day or two in sending you money. Before Mr. Wilcox went to Europe he made some provision for money, and left two of his intimate friends, who were with me, trustees of the property, to provide money while he was gone. One of these, who also became a warm friend to me, Mr. Jones, the Vice President, died about a month ago, and the money provided has been spent. When I went last Saturday for my check, the Treasurer said that he would rather I would delay a few days, and if I was pressed come on Tuesday—today—and he would pay me. Yesterday Mr. Wilcox went to Mount Vernon with me, and examined my management since I commenced, May 1ˢᵗ, and he was more than pleased, he was very complimentary. <u>Every thing</u> worked to my <u>entire</u> satisfaction. The arrangements made were very important. You remember that I told you, that my continued success depended entirely upon my being able to manage the property to the satisfaction of Mr. Wilcox. He told me and my friends yesterday that I had his entire confidence, and he expressed his entire confidence and satisfaction in my management of the property. I am to see him tomorrow on money matters, and I will write you after I have seen him.

With tenderest love and kisses for you and Alice.
Y. H.

Greenleaf was here a short time this morning on his way to Maine. He will stop on his way back. He is looking well. Y. H.

Continue to pray that God will so prosper me that we may soon be united.

Y. H.

———

Earlville Sep. 13. /91

My Darling Husband.

As usual the day is waning before I begin to write. Like all the other days sabbath has its round of duties though they differ somewhat from those of the week.

I have not felt quite strong in the last few days from a cold and other causes. for this reason I treated myself to a nap after church and it was past 2 o'clock when we had dined. After dinner I treated pony to a little outing by leading him about to feed on the fresh grass of which he is so fond. I do not like to drive on Sunday but am sorry for the little fellow shut up in a not over clean stable.

After he was cared for I indulged in a little reading—with the rest have finished the little volume on Sanctification begun some days ago. The one which you sent Alice. It is needless to say that I like it because it is written from such a standpoint that no one with any love for the Master can fail to like it. If all sanctification teaching was on that line there would be no need for schisms in the church on its account. all christians of all churches can say amen to it and it is as old as christianity, though he has expressed in a very happy manner the feeling which so many christians hold somewhat vaguely and which many a devout soul has experienced without the power of explaining it. The other one—"Love, the Supreme Life," I read in the early summer and was much pleased with it. I received from you this morning a letter enclosing check which allays my anxiety in regard to your salary altho you do not definitely say that it has been paid but I infer as much.

I am intensely desirous to know whether we shall be able to go to you this month. I am expecting it but can not help realizing that there are many things which might prevent.

I dare not permit expectation and desire to attain their full sway till I hold the money in hand or know that it is on the way—once I could not have done this but this last few years have been a schoolmistress to me in some respects. I must not write more now for am anxious to write a short letter to your sister Mary. I presume that she is looking for us to be there soon. I am very anxious to see her and her family but I fear that we shall be disappointed on account of the lateness of our leaving here and the increased expense unless it should be on our direct route and we are able to get stop over privileges which is uncertain.

With loving kisses
Emma

[letterhead] John E. Bryant,
38 Broad St.
Room 35.

New York, Sept 25, 1891

My Darling:

I send you enclosed my check for $20, and hope the early part of next week to send the balance of what you will require to reach New York.

If any thing should happen to prevent you from coming on the train you expect, and I am thus prevented from meeting you at depot, you had better go to 22 7th St.—near Cooper Union, which is corner of 4th Ave. & 8th St. That is the home of Bro Layton, my pastor, and if anything prevents me from meeting you, that is, I think, the best place for you to go, for they are good friends, and will make it pleasant for you.

I expect however to meet you at depot.

You wrote that if you stop to see Mary you would come by Erie R.R. If you do not stop to see her, you had better come by New York Central. The depot of the Central here is <u>much</u> more convenient.

Upon reflection I think that if you fail to come, as you expect, you had better remain at depot for me. There is a good waiting room, and I will meet you there. Should anything prevent, you can telegraph me at my New York office, or at night at my boarding house, 110, East 10th Street. If then I fail to meet you, you had better go to Bro. Layton's 22 7th Street, the parsonage, next door to the church. But we had better make such arrangements that we will not fail to meet at the depot on arrival of the train.

I fear that the time is so short that you will not be able to get here at the time mentioned, and stop with Mary. It will be no killing matter if you do not reach here Oct. 10, but as my birthday is Oct. 13—you know I will be 40 years old[5]—it will be pleasant for me to have you and Alice with me; but I do not want you to make yourself sick in the effort to come. I think the way is now open for me to send you the money next week, and if you do not get ready, why take the time. I will leave that entirely to you.

In a letter received today, you ask me about our sewing machine treadle. The company is going forward with its business, and gaining Mr. Haight— a wealthy gentleman had a considerable amount of the stock, and is giving his personal attention to the management. I have confidence in the Company; but matters have not moved as rapidly as I expected. I hold my stock, but there is now no sale. I secured a loan on it that helped me in my struggle.

In a recent letter you asked me to tell you some place in the New Testament that promised riches to the child of God. I know of no such promise there, and I have never claimed that. What I do say is that Christ himself said that if I will seek <u>first</u> the kingdom of God and <u>his</u> <u>righteousness</u>, all "these things" shall be added. (Math. 6–33) Now these things clearly relates to food, shelter and clothing. Again Paul says: "Be careful for nothing; but in every thing by prayer and supplication with thanksgiving let your requests be made known unto God." Phil[ippians]. 4–6.

"But my God shall supply all your need according to his riches in glory by Christ Jesus." Phil. 4–19.

Now these clearly refer to temporal affairs, as the context shows.

But there is another great fact.

The Bible clearly shows, and teaches that God, the Holy Spirit, will dwell in the human soul. So that, we may have God in us—a part of our very being. Who can limit the power of God in the human soul? I have come to understand my experience of 1875, and of Nov. 11th 1888 more clearly. It was God manifesting His presence in my soul. The experience of 1868, which I call conversion, and that of 1875, and of 1888, were not alike in their manifestations, but it was the same Spirit. Since Nov. 11, 1888, for reasons, which I will fully explain to you when we are united, if you desire to have me do so, I have come to understand the matter better, and now I am moving to a success never dreamed of, as you shall see with your own eyes.

When we are united you shall, I believe, understand that our Father is a real Father, if we only comply with the conditions, and that He can give us success, or hinder us, and that "All things work together for good to them that love God." [Romans 8:28]

---

[5] John was fifty-five years old in 1891.

If you desire to know why God has heretofore dealt with me as He has, I can give you what I believe to be the reason; but if you wish to put all these things behind, as we move into a happy future, let it be so. I will try and please you.

One thing is certain here is $20. When I send more money that will be certain. When you arrive here, that will be certain. I rejoice in a knowledge that God is with me, and is leading me. To me that is as certain, as that I am sending you money.

And now putting aside all differences of opinion or judgement, we will prepare for a happy union, and then, hand in hand, we will go on into the future, as God leads, until we cross the river.

With tenderest love and kisses for you and Alice.
Y. H.

You have not acknowledged the receipt of the last $10 I sent—last week—Did it come to hand?

———

Earlville Oct. 11 "/91
Sabbath Eve

My Darling Husband.

I find it hard to hold myself back from starting at once now that I have the funds to go and two weeks seems a long time to wait after this weary waiting of five years. For you I feel it even more than for myself for everyday and every hour of the day will be so filled with the unavoidable preparations for going that the time will perhaps seem shorter to me than to you. If I followed my inclinations, to-morrow would see me on the way to you with no stops for friends or shopping, but I realises [*sic*] that by so doing I would fail to see Mary and should also reach you in an unprepared condition that would to some degree dim the pleasure of our meeting because I should be as illy prepared for church or to meet your friends. So I must try to restrain my impatience and ask God to keep you safely and bring us in health and safety to each other at the end of the two weeks. Saturday the 24th I confidently hope and expect to be with you and shall be most happy to visit at your pastor's as you suggest. That gives me one week for work and packing and one week for Chicago, the journey to New York and the visit with Mary. I fear that it will be impossible for me to leave here earlier than Tuesday the 20. though I shall go a day earlier if possible. I must have two days in Chicago, if possible, leaving there on Thursday at the latest which will barely give a day at Mary's in Indiana and take me to you on Sat. I shall try to plan to reach you early in the day, so that if I am delayed by any failure to make connections it can not throw me into the night or into Sunday morning. Sister and I went to the Baptist Church this morning. heard a very good sermon from a young theological student from Chicago.

Can you realise [*sic*] that two weeks from to-day will see us together God willing? While we may be very impatient then [*sic*] two weeks there will be a world of pleasure in the knowledge that the time is fixed and that there is a definite date when we hope to see each other. Next week you will think of me on the way to you. I shall make just as little stop as possible after I am once on the way. Alice has already gone into Chicago. She has long been promised the visit there and I foresaw that I could not possibly go, for we could not go until we had our money and our preparations were all made and then I could not wait to visit, so as soon as I rec'd the $20 from you I wrote Miss Engleman to know when it would be agreeable to receive her. She fixed upon Thursday last and I sat up all night and until nearly 4 o'clock Thusday [*sic*] morning in order to finish her sewing. She worked hard herslef [*sic*] also and only went to bed at 11 o'clock at my insistence. I was very glad however that I perserverd [*sic*] and that she started at the time fixed upon as she reached there just in season for several pleasant things. . . .

I am especially pleased by the opportunity [for her] to attend the Mt. Holyoke Alumnae banquet. Such opportunities come but rarely and are especially valuable to a girl like Alice who has but just emerged from her own college life. I have written to Dr. Fuller's family telling them where she is and asking them to call on her and I presume that she will visit them. The Thompson's of whom she spoke are a Chicago family who lived two or three years in Athens during our stay there and whose children went to my school. . . .

The day she left for Chicago her uncle gave her a beautiful gold watch and chain. She was very proud and happy over it as you may imagine and I was myself much pleased as I am sure you will be. . . . It is beautifully marked on the outside with name and date. . . .

Over and over the joyful thought comes to me that only one more sabbath intervenes before I will be with you. . . . May your dreams be sweet and may God keep you in his loving-kindness in these remaining days of our separation.

Lovingly
Emma

Monday Morn. I have just rec'd yours of Sat. and am grieved beyond expression that I must disappoint you in regard to being with you this week. . . . Now let me tell you how much I have to do and I think you will yourself feel that it is useless for me to attempt to start before next week unless you are ill in which case telegraph me and I shall go at once. I have not a single dress suitable to put on at this season of the year for church or street—nothing at all to put on my shoulders for a wrap—not a warm skirt even for travelling—all these are to be done this week beside one whole day at packing . . . and good bye calls that cannot be omitted for Earlville people have now as always treated me with great friendship making me at home and inviting sister and myself to a good many parties, so to leave without making good bye calls would be very inexcusable. . . . The only help I can obtain is the [illegible] of my dress which is in a dressmaker's hands. besides these I have to finish a wrapper for morning wear which I must have immediately on my arrival in N.Y. and which Alice has cut and partly made for me. The last time . . . I was unable to visit Miss Engleman and Miss Merrick at all altho' they were expecting us and Miss E. plead[ed] hard for us to stay. I felt that after all their politeness to us at the time of the convention and the complimentary tickets to La Crosse which she got for us I was treating them very rudely and I have felt badly about it ever since. It left that mortified unhappy feeling which a rude or inappreciative act always does and I determined that nothing but illness should cause me to repeat it. Now that Alice is with them and we are under renewed obligations . . . I also feel that I ought to call on Mrs. Fuller. . . . The money which you have sent has all been received and as liberal as your provision has been I shall . . . be obliged to buy an inferior cloak in Chicago unless it would be possible for you to send me a little more at Chicago. I have tried to be very prudent and I think that I have been, but Alice and I both were so entirely out of both outside and inside clothing, of wraps and bonnets and hosiery that it has taken more than I anticipated. I shall not dare to calculate on less than fifty dollars to meet my expenses from Chicago to N.Y. on account of the stop in Indiana and danger of delays and extra expenses. I must send money this morning to Athens to have my furniture sent from there. . . . I gave Alice fifty dollars to take into Chicago. . . . she will probably need it all. . . . I have still on hand the check for $80 and not much more. The season of the year is such that I shall be obliged to purchase in Chicago a long heavy winter cloak which will be my dress cloak for all winter and I must make here before a [sic] go a broadcloth cape for the middle of the day and warm days where I can not wear anything heavy. I have neither the strength to carry a heavy cloak when it is warm nor the endurance to expose myself without one when it is cold. Sister thinks I can not purchase such a cloak as I need for less than $30, but I shall purchase according to my funds and will not cramp myself for money to go with even if I hurt my pride a little by buying an inferior cloak. so do not worry if you cannot conveniently send a little more to Chicago. . . . Try not to be so disappointed that it will dim your joy when I do see you. I believe that lack of a real loving greeting when I get there would be like a killing frost to the autumn blooms. . . . O, that the Lord may keep us all in safety and bring us together in joy and love. I believe He will.

Emma

I enclose Mary's letter. . . .

[October 21, 1891?]
Chicago Wed. night

My Darling.

My tickets are purchased and I am at last ready to start. I propose to leave here at 7.30 to-morrow (Thursday) morning on an accommodation train, the only one stopping at Kingsland, reach that place at 1.30 and expect Jo to meet me there, will remain with them Thursday night and leave Kingsland at 1.30 P.M. Friday going to Decatur where I will be obliged to wait four hours for the through train which reaches there at 6 P.M. will take the sleeper there and can not reach N.Y. till 8 o'clock Saturday evening.

I am disappointed by this as I have hoped to be there in the morning. You have several times spoken as if it is possible that you may not meet us at [the] train. I think if cannot well to give us directions for such an emergency but remember that it would be very forlorn for us to find ourselves alone in N.Y. after dark. I should almost feel that it took away much of the pleasure of our meeting if we do not see you at the train. I hope that you will meet us in [illegible] to cross the ferry with us. So please for this once lay aside all other engagements and start with <u>plenty of time to spare</u> that there may be no risk about it. I do not think that it will be necessary to telegraph you as we are going by the Erie road and are to reach there at 8 P.M. Saturday. Should anything change our plans I will [illegible] telegraph you—but if you hear nothing from me expect me at that time. Hoping soon to express my love in person

Emma

[Emma and John were reunited in New York.]

———

Earlville Oct. 16. "/94

My Darling.

There has been so little to write till now that I did not write yesterday. I am waiting here almost impatiently for O'Neil to come from Ottawa and settle what is to come to me from dear Sister's personal effects. As I have written you before there is no legal claim whatever against the estate. I learn this through Mr. Haight who is thoroughly cognizant of the business of the family, having [illegible] everything up and consulted the register of deeds and taken abstracts on account of the loan of money by the bank to sister & Mr. Browne. Mr. Haight will do all that he can to assist me and is in a situation to do all that anyone can do. I am writing somewhat hastily now as this must go in this morning's mail. I have just received a very kind letter of sympathy from Mr. Zeller in which he says that it will be difficult for him to come to Earlville now altho' he will do so if he can be of assistance to me. The condition of affairs being such as it is he could not and might even arouse the ill will or suspicion of O'Neil that he had come for the purpose of even interference. Mr. Zeller's letter also contains a most cordial invitation for me to go to Spring Bay to visit his mother. he says that she is feeble and there is very little hope that she will be able to go to the wedding.[6] The route lies through Ottawa and I had already decided to go there before leaving for home in order to see Sister's friends there who were with her near the last and to learn if there were any last messages left for brother or myself as I feel that there must have been. I think that the expense from there will not be very great. Mr. Zeller will meet me at Peoria. I am very anxious to go and, believing that it would meet with your approval and please Alice, I have written accepting the invitation, knowing that there was no time to consult you. I hope that I shall receive money from you to-morrow to enable me to go at the earliest time that

———

[6] Alice and Julius Zeller are now engaged and plan to be married in January 1895.

I am through with my business here. . . . Pray for [me] darling and give a great deal of love to Alice. remember [me] to Joseph and other friends.

Most lovingly—
Emma

[Wedding invitation]

Mr. and Mrs. John E. Bryant
invite you to be present
at the marriage of their daughter
Alice
to
Mr. Julius Christian Zeller,
Tuesday, January first,
eighteen hundred and ninety-five,
at twelve o'clock noon,
327 South Fifth Avenue
Mount Vernon New York

[Unidentified clipping]

"A New Year's Wedding"

An Estimable Young Couple Link Their Future Together at the Commencement of the New Year. . . . Much interest was manifested in this wedding owing to the prominence of the bride's father, Col. John E. Bryant, of the Board of Directors and Manager of the Mount Vernon Suburban Land Company and the Board of Directors and Secretary of the Record Publishing Company of this city, the bride's prominence in church and society work in this community and the fact that Mrs. Bryant has been favorably known in connection with her zealous church and temperance work. . . .

Mr. Julius Christian Zeller, the fortunate man who won so charming and talented a wife, is a rising young minister belonging to the Illinois Conference of the Methodist Episcopal Church, and although actively at work in his chosen field, has yet his theological studies to complete. . . . Mr. and Mrs. Zeller left the city . . . [and] will proceed to their new home in Kickapoo [Illinois]. . . .

Mt. Vernon May 25, 95
Saturday Morn.

My Precious Daughter

Your little letter so full of the love and appreciation that makes my heart young and puts fresh strength and promise into my life came Thursday afternoon and the box went out by first express Friday (yesterday) morning so I feel quite sure that it will reach you before the 30. I was just finishing the cape when I rec'd your letter. . . . Don't worry about the sewing I may do for you—just enjoy it as I enjoy the doing of it. . . . Every day I am thinking and planning to go to you and were it not for leaving your papa the thought would be unmixed joy. Let us pray earnestly and in much faith that he maybe enabled to go to visit you. . . . I am anxious lest you may overdo Decoration day. Do be very careful.

Tuesday Morn—To speak again of Decoration Day . . . don't fuss over the ice cream in any way. A miscarriage would mean trouble and anxiety through the balance of your child bearing. Again I say whatever comes <u>do be careful</u> [double underline]. It means much for you and your husband for all the future. . . .

Father drove up and asked if I wanted to go to ride. It was a most charming afternoon and a ride was an unusual treat but I told him <u>no</u>, as that box must go out that evening but when he told me that he thought Friday morning would be sufficiently early I had not the moral courage to stay at home so I put by sewing and went. [We] had a most delightful ride going to East Chester and viewing the recent improvements there then to Pelham Manor where he had business and thence home through Durham Park and Vernon Park. I have not spent as pleasant two hours in a long time. There was one thing only to mar the pleasure of the drive and as we did all we could for the poor horses I tried not to let even that mar the recollection of a lovely afternoon. As we were driving towards the city on 3d. street we passed an overloaded team [in] which a span of horses were making painful and unavailing effort to drive over a road covered with broken stone. I begged your father to stop and let me get out feeling that my presence and entreaties might prevent the horses from being beaten and possibly persuade them to take off a portion of the load as your father would not consent to that we drove to the police station and your father went in and sent out a policemen to look after the matter. I felt however that the poor horses probably suffered the urging and beating before any help reached them and regretted that I did not remain there while B. drove to the station.

I am constantly reminded of our Saviour's words that the love of money is the root of all—The greed to grow rich

Monday Evening—You see I got no farther Saturday morning than "the greed to grow rich" and all my time since then seems to have been preempted for something other than writing. What I was about saying was that the greed to grow rich was at the bottom of more of the sin and cruelty of the world and even the poor dumb creatures must suffer from the avarice. . . .

Since I began this we have had your second letter and enjoyed it greatly. . . . Many thanks to yourself and Julius for the money order and for the kind thoughts that prompted it. If I do not go to Prohibition Park I shall use it for something that can keep, probably some coveted book. If it was not for the anticipation of criticisms upon republicans your papa would go with me to the Park which would make of it a lovely outing. I can not help wishing that our speakers would confine themselves to appeals for prohibition and leave the criticisms of other parties out of all meetings even those strictly political. I went with such anticipation of pleasure to hear Mrs. Mary Cleament Leavitt, our round the world mis.[sionary] and your father left Teacher's meeting to come and reached there just in season to hear his party unpleasantly commented upon. I was sorry that I had urged him to go. Still in some ways the wrongs will come right and the work will go on.

I shall be very glad indeed if you go where there is a W.C.T.U. It will be a pleasure to you to meet with them and a pleasure to them to be able to feel that the pastor's wife is in touch with them. I sent to-day some papers and leaflets—do not know whether the leaflets are at all what you want but hope you may be able to get some gleanings from them for your work. It is certainly Christ's work and I am sure he will bless you in it. . . .

> With a great deal of love to both
> Mama

My Darling Alice—Your mother closed her letter abruptly that I might take it for the mail. . . . We wish you could come here but under the circumstances it seems better for your mother to go and for me if possible. . . . I am interested in your work and am glad that you can help. May God bless and help you.

> With love & kisses
> Y. F.

Alexandria Ind. Sep. 10. /95
Sunday 7.35

My Precious Husband.

I took out paper and pencil at the place thinking I might have a few minutes to write before train started again but we are already in motion so my chirography may be even more [*sic*] than usual. . . . After bathing face and hands which was all the ablution possible and combing my hair I felt quite refreshed at Muncie Ind.—there was a stop of twenty minutes and I went out and had a good cup of coffee & a sandwich coming back on the train and finishing my breakfast with some plain cream cakes and delicious pears put up for me by sister Mary so that I now feel quite fortified for the day's trip.[7] I am quite free from the cars sickness from which I used to suffer and recognize in it some of the compensation of age (for you know I am growing old even though you are not) If at fifty I have possibly less keen pleasures I also suffer less, though I fear I am not much less fee[l]ing than I was in my earlier life. Wonder whether the time will ever come when you and I will not be ready to draw sword and rush into the fight in defense of our conviction.

It is a great joy to me to know that every minute takes me nearer to Alice. how happy I should be if you were with me. it will be one sorrow in the cup of joy for both of us that you are not with me.

Peoria—Arrived safely after a very warm day in a crowded car—found dear Alice waiting at depot for me. Luckily I had telegraphed Dr. Zeller when I would be in so she knew just what train to meet. She sends love and says you will hear from us soon.

We came to the [illegible] and have had lunch and are going now directly out to Kickapoo.

Lovingly Emma

---

[7] En route to visit Alice, Emma had a brief stopover visit with John's sister Mary and her family.

Kickapoo Sep. 12. 93 [1895]
Thursday Eve.

My Darling Husband.

I am just now monarch of all I survey, Alice and Julius having gone out to ride. I was invited to accompany them but chose to stay home to write you. My trunk has just arrived being brought up by a merchant who had gone for goods. . . . As I wrote you Alice met me at the depot. . . . She seems amazingly strong and well. . . . I feel great courage that she will have an easy confinement because she has lived so healthfully and worked and driven so constantly. Her great safeguard from overdoing is that she usually lies down an hour or two every day between breakfast and her late dinner. . . . They seem very happy and Alice tells me that she feels no regret that they married when they did but thinks it was just the right thing to do. The baby is I think quite an unintentional responsibility. . . .

I trust that I shall very soon hear from you. I want to know how all things are going—how the mission work prospers and whether the boys have any work yet. Remember me to them and tell them I am thinking about them and praying for them. Much love to all the family and to all enquiring friends. . . . May the dear Lord keep you very safely and bless you abundantly

Your loving wife
Emma. . . .

————

Hennepin [Illinois] Oct. 13. "95
Sabbath Ev'g.

My Precious Husband

Day before yesterday it dawned upon me, or rather Alice called it to my mind that to-day is your birthday—it was then too late to write a letter to reach you to-day. . . . May you have many more birthdays my darling and may you always be as conscious of God's loving care over you as you are today. How it takes the sting out of approaching age to know that we are rapidly approaching that eternity where our youth and strength will be renewed and where feebleness will be impossible.

How I wish that I could be with you this evening. I scarcely dare look forward to being away from you for months longer. Please write me whether you anticipate coming to spend Christmas with us. I shall be more disappointed than I can tell if you are not able to come at all while I am here. I feel almost as if I can not be denied this visit of yours to Alice. She is much pleasanter situated, I think, here than she was in Kickapoo.[8]

If you see a time before Christmas that you can come take advantage of that—come whenever you can, soon or late, but do come. I have thought of you and the West Mt. Vernon Mission this evening and wondered if you were there. . . . Let us remember the days when we used to write each other daily and at least write twice weekly. I will try to write you on Sunday and once in the middle of the week. . . . there is a great pleasure I think in looking forward to a certainty of hearing from those we love at some fixed time. The Cong.[regational] church here are [sic] holding revival services. I have been to none of the services save a woman's meeting this afternoon. It is probably the last meeting of any kind that I shall attend until after Alice's confinement. I am hoping that she may keep up one week longer but can scarcely expect it. I hope that you will be as much as possible in prayer for her this week. I dread it greatly altho I have no reason to anticipate anything unfavorable. . . . I am glad that you are so pleasantly and comfortably situated and I have no doubt that things will go equally smooth after my return but I should be unhappy to think of boarding anywhere longer than until next May. I feel that it would be a great mistake at our ages to give up our own independent home. As far as economy is concerned I can only say what I have so often said before—that you are mistaken in supposing that there is any economy in it. Give me the forty dollars per month that you will be paying Joseph and the money that you will pay for fruit and other extras and I will guarantee as good board as you have now in case [sic] we can rent with them and thus reduce our rent to about fifteen dollars per month. In any aspect of the case the gain made would be dearly bought by the sacrifice of our own home—your business and christian work so completely engross your time that if we were boarding I should scarcely see anything of you. It is possible that we may take our dinner with them but that can be easily settled when the time comes. . . .

With loving kisses
Emma

I enclose a letter from O'Neil. . . .

---

[8] The Methodist General Conference has assigned Julius to a new parish; Emma assisted in the move.

Hennepin
Sunday Night
[October 28, 1895]

My Darling.

This is and has been all day a very anxious time with me and I presume that, ere this reaches you, you will learn by telegraph of the issue. God be merciful to our daughter and take her safely through. . . .

Monday 11:23 A.M. Long before this letter reaches you your anxiety will have been relieved by telegram. It almost broke my heart to see our poor child suffer as she did. she had very severe labor indeed almost more than she could bear. Her physicians could not rec've their telegram in season to come yesterday morning after all . . . still they reached here sufficiently early. they came a little before five o'clock last evening and altho' she had been ill all day and all of Sat. night she had not suffered a great deal at least had no agonizing pain but about dark they increased and from late evening till the babe was born at 5.45 this morning she had scarce any intervals of rest from the most excruciating pains. . . . It was not much over a half hour later that baby came—a fine plump girl weighing eight lbs. I never felt in all my life perhaps such a load lifted from my mind. it seemed heavenly to see the dear child revived and safe. . . . Alice sends her love and says she wishes you were here. . . .

Much love to all and many kisses to you, my darling husband
Emma

———

Hennepin Nov. 11th '95

My Precious Husband.

All day you have been much in my mind and I had hoped for a little uninterrupted time for writing you. . . . I am keeping very well and not at all afraid of breaking down but I have lost so much sleep that of late I have become alarmed lest I may fall asleep some time with the baby in my arms and some harm come to it. . . . No day perhaps since I left you have you been so constantly in my mind. I have had no time for retirement for especial prayer and none for reading of the word till this evening when I read the 18. chap. of Acts and the first 12 verses of the 19.th In the 18th we learn of God's divine voice to him which perhaps was not more plain than God's voice to you on the day of which this is the anniversary and in the 19th the word Acts rec[ords] of the miracles wrought through him. More and more as I read the word I feel that the manifestations of the Holy Ghost then were largely different from those of the same Holy Ghost now and that they <u>were</u> different because the needs of that time were different from the needs of this. The direct voice of God was a frequent thing then while now it is once or twice perhaps in a lifetime and that only to very few people.

But he speaks constantly and authoritatively through the Scripture and the promptings of our conscience to every christian. More and more clearly I realize that there is a difference between being led by the Spirit and infallibility but as this latter thought has no bearing upon your experience of answered prayer Nov. 11. I will not touch upon it further. . . .

In all of Alice's severe illness there are many traces of the loving kindness of the Lord and I feel that as He has guided us as He has been with our child and that her steps have been guided by the Lord at all the great turning points of her life. I find the tie between her and her husband very close and tender and believe that they are to each other what God has intended for husband and wife to be and that this hardship and early burdens will not be to their detriment. . . . May the dear Lord bless and keep you, guide us both as to the time of my home going and bring you to me here and above all keep and sustain you in strength of body and vigor of spiritual life in the months of absence the one from the other.

With loving kisses
Emma

———

Hennepin Dec. 6th 95

My Precious Husband.

The day seemed brighter and life a little sweeter when I came in this afternoon and learned that there was a letter from you. Altho' I realize just how busy you are I do get a little low spirited when there has been a long interval between your letters. . . . I cannot be even a little bit sorry that you miss me and need me. I shall hope for much time to help you on my return—more, at least, because of the boarding. Indeed there is the one bright spot about boarding—that it will give me more time from the many things that I feel to

be laid upon me. I have been out this afternoon to W.C.T.U. mother's meeting—the first time that have been. . . .

I expect to be first class authority on babies when I return. When baby is
well she is the sweetest, happiest baby ever born—will lie down awake or lie
and go to sleep by herself as good as a kitten—and when she is hungry or in
pain she speaks out her mind very plainly. this is the only resemblance to her
grandma that I have yet been able to trace.

Monday Morning—. . . We are delighted to be able to hope for your coming
in Jan. or Feb. If any urgency to you to come this winter gives you an unpleasant season of the year for your visit when you might come at a pleasanter time
I shall greatly regret it . . . beside that the visit to Alice now may mean more
to you and her than it would just after she had been home. I have tried to lay
this whole matter on the Lord who knows our necessities and how much this
visit means to all of us. . . .

> With much love from all and many kisses from
> Wifie

———

Hennepin Jan. 1. 1896

My Precious Husband.

I wish you a happy New Year. May it be a happy beginning of one of the
best years of your life. . . . There has been a minor share of sadness with me
all day because of your absence and Alice and Julius have not been thoughtless about you. they send much love and their extreme regrets that you could
not be with us. They wished me to say that they should have deferred the
baptzing [*sic*] of baby till you were here had it not been for their great desire
to have the baptism on this anniversary day and before Julius baptized any
other baby. The ceremony of baptism was here at home after dinner at about
five o'clock and seemed to me a sweet and solemn service notwithstanding my
belief about infant baptism and the place given it in the churches. much of the
ritual was omitted which was an improvement in my eyes and ears.[9] The name
[of the baby] is Miriam Irene. As long as they do not think it best to name

———

[9] Emma shared the Baptist Church's opposition to infant baptism, which was one reason
she refused membership in the Methodist Church.

her for any one there is no name perhaps that would have suited me better than Miriam and I trust that she will grow up to be a strong brave woman like Miriam of old.[10] She has been thriving so well of late and very good natured.

. . .

I am looking forward with eager anticipation to seeing you very soon.

With loving kisses
Emma

Love to Joseph's family—

I thought of you on the last night of the Old Year and imagined you in Watch Night service and hoped for a blessing from you.

Hennepin Jan. 30 of 96

My Precious Husband

This will be the fifth letter crowded into the space of a little more than an hour and it must be very brief indeed. . . . I have already written that I expect to leave here Monday Feb. 10. Julius goes away next Tuesday and cannot be back till Sat. and I shall if possible leave the following Monday. I am most impatient to be with you—never more so. About a house—the more I think of it the less probable it seems to me that a single house can be found comfortably accommodating both families for housekeeping. I can not help feeling that when you and I talk everything over you will decide on a house by ourselves. Sometimes I think it would be better to tell Joseph to engage whatever house suits him and if when the time comes we decide to board we will accommodate ourselves to what they have, then leaving ourselves independent. of course I may not see it in that light after I have talked it over with you but it seems so to me now. I dont like the idea of putting ourselves under obligation to Joseph by any delay which he may incur in waiting for me or in consulting our wishes as to a house.

I do not think now that I shall take time to go to Earlville, unless something now unforeseen influences me and I shall probably be home the same week in which I start from here. . . . Alice does not know that I am writing or

---

[10] Miriam, a prophet, was the sister of Moses and Aaron in the books of Exodus and Numbers in the Old Testament.

she would send love—baby has been suffering a good deal with earache—it is very hard for the poor little thing and for us, too.

> With a great deal of love
> Emma

———

> Hennepin, Ill.
> July 26 ' 96

Dearest papa

Mama and Emma both complain that I do not say enough of the baby, and probably you feel like entering the same complaint. I am sure I was not aware that I was negligent on that point for she is so constantly in my thoughts. She has been much harder to take care of since my return, I think that is due to several causes—[illegible], heat, teething and lack of company. . . .

I am very anxious, papa, to have you write your biography for Miriam, entering very fully into your war and reconstruction experiences—as well as your later experiences in mission work etc. Can't you do it? It will mean a great, great deal to her and to all your descendents. I am greatly in fear that your Atlanta things will be lost and there is so much there relating to your early life that I should so much prize. . . .

Julius joins me in love to both. . . .

> Ever your loving
> Daughter

LETTERS: 1897–1900

Many issues of the Progressive Era, such as women's suffrage, social justice, and social purity, remained Emma's concerns—and causes that she continued to support through the Woman's Christian Temperance Union. With the Bethany Mission in Mount Vernon, the Bryants worked together to make viable the "social gospel," which linked institutional churches to the needs of street people. While neither lived to see the prohibition amendment to the United States Constitution in 1917, they continued in their fervent belief that alcohol was a source of much human misery. Seeing them linked, the liquor industry opposed both women's suffrage and prohibition, thus incurring Emma's animosity. JEB's faith in the efficacy of politics as an avenue for change in society continued through his final days, as did his work with the Republican Party.

The health problems that had followed Emma over the course of her adult life plagued her last years with more asthma, bronchitis, and eventually diagnosed tuberculosis. These letters document her stays in Liberty, New York, where she sought medical treatment at the Loomis Sanitarium for Consumptives.[1]

John also succumbed to the realities of age and illness. The boundless energy of his youth gave way to fatigue and eventually cancer, from which he died in 1900. JEB related his last hospital stay in his own diary, which then includes Emma's entries for the remainder of the year. The devoted love between them endured to the end. As she was bereft without him, this diary records the final, touching chronicle of her sorrow.

---

[1] Alfred Loomis advocated treatment for tuberculosis in the New York Adirondacks. The Loomis Sanitarium was named in his honor. See Sheila Rothman, *Living in the Shadow of Death: Tuberculosis and the Social Experience of Illness in American History* (New York: Basic Books, 1994), 156, 207.

Mount Vernon Jan 1. 97

My Precious Daughter.

Altho' tis near 10 o'clock I will at least begin a letter in answer to your last received yesterday. I wish you and Julius and Miriam a Happy New Year— one filled full of the very best and sweetest things in life, the sunshine and the shadow, if shadow <u>must</u> come into your lives as it does in all—in just such proportion as shall make this coming year one precious to be remembered in after life.

Beauty and I are all alone unless we reckon in the canary bird. . . . I am left at home to nurse a fresh cold—not an inspiring occupation. I went out with your papa this afternoon to attend the reception of the hospital management, just reopened to-day. As you have perhaps learned from the Record there has been no hospital here for a long time. yesterday was the reopening and your papa and I went in for a little while.

We were much interested in your list of Christmas gifts and sorry that ours should have been so far behind. . . . You ask abt. the book rec'd by us. It is a handsome book, good paper and good print and I anticipate a good deal of pleasure in reading it. I had the rare treat last night of listening while your father read the first few pages. Many thanks to both of you for it.

Sunday night—I felt too ill and "shifless" as the old darkey woman expresses it to resume writing [the] next day. . . . We are having heavy foggy weather and I have staid [sic] closely in-doors—even keeping my bed till noon which is an almost unprecedented thing for me to do. Your papa is at the mission and the remainder of the household are at church. I can in imagination look in upon you alone and my heart gives a great bound to be with you. I wonder often whether your father and I will make the contemplated visit this year. [I] cannot quite see how but still cling to the hope. . . .

One week from to-night our mission has a public meeting at the First M.[ethodist] E.[piscopal] Church to be addressed by Dr. Berchtel. It is for the purpose of raising money to carry on the work. . . . Your father's pecuniary responsibilities and the drain upon his strength which this and all his other work entails press upon me sometimes with such force that I feel as if I can not bear it. There is only one refuge and that is the love and power of my dear Heavenly Father and I rest myself, burdens and all, in his arms and go on strengthened and helped to do the little that I can do towards carrying this mountain of work that your father has assumed. He insists that he is not

overworking and says that he rises perfectly refreshed and I sometimes dare
to hope that God will work the miracle in his case of suspending the ordinary
laws of nature according to his faith. If he does I shall be able in some measure to understand the philosophy of Christian Science healing, of which
there are too many well-attested case[s] to entirely brush it aside as nonsense. . . . Dont think that I am becoming Christian Scientist. I still preserve
my old attitude towards it and am afraid that if I get where that is the only
thing left for me I shall have to die—not because I would rather die than be
cured by them but because of the impossibility of putting myself sufficiently
in touch with their theories to enable them to do anything for me, if there is
any power in them. . . .

Your papa has just returned and I will close. . . . With a great deal of love
to all and kisses to Miriam

Your loving Mamma. . . .

———

Report of Bethany Mission
and Christian Home
for 1897
14 North Bond Street
Mount Vernon, N.Y.

BETHANY MISSION AND CHRISTIAN HOME—

Bethany Mission and Christian Home, founded in September 1895, to
meet a want long recognized by the Christian public of this city, herewith
offers the report of its work for the year just past January, 1897 to January,
1898. During that time it has housed and, in most cases, fed five hundred and
sixty-nine (569) men who have sought its shelter. To the full extent of its
accommodations it has received every applicant who has sought food or lodging and shown a willingness to work for it. Where repentance and a desire to
reform has been manifested, the men have been received as members of the
Home, employment has been given or secured and they have been encouraged to remain until they were established in Christian life.

SCOPE OF THE WORK—

The Mission seeks to save the perishing through the power of Christ and
the exercise of Christian sympathy and aid. Its object is to diminish the
amount of human misery and sin and to add to the aggregate of righteousness

and prosperity; its beneficiaries are taken from the ranks of those who, through vice or misfortune, or both, are a menace and a burden to the community; in so far as its efforts are successful, they are restored to society, clothed and in their right minds.

NEEDS—

This work can be successfully accomplished only in the measure in which the Christian public of Mount Vernon recognizes the work as *theirs*, and aids it by material help and by their sympathy and co-operation.

The expenses for rent, fuel, water, light and food are necessarily far in excess of the income from the sale of kindling which is the only industry attempted thus far. The expenses have been kept at the lowest practicable point; for the table a sufficiency of wholesome but plain food has been provided; to do less than this would defeat the object sought. All the work of the household is done by the men themselves, thus reducing the expenses to the minimum and giving employment to the largest number. Prior to 1897 nearly four hundred dollars were spent on building, repairs and furnishing, being nearly half the indebtedness up to January, 1897. To meet this indebtedness $434 has been donated in the past year and is included in the gross receipts in treasurer's report, herewith appended.

RESULTS—

The question will naturally be asked what has thus far been accomplished? To this it can be answered: Upon the paths of seven hundred and seventy-seven (777) men who were walking in darkness the light of the Gospel has shone. . . . The experience of two years has proven, beyond a cavil that an encouragingly large number of those who are "upon the road" are willing to work; shirking, laziness and dishonesty have been surprisingly rare. . . .

ACKNOWLEDGMENT—

To all who have been in any way assisted in this work of applied christianity, Bethany Mission returns its most sincere thanks, and earnestly bespeaks, for the future, the material aid and christian sympathy of all lovers of our Lord Jesus Christ and of their fellow men.

JOHN E. BRYANT, Superintendent.

EMMA SPAULDING-BRYANT, Asst. Supt.[2]

---

[2] Note that Emma here records her name with a hyphen; compare to page 394.

FINANCIAL STATEMENT
January 1, 1897, to January 1, 1898

Disbursements

> Meals . . . Wood, tools, etc. . . . Wages . . . Rent . . . Water, gas and coal
> . . . Miscellaneous expenses . . . Total—$4,037.46

Receipts

> Wood . . . Cash payments for board . . . Collections, donations,
> subscriptions . . . Cash from loan . . . Total—$4,037.46

EMMA SPAULDING-BRYANT,

Treasurer.

———

Mt. Vernon Jan. 2. 1898

Dearest Alice

A Happy New Year to you, to Julius and to Miriam and any who may be in your household. I wanted to write New Year's day but had no time, these are very busy days with me. Our moving and settling consumed so much time that I fell badly behind in my mission work and have never quite caught up and the close of the year always involves a good deal of extra work and this year more than usual owing to the Christmas circular and that to the wood customers.[3] We are having a genuine winter now—both Christmas and New Year days were very cold. this has been just such a day as I should have enjoyed a few years ago—clear and crisp and cold.

I halted between two opinions for a few minutes this morning as to whether I would go to my own church or with your father, but I could not bear to be away from him on the first sabbath of the year and so went with him to the Methodist and went to the communion with him as I do when I am there at that time. . . .

---

[3] As said in the report, the mission's employment for the men was selling firewood.

I am growing very sleepy and I have recently had so much trouble to sleep that feel that I ought not to sit till that sleepy time passes even to write you. . . .

> With a great deal of love to all
> Mamma

Monday Morning—Your letter was devoured at the breakfast table this morning by the twain of us, i.e. I read aloud while your father ate. I am in as great a puzzle now about my christmas china as you probably are. I wrote you without a doubt that it was from you. . . . I am so glad that you enjoy the machine so much—it is a great delight to us. If I could have sent it a year ago as I longed to do I could not have sent nearly as nice a one as this. So it may be with some of other waiting. God only keeps us waiting that our joy may be the greater by and by. . . .

> Spring Bay,
> Woodford Co., Ill.
> June 30, '98

My Dear Mr. Bryant,

Several days ago Alice informed me of your indisposition and the operation you were about to undergo. I have felt very solicitous concerning your condition and especially in the absence of any letter from Alice for nearly a week. However I infer that you are much better and have passed any serious danger, else Alice would have wired me, as I directed her to do. I trust and pray that my inference may be the correct one and that you are not only rapidly recovering from the effects of the operation, but that it will result in permanent benefit and restored health to you.

You have certainly been leading a most active life for your advancing years and I have often feared lest your many burdens and responsibilities would consume your strength and wonderful vitality and rob you of much of the pleasure of the retrospective period of ones life. Whether your illness has been at all providential, in that it will convince you to take a short respite of rest, I know not, but I cannot help but feel that you need and should take a rest. . . . I have observed with admiration the earnest zeal and enthusiastic activity you displayed in the management of the mission and all your business affairs. . . .

I hope that the mission and your business affairs will not become demoralized during your illness and that when you are able to resume your place again things may go on as before. I trust that this letter will find you steadily improving and Mrs. Bryant quite well. . . .

With much love,
Julius C. Zeller.

————

Liberty[4] Nov. 11. 1898
Thursday 12.25

My precious husband.

Will write you briefly to-day for I must write Alice to whom I have written nothing since my letter telling her the hard news of the Dr's diagnosis of my case. I feel that it must have come to her with a great shock and I must try to write something which may cheer her up a little. I wonder that I do not hear from her—have you heard nothing? please <u>dont forget</u> to remail the letters that may come for me. It is so hard to be here alone and not even to hear from those so dear to me. <u>dont let my letters</u> get lost or pigeon-holed.

Last night was a howling pandemonium of wind after an all day rain storm of the day before. To-day the wind is but little abated and I had wishes to disregard the Dr's orders or go to his office for the inhalation treatment to-day, and I chose the latter. It was too inclement to attempt to walk and I rode down with Mr. Carrier and he engaged to come after me the same man whom you hired the horse of and he came in an open wagon with the same horse. Luckily I was well bundled and got home without feeling badly chilled. I asked if it wasn't the same horse and the man apologized by saying it was the only one in the stable or he wouldn't have taken it. I couldn't blame Mr. Carrier for patronizing him however—for there is a dearth of any hacks here except those long ominibusses [*sic*] and those may go from the depot with a load of passengers and are not to be relied on. About the inhaler if I am to make any point of following Dr. Stubberts orders I expect you had best to get it as soon as you are able because I am now at great expense in going to the Dr's office.

————

4 Liberty, New York, where Emma was treated in the Loomis Sanitarium by Dr. J. Edward Stubbert.

The first time I walked down and Mr. Carrier brought me home. I was inhaling when he came and at his own suggestion he took my prescriptions to the drug store and had them filled and drove back for me to the Dr's office—he charged me fifty cents for it.

I was amazed. I rode down with him this morning and do not know what he will charge me—as he was going anyway I hope it will not be more than a quarter, but I asked him to engage a hack to bring me back for a quarter and that is the way I fell into the hands of your knight of the living and came home behind his fast steed.

So you see that every trip to the Dr's office is rather an expensive affair. I have a new prescription to-day which means more money. I sometimes feel as if I might as well have saved the expense of Dr. and medicine but do not know. I am somewhat encouraged because notwithstanding the cold weather that we haven [sic] had I think my lungs really do feel somewhat better. I can inflate them pretty well and I expectorate but little. If there is no change for the worse for a week or two I shall be really quite encouraged—still it is too early to judge anything yet.

O, my darling, how I long to see you! I grieve to think of you alone working so hard to keep me here. God sustain you and help you. Sometimes I think that the things I have sent for will make so big a bundle that you may as well put them in a dry goods box and send by freight. It would not take long to come so short a distance—in that case I wish you would put in the largest blue and white bed spread the one that is on our bed. The large blue comfortable lined with white would take its place for you. The bed covers here are so narrow that there is not enough to tuck in. Be sure not to forget the red blanket from the bed that I slept in. I want to wrap my feet and lap in on the piazza. About the inhaler I have thought that perhaps if you should take the address of it to Dr. Sleight she could and would get for you at physicians prices even if she had it expressed to Mr. Vernon as if it was for herself you could afford to send it from there here if she got a large reduction as I think Drs do. perhaps she could even get it at the rental of 5.00 per month and reduced rate if bought with rent paid to apply though of that I should be less certain. It does seem to me that it ought not to cost more than $15 or $20 at outside.

Now it is near dinner time and I must lay aside writing. . . . Please dont forget the papers, my own and the Chronicle-Record. I feel so cut off from home. I heard this morning at the office people talking of another murder of negroes in N.C. Have not seen the paper yet. one or more of the men spoke of the death of negroes as not counting. one of these spoke of Wilmington as his old home.[5]

> And now once more Good bye and may the dear Lord keep you my loved husband.
> Emma

[perpendicular line drawn through paragraphs of instructions]

———

Liberty Nov. 15. 98
Tuesday P.M.

My Precious Husband.

Your letter of Sunday reached me early this morning having come up late from the office Monday night. It is such a blessing to hear from you and to know that you are well. I scarcely dare think of the long winter that must intervene before I can be home with you even at the earliest, but if that or even a whole year can return me to you restored in health we will both be content I know. I did not realize how precious life was to me till this separation has shown me how much you must need me by my own need of you. God keep you darling and be very near to you in these lonely days. if you wake in the night put up a prayer for me. I am often awake and lonely though I think I sleep better than at first. [I] am not at all troubled by a cough at night and I think you will observe a good deal of improvement in me when you come.

I had nice letters to-day from Greenleaf and from Cora[6] and from Mrs. Leyon from our Union. I think I will send you Mrs. Leyons' letter but you will please returne [sic] it. I feel strengthened and helped by the prayer of so many christians and the kind remembrances of my friends. Please remember me to Mary & Agnes Bigelow when you see them to Mrs. Leyons and all the other friends. . . . My greater difficulty just now is to get my room warmed up in the morning in season to get up. I had a serious talk with Mrs. Carrin this morning about it and think they will do their best. I think I took a little cold this morning in walking out as the roads are very damp. I had on

———

[5] The Wilmington "race riot" was violence perpetrated by white supremacy advocates against African American citizens and property in Wilmington, North Carolina.
[6] Emma's brother Greenleaf married Cora Ada Smith on February 8, 1893.

my arctics but there must have been dampness rising from the ground. This afternoon I have some fever, but think it will all pass away. my fever has never been entirely cured. The Dr. says it proceeds partly from the lungs. I am getting back my strength and if we had dry roads think I could take quite long walks. as soon as the heavy wraps come I shall try to sit on the porch a good deal. if the dress skirt can not be sent with the other things without injuring it you can bring it with you whenever you come. there is not haste about it as it makes very little difference what I wear just now. I hope you have Alice's letters before this. I felt both touched and happy by her offer to come to me if I need her. Julius wrote the same saying he would have his sister keep house for him and take care of little Miriam. I should not of course send for her unless hopelessly ill but it is a comfort to know that I should not have to go out of life withou[t] seeing her should God call me. I had thought before that letter that she could not possibly come to me on account of the children and her home duties. I was delighted to know that there are so many more pleasant features about their new charge than at first appeared. . . .

Mrs. Carrin has bought [*sic*] a pair of heavy blankets for my bed and I hope to keep warm nights. The weather is very changeable much of it cold and raw. . . .

I love you, darling, with all my heart and it would seem like paradise to be with you in our own little home again. God keep you, darling, and save you from sickness.

Lovingly
Emma

Mt Vernon
Nov. 27th 1898

My Dear Alice:

I have received yours of the 6th and 14th, but the constant press of business has prevented me in answering until now. We had a fearful blizzard last night and today, and I am home this evening and take the time to write you.

I was very glad to hear from you, but sorry for the sad occasion of the letters. At one time I was fearful that your mother would not recover. She was very sick indeed—very dangerously sick. She came very near having pneumonia, and, if she had, she could not possibly have lived in my judgement.

Her summer was a hard one. I saw before you left that she was doing too much, but there did not seem any way to prevent it. After you left, she should have rested, but she could not, as we thought. Then Mrs. Hoffman insisted upon her taking the chairmanship of a booth at the Bureau of Charities fair. She was very anxious for the W.C.T.U to take part in the fair, and they would not unless she would be chairman of the committee. Under all the circumstances she did not feel like declining. She took a severe cold the first week she commenced to canvass for groceries for the booth, and I think went out every day with her severe cold. I was so very busy that I did not know how things were and I have been in the habit, as you know, of not interfering in any thing she really set[s] her heart upon doing, and so I did not realize that she was sick until she was in bed. As soon as I did every thing was done for her that could be, and, at length, I took her to Liberty. She commenced to gain immediately, and there is strong reason for hoping that she will entirely recover. When the Dr. at Liberty examined her lungs, he said she would recover, if she had vitality enough to stand the climate. The test he says will be when the clear cold weather of December comes. We will continue to hope and pray. Very many are praying for her recovery.

We appreciated your kindness very much in sending the check to your mother, and thank you both very heartily.

It is a very nice thing to have the telephone in your house. It must be very valuable. What does it cost?

I am glad you like your place so well, and hope it will prove to be satisfactory. How far are you from Chicago, and does Julius go there to attend the University?

I am glad you all have recovered from your illness, as I judge you have by what you write. I was troubled about you all.

I am also very glad that Miriam gives you but little trouble now. I trust she will out-grow the nervousness. I judge that baby (when will you name her, and what will be her name?) continues to be very good.[7] I think Miriam had a very good reason for not wishing to kiss her grandfather. She must have a remarkably good memory.

With love to you all
Y. F.

---

[7] Alice and Julius named their second child Dorothy Spaulding Zeller.

Liberty Feb. 10. 1899

My darling Husband.

I am much surprised and very sorry to know that you had heard nothing from me up to Wed. night. . . . I have only missed one day in mailing a letter to you, I have certainly not intended to leave you in any more suspense and anxiety than is unavoidable.

It may be very selfish to be glad that you miss me and yet your letter has made me very happy. Your words of love are very sweet to me and find in my heart as ready a response as in those days of our early love so precious in memory to both of us. I believe, my darling, that I shall be spared to you for some years yet even if I do not regain all my former vigor or strength. I may be obliged to live more carefully than I have done in the past but we will become accustomed to that and it will not I trust mar our happiness. God keep you safely, darling. I am often anxious for your health and one of the greatest trials of my own illness has been that it has hindered me from being helpful to you as I desired. I am glad to know that I am remembered at evening prayers at the Mission and I know that God hears and answers prayer and that he will spare me unless there is something that in His father heart and omniscience is better for us both. It is a comfort to me often and often when I am troubled and anxious to be able to say "God knows." If it was only knowledge without love there would be no comfort in it but I am sure that love as well as wisdom is infinite. If you come to-morrow night I shall see you before you receive this letter. As much as I desire to see you I almost hope that you will wait one week and make your plans to meet me Saturday week at whatever station I should take the train for Madison, or rather at Wehawken to go with me from there, in case I do make the change. I have written this evening to Mrs. Malloy, mentioning Bro. Peck and wife and have also written to an address in Morristown.[8] Do you know if Madison is on the R.R. if we had to go by stage or carriage there would be much exposure about it that it might be better to stop at Morristown. If you have an opportunity please enquire whether the village or town of Madison is well provided with sidewalks as an opportunity to walk without stumbling along in the snow as what I most want next to be a good climate. Miss Wilkes is expected week from to-morrow. I have thought if all arrangements could be made for me to go that day it might be

---

[8] Madison, Morristown, and Weehawken are all in New Jersey.

best. I shall have an opportunity to consult Dr. S.[tubbert] about it early next week, probably Wednesday. I presume if I do go next week I would be unable to decide early enough to write. Will make a rough calculation of money I should need and if you can send it and I decided to go on hearing from Mrs. Malloy I could telegraph you. I have about money enough left to pay board next Thursday there would be 2^{oo} more due him probably 8^{oo} due Dr. S. beside 5^{oo} for inhaler and money for my journey. If you cannot send this even I must of course wait a little. I think I could get away with 20^{oo}. I must close my writing at once as it began to be cold in the dining room where I am writing. my room has been so cold for two days that I have been unable to stay in it long enough to take my inhalation. yesterday I missed them altogeth[er] and to-day have had them only once. shall inhale before I return if room is warm enough but fear it will not be.

Please remember me to Bro Peck and wife, G[e]orge and all enquiring friends. I sent you letter yesterday enclosing one from Alice.

Lovingly
Emma

about my health would be doing well if the weather was not so extremely cold. this is unfavorable but am most thankful that am able to be down stairs

————

Magnolia, Ill.
Feb. 13 '99

Dearest mama.

I was unable to write yesterday as I went to Strawn with Julius. Although the thermometer was below zero I was not at all uncomfortable for I was well bundled up and we had a hot brick and a lantern at our feet. Kate and I expect to drive to Hennepin to-morrow to get some lard and sausage from Huks Bros.

Monday evening—I am home from church and must not write very long as it is now 10:30. I have given up the trip to Hennepin for a few days as Julius thinks we ought to do some visiting among the people in behalf of the meetings. He had a very small attendance all last week on account of the weather. The thermometer was down as far as 25° below zero one morning and was 20 several times. How I wish I could be with you on your birthday. I hope you will like our gift and that it will reach you safely. We have ordered a copy of the "Spaulding Memorial" to be sent you.[9] Write me how you like it and whether it is up to your expectations. I feel troubled about your discomforts at Liberty. I did not know you had changed your room to one higher up. You ought not to have done it. I think as you are feeling that it would be better for you to try Morristown or some such place where you can have more comfort and be nearer home. You speak of going there before returning to Mount Vernon. You surely do not mean to go back there instead of coming here this spring. . . .

I feel so anxious to know how you are feeling. Be sure and tell me just exactly how you are. Do not overdo yourself in writing. Write me just a few words when you are not feeling well. Julius joins me in love and birthday wishes for many more happy returns of the day.

> Your loving,
> Alice

Be sure and let us know if there is <u>anything</u> we can do for you.

———

> My Office.
> 12 Night Mar. 10 /99

My Darling Wife.

I realize that I am sadly neglecting you in writing, but I am in no other way. I have been trying to write more frequently, but it seems almost impossible. I am up late every night, and yet neglect many things. . . .

You[r] letters do me much good. I cannot tell you how much I appreciate them. I too am looking to the time of our home coming. We will be very happy. I am delighted that you will spend the summer with me. I can stand the winter with you visiting Alice, but to spend the summer there, and, probably, an other winter at Madison or Liberty, would be rather hard; but I am told that all things work together for good to them that love God, and I know that I love God, and so I must believe that all things will work for our good, if we continue to love God, and in faith and trust I do the best I can.

———

[9] Charles Warren Spalding, *The Spalding Memorial: A Genealogical History of Edward Spalding of Virginia and the Massachusetts Bay and His Descendents,* 2 vols. (Chicago: American Publishers' Association, 1897).

I enclose a check for ten dollars. I will send an other in a few days. I want you to do just what seems best for your health. That is the thing to be done. It seems a providence that led you to Liberty and to Dr. Stubbuck [*sic*]. My advice is to follow his advice until you make an other move. Of course we can not spend money lavishly; but what is the use of money, if you die. God has been very good to me. He has enabled me to provide the money this far, and I have faith to believe that He will, if I continue to seek first His kingdom and His righteousness. I know you are prudent, and I will continue to try and send what you need, and we will continue to trust God in all things.

I have neglected to write that aunt Harriet is dead; died a week ago last Saturday. Joseph went, but got there after her death. Hattie got there before she died.

I have many other things to write, but I must go home and to bed. Will <u>try</u> to do better next time.

With warmest love and kisses.
Y. H.

Liberty Mch. 19. 1899

My Darling.

We have had a Sunday of heavy fog following an all day snow storm yesterday and now at 5 P.M. the wind is blowing and snow falling. . . . I can not say that I dislike these storms as long as I am comfortably housed but my heart aches for the homeless who are cold and hungry. God help them by opening the hearts and pocket books of those who have something to give. As I look out of my window to see the flakes go whirling merrily about it is hard to realize that the immense drifts which imprisoned one of the western trains for two or three weeks and had then I think to be abandoned while the passengers were gotten out in some other way was composed of just such little particles of snow, and so the p[h]rase snowed under as used in politics is a happy one—just an accumulation of little individual ballots, so small and insignificant each by itself, so mighty in the aggregate. My <u>soul</u> looks eagerly forward to the time when a christian woman will count one at the polls as well as the lowest bar worn loafer—that the lowest woman will then have the power to vote as well as the lowest man can not annul the gain unless the time should come when the bad women out number the good of which I have no

fear.[10] By the way did you see the copy of document sent by the Colorado legislature to all the states of the Union and I think to Congress also, speaking
in the highest terms of the result of woman suffrage in Colorado often and
recommending it, after their long experince [sic] of it, to other states?[11]. . .

I am much interested in Cabot's history of the Spanish-American war,[12]
especially the first chap—(in Feb. no.) which goes back seventy years to the
efforts of Bolivar to assist the Cubans to their freedom, which, shame to say,
were frustrated by this country which sustained the Spanish power in Cuba
because the South were [sic] unwilling to have free negroes so near their
Atlantic border, so that not only did we pay the price for American Slavery by
all the horror of the Civil War but again now by this Spanish-American war.[13]
Then Cuba could have been freed without our help and we would not permit
it. now it has been accomplished by the blood of our sons. "The mills of God
grind slowly but they grind exceeding small" If you have not read this chapter in the Feb Harper I would advise you to do so. Cabot is a fine writer and
it is important history with which he is dealing. How true it is that "God
maketh the wrath of man to praise Him and the remainder he restraineth"
Somehow, sometime God's purposes are wrought out though often in blood
and anguish when it might have been done in far easier ways had statesmen
only faith enough in God to do the right thing trusting God for the outcome.
I must give you a little quotation from this same chapter which impresses me
as especially forceful. Speaking of the action of the U.S. in stopping the movement for the liberation of the Spanish colonies and its assumption that the
question was thereby settled he says "Cuba was held under Spanish rule, and
the question which had received the wrong answer began almost at once to
make itself heard, after the awkward fashion of questions which which [sic]
men pretend to have disposed of, but which are still restlessly seeking the
right and final answer, and, without respect for policies or vested interests,
keep knocking and crying at the door" This is not only terse, vigorous
English but, God's own truth and as applicable and as applicable [sic] to the
questions of Woman Suffrage and the prohibition of the liquor traffic as to the

---

[10] Logic used by some suffragists was that progressive women surely deserved the vote as
much or more than the male dregs of society, and women would counteract their voice in
politics.

[11] The state of Colorado granted women the vote in 1893.

[12] Henry Cabot Lodge, *The War with Spain* (New York: Harper & Brothers, 1899).

[13] Spanish-American War, April–August 1898; the United States Congress ratified Treaty
of Paris, February 6, 1899.

liberation of Cuba. I wonder often why it is that intelligent Christian people who really desire the removal of the saloon as a legalized institution can cherish such abject cowardice about it, how they can believe that there is a God, all-powerful and all-good and that puny mortals can thwart his plans. It is true that God's plan must be worked out through individuals consciously or unconsciously, willingly or unwillingly but in some way and in some time. I would not part with the <u>absolute faith</u> in the final triumph of righteousness even in this world for the wealth of the millionaire, and I do count money I will confess. Without that faith I think life would be hardly worth living here and I am afraid I should almost or quite lose my hold on eternal life. I cannot remember, either, a period in my life when this faith was not in me. Just as soon as I was old enough to think at all on these subjects I think I had the same absolute faith that I have now. Possibly the fact that I cannot remember the time when God was not present with me on these fundamental lines and because my conscious christian life has been so largely the deepening and strengthening of these forces of my nature may be one of the reasons that my experience has been so destitute of signs and wonders that for very many years I stumbled over the fact that it was so unlike that of most other christians. I have of late years tried and I think successfully to come out from under that cloud, trusting God for the right kind of experience as well as for all else. It is nearly 8 o'clock and I suppose the brothers at the Mission are singing the old tunes now which I would so much like to listen to. Please remember me to them and tell them that my thoughts and prayers often go out and up for them and for those who have been there in the past and are now so widely scattered.

I ought to write at least one more letter to-night and want to go down stairs for a few minutes as well as take my inhalation before retiring. All my days now are brightened by the thought of the home going. I feel that it can hardly be more than four weeks now before I can step over our own threshold. I am thinking somewhat of spending a couple [of] days with Greenleaf and Cora before I go home. There will be so much to do when I once get there that it will not be easy to find time to leave when I am once home and I am very anxious to make them a little visit. What do you think of it? . . . I am anticipating a very happy summer. never in our married life have I been more eager to return to you or looked forward to it with more joyous anticipation.

May God keep you [and] bless you.
Emma

Wakefield N.Y. City
March 27, 1899
Tarrytown-on-Hudson.

My dear Mrs. Bryant:

At the Westchester County Woman's Christian Temperance Union School of Methods held at Tarrytown, I was requested to write you a few lines thereby expressing the love and appreciation of your White Ribbon Sisters. We are indeed very sorry that you have been so sick and thus compelled for the time to give up the work we all so much love, but pray our kind and loving Father will give you back to us stronger than you have ever yet been. We very much regretted having to accept your resignation as County Supt. of Mothers' Meetings as we all knew how greatly interested you were in this work and remembered with much pleasure the excellent papers you had furnished for our County gatherings, upon this subject. Mrs. Nicholas Le Page of Mt. Vernon was appointed Supt. and I trust she will be as much interested in this work as you have been. . . . Much was said in regard to the bill to come before our State Legislature repealing the Scientific Temperance Instruction law. The saloon element as usual are trying to have this instruction to the young stopped and I fear we are in for a big warfare.

Miss Rollins wishes me to give you her love and wants you to know she prays for your recovery. At our meeting at Tarrytown ten minutes were devoted to prayer for you [and others who are ill]. . . . One by one God takes the workers and we are left to fill up the gaps and carry the work on to victory. God help us to be as faithful as these who have carried the work thus far. Kindly accept my love and many prayers that you may soon be able to do some more work for the Master.

Yours lovingly,
Victoria S. Bell,
Cor. Secretary.

———

Liberty Apr. 27. 1899
Thursday A.M.

My Darling.

At last there is nothing in the way of my home going Saturday if the weather is favorable and the necessary funds come in season for me to pack to-morrow. If from that or any other cause I am unable to go on the early train I may go on the 2.51 P.M. Sat. rather than not to be with you Sunday, altho' I think it would be something of a risk to expose myself to the night air at the very first. I would much rather go on morning train. . . . I shall not take the time to write much this morning as I want to paint some little souvenir to leave for two of the ladies who have done me many favors and to finish some other work beside. I am almost forgetting to tell you that I saw the Dr. this morning and he does not disapprove of my going Saturday. Please be sure to let Mrs. Mapen know as soon as you have sent for me so that she will have the room thoroughly aired and warmed. I am in such haste to be with you, darling. I enclose in this a letter just received from Alice—dont pigeon hole it as I shall want to reply to it Sunday.

> With loving kisses and the hope soon to see you
> Emma

12,15—Have just rec'd your telegram and am very happy—shall <u>not</u> telegraph you Saturday unless something prevents me from starting Saturday morning, what I do not anticipate. God grant that nothing may hinder us from meeting at Weehawken Sat. forenoon.

[Series of telegraphs sent from John in Mount Vernon to Emma in Liberty]

THE WESTERN UNION TELEGRAPH COMPANY. . . .
RECEIVED . . .
DATED
TO Mrs. J. E. Bryant
c/o J. B. Carrier

Oct 21 1899
Business detains me
cannot go to Liberty tomorrow
write you

Y. H.

Oct 28 1899
I send check today and write.

Y. H.

Nov 9 1899
Have the examination
am well write you

Y. H.

Nov 11 1899
Cannot come today come next Saturday certain
send check today

Y H

Nov 18 1899
Am on my way to Liberty.

Y. H.

————

Manteno, Ill.
Nov. 5 '99

Dearest mama—

I am very sorry to have deprived you of one of your weekly letters, but I have been working very hard to get fully settled down and have been suffering with a cough and enlarged tonsils ever since I came. We are beginning to feel at home now and have a very pretty house in fact the very prettiest we have ever had. . . .

Julius got a postal from George on his return from a trip to the White House. He has found that he will get no pay from the state until the Asylum is finished and he feels very much incensed about the matter. McKinley will send him to the Philippines at $1800 with a prospect of rapid promotion.[14] I rather think he will go. Little George Zeller, Aleck's sixteen year old boy went a few years ago.

When McKinley was in Peoria recently George had quite a talk with Sen. Long[15] and told him that his brother married the daughter of an old schoolmate (?) of his whose name after her marriage was Bryant and he did not remember her maiden name. Long said, "I know what it was, it was

————

[14] The American-Philippine War began in February 1899 when Filipinos realized that the United States would not grant their independence after the Spanish-American War.

[15] John D. Long, native of Buckfield, secretary of the navy in the McKinley administration.

Spaulding and if I am not mistaken her first name was Emma, she was of the very best blood of the old commonwealth." He also spoke very kindly of papa and wished to be remembered to you. . . .

The children that take care of Miriam and Dorothy are a boy of twelve and a girl of nine, both very careful children. They have been in the habit of taking care of the preacher's children for a number of years. They are Canadians and very pretty children with curly black hair.

I must close now as it is nearly church time. . . .

Julius joins in much love to both.

Your loving
Alice. . . .

———

Liberty Nov. 20. 1899

My Precious Husband

Never more precious to me in all the rapture of our youthful love than in this year of sickness and separation. It is not yet nine o'clock and I presume you are still on your homeward way. I fear that it will be more than ever lonely to you now. God bless you, my darling, and keep you in His own peace.

I am feeling better than when you left and drank a cup a [*sic*] warm drink at tea time which relieved a little the faintness of my stomach. . . .

Did you remember to send the prescription to Alice for her tonsils? If not please put it in an envelope <u>immediately</u> with a line that it is from Dr. S. for her inflamed tonsils and that he does not advise their removal in the case of adults unless under extraordinary circumstances.

Lovingly.
Emma

———

Liberty Jan. 12. 1900

My Darling.

Your long letter, rec'd Tuesday gave me great pleasure. . . .

I sympathize fully with your need of sympathy and of some one to talk with on your temperance work as well as with your longing to say something on it in the house of God and the difficulties in the way. In your case the situation is doubly hard because you are between upper and nether millstones of the callous indifference of the main body of the church and the sincere belief of the prohibitionist that it is scarcely possible for you to be a temperance man and not walk with them. . . .

I have some glimmerings I believe of God's workings with me personally but why you must be left in loneliness and in need of love and sympathy are more difficult to recognize—but on these two things my soul is anchored. God loves us and we love one another, and while these two things are sure there is always sunlight. I believe that I shall be home again in comfortable health next summer and if God offers the way for me to go South who knows but what it may give me, as it used to Nannie, several years of uplift in which I can remain with you and we can work together. As bad as my illness is there are so many things that might have been infinitely worse that I dare not be unhappy. My most earnest pleading with God is that your life and health may be spared. don't make such another overstrain as you did at the last election, remember what loss of power to work would mean to you and to all the objects that you hold most dear. This first dinner bell has rung, yes, and the second. I must bid you a loving good bye and hurry down.

> Lovingly
> Emma

———

> Liberty Jan. 21. 1900
> Sunday Morning

My Darling.

This week or at least since Wednesday has been a lonely one to me for I have not had a line from you. . . . I know that you have been busy and overwrought and I fear you have not provided yourself yet with those postals on which to write just a line while you wait for dinner. I imagine that you are in the very thick of the fight in city politics and I send out to you many a prayerful thought in your struggle. I realize that you have arrayed against you the power of the eighty saloons of the city and the indifference of the majority of even good people along with the conservation's of capital—a truly formidable combination with which only God is strong enough to cope. That He will do it through His servants we know but how long the fight will be on we fortunately do not know. God bless and help you.

Yesterday was another day of fog and steaming dampness from sky and earth but in the night there came a good wind and to-day is bright and sunny. I shall try to get out a little after dinner if not earlier; last night was like the previous one, comfortable for a few hours and the balance naps caught between the times of coughing propped up by pillows and everything else at hand. I can scarce expect much else for some time to come, the night or two before this last cold I had been so happy to lie on a single pillow—but I am most grateful to have had no fever in this last attack and to be able to dispense as soon with the service of a nurse for the money question has come to be a much more serious question than it was at any time last year, because then my Dr's bills were paid soon after they become [*sic*] due, now his bill and the Sanitarium bill for inhaler aggregate over fifty dollars; with no money to meet this or take me South the outlook is very dark <u>humanly speaking</u>. I also owe my nurse 5^{00} or thereabouts—do not yet know just what. In the Dr's case I only asked a temporary delay, expecting to go South at once. It is seven weeks since then and I dont know what he thinks; with the very slight prospect that there is for me to get South will it not be best to send, if possible, 10^{00} in your next order to begin the payment of the Dr's bill? . . . It often seems to me that as I am doing so poorly here that I might as well go home though I presume the Dr. would not think so, at any rate I should not go unless you approved. When the air is clear and crisp I feel that it is better here but at other times I feel differently. . . .

The book of Daily Texts which you brought me Christmas has been a great inspiration and comfort to me. I have never had but one of the kind before that at all met my needs and that I gave away to a sick friend many years ago in the hope that it would comfort her as it had done me. This is much fuller and better than that was and the scripture texts are so enforced and vitalized by the experience and inspired thought of the authors quoted that it is much more helpful to me than the text alone. . . . I think would be as enjoyable to you as it is to me. I thought of you when I read this. ["]There is a plan working in our lives; and if we keep our hearts quiet and our eyes open, it all works together; and if we don't it all fights together, and goes on fighting till it comes right, somehow, somewhere" I shall mark those passages that especially appeal to me and are helpful to me in times of great stress and so it will be more valuable to me year by year and, perhaps, may be a help and comfort to you or Alice after I am gone, should I go first. I have greatly delayed in writing because I rose only in time for dinner to-day (Monday) having had a hard night and this afternoon after coming in from the sun parlor the fires had gone out and my room was too cold to sit in. . . .

Lovingly. Emma

Telegram rec'd about my state of health now. I think that it is about the same as when I went with you to the Dr's office on Nov. 20.—but I am only judging by my cough and other feelings. it may not be so bad. God knows and I am trusting Him.

Liberty Feb. 10. 1900

My Darling.

I am so sorry to learn that you are suffering from neuralgia in even so slight a form. If you need me do not hesitate one minute to telegraph me and I will come at once. When the messenger boy came I had great hope that it was to say that you would be here to-night. my sorrow for your illness and my absence from you swallow up all other disappointment. Did you receive a telegram from Julius or Alice?

I have just received such a good letter from both of them and draft for fifty dollars for my journey so that as soon as you are well enough to make it entirely safe for me to go so far away I shall be ready.[16] If you are perfectly able to come Tuesday it will still take me there in good season. I shall keep the draft without cashing till you come. . . .

I love you very warmly and long to be with you to-morrow in the little home. Remember if you need me I haven't the least fear of going to you. Did I tell you that my last examination of sputum, showed no tubercle bacilli but some pus germ of bronchitis. this is as I believed, while there is some tuberculosis it is largely bronchitis chronic of course and slowly leading to the same end but giving me a chance for many years of life.

With loving kisses
Emma

Dont run any risks in your health and dont fail to send for me if I am needed

----

[16] Alice and Julius felt that a warmer climate would benefit Emma's health; they wanted to assist in expenses for her trip to Quitman, Georgia.

[February 19, 1900]

Precious mama.

I do not know what to write or what to say. How can I say anything to comfort you. Underneath you are the Everlasting Arms and you know my own heart is breaking.[17] Oh my precious father—to think he should go this way—and I have always had a strong hope he would be able to pay his debts and be prosperous before he died.[18] But he is beyond all his cares and dreadful burdens now, he is reaping the reward of all his self-sacrifice for others.

What a beautiful life his was, so noble, so gentle. "I have fought the good fight," how truly he can say it now. God help you. I can not go, but I will send my most precious possession and I know Julius can do more for you than I could.[19] I feel as if you <u>must</u> come to us, but you and Julius can plan as to what is best. If I could only be with you.

Your loving,
Alice.

———

[letterhead]
Grand View Heights,
J. D. Carrier, Prop.

Liberty, N. Y.,
_____189_

My Dear Mrs Bryant

We received a letter from Mr B. this morning saying how well you stood the trip home. I am so glad to hear that you are none the worse for it, and that

---

[17] JEB died on February 18, 1900. Alice later recounted that Emma "loved my father deeply, and stood by him most loyally. When my father was operated on for cancer in New York he asked that my mother be allowed to have a cot in his room at night. 'Doctor she stood loyally by me all those dark days in the south, let her stay with me now.' Much to the amazement of the nurses, the surgeon in charge of the hospital consented."

[18] JEB's last will and testament revealed an estate of $2,000, inadequate to cover his remaining debts.

[19] Alice was six months pregnant with twins; one son died at birth, the other was her third child and the only son who lived, Raymond Bryant Zeller.

you had not gone too far away to make it impossible for you to be with your Husband through his trouble—it is a great satisfaction to you I know to be near him just now. . . .

We all speak of you very often and miss our "Little Mother" beyond everything—we sincerely hope that Mr B. will come through all right and that strength will be given to you both sufficient to sustain you.

We all join in sending our love and best wishes to you

Yours Sincerely
Emma A. Carrier

Feb 19th 1900

[Bill from Grand View House]

> Liberty, N.Y. Feb 14 1900
>
> | To board for Mr Bryant | $ 2.50 |
> |---|---|
> | Two weeks bord [*sic*] Mrs. Bryant | 18.00 |
> | board 1 and 2 meals | 2.14 |
> | | $22.65 |
>
> Recd Payment
> J. B. Carrier

Manteno Ill.
March 4 '00

Dearest mama.

. . . Julius did not hesitate one moment about going, but as soon as the telegram was received began to make his arrangements. I can not tell you what a comfort he has been since we heard of the first operation, so thoughtful, so ready to plan to be helpful whatever emergency might arise.

Somehow I can not feel that papa has gone. It seems as though his spirit is with me and that in some other world he is living the same grand good life he did here, only free from the limitations which so hemmed him in and surrounded him. He died while he still believed that his business political and religious work would yet have some grand outcome. He had not lost his hopeful view of life. But to have lived to be a helpless cripple, dependent upon the care of others would have been more than his proud spirit could have borne.

To have cared for him and to have had the blessing of his presence in our house would have been a comfort to me. To have been able to write down the story of his life and to have had him tell his grandchildren some of the wonderful stories of his life would have been the realization of a dream of many years. But I believe he is happier as it is. He indeed now "knows the truth" and he can settle some of the religious truths that perplexed him in this life. The language of that Country is not strange to him and he will be able immediately to enter into its mysteries. . . .

Lovingly—
Alice. . . .

———

[letterhead]
Nathan Nutting, M.D.
210 South Second Avenue,
Mount Vernon, N.Y.

Sept 3rd 1900

Mrs. E. S. Bryant.
My Dear Madame:—

I beg to acknowledge your favor of Aug 28th, and in response thereto I enclose bill as requested.[20]

I do not recall the date when the Col. first called my attention to the small tumor in the groin. When I found that they were making their appearance elsewhere, I, at once, refered [sic] him to Dr. Ostrom. At that time there was no question in my mind as to the final result. The only question was, "How long."

Trusting that this will find you in improved health, I am,

Very Respectfully
Nathan Nutting

---

[20] Nathan Nutting, M.D., bill for professional services, $4.00, dated January 1, 1900.

[Emma's handwriting across the top of letter]
And money sent Sept, 13

[Unidentified clipping]

MOUNT VERNON, N.Y. FRIDAY, MARCH 16, 1900

Resolutions of Respect
First Ward Republican Association Adopt [*sic*] Resolution of Respect for Col
Bryant.

At a meeting of the First Ward Republican Association held in Lincoln
Hall on Tuesday evening Mr. Edwin A. Horn offered the following resolutions on the death of Colonel John E. Bryant:

"WHEREAS, It pleased God to call home Colonel John E. Bryant, one
of the foremost public spirited citizens of Mount Vernon, a Christian gentleman of strong convictions, firm courage, and indefatigable energy, be it

"*Resolved.* That in the death of Colonel John E Bryant the First Ward
Republican Association loses a conscientious advisor, an upright counselor,
and an energetic worker from the time he made his home among us. Serving
as Vice-President, President and almost continuously as a member of the
Executive, Finance and Campaign Committees and as a delegate to many
conventions and to the City Committee, he filled, with honor to himself and
the Association those positions of trust and responsibility to which he was
elected; and be it further

"*Resolved,* That while we express our sincere sorrow at the vacancy caused
in our ranks by his calling away, we are thankful to have been permitted to
associate and labor with and be inspired to better motives by a man of such
high character and integrity as was John E. Bryant" . . . .

[JEB's diary; mostly his entries until 18 February 1900, when Emma continues. Selected entries.]

January

1—   Attended watch night service at First Methodist Church Mt. Vernon
       N.Y.

14—   1st Me E. Ch Rev J C Peck pastor—Rev Joseph Pullman P.E.
        Les[son] Heb[rews] 1+2+4 Luke 22+
        Text Matt[hew] 22+42
        What think ye of Christ Very good sermon

20—   1 P.M. Reform Club 5th Ave & 27th St. N.E. Cor.
        Sewer Bill

21—   1st M E Ch Rev Geo C. Peck pastor
        Lesson Acts 26+9–16
        Text Acts 26+29
        I <u>was not disobedient</u> unto the heavenly vision—Not <u>Disobedient</u>

28—   At Liberty with Mrs. B

<u>February</u>

10—   [ESB] This is the day on which my dear husband was to come to
        Liberty and on Monday I was to go with him to New York to take
        the train for Quitman, Ga. instead I rec'd in the afternoon a telegram
        that he was unable to come owing to slight attack of neuralgia.
        Hoped to come Tuesday following

11—   [JEB] Went to New York to see Dr. Ostrom by advice of Dr.
        Nutting of Mt Vernon to ascertain the cause of my illness. He pro-
        nounced it cancer and said it would be necessary for me to have an
        operation performed. I go to Hahnemann Hospital next Saturday.

13—   [ESB] I received a letter from my darling on this date telling me
        what is written in his entry of yesterday except that he did not say that
        the Dr. pronounced it cancer and saying that he wished he could see
        me but that it was impossible. I telegraphed at once that I should go
        home Thursday and wrote Mrs. Smith of 12 W. 38. St to ask if she
        could entertain me over Sunday

15—   [JEB] Mrs Bryant came home from Liberty to be with me at oper-
        ation in hospital

17—   Came to Hahnemann Hospital Park Ave & 67th St New York City
        this afternoon in a severe snow storm Mrs. Bryant came with me.
        She went to spend the night with Mrs. Smith

18—   At Hahnemann Hospital N.Y.C. [JEB's last entry]

[ESB] The last entry made by my darling and the last lines ever written by him except the signature to his will written the following day and his signature to a R.R. pass. I make this entry Sunday Mch. 11 (my darlings second Sunday in Heaven) at the home of Mrs. Swart—226 So. 2d Ave. I went to him at hospital this noon

19— I am filling in these pages from memory. This Sabbath afternoon (Mch. 11) Sat Feb 10 I rec'd telegram of which I have made note under that date. I slept on cot in this room last night. Dr. Ostrom twice refused our pleadings that I be permitted to remain night with him. at one this afternoon the operation was performed and God graciously answered my prayers to move the surgeon's heart to permit me to stay with him night & day

20— The operation yesterday was much more serious than anticipated and necessitated the severing of both femoral artery and femoral veins through which circulation of leg flows—every effort is being made by elevation of limb and by massage to save limb. yesterday morning Ben Fairchild came in to arrange business matters—is to draw up will.

21— Before the operation Monday we had a very precious season of prayer together and my precious husband talked to God as clearly and really as if he had seen Him face to face. Most fervently he prayed for Alice and Julius and their babies, for his "dear wife" that God would deal tenderly with her and raise up friends to her if he should be taken—for his brother and sister and kindred and for the mission and the reform in politics for which he was striving

24— I was unable to fill in from memory the history of all these sad days in which my precious husband has suffered so much with such bravery and cheerfulness. Last Sunday Mrs. Smith came to see him for a few minutes since then no one has been admitted. Everybody is interested in him. the house Dr. said that there had not been in years such another patient

25— I was very hopeful this morning but when the wrappings were removed from the limb this afternoon I recognized the awful truth that it had begun to mortify. it will be removed to-morrow. he is brave and cheerful and says he will be perfectly satisfied if he can get well to work for the Lord without his limb. God is ever present. Brother Peck has been telegraphed for

26—   Bro Peck came this morning. B. talked alone with him and then we had prayer together after which we were mostly alone and he rested what he could before the second operation. we both knew that he was facing great danger but still we were hopeful. again we had prayers together, necessarily briefer than before. [illegible] and at 1 P.M. he was lifted to the car and went again to the operating room calling out cheerily to me at the [illegible] as it went up.

27—   After the operation yesterday we worked over him till 9 P.M. after that he had a comfortable night and this morning a strong pulse and we were encouraged, but during the morning the secondary shock began and he suffered acutely till he passed over the river at 4 P.M. His last words so far as I am conscious were "I am very much exhausted—can't you let me rest a few minutes"

28—   After the passing away yesterday I wired Greenleaf and he was too ill to come. I could not get communication with Mr. Fairchild but Mr. Knight [JEB's partner] came in just as I was sending a message to him. he seemed to have been sent of the Lord and was most helpful to me. Cora came before I left and at Mount Vernon Carrie came in to stay with me and before I slept came telegram from Julius that he would be with me on Thursday.

29—   Julius was delayed and reached here late at night

30—   Julius and I were up till near one last night. To-day were the funeral services of my precious husband. The honorary pallbearers were D. W. Whitman, F. M. Tichemon, Dawson, Archer, Judge Mills & Noel Blakeman

March

3—   This morning we laid away the dear casket of flesh in Woodlawn Cemetery. I cannot associate him with that little mound of earth. I can only think of the strong brave spirit free and happy.
Julius, Cora, cousin Joseph and I, Mr. Peck, Mr. Fairchild (Ben) and Mr. Knight were all who went.

4—   Julius went to-day to dine at John Fairchilds and I dined with cousin Carrie and Joseph—but most of the day was at home alone. as dusk came on it was hard to believe that B. was not coming in

from the Mission and that we should not be sitting down to our little tea together

5—   To-day began the looking over of papers and the preparation for
       breaking up the little home that has been so dear to us

9—   All this week has been very full of work with calls from many dear
       friends.

10—   Mrs. Swart has husband and Mrs. Laveny called to take me to Mrs.
       Swarts this evening. I am deeply touched by the kindness of Mrs.
       Swart and felt as I walked into her pleasant home that my husband's
       spirit was near and happy in the kindness shown me.

11—   Julius went Saturday to visit Greenleaf and Cora. I felt strong desire
       to sit once more in the old seat at church where I have so long sat
       with B. Mrs. Swart kindly asked Mr. Edison Lewis to take me in
       carriage with his family. Mrs. Swart sat in B's place beside me in
       church. Bro. Peck preached from the text—"He saved others him-
       self he could not save" many thoughts of the sermon reminded me of
       my darling

12—   Cora and Greenleaf and Julius all came to-day but singly, no two
       together. Cora will stay with me until we are through here. Greenleaf
       and Julius went to call on Mr. Ben Fairchild at Pelham Heights and
       Greenleaf took train for city from there.

13—   Very busy packing. . . .

15—   Julius got the furniture off to-day and started for home in a snow
       storm. am obliged to remain behind to settle business. an attempt at a
       meeting of Directors of Bethany Mission at Mr. Swarts to-night. Mr.
       Peck, Mr. Whitmore, Mr. Bacon and Mr. and Mrs. Swart present.

16—   Letter from Julius
       Felt quite ill last night and exhausted this morning, went to house
       after dinner, spent after in collecting remnant of dishes etc. and dis-
       posing of same to second hand dealer. Mr. Fairchilds clerk called to
       tell me that I must go to White Plains to-morrow to probate will.
       Mrs. Swart came for me and we drove to see Mr. Knight—he will
       go with me. Mr. Ben Fairchild called this eve. Will call again
       Monday morning

17—   Went to White Plains and when we reached there found that the clerk had left the will behind in New York. This and an error in the paper sent to Alice to sign made our trip useless

19—   Went in the rain to-day to the old home and from there to John Fairchilds pretty home where Mammie met us at the door. Ben called this morning before I left Mr. Swart's. The waiver returned from Alice had to be returned on account of informality in signing and I am likely to be detained all the week here. The missing check was in check book as I hoped.

23—   Went to-day to White Plains to probate will—this second attempt was successful. . . .

24—   Wrote Dr. Ostrom saying that his bill (175) was turned over to Mr. Fairchild

25—   Feeling very ill to-day—kept bed till noon. sent for Dr. Slieght who came in afternoon.

26—   Dull in the morning with snow in the afternoon. had planned to go to Fort Hamilton but am feeling very badly and that with unfavorable weather will detain me. wrote long letter to Alice to mail with one written Julius previously.

27—   Came to-day to visit Cora and Greenleaf till I go to Alice and Julius. a lovely day and I feel much better than for last two days. . . . Am feeling very tired this evening.

29—   Symptoms of fresh cold—coughed a good deal last night. wrote Mr. Wilcox have been reading "Hugh Wynne free quaker" by Weir Mitchell

31—   Am improving slowly but surely I think

April

1—   With Greenleaf and Cora a very quiet Sunday

5—   Walked to library—took out "The Enchanted Typewriter" by John Kendrick Bangs

14—   Came this afternoon to Mount Vernon to spend Sunday with Carrie, go over my trunks and find, if possible, B's commission in army and discharge papers.

15— A beautiful Easter Sunday morning and my second church attendance since Nov. 4, the first being in Mt. Vernon (where I now am)
the second Sunday after my darling's going away. Carrie went with
me this morning and we sat in the old pew, cousin Joseph in B's seat.
as I looked at the altar decorations I thought of the keen enjoyment
which B. always had in all such occasions and I was comforted on the
way there by the thought that he had seen the risen Lord himself
while we grope after Him darkly.

16— Yesterday's text from Luke 24. 5, 6 with the thoughts brought out
from it that no good dies and that death is but the portal of eternal
life was the tonic that my ears, (tempted to weariness since the going
of the loved one whose presence always brought inspiration into my
life) needed that Easter morn. I felt refreshed and strengthened for
continuing life's struggle a little longer and glad that I had not
yielded to the desire felt of late to put on the mourning weeds.

21— Said to-day a last good-bye to dear Mount Vernon. Have been all the
week with Carrie and Joseph and now am at Fort Hamilton with
Greenleaf & Cora. stopped at Woodlawn and planted pansies at the
head of the mound that holds all earthly of my darling—

24— Greenleaf and Cora went with me to Grand Central depot and I left
at one o'clock by N.Y. Central for Manteno—

25— A very comfortable trip yesterday and to-day—and two days of
beautiful weather. Reached Manteno at five in the afternoon and
found Julius at the train. Alice and the babies met me at the door of
the parsonage. It is very sweet to be with them.

May

12— Have made no entries since I came here—am moved now into my
very pleasant front chamber where the birds in the tree tops are company. . . . This climate does not seem to agree with me. . . .

13— A beautiful day—my second—no third Sunday in Manteno. Have
not yet been able to go to church. sat out under trees a few hours.

20— My first church attendance in Manteno.

30— I have longed this Decoration Day to know if my darling's grave has been remembered. I wonder if I shall be called to go to him before another Decoration Day. It is very lonely without him and can never be less so I think. No other love has ever been like his or can be.

June

12— Walked to town for mail and shopping. suffer good deal of distress daily for breath—bronchial tubes much inflamed.

17— Presiding Elder Williams preached to-day—communion season. In afternoon read Life of Bishop Taylor which deeply interests me. This evening have looked over some of my Athens letters before destroying and spent some time on old diaries of both Bs and mine

21— W.C.T.U. county convention began its sessions at noon to-day in Presbyterian church

22— Second day of convention—cold and damp. missed the meetings except closing half hour from that reason. . . .

23— Am feeling less asthmatic trouble this morning than at almost any other time since I came here. attribute it to medicine from Dr. Gulick

25— All day we have been looking to Alices confinement as very near at hand. God bless and keep her.

26— Our thirty sixth wedding anniversary. My heart longs for his love and his companionship. will another anniversary find me here and if not here shall we be together, in one of the many mansions? God grant it

27— Alice was delivered at 9 A.M. of a fine eight lb. boy and at 8:30 P.M. of another son dead at birth—and weighing seven lbs. . . . Alice we hope is doing well. wrote Greenleaf & Cora. . . .

28— Julius started this morning with the little dead body to Spring Bay. . . . Alice doing well but grieved over loss as all are

July

4— Very warm. Alice still in bed—baby boy one week old to-day. . . . I think it was one year ago to-day that my dear husband and I had such a lovely day together, going first to Glen Island in search of the yachts and not finding them there to (I think) Hudson Bay Park where we did find them—then to N.Y. from New Rochelle by steam cars, dinner in N.Y. and the afternoon at Central Park. how precious is every recollection of it now—when shall I see him?

13— "and the Lord shall guide thee continually and satisfy thy soul in drought. ["] precious promise. I can think of nothing else that so typifies the barrenness that has come into my life by my darling's death as this simelie [*sic*] of drought, as the thirsty earth is parched and all vegetation withers so my very soul longs for my husband's tender love. God grant that my soul may be satisfied in Christ, my Lord, and that the twain of us may be permitted to dwell in the light of His countenance through all eternity.

14— I went yesterday, Friday to W.C.T.U. . . . .

26— Rec'd from Milo Stevens & Co. blanks in regard to property of which I sent on to Mr. Knight to be filled out in Mount Vernon. . . . my case will be complete and that there is prospect of an early granting of pension.

18— Letter from Carrie . . . she writes that Beauty is very thin and eats scarcely anything. poor little fellow—I am so very sorry. have sent Carrie one dollar and asked her to buy him milk and meat. I think of him as watching day by day for the Master and Mistress that never come.

August

2— I seldom feel like writing here now-a-days—life is very lonely. I can not say bare for there is still opportunity of service, still sweetness and I am assured that the Master is keeping me out of Heaven only because I need so much polishing & chastening to fit me for the life there. God help me to be a more apt pupil

4— Rec'd word to-day from Milo Stevens & Co. that my pension evidence is all in and my claim now awaits the action of the department.

10— Attended W.C.T.U. meeting at Mrs. Bell's and rode home with Miss Jackson

11— Observance of Old Home Week at the "Old Church on the Hill" Buckfield Maine. Orator John D. Long—. . . .

24— letter from Cora this week. Greenleaf in Maine—he attended Old Home Exercises at Buckfield, Cora writes.

September

17— To-day I found in a pkg. of old letters one written by my darling from Beaufort S.C. in October 1865 just before he returned to take me south.

18— This morning Julius left for annual Conference at Peoria. only Alice, the children and myself at home. I have not been nearly as well as usual for some days but am more comfortable to-day.

23— Julius still at Conference. Alice preached in morning and assisted in Epworth League service at night. . . .

24— Alice and all the children started at 7 this morning for Spring Bay. . . . Mrs. Phoebe Paine is staying with me during Alice's absence.

25— I went to Dr. Gulicks office to learn result of examination of sputum. it confirms what the last few weeks had already indicated to me that my disease is now consumption. I fear that the knowledge has been hard to Alice who [illegible] before she left, as I fancied from her unwillingness to leave me.

October

24— Rec'd a Maroa paper to-day with news of Mr. Persinger's death. . . . a merciful release from sufferings by cancer through a paralysis of the nerves of respiration. he died a week ago, Wednesday, 17.

November

10— Our first flurry of snow this morning. papers bring news of blizzards and heavy snow in the east.

12— Letter from Mrs. Mapu telling me of the respect shown to my dear ones memory in the parade before presidential election. It is a happy thought to know that he was remembered in the midst of all the excitement.

dear little Beauty has forclosed [*sic*] his watch.

15— Have written Mr. Fairchild to-day asking whether he has talked with Mr. Stykes about C. Rec. stock, office furniture, balance due from ch. Rec. and sending Dr. Ostrom's letter. Ground covered with snow

21— . . . letter yesterday from Emma Stevens and to-day from Carrie both telling me that dear little Beauty had been chloroformed to put him out of suffering several days also letter from Mrs. Mapu telling of same. dear faithful little kittie

27— Called at Dr. Gulick's office to learn result of examination of sputum. tuberculosis bacillii [*sic*] were present and Dr. pronounces it, as I expected, consumption

December

10— Clear and cold—. . . worked on Christmas lace for Alice, ladies here in evening cracking nuts for Christmas sale

18— "But the God of all grace, who hath called us unto his eternal glory by Christ Jesus, after that ye have suffered awhile, make you perfect, etablish [*sic*], strengthen, settle you["]—I Peter 5.10.

My heart rejoices this morning as I read these words and realize anew that I am really called unto eternal glory. God keep me to make my calling about election eve.

20— Mailed letter to Greenleaf and to Mr. Wm Archer in regard to estate matters, especially Record stock.

A beautiful day, almost like autumn. walked to town and bought paint brushes. am working on little copy of violet to send Cora.

25— Dined with Alice and Julius at home of Mr. Dole—a large family reunion of the Dole relatives with a few friends—eighty-one present including children. How bright was last Christmas and how saddened it would have been could we have known that it was our last together on earth. will our reunion be before another Christmas? I think so. dear baby has been quite ill for several days.

26—   Christmas day brought to me letter from dear sister Cora. . . .
        It came to-day with letter from dear brother and money order for me
        from him of $10. He has been [illegible] and a good brother to me
        . . . bless him and I thank God from my very heart for the love of
        kindred—how it comforts my heart in these days of sorrow.

27—   from Thelda has come a Christmas pkge. with little gift for me, dear
        girl.
        I would love to see her. From Julius and Alice I received most
        acceptable Christmas present of two books. . . . Am much disap-
        pointed not to have been able yet to frame the painting for Julius as
        I desired.

28—   A lovely clear day. I walked to express office to send off little paint-
        ings to Greenleaf and Cora and in the afternoon went to bible read-
        ing at church led by the evangelist Annie Gleason, assisted by the
        singer who goes with her, Miss Merritt.
        Subject providing prayer-service was helpful and pleasant to me.
        Wrote Mr. Fairchild in regard to estate matters, especially Mr.
        Laytem's bill

29—   another glorious morning—waiting in bed while I wait for breakfast.

31—   A year ago to-night I was at Liberty and my darling in Mount
        Vernon at watch night service which he loved so much. How
        changed our lives since then, he is strong and well in that city where
        there is neither sickness or sorrow and I am just waiting with Julius
        and Alice and the babies till the call comes. a few months ago I
        thought that it would not be long to wait, now it seems otherwise. but
        God is good and His way is best. All but myself and the children are
        at watch night service to-night. . . . I wonder if my darling looks
        down from Heaven upon the service here to-night.

[There is no extant diary for the following year. Emma died on May 2, 1901.]

EPILOGUE

Emma Frances Spaulding Bryant. b. February 16, 1844; d. May 2, 1901. Daughter of Capt. James and Cynthia Bray Spaulding. Wife of carpetbagger John Emory Bryant. Mother of Emma Alice Bryant Zeller.

Emma's story is more than these bare statistics of her life as defined by others. The portrait which emerges from the reading of her correspondence and diaries reveals a truer sense of her own being: a woman of character, strength, and remarkable tenacity. From the single threads of her life's influences and experiences, she wove an extraordinary fabric and left an enduring legacy.

Emma was born into a tightly knit family group. As a descendant of one of the town's founding families and the daughter of a prominent town official in the town of Buckfield, Maine, there was never a doubt regarding the security of her identity or the future she could anticipate. Spaulding cousins, aunts, and uncles were part of her extended family and she maintained ties with them through prodigious letter writing. Within the nuclear family, deep affection bound them together. Emma mourned when her sister Zilpha died at the age of thirty and remembered the day of that death in later diaries. She never found consolation for the death of her mother, six months after her own marriage in 1864, nor did she cease to grieve that Cynthia Bray Spaulding's health had vanished before their eyes in her last years.

Sorrow in the loss of loved ones would be, in fact, an ongoing feature of Emma's life. Her first pregnancy ended with miscarriage, "the hopes of an heir blighted," she wrote darkly. Then, her firstborn and only son, born with spina bifida, lived only a few days. Emma's anguished musings reached out for comfort from her absent husband: "The day is lonely and I can but think longingly of the little babe that would have made all the days so short and cheery—but . . . God has other work on earth for me to do. I often find myself conjecturing what that work shall be—whether the blessed work of rearing other children of our own flesh (tho none could quite fill the void it seems to me left by our first-born darling) or some other work which I have not looked forward to or desired—He only knows." (April 18, 1869)

The Spauldings expected that their children would be educated. From its earliest days, Buckfield had provided for schools for its residents; Emma's uncle arranged for the hiring of itinerant scholar and teacher John Emory Bryant. Emma studied first in John's classroom and then went on to college, there finding a setting that brought the promise of what womanhood would be for her. Maine Wesleyan Seminary and Female College vowed that "for healthfulness, beauty of scenery, and freedom from vicious and disturbing influences, there is no better location for a school in New England." With *en loco parentis* understood, parents could be "assured that their sons and daughters" would find there not only a "safe and pleasant home," but a "judicious and firm discipline," where a "strong moral and religious influence is constantly exerted."[1]

In those bucolic surroundings, with the atmosphere of security and freedom to grow, Emma became a young woman of strong conviction, loved by her friends and remembered as "the most conscientious and truthful person" one could know. It seemed that she had a multitude of pals devoted to her. Emma would name her only surviving child Emma Alice, remembering her dearest "chummie," Alice White, also a native of Buckfield, whose early death effected another painful loss.

The college at Kents Hill sought for its female students a classical education comparable to that offered to males. The rigors of that scholasticism left Emma with a desire for involvement in the politics of the day as well as an appetite for reading in biography, history, theology, and current medical and social trends. The Chautauqua reading program became one source of her continuing education.

Emma's expectations for the future were surely high when the dashing young captain and her former teacher courted her. John Bryant having already shown himself to be a hothead and demanding as a person, she had some ambivalence. Their courtship, primarily by mail during the Civil War, was a harbinger of the marriage his career would necessitate. But little of that could be known then—his plans for a law career in Maine reassured her, while his triumph over accusers in his court-martial trial and exoneration through daring military exploits must have seemed convincing. She could not have known how many times she would inquire: "I feel quite sure that the charges . . . as regards yourself must be untrue, are they not?" (April 18, 1869)[2]

---

[1] *Catalogue of the Officers and Students of the Maine Wesleyan Seminary and Female College, Kent's Hill, Readfield, 1863–64* (Portland, Maine: B. Thurston, 1864), 28–31.

[2] See *Carpetbagger of Conscience*, 180–83; and vii–xiii of the 1999 edition, for an extended evaluation of JEB's career.

During the wartime correspondence, her anxiety may be seen, however, in her admonition that he should eschew revenge and seek a Christian life of prayer and faith, advice he accepted only later in his life. Emma showed herself keenly conditioned by a pietistic Baptist faith, presumably from her upbringing, held securely despite the majority Universalist congregation in Buckfield and John's ties to the Methodist church. This bedrock foundation carried her through her entire life, giving her consolation in sorrow and growing stronger in adversity. Prayer became her coping mechanism for release of events beyond her control, particularly in her husband's affairs.

Finding such a comfort in spirituality was not unusual, but Emma's confidence in challenging the tenets of that religion was indeed remarkable. While she accepted the Baptist prohibition against the theater and smoking, the measure of her intellectual openness was her willingness to analyze everything handed down in tradition, regardless of its source. Influenced by her readings in reform literature, Emma deftly instructed even pastors in her Sunday School class on interpreting Genesis 1:26–27 to understand "dominion" as shared by "male and female," both having been created in "the image of God." She also urged this reading as enlightenment for her husband. (March 27, 1887)

If her own conscience demanded deviation, Emma would not be bound by any of society's strictures. Alice recalled that the neighbors were horrified to discover that Emma had discarded the customary "long heavy muslin chemises" for "gauze underwear." Regularly, she seemed to experiment with new methods or medicines, frequently reporting her conclusions to John.

The seriousness of some of her causes should not obscure the light side of Emma's personality. Clearly, her college chums saw her as carefree and adventuresome. In Illinois, she was invited "out to tea with a party of young people," by which she was "flattered." While her host claimed that she thought her "about as young as any of them," Emma reckoned that the lack of a generation gap was due to her "sentiment upon the woman question." (June 19, 1880) Indeed, the "woman question" came to embody many aspects of the philosophy life was providing her. Once awakened to misogyny as the source of so many obstacles placed before women, Emma was unafraid to venture into these untested waters. Surely the tenets of prescribed gender roles had been prominent in her training. The patriarchal nineteenth century called for male superiority, with the husband as head of household, breadwinner, public and professional persona of the family. But Emma's own experience did not match these expectations. It was the realities of her life that made her an ardent feminist.

So often absent, John could hardly function as head of household. Emma was forced to solve all the immediate problems of daily existence: how to treat a sudden illness, when to call the doctor, security at night (she always carried a revolver to the door), even where she would live. Gradually, the weight of her responsibility built the realization that John "could not make decisions for her" or "plan for me at all at your present distance from me." (March 28, 1883)

Emma's indigent existence taught her the crippling effects of dependency and shattered any expectation that her husband would be the breadwinner. Years of penny-pinching and deprivation for his priorities led to her acknowledgment that this rule of society was also invalid. If her daughter would be educated, she would have to secure it by her own work. There can be little doubt she was grateful for her own college education, which enabled her to recapture the expertise she had enjoyed as a student. Keenly aware that she was beginning in her middle years with little formal instruction in teaching methods, she nevertheless took the wise course of apprenticeship, which finally led to her own classroom. John could not dissuade her from the confidence that this was the correct path. The " . . . obvious work for me . . . now," she wrote, is to " . . . attend to Emma's [Alice] development and my own restoration to health, and to reviewing my mathematics (a subject 'which I love myself') and learning the best methods of teaching by watching those who know how to teach and by trying my hand, as I am doing. . . ." (March 28, 1883)

Their occasional crises between husband and wife offer windows on the contest of wills and Emma's growing self-esteem. The incident in 1873 in which she sought medical treatment, and her frank discussion of her treatment, was such an opening. She seemed taken aback that her husband should question her fidelity and honor to their marriage vows. "Do you think that I have no love of my <u>own</u> virtue, no pride, no <u>temper</u> or <u>will</u> of my own that you fancied me so helpless in his hands?" Clearly, John had assumed the worst: if another man—even a physician—had viewed her body, she was a fallen woman. "Freedom of the wife," he wrote suspiciously, could lead to "free love." And what, Emma retorted, does "freedom for the husband lead to?" Did he ask her to be his "inferior," his "obedient child?" To this she answered, "<u>Never.</u> I will be your true, loving wife your companion and equal in every and the fullest sense . . . nothing <u>less</u> and nothing <u>else</u>." (August 7, 1873)

Here JEB skated on thin ice. His own free-style travels and associations with other women merely illustrated another nineteenth-century convention: males lived by a different standard from that expected of their wives. Did John have sexual encounters with other women? What was his relationship to "the Countess"? Who can know. Emma never looked back. She accepted his version of reality—but insisted that he grant her the same trust. "I have never lived with you on other terms than those of the most perfect <u>love</u> and <u>trust</u> and <u>equality</u>. I <u>never intend</u> to live <u>with you on other terms</u>." (August 7, 1873)

Emma's thinking was wonderfully inclusive. Her logic reflects the natural rights argument claimed by the first generation of early feminists. " . . . It is always unfortunate," she wrote, "when a woman needs to assert that which she should simply <u>use</u> as her natural inheritance. . . ." Rights and equality were the heritage of one's humanity. "I have for many years believed that the germs of human nature, the essentials of it I may say, are the same everywhere, and all experience and observation confirms that view," she wrote, and "both sexes" have all these essential elements. "It is because I was born with a respect for the <u>inherent rights of every person</u>, for the right of each person to judge for him or herself what God requires of them, and do you suppose that I grant all this to you, as you know and the Father knows I have, and feel within me none of those rights?" (March 28, 1883)

Within the Woman's Christian Temperance Union, Emma had the opportunity to combine some strongly held elements of belief. In the 1890s, the WCTU effectively combined the causes of temperance with support for women's suffrage. Perhaps this was also an avenue for accommodation with her husband, who had long held temperance views and was committed to abstinence for himself.

The domicile question, however, provided one of the most taxing issues between them, for Emma's ever-recurring dilemma was where she would reside. The financial impossibility of owning their own home, plus the itinerant nature of John's political career, made the question a raw, never-ending worry. In 1883, the decision brought a sharp exchange of viewpoints and statement of will. "When you asked me to marry you, you asked me if I could lie happy in your arms, you did not ask me if I would obey you, if I would yield up to you my individual liberties and right of judgement. You knew me too well to ask such a question, and it is very unfair now to attempt to claim what never belonged to you and was never given you." (April 3, 1883)

Letters between them were her venue for thinking through the options for a new residence, but when her husband sought to short-circuit the process by his pronouncements, her response was immediate and vehement. "I can tell you, darling, what will very greatly improve my health. To have my husband remember that God has given me brains and judgement and feeling of responsibility, as well as to himself, and to cease to <u>distress</u> and <u>chafe</u> me by opposing every plan that I make, and by attempting to think for me." (March 28, 1883)

The difficulty in solving this problem carried over into their divergent interpretations of the years when necessity required deprivation and struggle. John's facile admonishment not to "trouble" herself with worries for the future wounded her. "Do you think, husband mine, that God would have thus cared for us in these past years if I had not 'troubled' myself by planning and working and economizing. If while you were struggling in the north I had drifted along without exercising my judgement. . . ." (March 28, 1883)

The home the Bryants shared in Mount Vernon during their last years therefore provided Emma special comfort. The solace she felt can only be imagined after her decades of hotels, boarding in the homes of others, packing and unpacking trunks, moving and starting over yet again. With a heart broken by John's death she gave up "the little home" that had "been so dear to us." (March 5, 1900)

With many lessons learned from the vicissitudes of her life, even with her willingness to question whatever the source of authority, still it is not surprising to know of Emma's desolation after her husband's demise. Through it all she had loved John, had shared his passion for social justice, had believed with him in the causes of political reform and education, had struggled with his weakness and assisted him in his need. Together they had loved their daughter and seen her blossom under Emma's guardianship to be a confident, able woman. But without her husband—the relationship she had insisted be formulated on equality and mutual respect—she was left at last with "days of sorrow." "No other love has ever been like his," she wrote, "or can be." (May 30, 1900) The faith that had sustained her through her life reached beyond: "God grant," she wrote, " . . . that the twain of us may be permitted to dwell in the light of His countenance through all eternity." (July 13, 1900)

Emma's narrative has all the drama of fiction: a strong woman; a difficult life; an ambitious, political husband; a long-suffering wife; a happy ending of love and devotion. But sentimentality does her a disservice. Rather she might claim the mantle reserved for the heroic—an intelligent, courageous person with a mind of her own, gleaning new insight as she challenged the bankrupt doctrine of woman's subservience. In an intensely political climate of sectional mistrust and hostility, she had survived and triumphed. In a repressive century of male domination, she refused its rigors in the most difficult setting of all—her own home. In a marriage to an idealistic public person—a marriage characterized by separation and hardship—she achieved deep bonds of devotion while learning the essential lesson of self-sufficiency. For her daughter she insured the vital elements for success in education and an independent spirit.

Emma Frances Spaulding Bryant's legacy is simple but profound: acceptance of life as it comes with the courage to challenge the old and embrace the new; faithfulness in relationship; nurturing of talent; fulfillment in work; and respect for the equality of all persons—all guaranteed by genuine spiritual depth. A life lived with integrity.

SELECTED BIBLIOGRAPHY

Manuscript Collections

Blodgett, Foster. Papers. Special Collections, University of Georgia Library, Athens, Ga.

Brown, Joseph Emerson. Papers. Felix Hargrett Collection, University of Georgia Library, Athens, Ga.

Bryant, John Emory. Correspondence. Maine State Archives, Augusta, Maine.

_____. Correspondence and Papers. American Missionary Association Archives, Amistad Research Center, New Orleans, La.

_____. Papers. Rare Book, Manuscript, and Special Collections, Duke University, Durham, N.C.

Bullock, Governor Rufus. Correspondence. Georgia Department of Archives and History, Atlanta, Ga.

Chandler, William E. Papers. Library of Congress, Washington, D.C.

DeRenne Collection. Special Collections, University of Georgia Library, Athens, Ga.

Farrow, Henry P. Papers. Special Collections, University of Georgia Library, Athens, Ga.

Hayes, Rutherford B. Papers. Rutherford B. Hayes Presidential Center, Fremont, Ohio.

Howard, O. O. Papers. Special Collections, Bowdoin College Library, Brunswick, Maine.

Reconstruction File. Georgia Department of Archives and History, Atlanta, Ga.

Tourgée, Albion Winegar. Papers. Chautauqua County Historical Society, Westfield, N.Y. Microfilm copy, University of North Carolina Library, Chapel Hill, N.C.

Documents

"Birth and Death Records." Municipal Center, Town of Buckfield, Maine.

Chandler, Allen D., comp. *The Confederate Records of the State of Georgia.* Atlanta, Ga., 1911.

Congressional Globe. 41st Congress, 2d session, 42, part 6. Washington, D.C., 1870.

Custom House Nominations, Savannah, Ga. Record Group 56, Treasury Department. National Archives, Washington, D.C., June 1871–October 1877.

General Court Martial, [Proceedings in the case of] Capt. John E. Bryant, Co. "C," 8th Maine Vols., Headquarters, U.S. Forces, Port Royal Island, Beaufort, S.C., January 23, 1863. National Archives, Washington, D.C.

Journal of the House of Representatives of the State of Georgia, 1868–1870. Macon, Ga., 1870.

Journal of the Senate of the State of Georgia, 1868–1869. Macon, Ga., 1869.

Last Will and Testament, and Accompanying Documents, of John Emory Bryant. Surrogates' Court, County of Westchester, State of New York.

Monroe, David S., ed. *Journal of the General Conference of the Methodist Episcopal Church, Held in Philadelphia, Pa., May 1–28, 1884.* New York: Phillips & Hunt, 1884.

Registers and Letters Received by the Commissioner of the Bureau of Refugees, Freedmen, and Abandoned Lands, 1865–1872. Microcopy 752. National Archives, Washington, D.C.

U.S. House of Representatives. *Miscellaneous Documents.* 40th Congress, 3d session. Washington, D.C., 1869.

U.S. House of Representatives. *Report of the Joint Committee on Reconstruction.* 39th Congress, 1st session, pt. 3. Washington, D.C., 1866.

U.S. Senate. *Index to the Reports of the Committees of the Senate of the United States.* 41st Congress, 2d session, Washington, D.C., 1870.

U.S. Statutes at Large, Washington, D.C., 1868.

War of the Rebellion, Official Records of the Union and Confederate Armies. Washington, D.C., 1894–1900.

NEWSPAPERS

Athens Blade. 1879–80, scattered issues.
Athens Southern Banner. 1869–72.
Atlanta Constitution. 1868–1900.
Atlanta Daily New Era. 1866–68.
Atlanta Methodist Advocate. 1869–83.
Atlanta Southern Advance. 1882–86, scattered issues.
Atlanta Weekly Defiance. October 3, 1885.

Augusta Constitutionalist. December 1867–February 1868.

Augusta Daily Press. January–April 1869.

Augusta Loyal Georgian. 1866–68, scattered issues.

Augusta National Republican. July–December 1868.

Macon Daily Telegraph. 1865, scattered issues.

Macon Georgia Weekly Telegraph. 1860–63; 1865–68.

New York Times. 1862–63; 1880–89.

PRINTED PRIMARY SOURCES

Ames, Blanche Butler, comp. *Chronicles from the Nineteenth Century: Family Letters of Blanche Butler and Adelbert Ames.* 2 vols. Clinton, Mass.: Colonial Press, 1957.

Avery, Isaac Wheeler. *The City of Atlanta.* Louisville: Inter-state Publishing, 1892–1893.

————. *The History of the State of Georgia from 1850 to 1881.* New York: Brown & Derby, 1881.

Buhle, Mari Jo, and Paul Buhle, eds. *The Concise History of Woman Suffrage: Selections from the Classic Work of Stanton, Anthony, Gage, and Harper.* Urbana: University of Illinois Press, 1978.

Caldwell, John H. *Reminiscences of the Reconstruction of Church and State in Georgia.* Wilmington, Del.: Thomas, 1895.

Catalogue of the Officers and Students of the Maine Wesleyan Seminary and Female College, Kent's Hill, Readfield, 1863–64. Portland, Maine: B. Thurston, 1864.

Cole, Alfred, and Charles F. Whitman. *A History of Buckfield Oxford County, Maine from the Earliest Exploration to the Close of the Year 1900.* Lewiston, Maine: The Journal Printshop, 1915.

DuBois, Ellen Carol. *Elizabeth Cady Stanton/Susan B. Anthony: Correspondence, Writings, Speeches.* New York: Schocken Books, 1981.

French, E. R. *History of the Maine Wesleyan Seminar.* Portland, Maine: Smith & Sale, 1919.

Higginson, Thomas Wentworth. *Army Life in the Black Regiment.* Boston: Fields, Osgood, 1870. Reprint, East Lansing: Michigan State University Press, 1960.

Reed, Wallace Putman. *History of Atlanta, Georgia.* Syracuse, N.Y.: Mason, 1889.

Sibley, John Langdon. *History of the Town of Union, in the County of Lincoln, Maine.* Boston: Mussey, 1851.

Spalding, Charles Warren. *The Spalding Memorial: A Genealogical History of Edward Spalding of Virginia and the Massachusetts Bay and His Descendents,* 2 vols. Chicago: American Publishers' Association, 1897.

Stearns, Charles. *The Black Man of the South and the Rebels.* New York: American News, 1872

Tourgée, Albion W. *A Fool's Errand, by One of the Fools.* New York: Fords, Howard & Herbert, 1879.

Tunnell, Ted. *Carpetbagger from Vermont: The Autobiography of Marshall Harvey Twitchell.* Baton Rouge: Louisiana State University Press, 1989.

Whitman, William E. S., and Charles H. True. *Maine in the War for the Union.* Lewiston, Maine: Dingley, 1865.

Monographs

Anderson, Eric, and Alfred A. Moss, Jr., eds. *The Facts of Reconstruction: Essays in Honor of John Hope Franklin.* Baton Rouge: Lousiana State University Press, 1991.

Beale, Howard K. *The Critical Year: A Study of Andrew Johnson and Reconstruction.* New York: Ungar, 1958.

Belz, Herman. *A New Birth of Freedom: The Republican Party and Freedmen's Rights, 1861–1866.* Westport, Conn.: Greenwood Press, 1976; New York: Fordham University Press, 2000.

———. *Reconstructing the Union: Theory and Policy during the Civil War.* Ithaca, N.Y.: Cornell University Press, 1969.

Bentley, George R. *A History of the Freedmen's Bureau.* Philadelphia: University of Pennsylvania Press, 1955.

Berry, Mary Frances. *Military Necessity and Civil Rights Policy: Black Citizenship and the Constitution, 1861–1868.* Port Washington, N.Y.: Kennikat Press, 1977.

Bryant, Jonathan M. *How Curious a Land: Conflict and Change in Greene County, Georgia, 1850–1885.* Chapel Hill: University of North Carolina Press, 1996.

Butchart, Ronald E. *Northern Schools, Southern Blacks, and Reconstruction: Freedmen's Education, 1862–1875.* Westport, Conn.: Greenwood Press, 1980.

Carse, Robert. *Department of the South: Hilton Head Island in the Civil War.* Columbia, S.C.: State Printing, 1961.

Carter, Dan T. *When the War Was Over: The Failure of Self-Reconstruction in the South, 1865–1867.* Baton Rouge; Louisiana State University Press, 1985.

Cimbala, Paul. *Under the Guardianship of the Nation: The Freedmen's Bureau and the Reconstruction of Georgia.* Athens: University of Georgia Press, 1997.

Clinton, Catherine. *The Other Civil War: American Women in the Nineteenth Century.* New York: Hill & Wang, 1999.

Coffman, Tom. *Nation Within: The Story of America's Annexation of the Nation of Hawai'i.* Kane'ohe, Hawaii: EpiCenter, 1998.

Cogan, Frances B. *All-American Girl: The Ideal of Real Womanhood in Mid-Nineteenth-Century America.* Athens: University of Georgia Press, 1989.

Coleman, Kenneth, ed., *A History of Georgia.* Athens: University of Georgia Press, 1977.

Coulter, E. Merton. *Negro Legislators in Georgia during the Reconstruction Period.* Athens: Georgia Historical Quarterly, 1968.

Crapol, Edward P. *James G. Blaine: Architect of Empire.* Wilmington, Del.: Scholarly Resources, 2000.

Crow, Jeffery, Paul D. Escott, and Charles L. Flynn Jr., eds. *Race, Class, and Politics in Southern History: Essays in Honor of Robert R. Durden.* Baton Rouge: Louisiana State University Press, 1989.

Current, Richard N. *Northernizing the South.* Athens: University of Georgia Press, 1983.

——. *Those Terrible Carpetbaggers.* New York: Oxford, 1988.

Currie-McDaniel, Ruth. *Carpetbagger of Conscience: A Biography of John Emory Bryant.* Athens: University of Georgia Press, 1987; New York: Fordham University Press, 1999.

Degler, Carl N. *At Odds: Women and the Family in America.* New York: Oxford University Press, 1980.

DeSantis, Vincent P. *Republicans Face the Southern Question: The New Departure Years, 1877–1897.* Baltimore: Johns Hopkins University Press, 1959.

Drago, Edmond L. *Black Politicians and Reconstruction in Georgia: A Splendid Failure.* Baton Rouge: Louisiana State University Press, 1982; Athens: University of Georgia Press, 1992.

Duberman, Martin B., ed. *The Antislavery Vanguard: New Essays on the Abolitionists.* Princeton: Princeton University Press, 1965.

Duncan, Russell. *Entrepreneur for Equality: Governor Rufus Bullock, Commerce, and Race in Post-Civil War Georgia.* Athens: University of Georgia Press, 1994.

Edelstein, Tilden G. *Strange Enthusiasm: A Life of Thomas Wentworth Higginson.* New Haven: Yale University Press, 1968.

Fleming, Walter Lynwood. *The Sequel of Appomattox: A Chronicle of the Reunion of the States.* New Haven: Yale University Press, 1920.

Foner, Eric. *Free Soil, Free Labor, Free Men: The Ideology of the Republican Party before the Civil War.* New York: Oxford University Press, 1970.

_____. *Politics and Ideology in the Age of the Civil War.* New York: Oxford University Press, 1980.

_____. *Reconstruction: America's Unfinished Revolution, 1863–1877.* New York: Harper & Row, 1988.

Frankel, Noralee, and Nancy S. Dye, eds. *Gender, Class, Race, and Reform in the Progressive Era.* Lexington: University of Kentucky Press, 1991.

Frederickson, George M. *The Black Image in the White Mind: The Debate on Afro-American Character and Destiny, 1817–1914.* New York: Harper & Row, 1971.

_____. *The Inner Civil War: Northern Intellectuals and the Crisis of the Union.* New York: Harper & Row, 1965.

Gillette, William. *Retreat from Reconstruction, 1865–1879.* Baton Rouge: Louisiana State University Press, 1979.

Gilmore, Glenda Elizabeth. *Gender and Jim Crow: Women and the Politics of White Supremacy in North Carolina, 1898–1920.* Chapel Hill: University of North Carolina Press, 1996.

Goldsmith, Barbara. *Other Powers: The Age of Suffrage, Spiritualism, and the Scandalous Victoria Woodhull.* New York: Alfred A. Knopf, 1998.

Gravely, William B. *Gilbert Haven, Methodist Abolitionist: A Study in Race, Religion, and Reform, 1850–1880.* Nashville: Abingdon, 1971.

Griffith, Elisabeth. *In Her Own Right: The Life of Elizabeth Cady Stanton.* New York: Oxford University Press, 1984.

Hirshon, Stanley P. *Farewell to the Bloody Shirt: Northern Republicans and the Southern Negro, 1877–1893.* Bloomington: Indiana University Press, 1962.

Inscoe, John C., ed. *Georgia in Black and White: Explorations in the Race Relations of a Southern State, 1865–1950.* Athens: University of Georgia Press, 1994.

Jones, Jacqueline. *Soldiers of Light and Love: Northern Teachers and Georgia Blacks, 1865–1873.* Chapel Hill: University of North Carolina Press, 1980.

Kerber, Linda K., Alice Kessler-Harris, and Kathryn Kish Sklar, eds. *United States History as Women's History: New Feminist Essays.* Chapel Hill: University of North Carolina Press, 1995.

Kousser, J. Morgan, and James M. McPherson, eds. *Race, Region, and Reconstruction: Essays in Honor of C. Vann Woodward.* New York: Oxford University Press, 1982.

Litwack, Leon F. *Been in the Storm So Long: The Aftermath of Slavery.* New York: Knopf, 1979.

Mayer, George H. *The Republican Party, 1854–1966.* New York: Oxford University Press, 1967.

McFeely, William S. *Grant: A Biography.* New York: Norton, 1981.

————. *Yankee Stepfather: General O. O. Howard and the Freedman.* New Haven: Yale University Press, 1968.

McPherson, James M. *The Abolitionist Legacy: From Reconstruction to the NAACP.* Princeton: Princeton University Press, 1975.

————. *The Negro's Civil War.* New York: Vintage, 1967.

————. *Ordeal by Fire: The Civil War and Reconstruction.* New York: Knopf, 1982.

————. *The Struggle for Equality: Abolitionists and the Negro in the Civil War and Reconstruction.* Princeton: Princeton University Press, 1964.

Mohr, James C., ed., and Richard E. Winslow III, assoc. ed. *The Cormany Diaries: A Northern Family in the Civil War.* Pittsburgh: University of Pittsburgh Press, 1982.

Montgomery, David. *Beyond Equality: Labor and Radical Republicans, 1862–1872.* New York: Knopf, 1967.

Morris, Robert. *Reading, 'Riting, and Reconstruction: The Education of Freedmen in the South, 1861–1870.* Chicago: University of Chicago Press, 1981.

Morrow, Ralph E. *Northern Methodism and Reconstruction.* East Lansing: Michigan State University Press, 1956.

Nathans, Elizabeth Studley. *Losing the Peace: Georgia Republicans and Reconstruction, 1865–1871.* Baton Rouge: Louisiana State University Press, 1968.

Olsen, Otto H. *Carpetbagger's Crusade: The Life of Albion Winegar Tourgée.* Baltimore: Johns Hopkins University Press, 1965.

————. *Reconstruction and Redemption in the South.* Baton Rouge: Louisiana State University Press, 1980.

Parks, Joseph H. *Joseph E. Brown of Georgia.* Baton Rouge: Louisiana State University Press, 1977.

Perman, Michael. *Reunion without Compromise: The South and Reconstruction, 1865–1868.* Cambridge: Cambridge University Press, 1973.

————. *The Road to Redemption: Southern Politics, 1869–1879.* Chapel Hill: University of North Carolina Press, 1984.

Powell, Lawrence N. *New Masters: Northern Planters in the Civil War and Reconstruction.* New Haven: Yale University Press, 1980; New York: Fordham University Press, 1998.

Rable, George C. *But There Was No Place: The Role of Violence in the Politics of Reconstruction.* Athens: University of Georgia Press, 1984.

Randall, J. G., and David Donald. *The Civil War and Reconstruction,* 2d ed. Boston: Heath, 1961.

Reagan, Alice E. *H. I. Kimball, Entrepreneur.* Atlanta: Cherokee, 1983.

Reidy, Joseph P. *From Slavery to Agrarian Capitalism in the Cotton Plantation South: Central Georgia, 1800–1880.* Chapel Hill: University of North Carolina Press, 1992.

Roark, James L. *Masters without Slaves: Southern Planters in the Civil War and Reconstruction.* New York: Norton, 1977.

Rose, Willie Lee. *Rehearsal for Reconstruction: The Port Royal Experiment.* New York: Vintage, 1964.

Rothman, Shelia M. *Living in the Shadow of Death: Tuberculosis and the Social Experience of Illness in American History.* New York: Basic Books, 1994.

Shadgett, Olive Hall. *The Republican Party in Georgia from Reconstruction through 1900.* Athens: University of Georgia Press, 1964.

Small, Walter Herbert. *Early New England Schools.* Boston: Ginn, 1914.

Stampp, Kenneth M., and Leon F. Litwack, eds. *Reconstruction: An Anthology of Revisionist Writings.* Baton Rouge: Louisiana State University Press, 1969.

Swint, Henry Lee. *The Northern Teacher in the South, 1862–1870.* New York: Octagon Books, 1967.

Talmadge, John E. *Rebecca Latimer Felton: Nine Stormy Decades.* Athens: University of Georgia Press, 1960.

Thompson, Clara Mildred. *Reconstruction in Georgia: Economic, Social, and Political, 1865–1872.* New York: Columbia University Press, 1915.

Tunnell, Ted. *Edge of the Sword: The Ordeal of Carpetbagger Marshall H. Twitchell in the Civil War and Reconstruction.* Baton Rouge: Louisiana State University Press, 2001.

Tyler, Alice Felt. *Freedom's Ferment: Phases of America Social History to 1860.* Minneapolis: University of Minnesota Press, 1944.

Woodward, C. Vann. *American Counterpoint: Slavery and Racism in the North-South Dialogue.* Boston: Little, Brown, 1971.

——. *The Burden of Southern History,* rev. ed. New York: Mentor, 1960.

——. *Origins of the New South, 1877–1913.* Baton Rouge: Louisiana State University Press, 1967.

_____. *Reunion and Reaction: The Compromise of 1877 and the End of Reconstruction.* Boston: Little, Brown, 1951.

ARTICLES IN BOOKS OR PERIODICAL LITERATURE

Abbott, Richard. "The Republican Party Press in Reconstruction Georgia, 1877–1874." *Journal of Southern History* 41, no. 4 (November 1995): 725–60.

Belz, Herman. "The Freedmen's Bureau Act of 1865 and the Principle of No Discrimination According to Color." *Civil War History* 21, no. 3 (September 1975): 197–217.

Brandon, William P. "Calling the Georgia Constitutional Convention of 1877." *Georgia Historical Quarterly* 17 (September 1933): 189–203.

Carter, Dan T. "Anatomy of Fear: The Christmas Day Insurrection Scare of 1865." *Journal of Southern History* 42 (August 1976): 345–64.

Cason, Roberta F. "The Loyal League in Georgia." *Georgia Historical Quarterly* 20 (June 1936): 125–53.

Cimbala, Paul. "The Talisman Power: Davis Tillson, the Freedmen's Bureau, and Free Labor in Reconstruction Georgia, 1865–1866." *Civil War History* 28, no. 2 (June 1982): 153–71.

Coleman, Kenneth. "The Georgia Gubernatorial Election of 1880." *Georgia Historical Quarterly* 25 (June 1941): 89–117.

Coulter, E. Merton. "Henry M. Turner, Georgia Negro Preacher-Politician during the Reconstruction Era." *Georgia Historical Quarterly* 48 (December 1964): 371–410.

Currie-McDaniel, Ruth. "Black Power in Georgia: William A. Pledger and the Takeover of the Republican Party." *Georgia Historical Quarterly* 62 (fall 1978): 225–39.

_____. "Courtship and Marriage in the Nineteenth Century: Albion and Emma Tourgée, a Case Study." *North Carolina Historical Review* 61 (July 1984): 285–310.

_____. "Northern Women in the South, 1860–1880." *Georgia Historical Quarterly* 76 (spring 1992): 284–312.

_____. "The Wives of the Carpetbaggers." In *Race, Class, and Politics in Southern History: Essays in Honor of Robert F. Durden,* edited by Jeffery J. Crow, Paul D. Escott, and Charles L. Flynn Jr. Baton Rouge: Louisiana State University Press, 1989.

Curry, Richard O. "The Abolitionists and Reconstruction: A Critical Appraisal." *Journal of Southern History* 34 (November 1968): 527–45.

Daniell, Elizabeth Otto. "The Ashburn Murder Case in Georgia Reconstruction, 1868." *Georgia Historical Quarterly* 59 (fall 1975): 296–312.

Davis, David Brion. "The Emergence of Immediatism in British and American Antislavery Thought." *Mississippi University Historical Review* 49 (September 1962): 209–30.

Friedel, Frank. "The Loyal Publication Society." *Mississippi Valley Historical Review* 26 (December 1939): 359–76.

Harris, William C. "The Creed of the Carpetbaggers: The Case of Mississippi." *Journal of Southern History* 40 (May 1974): 199–224.

Herndon, Jane. "Henry McNeal Turner's African Dream: A Re-evaluation." *Mississippi Quarterly* 22, no. 4 (1969): 327–36.

Holt, Shan: "The Anatomy of a Marriage: Letters of Emma Spaulding Bryant, 1873." *Signs: Journal of Women in Culture and Society* 17, no. 1 (fall 1991), 187–204.

Kenney, Alycia. "Health Resorts and Medical Tourism: Sanitariums as Business Ventures in Asheville, North Carolina, 1880–1900." Unpublished paper, 2003.

Kinkaid, Larry. "Victims of Circumstance: An Interpretation of Changing Attitudes toward Republican Policy Makers and Reconstruction." *Journal of American History* 57 (June 1970): 48–66.

Klingman, Peter, and David Keithman. "Negro Dissidence and the Republican Party, 1864–1872." *Phylon* 40 (June 1979): 172–82.

Kolchin, Peter. "Scalawags, Carpetbaggers, and Reconstruction: A Quantitative Look at Southern Congressional Politics, 1868–1872." *Journal of Southern History* 45 (February 1979): 63–78.

Lebsock, Suzanne D. "Radical Reconstruction and the Property Rights of Southern Women." *Journal of Southern History* 43 (May 1977): 195–216.

McPherson, James M. "Coercion or Conciliation: Abolitionists Debate President Hayes' Southern Policy." *New England Quarterly* 39 (December 1966): 474–97.

———. "Many Abolitionists Fought On after the Civil War." *University: A Princeton Quarterly*, no. 39 (winter 1968–69): 14–18, 30–34.

Moore, James Tice. "Redeemers Reconsidered: Change and Continuity in the Democratic South, 1870–1900." *Journal of Southern History* 44 (August 1978): 357–78.

Murphy, William F. "A Note on the Significance of Names." *Psychoanalytic Quarterly* 26 (1957): 91–106.

Paludan, Phillip S. "The American Civil War Considered as Crisis in Law and Order." *American Historical Review* 77, no. 4 (October 1972): 1013–34.

Pease, William H., and Jane H. Pease. "Antislavery Ambivalence: Immediatism, Expediency, Race." *American Quarterly* 17 (1965): 682–95.

Powell, Lawrence N. "The American Land Company and Agency: John A. Andrew and the Northernization of the South." *Civil War History* 21, no. 4 (December 1975): 293–308.

———. "The Politics of Livelihood: Carpetbaggers in the Deep South." *Regions, Races, and Reconstruction: Essays in Honor of C. Vann Woodward*, edited by James M. McPherson and J. Morgan Kousser. New York: Oxford University Press, 1982.

Rable, George C. "Bourbonism, Reconstruction, and the Persistence of Southern Distinctiveness." *Civil War History* 26, no. 4 (December 1980): 135–53.

———. "Southern Interests and the Election of 1876: A Reappraisal." *Civil War History* 26, no. 4 (December 1980): 347–61.

Redkey, Edwin S. "Bishop Turner's African Dream." *Journal of American History* 54 (September 1967): 271–90.

Riddleburger, Patrick W. "The Radicals' Abandonment of the Negro During Reconstruction." *Journal of Negro History* 45 (April 1960): 88–102.

Russ, William Adam, Jr. "Radical Disfranchisement in Georgia, 1867–1871." *Georgia Historical Quarterly* 19 (September 1935): 175–209.

Savitt, Todd. "Politics in Medicine: The Georgia Freedmen's Bureau and the Organization of Health Care, 1865–1866." *Civil War History* 28, no. 1 (March 1982): 45–64.

Sproat, John G. "Blueprint for Radical Reconstruction." *Journal of Southern History* 23 (February 1957): 25–44.

Talmadge, John E. "The Death Blow to Independentism in Georgia." *Georgia Historical Quarterly* 39 (December 1955): 37–47.

Thomas, John L. "Romantic Reform in America, 1815–1865." *American Quarterly* 17 (winter 1965): 656–81.

Ward, Judson C., Jr. "The Election of 1880 and Its Impact on Atlanta." *Atlanta Historical Society Journal* 25 (spring 1981): 5–15.

———. "The New Departure Democrats of Georgia: An Interpretation." *Georgia Historical Quarterly* 41 (September 1957): 227–36.

———. "The Republican Party in Bourbon Georgia, 1872–1890." *Journal of Southern History* 9 (May 1943): 196–209.

Weisberger, Bernard A. "The Dark and Bloody Ground of Reconstruction
    Historiography." *Journal of Southern History* 25 (November 1959):
    427–47.
Woodward, C. Vann. "Bourbonism in Georgia." *North Carolina Historical
    Review* 16 (January 1939): 25–35.
Wynne, Lewis N. "The Bourbon Triumvirate: A Reconsideration." *Atlanta
    Historical Society* 24 (summer 1980): 39–55.

REFERENCE WORKS

Coleman, Kenneth, and Charles S. Gurr, eds. *Dictionary of Georgia Biography.*
    2 vols. Athens: University of Georgia Press, 1983.
Coppens, Linda Miles. *What American Women Did, 1789–1920: A Year-by-
    Year Reference.* Jefferson, N.C.: McFarland, 2001.
Faust, Patricia L., ed. *Historical Times: Illustrated Encyclopedia of the Civil War.*
    New York: Harper & Row, 1986.
Simpson, Mathew, ed. *Cyclopedia of Methodism.* 4th rev. ed. Philadelphia:
    Everts, 1881.

UNPUBLISHED THESES

Bhurtel, Shyam Krishna. "Colonel Alfred Eliab Buck: Carpetbagger in
    Alabama and Georgia." Ph.D. diss., Auburn University, 1981.
Bloom, Charles G. "The Georgia Election of April, 1868: A Reexamination
    of the Politics of Georgia Reconstruction." M.A. thesis, University of
    Chicago, 1963.
Hume, Richard L. "The 'Black and Tan' Constitutional Conventions of
    1867–1869 in Ten Former Confederate States: A Study of Their
    Membership." Ph.D. diss., University of Washington, 1969.
Smith, Allen Chandler. "The Republican Party in Georgia, 1867–1871."
    M.A. thesis, Duke University, 1937.
Smith, Wallace Calvin. "Rufus B. Bullock and the Third Reconstruction of
    Georgia, 1867–1871." M.A. thesis, University of North Carolina, 1964.
Stipe, Carl Evans. "Colonel Alfred Eliab Buck." M.A. thesis, Emory
    University, 1944.
Ward, Judson Clements, Jr. "Georgia under the Bourbon Democrats,
    1872–1890." Ph.D. diss., University of North Carolina, 1947.

INDEX

Sherman, Mrs. Josiah, 121–25, 129, 132,
134–35, 142–44, 147, 151, 153, 155,
169–70, 213, 215, 226–27, 230–31, 234,
243, 245–46, 253, 255, 257–58, 284,
289, 291
Sherman, Lizzie, 128
Sherman, Thomas West, 14
Sleight, Dr., 444, 469
Small, Miss, 341
Smith, Mr., 149, 334–35
Smith, Mrs., 82, 84, 95, 113–14, 116–17,
337, 465–66
Smyth, Thomas Alfred, 75
Smythe, W. H., 259, 263
Sons of Temperance, 411
Southern Advance Association, 248, 283,
289, 326, 402
Spalding, Charles Warren, 4n, 450n
Spalding, Mary Kellogg Ramsdell, 120,
121, 125
Spalding, Volney, 119, 123, 125–26, 212,
215–16, 218–20, 222–23, 227–32, 237,
239–40, 242, 244–45, 250, 258, 287,
289, 293, 296, 301, 303, 323, 325–26,
330
Spanish-American War, 452
Spaulding, Cynthia Bray, 5, 20, 38, 98, 130,
217, 249, 314, 477
Spaulding, Benjamin, 6
Spaulding, Clarinda, 6, 9, 68, 83, 171
Spaulding, Cora Ada Smith, 445, 453,
467–71, 473, 475
Spaulding, Dastine, 6, 7, 9
Spaulding, James, 5, 79, 85, 93–94, 97, 99,
125, 130–32, 135, 177–78, 213, 249,
264, 268, 281–82, 329, 477
Spaulding, James Greenleaf, 5, 24, 58, 68,
73, 107–10, 112, 125, 179, 186–87,
189–92, 194, 196, 198, 200, 204, 206,
210, 298, 372, 374, 377–80, 383, 416,
445, 453, 467–71, 473–75
Spaulding, Margaretta Jane. See Browne,
Margaretta Jane.
Spaulding, Mary, 199
Spaulding, Nancy W. Hines, 107–10, 179,
186–87, 192–93, 196, 198, 200, 295,
298, 33–35, 372, 379–80, 458
Spaulding, Zilpha Prince, 5, 16
Speer, Emory, 304

Spence, Dr. John F. 362, 365–66, 373–74,
351, 354, 379, 412
Spencer, Mr., 286
Srance, Prof., 113
Stanton, Edwin McMasters, 75
Stanton, Elizabeth Cady, 1, 167n, 172n, 316n
Stanton, S. T., 225
Stearns, Charles, 128
Stearns, Etta, 128
Steedman, James B., 83
Stephens, Joseph, 27
Stevens, Emma, 474
Stevens, Joseph, 13, 46
Stickel, Mrs., 87
Stocer, Mrs., 300
Stokes, M. H., 301–303, 305–308, 310–13,
336, 358
Stone, Lucy, 167n
Strickland, Augustus H. (Lee), 10, 15
Strong, Major, 33
Stubbert, Dr. J. Edward, 443, 449, 451, 457
Stykes, Mr., 474–75
Swart, Mr., 469
Swart, Mrs., 466, 468
Swign, Dr., 221

Tanner, Dr., 320
Taylor, Bishop, 471
Tennessee Wesleyan College, 345n
Thomas, George S., 258
Thomas, Senator, 161
Thompson, Miss. See Saxton, Rufus, Mrs.
Thompson, Mr., 203, 422
Thompson, Mrs., 203, 422
Thurman, Bro., 359, 364, 383, 392
Tichemon, F. M., 467
Tilden, Samuel J., 179, 201, 205
Tillman, Bessie, 395
Tillson, Davis, 78, 81–83, 86, 88, 90, 95
Tourgée, Albion, 248, 251
Turpin, Mrs., 138, 141–42

U.S. Grant Memorial University, 340,
345n, 389n
Union League, 212, 232, 239, 245, 283,
293, 332, 338, 345
Union League Club, 225, 232
Union Signal, The, 378
University of Chattanooga, 389n

RECONSTRUCTING AMERICA SERIES
Paul A. Cimbala, series editor